Jesus of Nazareth

Gerhard Lohfink

Jesus of Nazareth

What He Wanted,
Who He Was

Translated by

Linda M. Maloney

A Michael Glazier Book

LITURGICAL PRESS
Collegeville, Minnesota

www.litpress.org

A Michael Glazier Book published by Liturgical Press

This volume was originally published in German as *Jesus von Nazaret. Was er wollte, wer er war* (Freiburg i.B.: Herder, 2011).

ISBN 978-0-8146-8308-8

1	2	3	4	5	6	7	8	9

Library of Congress Cataloging-in-Publication Data

Lohfink, Gerhard, 1934–
      [Jesus von Nazaret. English]
      Jesus of Nazareth : what He wanted, who He was / Gerhard Lohfink ; translated by Linda M. Maloney.
           p.   cm.
      "A Michael Glazier book."
      Includes bibliographical references and index.
      ISBN 978-0-8146-8058-2 — ISBN 978-0-8146-8059-9 (ebook)
           1. Jesus Christ—Historicity.   2. Jesus Christ—Person and offices.
      I. Maloney, Linda M.   II. Title.

      BT303.2.L6413   2012
      232—dc23

                                                                    2012020860

To the memory of
Father Heinrich Bacht, SJ

. . . ponder daily over death and life,

if thou mightest find it,

and let thy bearing be joyous

and go not out of the world

without first having publicly testified

thy love and reverence

for the Author of Christianity.

—Matthias Claudius, Letter "To my son Johannes," 1799

Contents

Preface

There are innumerable books about Jesus. The reason is obvious: we can never finish with him, and every age must encounter him anew. Some of the many Jesus books are very good. Some are very bad. The bad ones are bad because they are far from understanding that the real "historical Jesus" cannot be grasped independently of faith in him. Which faith? That of the first witnesses and those who handed on the story, those who had to describe "accurately" or, better, "faithfully to the person" what had encountered them in Jesus.

Historical criticism is indispensable to research on Jesus. It illuminates the world in which Jesus lived, and still more, it works out the relationships among the sources of the gospels, illuminates the various layers of tradition, and thus sharpens our perception of what the evangelists wanted to say about Jesus in their "final text." Historical criticism inquires persistently about what happened, and thus it demonstrates that Christianity is about real history and not about myths or ideologies. But when biblical critics measure Jesus only by their own prior understanding, deciding ahead of time what is "historically possible" and what is "historically impossible," they exceed their own limitations.

Nowadays Jesus is far too often made to be merely a prophet, a gifted charismatic, a radical social revolutionary, a successful healer, a benevolent social worker, or even only a pious rabbi. The real claim of what is shown and expressed in Jesus is set aside, and the inevitable consequence is the assertion that the early Christian communities "deified" him.

The present book refuses to join in such reductionism, which goes contrary to the perceptions of the first witnesses and those who handed on the tradition. Its method is altogether historical and critical—historical research must always be critical—but at the same time it agrees with Karl Barth's statement in his commentary on Romans: "For me, historical criticism has to be more critical!"

This book intends to be serious about the fact that Jesus was a Jew and lived entirely in and out of Israel's faith experiences, but at the same time he brought those experiences to their goal and fulfillment. Those who want to really understand Jesus and what he was cannot avoid allowing themselves to be drawn into this faith.

I desire nothing more than that this book will help many people today to approach the real Jesus by making critical distinctions and yet at the same time remaining open and full of trust.

Gerhard Lohfink
Bad Tölz
September 2011

Acknowledgments

This book is dedicated to the memory of Father Heinrich Bacht, SJ (1910–1986), in gratitude. He was professor of fundamental theology at the St. Georgen College of Philosophy and Theology in Frankfurt, and it was he who showed me the path to priesthood.

As I was writing this book there were four books on my desk that I repeatedly consulted: Peter Stuhlmacher, *Biblische Theologie des Neuen Testaments*, vol. 1 (Göttingen: Vandenhoeck & Ruprecht, 1992), and Martin Hengel and Anna Maria Schwemer, *Jesus und das Judentum* (Tübingen: Mohr Siebeck, 2007), as well as the two-volume book on Jesus by Pope Benedict XVI. Those four books were both an aid and a great joy to me.

My own book would not have come into being without the urging of my student and friend, Professor Dr. Marius Reiser. I thank him for many suggestions. Originally we intended a common project, but it may be as well that two different books came of it. They shed light on the same subject from different points of view. Marius Reiser's book is titled *Der unbequeme Jesus* [*The Inconvenient Jesus*] and was published by the Neukirchener Verlag in 2011.

Heartfelt thanks for the English-language edition are due to my former doctoral student, the Rev. Dr. Linda Maloney. She contributed all her biblical scholarship skills and personal application to the translation. Without her and Mr. Hans Christoffersen, academic publisher of Liturgical Press, this English edition would never have seen the light of day.

I owe special thanks to my brother Norbert, professor emeritus of Old Testament at St. Georgen. He accompanied this book with his advice from the outset and constantly encouraged me. He continues to make Psalm 133 a reality.

Finally, my gratitude goes to Hans Pachner, faithful in fetching books for me, and to Hans Braun, my careful copyreader, as well as to my patient housemates Barbara Stadler and Manfred Lazar—and with these four also the great crowd of companions on the way in the Katholische Integrierte Gemeinde. I do not know how I could live without their friendship and their faith.

Gerhard Lohfink

Abbreviations

ACW	Ancient Christian Writers
ADPV	Abhandlungen des Deutschen Palästina-Vereins
AnBib	Analecta biblica
Ant.	Flavius Josephus, *Antiquities of the Jews*
ANTZ	Arbeiten zur neutestamentlichen Theologie und Zeitgeschichte
BDAG	Bauer, W., F. W. Danker, W. F. Arndt, and F. W. Gingrich. *Greek-English Lexicon of the New Testament and Other Early Christian Literature.* 3rd ed. Chicago, 1999.
BDS	Bonner dogmatische Studien
Bell.	Flavius Josephus, *The Jewish War*
BET	Beiträge zur biblischen Exegese und Theologie
BibS(N)	Biblische Studien (Neukirchen, 1951–)
BThS	Biblisch-theologische Studien
BTZ	*Berliner Theologische Zeitschrift*
BZ	*Biblische Zeitschrift*
CTM.PT	Calwer theologische Monographien, Reihe C., Praktische Theologie und Missionswissenschaft
Eccl. Hist.	Eusebius, *Ecclesiastical History*
EKK	Evangelisch-Katolischer Kommentar
EuA	*Erbe und Auftrag*
FB	Forschung zur Bibel
GTB	Gütersloher Taschenbücher Siebenstern
HNT	Handbuch zum Neuen Testament
HTKAT	Herders theologischer Kommentar zum Alten Testament

HTKNT	Herders theolorischer Kommentar zum Neuen Testament
HTR	*Harvard Theological Review*
JSHRZ	*Jüdische Schriften aus hellenistisch-römischer Zeit*
KEK	Kritisch-exegetischer Kommentar über das Neue Testament
LD	*Lectio divina*
LThK	*Lexikon für Theologie und Kirche*
NBL	*Neues Bibellexikon*
NRSV	New Revised Standard Version
NSKAT	Neuer Stuttgarter Kommentar, Altes Testament
NTS	*New Testament Studies*
ÖTK	Ökumenisher Taschenbuch-Kommentar
POxy	Oxyrhynchus Papyri
QD	Quaestiones disputatae
RST	Regensburger Studien zur Theologie
SANT	Studien zum Alten und Neuen Testament
SBAB	Stuttgarter biblische Aufsatzbände
SBS	Stuttgarter Bibelstudien
SBT	Studies in Biblical Theology
TGl	*Theologie und Glaube*
ThWAT	*Theologisches Wörterbuch zum Alten Testament.* Edited by G. J. Botterweck and Helmut Ringgren. Stuttgart, 1970–
TQ	*Theologische Quartalschrift*
TRE	*Theologische Realenzyklopädie.* Edited by G. Krause and G. Müller. Berlin, 1977–
TTZ	*Trierer theologische Zeitschrift*
UTB	Uni-Taschenbuchkommentar
WMANT	Wissenschaftliche Monographien zum Alten und Neuen Testament
WUNT	Wissenschaftliche Untersuchungen zum Neuen Testament
ZAW	*Zeitschrift für die alttestamentliche Wissenschaft*
ZNW	*Zeitschrift für die neutestamentliche Wissenschaft*
ZST	*Zeitschrift für systematische Theologie*
ZTK	*Zeitschrift für Theologie und Kirche*

Chapter 1

The So-Called Historical Jesus

Why is it that new books on the historical Jesus appear almost every year? Why aren't the gospels enough for Christians? It must have something to do with the curiosity of Western people and their eagerness to know "the facts." They want to know how it *really* happened. They want to illuminate the past to the last detail. They stand in line to see an exhibit that shows them the world of the pharaohs, the Celts, or the medieval court. When they finally get into the gallery they believe that they have reached the original: they see documented before their eyes the time and the people that are the subject of the exhibit.

They are looking for the same kind of access to Jesus in the gospels, and yet the gospels are closed to their thirst for knowledge. They are silent about many details of Jesus' life that would be of particular interest to the fact-hungry Jesus-seekers. And so they reach for the newest Jesus book . . .

But there is something else as well: since the time of the Enlightenment the gospels have been dissected as no other text of the world's literature has been. The people of the Enlightenment regarded what they said as having been inflated by dogma. The true figure of Jesus was painted over with ever-more glowing colors and his contours exalted to the level of the divine. Therefore it was thought necessary to remove the over-paintings and finally reveal the real Jesus, who would then emerge in his true colors and outlines.

So here again—and especially here—we find the lust for facts. What can we really know about Jesus? Who was the "historical" Jesus? How much of his life can be reconstructed? Which of his sayings in the gospels are authentic? What are his "own words," what are his "own original deeds"? Did Jesus and the apostles preach the same things, or did Jesus' message about God become, after Easter, the apostles' message about Jesus?

In and of itself it would be quite all right that the thirst for facts that has gripped the West since the Presocratics and the first Greek historians should extend to Jesus. We should, in fact, say that in the case of Jesus that curiosity is thoroughly justified. If it is true that in Jesus the eternal Word of God became flesh—entered radically into history—then Jesus must be open to all the techniques of historical research. Then he should certainly be the object of historical scholarship. Then it must be permissible to analyze all the texts about him, to probe them, to determine their genre, and to pursue the history of their traditions.

But the justified hunger for historical reconstruction has been associated for a long time with a radical critique of the gospels that seeks to discover the real Jesus not *with* the gospels but *against* them. In this very context there is constant talk about overpaintings and exaggerations of the person of Jesus by early Christian tradition. But this confuses two different things: what the gospel critics call dogmatic exaggerations are nothing other than "interpretations" of Jesus, and interpretation is not the same as exaggeration. Many Christians rightly reject such words as "exaggeration," "overpainting," "overdrawing," "mythologization," and "idolization." They should not be defensive, however, against the word "interpretation."

For the gospels must not be regarded as mere collections of "facts" about Jesus. They are not an assemblage of documents from a Jesus archive in the early Jerusalem community. Obviously the authors of the gospels had a multitude of traditions about Jesus at their disposal, but they used these traditions to *interpret* Jesus. They interpret his words, they interpret his deeds, they interpret his whole life. They interpret Jesus in every line, in every sentence.

May we take texts that are interpretation from beginning to end and filter them through the sieve of criticism in the hope that the "facts" will remain behind? May we—like people panning for gold—wash away the useless sand of the interpretations to get at the heavy gold of the facts? May we derive strata from narratives whose whole purpose is interpretation, in order to get at the "original"? In the end, after the removal of all secondary layers, would we arrive at pure facts? The questionable nature of such an interpretive technique in reality is revealed by a simple question: where is the truth—in the facts or in their interpretation? Or, to use the image of the gold panner again: are the *facts* the gold, or is it the right interpretation of the facts?[1]

Fact and Interpretation

What, after all, is a "fact"? The word is usually used with great confidence and without reflection, as if its meaning were obvious. But so-called facts are not that simple.

Of course the world is full of facts, and often we can speak of them as a matter of course. When, for example, an earthquake happens we can certainly call it a fact. But even such facts are already interpreted. The event of the earthquake is, of course, established by seismographs, its strength measured by the Richter scale, and the earthquake observers compare their measurements. But then geophysicists investigate the *kind* of quake it is, and distinguish between "collapse earthquakes" (when subterranean caves collapse), "volcanic earthquakes" (connected with volcanic eruptions), and, finally, "tectonic earthquakes" (when shifts take place within the earth's crust). The "fact" of an earthquake is thus fairly clear. It can be described in straightforward terms. And yet even such a description already contains more than a fair amount of interpretation—correct interpretation, we may suppose.

But not all facts are on this level. What does it mean when there is something like an "earthquake" in politics?—when, for example, a social landslide occurs or a political scandal becomes public? What does it mean when a politician is toppled—and no one wants to take responsibility? What is the fact here? What really happened, and what were only sham maneuvers staged for the public? What was mere opinion making, and what was deliberate disinformation?

Political events require interpretation, and a great deal more interpretation than purely physical phenomena. What really happened must be painstakingly researched, analyzed, and interpreted. But the recovery of the course of events always involves interpretation from the very start. Beyond all these difficulties there is ultimately also the question: who is the authoritative interpreter? And which interpretation will triumph in the end? Hence the quandary: is there any such thing as pure fact when the real actors are people, with their desires, interests, and passions? Is it not true that here every fact that appears is already bathed in interpretation from the outset, drenched in it through and through?

Jesus was apparently interpreted from the first moment of his appearance and in entirely different ways. There was the initially tentative but still believing interpretation of those who followed him. This culminated in the confession: "You are the Messiah, the Son of the living God" (Matt 16:16). Then there was the interpretation, quite ambivalent in many respects, by those who did not follow him but went out to see him, many of whom apparently thought he was the Baptizer returned or one of the earlier prophets (Matt 16:14). And finally there was the aroused reaction of his opponents, who were sure that he was driving out demons with the aid of the head demon (Mark 3:22). Interpretations, then, from the outset: which was correct? It is unavoidable, at the beginning of this book, to delve more fully into the relationship between "fact" and "interpretation."

The So-Called News

Let us begin with what appears to be the simplest kind of question: what is the nature of the facts communicated to us by the media? When a young person begins to read the newspaper seriously, or starts to gather information from news broadcasts, she or he may still believe that all the events in the world can be summarized in the daily news. Perhaps one might even be as naïve and innocent as Count Bobby, of whom it is said that one day he observed, quite astonished: "What a good thing it is that every day just enough happens in the world to fill a whole newspaper." But one day we awake from our childish faith that the events of the world can be adequately summed up in the daily news. At some point every critical newspaper reader, radio listener, television viewer, or internet user realizes that the media can only relate a tiny section of what is really happening in the world.

The "news," for example, that reaches newspaper readers in the United States or Germany, or those who are faithful followers of the nightly news is, from a purely geographical point of view, extremely limited. Lands like Burma or Burundi, Togo or Tanzania only appear occasionally in our media. What is presented to us as news from within our shores is in itself a profoundly limited selection. And what do we hear about our own country? We get what amounts to an excess of partisan quarrels and assessments of the social or economic situation, much of it in the form of statements prepared in cabinet departments, party headquarters, or the offices of interest groups. Then comes the "cultural" sector, where nearly every segment reflects the subjective opinion of the correspondent carried to an extreme. After that we get sports, which in Germany means mostly soccer, in the United States football, basketball, baseball, and maybe hockey. Then there are the usual sensational stories that are to the media like spice in the stew: news of terrorist acts, murders, robberies, rapes, affairs, explosions, mine disasters, fires, weather crises, plane crashes. And finally there are those stories that always seem a little odd, on the model of "man bites dog."

News programs of this sort are an unimaginably tiny and often subjective slice of reality. For what makes up the reality of world events is not first of all scurrilous doings, World Cup contests, accidents, and political quarrels, and not just movements in the social network and the economy.

Where do the real changes happen in the world?—the things that move peoples to the depth of their souls?—the things that petrify them or drive them forward?—that will incite this or that revolution or prevent it?—that destroy dreams or bestow new hope? Does any of that show up in the news? Can it be adequately shown?

A British computer scientist supposedly fed three hundred million so-called facts into a machine he programmed, nicely named "True Knowledge." He wanted to find out which was the most boring day of the twentieth century. The computer found it: it was April 11, 1954. On that day, supposedly, nothing important happened: no famous person was born; no celebrity died; nothing exploded; no war broke out; no house collapsed.[2]

The way the media think is clearly revealed in this absurd computer game: an event has to be something that shrieks, stinks, or explodes. Incidentally, April 11, 1954, was a Palm Sunday. In case it might have been that on that day even a few thousand believers took the beginning of Holy Week and the entry of Jesus into his city so much into their hearts that their lives were somehow changed, then on that day a great deal happened, and it was very important indeed.

The So-Called Fact

So the question we have already hinted at finally comes to the fore: what is a historical fact, after all? We are all too ready to speak of facts, realities, true reality, actual events, undeniable facts. For a while now, politicians have been wont to say, "The fact is that. . . ."

But what is a "fact"? How does something become a "fact"? Anyone who says "such-and-such is a fact" has already selected it from the endless stream of events, isolated it from the chaos of confused and interwoven sequences, sharply outlined it, and so already given it a conceptual label and interpretation. In other words: even the so-called pure fact, even the "naked reality" always arises out of an interpretive probe into reality.

Every "fact" has to be shaped into language and communicated (with paintings or films representing peripheral language phenomena). But to the extent that a "fact" becomes language it has already entered into a very particular horizon of understanding, into the broad field of preunderstanding. Interpretation has already begun one stage earlier. It starts with the reception of external sense impressions in our brain. Already, to a scarcely imaginable degree, there has been a process of selection, division, sorting, organizing, cataloging—and all this with the aid of models of experience that our brain has been constantly accumulating since we were embryos.

One Day in Capernaum

But so that I do not lose myself in a discussion of the theory of knowledge let me illustrate what I have said through the gospels—more precisely, through Mark 1:21-39. In this pericope, very close to the beginning of Mark's gospel, we read the following:

> They went to Capernaum, and when the sabbath came, he entered the synagogue and taught. They were astounded at his teaching, for he taught them as one having authority, and not as the scribes.
>
> Just then there was in their synagogue a man with an unclean spirit, and he cried out, "What have we to do with you, Jesus of Nazareth? You have come to destroy us. I know who you are, the Holy One of God." But Jesus rebuked him, saying, "Be silent, and come out of him!" And the unclean spirit, convulsing him and crying with a loud voice, came out of him. They were all amazed, and they kept on asking one another, "What is this? A new teaching—with authority! He commands even the unclean spirits, and they obey him." At once his fame began to spread throughout the surrounding region of Galilee.
>
> As soon as they left the synagogue, they entered the house of Simon and Andrew, with James and John. Now Simon's mother-in-law was in bed with a fever, and they told him about her at once.

He came and took her by the hand and lifted her up. Then the fever left her, and she began to serve them.

That evening, at sunset, they brought to him all who were sick or possessed with demons. And the whole city was gathered around the door. And he cured many who were sick with various diseases, and cast out many demons; and he would not permit the demons to speak, because they knew him.

In the morning, while it was still very dark, he got up and went out to a deserted place, and there he prayed. And Simon and his companions hunted for him. When they found him, they said to him, "Everyone is searching for you." He answered, "Let us go on to the neighboring villages, so that I may proclaim the message there also, for that is what I came out to do." And he went throughout Galilee, proclaiming the message in their synagogues and casting out demons. (Mark 1:21-39)[3]

We see immediately that this is a careful composition: everything takes place in Capernaum, and only in the last sentence does the event extend beyond that town.

It is not only the unity of place that is maintained throughout but the unity of time as well: the action begins on a Sabbath morning with the worship service in the synagogue. Jesus—still in the synagogue—heals a possessed person and then, with several disciples, goes to Peter's house, where he heals Peter's mother-in-law. On the Sabbath evening, as soon as it is permissible to carry sick people, a great crowd assembles outside the door of the house. Jesus heals many of them and then remains in Peter's house for the night. Early in the morning he leaves the house and prays in a retired place. The composition thus extends from the morning of the Sabbath to the morning of the following day. The individual events are carefully connected, especially by the "immediately" ("just then," "as soon as") that is so typical of Mark.

There is also an internal unity in what happens during this one day: Jesus' mighty deeds fill the whole of it. First he frees from possession, then from a feverish illness. First a man is healed, then a woman. In the evening the whole thing is expanded: now many are healed, some from possession and some from other illnesses.

Another motif that dominates the whole composition is Jesus' authoritative "teaching." The participants in the worship service are astounded at his way of interpreting Scripture. This authoritative attitude of Jesus is then linked directly to his power over demons. The people of Capernaum say, after the possessed man is healed: "What is this? A new teaching—with authority! He commands even the unclean spirits, and they obey him." At the end, then, in the final verse of the composition, the combination of powerful teaching and mastery over demons appears again, now summarized as "proclaiming."

But we should not look only at the structural lines of the composition. We must also appreciate the overall mood: Mark depicts a fully rounded day replete with holiness. It is certainly a day near the beginning of Jesus' activity. It is an example of many other days. It can be no accident that it is a Sabbath, for that means it is a day on which creation, according to the biblical idea, arrives at its perfection.

Of course, we cannot exclude the possibility that within the time of Jesus' public activity this one day, with all the events depicted, actually happened. That is certainly possible. But it is more probable that Mark here artistically distributed several pieces of tradition over a single day. He arranged disparate memories in such a way as to produce a full day's happenings—including the night that followed. He describes a day when people and relationships are healed, find rest, and are restored to balance. In this way he placed pieces of tradition that were already available to him and that had been already interpreted in the telling within a still broader context of interpretation.

The Role of Liturgy

But the process of interpretation goes still further. The gospels, after all, are not displaced texts floating somewhere in the air. They are the church's texts and their true "life situation" is the liturgy. There, they are celebrated as the word of God. There they are proclaimed as Gospel and authentically interpreted. In the Catholic Lectionary the Old Testament reading from Job 7:1-4, 6-7 is assigned to be read with the gospel on the Sunday when most of Mark 1:21-34 is proclaimed.[4] There, Job speaks of the misery of human life. He says that life is like hard servitude, full of disappointment and toil. People spend it like day laborers who have to work all day in the heat and long for the shadows of evening. But there is no rest even at night. Job spends his nights as a sick man who tosses back and forth on his bed and wishes for morning because the night is endless. His nights and days are empty and without hope. Because his life is empty it has no weight. It swiftly disappears, and the thread of existence is cut off.

That is the content and especially the tone of the reading that is assigned to accompany the gospel of the "day in Capernaum." Was Job right? Of course he was. The torturous suffering he describes courses through the world and always has. So the liturgy creates a sharp contrast on this Sunday between the Old Testament reading and the gospel, and apparently that contrast was deliberately aimed at.

Job spoke of how dark, empty, and hopeless human days are. Mark, in the gospel, describes a full and fulfilled day that is complete in itself and is full of health, holiness, and salvation. But that creates a still more profound interpretive context. Now we are speaking not only about the power of Jesus' preaching, and not only about his power over demons and sickness. Beyond that, we are speaking of his power over the world's chaos.

It is true that Mark's composition, viewed in itself, is not lacking in chaos. That is present throughout the day. It erupts in the man who begins to shout in the middle of the synagogue worship because he is being shaken by his demons. It appears in the illness of Peter's mother-in-law. It shows itself in the many sick people and those plagued by the demons of society, the people who are brought to Jesus in the evening.

The chaos of the world, the chaos of society, this whole disorder and confusion is thus already present even in Mark's composition. But through the liturgical composition—that is, through the church's official interpretation—this motif now stands out in full force. Now, for the first time, we grasp the real profundity of the Markan text. But now we also grasp the extent of the salvation that is happening here. The world is, in fact, alienated from itself and without hope. But with Jesus the state of things comes back to plumb, people sink into rest, chaos is transformed, the demons of society to which individuals are helplessly surrendered are banished. The evening and the morning are no longer full of disappointment but are overflowing with messianic salvation.

This salvation that fills the emptiness and eliminates chaos arises precisely from the fact that Jesus, with his Gospel, has set loose in the world a history that overturns everything, one to whose service people can surrender themselves. This is no longer arduous service like that spoken of in Job's lament but a service in freedom. Peter's mother-in-law is healed because she is touched by Jesus, the one who fulfills all history, and she immediately stands up and serves this new thing. It is a magnificent composition that Mark has created here; it reflects the whole of Jesus' activity. But in the light of the liturgy this composition emerges with a still greater depth of acuity.

It is probably clear by now what I am about here: the bits of tradition available to Mark had already interpreted events in the life of Jesus. Mark then, most certainly, again interpreted Jesus and his actions with his composition of the "day at Capernaum." The church's liturgy then deepens this interpretive process still further: it places Jesus against the background of the Old Testament. Only then can we understand him fully.

So what about the correlation between "fact" and "interpretation"? Where are the pure facts in the composition of Mark 1:21-39, prior to the level of interpretation? And even if we could isolate the pure facts from the interpretations, would they be any kind of help to us at all? But above all: where is the truth in Mark's composition? Is it to be found beyond the level of interpretation? Perhaps the following scenario can help us to get a little further.

A Thought Experiment

What if we imagine for a moment that the gospels had never been written, and that instead the first day of Jesus' public activity had been filmed by a hidden camera and everything said in connection with his appearance had been recorded by a concealed microphone. Image and sound were then combined into a film that is presented to us today, uncut and without commentary—with the claim that it offers us pure fact and is absolutely authentic. What would we know in that case?

Well, something: in this way we would perceive an immense number of details that are entirely absent from Mark's account, or only fragmentarily there. We would know how Peter's house looked, outside and inside. We would know how Sabbath worship was conducted in Capernaum. We would see sick people getting up again and shrieking possessed people suddenly becoming quiet. We would finally have original examples of the Aramaic spoken in Galilee in the first century. Above all, we would then have words of Jesus that we could be absolutely sure are authentic. But would we understand them? We would have no evangelists—that was the assumption behind our scenario—to interpret them for us. We would lack the whole context of interpretation that the New Testament and the communities of the early church place at our disposal.

And as regards the figure of Jesus himself: what would we see? We would see a man of the Near East, or more precisely a Near Eastern Jew, and we would learn that he is called Yeshua. He would—probably to our profound horror—look quite different from the way we had imagined him. He would be neither the sovereign Christ of the Byzantine apses nor the fettered man of sorrows of Gothic art nor the Apollonian hero of the Renaissance. His Aramaic language would be comprehensible to only a few specialists. A lot of his gestures and postures would seem strange to us. We would sense that he lived in a different civilization and a different culture.

And yet: everything we would see would be important, exciting, even disturbing. We would know, in the end, many details that biblical scholars have been working to discover for a very long time. But would we, with all that, know what actually happened back then? Would we know more than what the gospels already tell us? Would we now really know with certainty that Jesus drove out demons "by the finger of God" and that his healings were signs of the reign of God now coming to pass (Luke 11:20)? Would we know, because now we could see the external events, that here, in this person, the Logos of God had become present entirely and forever? Let me emphasize: we would know *nothing* of what really matters about Jesus, his mission, his task, the mystery of his person.

To really experience anything of that we would have to be able to see the whole public activity of Jesus, be able to survey everything he did, not only on the first day. Above all, we would have to be aware of the claim that underlay his preaching and healing. We would have to be informed about the reactions of his audience, especially those he made his mortal enemies. Here already, then, the filmed documentation of only the first day of Jesus' public activity would fall short. We would need a documentation of the whole period of his public work.

Fine; let's make that part of our scenario. We document on film everything that happened from the time Jesus left his parents' house until he was laid in his tomb—not only what happened to Jesus himself, but also among his friends and foes. That would mean that a lot of films would have to be running on a lot of screens alongside one another—and for about a year and a half. It would be an enormous burden of work just to watch it! We would not be able to hold out.

But suppose we did. Then the question would still remain: did this mega-documentation really help us? Could we, for example, even remotely grasp Jesus' claim without knowing the Old Testament? Can Jesus be understood without the Torah and the prophets, without Israel's experiences and hopes? Can Israel's hopes be understood outside the history of the faith of that people? And can Jesus be understood if we look at his life without having as our perspective the fact that here the history that has taken place between God and Israel has reached its last and decisive phase? But how can this dimension of the event be made visible by merely piling up facts, by a simple summary of external events? Here every medium that only shows us a series of external facts will fail us.

Documentary Films

Let us remain for a moment with the case of film, because we can learn a great deal from it. Every documentary filmmaker who understands her or his art would make a radical and decisive selection from the enormous quantity of filmed material we would have produced in our scenario and bring that selection into a carefully constructed composition—and so interpret it already. Perhaps she would interrupt the chronological sequence with flashbacks. Perhaps he would even build in visual allusions to the Old Testament to clarify events. In any case we can be sure that she would constantly introduce pieces of film that create connections by means of "quotations." In addition, he would hint at things in the background and give symbolic dimensions to individual events.

In other words: every good filmmaker would choose only a little from the overflowing mass of material available, bring that little into a coherent context, and create a great many semantic relationships between the individual parts of the film, and would do exactly the same with the available sound material. And in this way the filmmaker would interpret the whole event, perhaps without inserting a single word of commentary from anyone off screen or providing a single interpretive title. In any case, if no interpretation is given to an external event it cannot tell us anything.

And now comes the crucial question: did the authors of the gospels do anything different? Did they not cut, recombine, quote, allude, comment, interpret? Of course they did! And they did so using all the tools of a true narrative craft, because they knew that without interpretation there can be no understanding. Even the most accurate and strictly factual depiction of history cannot do without constant interpretation.

On 25 February 2004 a highly honored film on Claus Schenk Graf von Stauffenberg and his attempt to assassinate Hitler was shown on German television.[5] A commentator in the *Frankfurter Allgemeine Zeitung* wrote of this film:

> This is the most accurate film about Claus Schenk Graf von Stauffenberg's assassination attempt that has yet been produced, and it is the least complete. Those who view it this evening on television can

rely on the correctness of the scenery, the uniforms, and the chronology. The director, Jo Baier, not only reproduced exactly the events of 20 July already researched by the Gestapo and found in their detailed files. He has precisely reconstructed Hitler's barrack and the whole of the Führer's headquarters in the East Prussian swamps, down to the mosquitoes. We cannot say in the strict sense that Baier has forgotten anything. . . . Anyone who wants to know what a German officer named Stauffenberg did throughout the day of 20 July 1944 will be well served here.

But anyone who wants to know what the last day in the life of Claus Schenk Graf von Stauffenberg meant will feel lost. This has to do with the fact that this film is remarkably lacking in any kind of larger meaning. We could even say that it is a narrative without a context, a historical film with no history in it—and one that de-dramatizes history in the same remarkable way that dramas nowadays are de-historicized. We learn nothing of who Stauffenberg was or even who he might have been.[6]

This is the problem in a nutshell. To use another image: bare "facts" swirl chaotically through the universe in their billions. If no one organizes or interprets them they remain garbage, pure informational garbage. This informational trash has nothing to do with "history," not in the least. The so-called fact is a prior level, a partial element, but it is not yet history. Thousands of facts, in and of themselves, are not history. History is interpreted event. Historical knowledge organizes and interprets the infinite chaos of facts.

The Interpretive Community

But who does this work of interpretation—interpreting the chaotic factual material that pours out at us every day and every year? Of course it seems obvious to say that this is the work of individual historians, specialists in history, who search the archives, seek out contemporary witnesses, gather material, and then one day produce a book in which they have placed the gathered facts in a larger context, shed light on them from various sides, and so narrated a piece of history.

Oh, if only it were so simple! In reality, individual historians do not work alone. Alone, they are nearly helpless. They presuppose the work of many others; they examine a great number of prior works that have already been produced by others. They have to depend on the statements and interpretations of earlier historians. All by themselves they could never get an overview of the incalculable quantity of factual material, let alone organize it or interpret it. Besides, the documents the historian finds in the archives are for the most part already interpretations from the view and to the purpose of the witnesses of the time.

Thus, as with all serious research, there is something like a research community of historians. We need only think of the many dictionaries and reference works every historian has in her or his library. To put it more bluntly: there is something like an interpretive community of historians. Obviously, in this interpretive community as in all the scholarly professions, outsiders, contrary thinkers, oddballs, and blockheads try to make themselves heard. They too are necessary.

And of course there are struggles between groups, extreme positions, battles over positions, and quotation cartels, that is, groups of scholars who quote each other but persistently keep silence about the results of other groups' research. But above all, there is endless combat. That is inevitable in every serious field of research.

But despite the never-ending battle among historians, they form something like an interpretive community that, up to a point, even creates consensus. Otherwise the mainstream of historical research and the great scholarly standard works that are used throughout the world would be completely unthinkable.

So what is being called "interpretation" in this chapter does not fall from heaven and cannot be accomplished by lone individuals. "Interpretation" presupposes a community of interpretation. "Interpretation" presumes communication between people. "Interpretation," finally, in sociological terms, assumes a group that wants to secure its historical identity. And above all, "interpretation" presumes a "cultural memory" within that larger group.[7]

The People of God as Interpretive Community

Everything said so far about historical scholarship is, of course, true also of theology. Here the larger group that makes historical interpretation possible is the people of God. They were a narrative community from the very beginning. They told how God acted among them in ever new ways. And as a narrative community the people of God became a community of interpretation, a community that again and again renewed and purified its memory.

All that, incidentally, is true not only of the past. The church is still an interpretive community today. It is vital for it to look back at its own past, to examine it critically, and to try to understand the present on the basis of this critical retrospect. Only in that way can it take the next step into the future. At present the church, after causing infinite suffering to the Jews over centuries with its theology of Israel, has finally come to the point of revising its relationship with Judaism. This revision will profoundly change the church's life.

So what has been said in sketchy fashion about every kind of secular historical interpretation is true above all of interpretation in faith: faithful interpretation of history presumes the people of God as the interpretive community. It is not only about perceiving the church's own guilt but also about recognizing the deeds of God performed in his people and for the world through his people. Such perception and narration is impossible without an interpretive grasp grounded in faith. It is only possible when believers come together in believing communities, in the church.

But is there not widespread unease at this point, at least? Should not objections be heard? Interpretive understanding, interpretive recognition, interpretive perception, interpretation and more interpretation—is it not a fact that interpretation can also go horribly wrong? Is interpretation not something vague, subjective, irrational, arbitrary, more conjecture than knowledge? The objection is plausible, but it does not do justice to the phenomenon of interpretation because the interpretation of world and history is a fundamental process without which human beings cannot grasp reality at all.

There can be no perception of reality without an interpretive model. More than that: when people open their mouths and do not just put out animalistic sounds such as groaning and growling but use concepts, they are already interpreting their reality. Every language presumes an overarching interpretation of the world and is itself such an interpretation. Those who assign interpretation to the realm of the arbitrary call into question every field of scholarship, including the natural sciences. Still more, they question the value of every human discourse, because whenever we speak and construct sentences we are interpreting the reality that surrounds us.

The same is true of Jesus of Nazareth, and of him above all. He is unthinkable without Israel, the people of God, in whose tradition he lived, and he can therefore be adequately understood only in faith and out of the believing memory of the people of God. An understanding of Jesus demands the foundation that is Israel, that is the church. If we do not hold to the church's interpretive tradition and seek its genuine realm of experience again and again, then sooner or later the image of Jesus will disintegrate before us. Interpretation of him will become a matter of taste or at least be determined by the momentary horizon of the interpreter. We see this clearly in the many images of Jesus produced in the last several decades, each according to a shifting fashion. They show very little of the Jesus of the gospels but a great deal of the spirit of those who produce them.

So we see Jesus as an opium for the soul and as a political revolutionary. Here he is as the archetype of the unconscious, there a pop star. He appears as the first feminist and as the faithful advocate of bourgeois morality. Jesus is used by those who want to see nothing change in the church, and he is used as a weapon against the church. He is instrumentalized over and over again to confirm people's own desires and dreams. At present he must above all stand for the legitimation of universal tolerance, which is no longer interested in truth and therefore threatens to slide off into arbitrariness. For example:

The Parable of the Ten Young Women

For many centuries the interpretation of the parable of the ten young women in Matthew 25:1-13 was obvious to Christians: these virgins are supposed to go out to meet the bridegroom and adorn the marriage feast with their lamps. The wise among them had equipped themselves with surplus oil for their lamps, and in their prudence they had acted quite reasonably. One should imitate them. The foolish, on the other hand, fell short of what they were supposed to do. They had not prepared themselves in advance. They had not understood what was at stake. Therefore, they were still looking for oil when the feast was already beginning. In the end they were left standing outside the door.

Today the earlier church's view of the parable has been utterly reversed by many interpreters and preachers: the foolish young women for whom the door of the house remained closed embody people who are stigmatized, suffering, and humiliated. All sympathy belongs to them. We identify with them. The wise, on the other hand, have become offensive. Why didn't they share their oil?

In one interpretation of the parable that came to my hands some time ago[8] the "I do not know you" spoken by the bridegroom to the foolish virgins is seen as a "wounding reaction" and a "Darwinist mechanism of selection." And the wise young women in the parable, who could not give away their oil because otherwise the messianic feast of the reign of

God would lose its brilliance, are demeaned as unjust, lacking in solidarity, and egoistic about their own salvation. Still more, the concern of the wise for the festival of the reign of God is declared to be "concealed violence" against those who did not prepare themselves for the feast. In other words, those who went out to meet the bridegroom acted inappropriately toward those who were unprepared.

That shears the point off of Jesus' parable and perverts the whole thing. In the parable of the ten young women the issue is not one of solidarity, readiness to help, or tolerance, but something quite different: the neglected *kairos*, the hour not seized.

Church history shows how often Christians have failed to recognize their hour. Then a door closed and did not open again so quickly. Jesus had exactly the same experience: the majority of the people of God in his time did not recognize the crucial hour of God's action. The consequences were horrible. Zealots and fanatics shaped the program for the next decades in Jewish history. Jerusalem was destroyed. It was a historical moment not grasped, one that would have demanded wisdom and the highest degree of readiness from the people of God of that time!

Should Jesus not have spoken of such a danger of failing in his own objective? Should he not have warned against it? The fact that aid and tolerance are important does not exclude the reality that there is a judgment, one that we create for ourselves. Those who are called to follow Jesus cannot remain behind for the sake of others who do not want to go with them. They must go out—precisely so that the new ingathering under the reign of God may come to pass in the world.

There are numerous texts in the gospels that signal a parting of the ways. They have been off-putting to a whole generation of churchgoers and reveal the degree to which many theologians have forgotten the church—or else they unlock what is crucially Christian and call people to discipleship anew. One such text is this parable about the foolish and wise young women. It is like a sharp sword. No one can understand this parable unless she or he thinks of sin in terms of the history of the people of God, its crises, dangers, and decisions.

Romano Guardini once asked, in one of his university sermons: What does that mean, exactly—looking at Jesus? How can I see him? How can I encounter him? And Guardini continues: oddly enough, here we find repeated in almost the same way what was true of the religions' search for the hidden God: just as there have been many images of God, so also there are many images of Jesus. And as people have sought to take control of God, so also they try to take control of Jesus.[9]

Therefore, says Guardini, today especially the question becomes as urgent as it can possibly be: who can protect Jesus from us? Who will keep him free of the cunning and violence of our own ego, which does everything to avoid really following Jesus? His answer: the encounter with Jesus must not be left to subjective religious experience; "rather, there is a place assigned for it that is built correctly, in which he can be seen rightly and listened to, and that is the church."

This is the crucial point. We need only to add that the "place" that is the church that protects Jesus from our own interests is not something that has been prepared for him after the fact; it surrounds him from the outset. It is around him as the space belonging to the people of God, into which Jesus was born and in which he grew up, in which one day he followed the Baptizer to the Jordan to be baptized. Jesus comes out of Israel, and without the traditions of Israel he is unthinkable and cannot be understood.

But the place of the people of God, namely, the newly gathered, eschatological people of God, also surrounds what Christians have said about Jesus since Easter and Pentecost. The very first words of Jesus that were handed on, and the first accounts and stories that told what Jesus had done, were shaped within the "space" of the church. The Jesus tradition is grounded in the interpretive community that is "church."

It could not be otherwise, for we have seen that there is no such thing as a pure fact. Every fact that is told is already interpretation. Without interpretation, no event in our world can be understood. And when we are talking about the history between God and the world—still more, when the subject is the culminating point of that history, the fidelity of Jesus to his mission even to death, which set in motion a history of freedom that overturns everything—how could such an event be grasped and told without interpretation? We could also say: how could it be grasped and understood without faith?

A Radical Process of Division

But at this very point another objection arises, and we dare not evade it: I quoted Romano Guardini's question: who will protect Jesus from us? Who will preserve him from the "cunning . . . of our own ego," which does everything to avoid really following Jesus? And his answer was: the encounter with Jesus must not be left to subjective religious experience; a place is appointed for Jesus, one that is built in such a way that he can be rightly seen and listened to—and that place is the church.

Lovely, and quite right! But is it so simple, "the church"? Have there not been some totally different interpretations of Jesus within the church itself, interpretations that were mutually exclusive? We only have to think of the great christological battles that led to the councils of Nicaea (325) and Chalcedon (451).

But to review the lengthy history of christological interpretation carried out in the major councils of the ancient church would, in our context, take far too much time and be too complicated. Let me simplify things. Instead of looking at the great christological confrontations in the third, fourth, and fifth centuries, let us look at the pictures of Jesus produced by the so-called infancy gospels.

In the "Infancy Gospel of Thomas,"[10] for example, we read how the boy Jesus is playing at the ford of a brook; he diverts the flowing water into small pools and then, by his mere word, makes the muddy brew "clean." Jesus is practicing, so to speak, for his later activity. The son of a scribe is standing near; he takes a branch and lets the water Jesus had gathered flow out again. How does little Jesus react?

> When Jesus saw what he had done he was enraged and said to him: "You insolent, godless dunderhead, what harm did the pools and the water do to you? See, now you also shall wither like a tree and shall bear neither leaves nor fruit." And immediately that lad withered up completely; and Jesus departed and went into Joseph's house. But the parents of him that was withered took him away, bewailing his youth, and brought him to Joseph and reproached him: "What a child you have, who does such things." (2.2-3)

This writing, which originated in the second century CE, goes on in the same vein. Not only does it lack narrative skill and good taste, its Christology is also pathetic. A miracle child does whatever comes to mind and so shows himself to be a child of God.

There can be no question but that this gospel has its own image of Jesus, and a pretty miserable one. No doubt it was written with good intentions. It wanted to illustrate Jesus' divinity, his wisdom and miraculous power. As a result, it circulated widely in the ancient church. The Greek original was translated into Latin, Syriac, Georgian, Ethiopic, and Church Slavonic. Apparently it was favorite reading for many Christians, or people liked to tell the legends collected in it.

And this was only one part of the much larger production of gospels and sayings of the Lord. We have a great number of other gospels and revelatory writings, preserved entire or at least in fragments—for example, a Gospel of Peter; a Gospel of Thomas; a Gospel of Philip; an Infancy Gospel of James; various acts of the apostles, such as the Acts of Andrew and the Acts of John; as well as an Apocalypse of Peter, an Apocalypse of Paul, an Apocalypse of Thomas, and many other apocalyptic writings.

Certainly some of these were abstruse compositions that promised secret knowledge and could be rapidly dismissed. Others contained Docetic and Gnostic heresies, against which the church was in any case struggling to defend itself. But many of these writings certainly addressed the thoughts and feelings of the Christians of the time, especially their religious curiosity. Only against the background of all these so-called apocrypha can we discern the true quality of the New Testament, and above all the power of discernment exercised by those who created it. They had an inerrant instinct for the authentic Jesus tradition going back to the apostles.

This is the crucial point: the Infancy Gospel of Thomas and similar creations may have been widely read and popular in the ancient church; they may even have borne the names of apostles; but they were not acknowledged as apostolic writings. And that means that they were not accepted into the canon of the New Testament. The theological significance of that nonacceptance should not be underestimated. In principle, what happened here was a radical process of division—altogether comparable to the process of division that was taking place in the great christological discourses of the first councils.

This immense process of considering and choosing, of distinction and division, but above all the deliberate selection and assembly of the writings ultimately chosen as the canon of the New Testament was an "ecclesial" process. We could even call it "authorial activity," because the result was the composition, the authoring, of the *one* book that is the New Testament, which is more than a bundle of randomly associated writings.[11]

Obviously the authors of this process were concrete persons, often even clergy or others commissioned by the church in some fashion. But they were supported by all those among the people of God who believed with their whole being and who for that very reason possessed the gift of discernment. Without the faith instinct of the many, without the *sensus fidelium*, the process of coming-to-be of the New Testament as the final, concluding book of the Bible would have been impossible. What would have happened without this ultimate critical process of discernment is evident in the apocrypha, which over long stretches are bizarre, confused, and unhistorical. A constant rereading of the immense apocryphal Jesus literature from the ancient church is urgently needed, because only that can show us how unique and precious are the gospels of the New Testament canon.

Faith as Recognition

What does all that mean for a book about Jesus? It shows that for a scholar who works *theologically* it cannot be a question of reconstructing a "historical Jesus" against the New Testament and its interpretation of the figure of Jesus. Any theologian who does that exalts herself or himself above the first witnesses and the church and thus abandons any chance of understanding Jesus.

Of course that does not mean that no scholar who works purely in the history of religions may study Jesus. Nor does it mean that such a scholar could not say a great deal about Jesus that is illuminating. But if a scholar in the field of the history of religion uses her or his methods cleanly, it will be clear at some point that she or he has reached a limit. That limit, that boundary, runs precisely where the interpretation of Jesus in faith begins. Why?

Faith always includes knowledge; it includes recognition. Certainly this is not the kind of knowledge or recognition that can make the thing it considers an "object," standing over against it in distanced fashion and analyzing it impartially. In the natural sciences that kind of knowledge is fundamental and indeed indispensable. But there is another kind of human knowledge that occurs only in personal encounter. It responds to the other, surrenders itself to the other, and adopts the other's view of reality. In theology this kind of knowledge is called "faith."

Faith is true knowledge, true recognition, but a recognition of a different kind from that which analyzes, that is, literally, "dissolves." Encountering another as a person definitely does *not* mean "dissolving" that person, taking him or her apart psychologically and thus seizing power over the other, but seeing the other in her or his difference, even strangeness. Whoever wants to truly recognize another as a person must expect to encounter the unexpected and be led into a new world of which one previously had no idea—a world whose strangeness fascinates but also frightens.

The student of religions who uses refined methods and so approaches Jesus "critically" will at some time arrive at a point at which she or he recognizes "critically" that one must abandon the usual standards of criticism and surrender to the different nature of this so very different person in order to do him justice.

Precisely here lies the point, or the boundary, where historical criticism also arrives by itself, where it must surrender its normal standards. It is only a very limited sector within the possibilities of human knowledge. The most important things in human life, such as affection, love, fidelity, and devotion, are based on a different kind of knowledge. As soon as historical criticism arrives at this boundary and honestly admits it, it points beyond itself. And that is, in fact, its greatest and loveliest possibility. It is precisely at this point that it is most appropriate.

So a purely historical approach to Jesus, or one undertaken entirely in terms of the study of religions, is possible. But it has its limitations. This book gratefully makes use of the primarily historical studies of many biblical scholars. Beyond that, it has not the least hesitation in critically reconstructing the original meaning of Jesus' words and parables. A good deal of this book will be reconstruction. But I am convinced that in doing so I have no need to proceed against the knowledge of Jesus that belonged to the first witnesses or against the faith in Christ of the early communities.

Tensions within the Jesus Tradition

I am certainly aware that the theologians of the early church brought the Jesus tradition up to date and interpreted it in terms of their own historical situation. I am also aware, of course, that the gospels (like the traditions that preceded them) spoke of Jesus from very different perspectives. But in doing so they were not falsifying Jesus; they were formulating the unfathomable mystery of his life in deeper and deeper ways. It is, in fact, just this fruitful tension between the oldest layers of interpretation in the gospel tradition and newer layers that were added later that makes it possible for us really to understand Jesus.

To mention another example besides the interpretation of the "day in Capernaum," we find in John's gospel, clearly the latest of the four, a passage in which Jesus says to Philip, "Have I been with you all this time, Philip, and you still do not know me? Whoever has seen me has seen the Father. How can you say, 'Show us the Father'? Do you not believe that I am in the Father and the Father is in me?" (John 14:9-10). Jesus certainly never talked like that. This is meditative reflection on a claim that is present in Jesus constantly and wherever anything is said about him, though in other rhetorical genres and forms of discourse, but much more reservedly. And yet the language of the Johannine Jesus touches precisely what Jesus was. The two levels of tradition, the Synoptic and the Johannine, must not be set off against one another. We must not make the oldest interpretation a monopoly, because it is only the whole body of layers of interpretation that, in their unity, bring out the picture of the real Jesus.

In this book the weight will certainly lie on the oldest texts, that is, the oldest layers of meaning available to us. I will not explicate the Christology of the Gospel of John, but I will attempt to extract Jesus' claim and (to a degree) his self-understanding from the earliest possible texts. But this is not done *against* later Christologies; it is done *with* them and under their guidance. I am writing not as a student of religions but as a theologian. Nor am I putting up an "iron curtain" with watchtowers and barbed wire between words of Jesus that are certainly authentic and others whose authenticity cannot be demonstrated with the same assurance. Such drawing of boundaries, which is carried out among biblical scholars with an immense expenditure of intelligence and acuity, have a little whiff of silliness. Anyone who has thought about the oscillation between "fact and interpretation" can understand why in this book I will not constantly ask, to the point of exhaustion, whether Jesus really uttered a particular saying in precisely this form.

Pope Benedict XVI once summarized my concerns in this first chapter as follows: The Jesus of the gospels is "the only real historical Jesus."[12]

Chapter 2

The Proclamation of the Reign of God

If we want to talk about Jesus—what he wanted, and who he was—we must speak first and above all about the reign of God. The expression "reign of God" is less familiar than "kingdom of God," the phrase used most commonly in biblical translations, including the New Revised Standard Version. Martin Luther, in his epochal translation of the Bible into German in 1545, rendered the corresponding Greek expression as "kingdom of God [Gottesreich]," and that has remained the usual reading.

But, without making a rigid principle of it, we should prefer the translation "reign of God," or "rule of God," not only because the Nazis talked about a "Reich/kingdom" whenever occasion offered, so that in German-speaking countries the word still arouses a certain disgust in many people, but above all because "reign" or "rule" better reflects the underlying biblical concept.

A Little Bit of Philology

Where we speak of "kingdom" or "reign" (German translations use "Reich" and French ones "royaume"), the Greek has *basileia*. This refers primarily to the status of a king, the king's power, the king's rule, and, by derivation then, the spatial realm within which the king reigns. In Aramaic, the language Jesus spoke every day, the Greek *basileia* reflects the word *malkuta*. And *malkuta* is first of all the "king's *rule* or reign," and only secondarily the *extent* of the king's rule or a particular territory.

With Jesus the concept of "reign of God" has something utterly dynamic about it. The reign of God has an event-character. It is something that happens. It "comes" or "is coming." For that reason also we should prefer the concept of the "reign of God." But obviously the notion "kingdom of God" also reflects a certain aspect of the event, namely the realm within which God is establishing his rule. One can "go into" the *basileia* or "enter into" it (cf., e.g., Mark 9:47; 10:15).

So we have here a sample of philology. We actually need even more of it; it is simply unavoidable, because we still have that lovely saying a theologian once uttered, reflecting Matthew 19:24: "A camel cannot enter into theology's heavenly kingdom without first passing through the eye of the needle that is philology."

One more preliminary remark: in Israel the earliest time when people spoke of a "kingship of God" or "royal reign of God" was the monarchical period, that is, the time of David and Solomon.[1] This already shows us that the concept of God's royal reign had a relationship to actual society from the very beginning of its use: it would be a society in which God's kingship would be visible. In the Bible this concept never referred to something *purely* internal or *purely* in a future life. That was often ignored in later times. But people should have known that a king without a people is no king at all but a figure in a museum.

There was, of course, a good reason why the concept of the reign of God was often understood in the church as something purely future: the evangelist Matthew speaks, with very few exceptions, of the "kingdom of heaven" instead of the "kingdom of God." That led people astray into thinking of the kingdom of God as identical with heaven, a purely transcendent reality. But the Matthean kingdom of God is precisely *not* what the Bible calls "heaven." In the Judaism of the time "the heavens" could be a polite circumlocution for "God." People didn't want to speak the word "God" all the time. So the "kingdom of heaven" is nothing other than the "kingdom of God," and the kingdom of God is primarily and above all on earth.

One final observation: the abstraction "royal reign" (Hebrew *malkuth*) is relatively late. Originally people said, using a verb instead of an abstract noun, "God reigns as king." But after the crisis of the exile this cultic statement about God's eternal kingship slipped into a historical vortex, a historical dynamic. Now it could be said with much stronger emphasis that "The Lord *becomes* king."

This means that God is now definitively establishing in history, and specifically in the present crisis in Israel, the kingship that was always his. God's eternal royal reign is manifested in that God intervenes, redeems his people, and creates them anew. God becomes the judge and rescuer of his people—in that sense God *demonstrates* his rule and in that sense it can be said that God *is becoming* king.

So much for preliminary remarks! Now to the matter at hand.

The Preaching of the Baptizer

The word "eschatology" is familiar to everyone who is interested in theology. Eschatology is often understood to mean "doctrine about the last things." In classic Christian dogmatics eschatology deals with the death of the individual, judgment and purification after death, eternal blessedness—and ultimately the end of the world, its judgment, and the resurrection of the dead.

For a long time eschatology was the final tractate in dogmatics, concluding the whole subject. Consequently it had something distant, remote, and otherworldly about it. One *felt* as if it had very little to do with the present course of history. But when we talk about New Testament eschatology—and Jesus' proclamation of the reign of God is pure eschatology—it is very different. Here the "last things," that is, what will change and transform everything, happen not in the distant future but in the immediate days to come. These things are near; they are breathing down our necks.

This should make clear what we mean when we begin to talk about the eschatology of John the Baptizer, because with the Baptizer what eschatology means in the Bible leaps up before our eyes. If we understand the Baptizer's preaching of the end time we will better comprehend what Jesus meant by the reign of God, because, as we have said, Jesus' proclamation of the reign of God is pure eschatology.

So to begin with, the Baptizer's real audience is not the individual but the people of God, Israel. Obviously the Baptizer also spoke to individuals, and obviously it is individuals who have to decide to turn their lives around. Obviously every individual must confess her or his sins and be baptized in the Jordan.

But this process in which every individual is involved is first and foremost about Israel. The Baptizer does not address humanity in general or sinners in general but the descendants of Abraham, the people of God. Israel has squandered its calling, and therefore God will now judge his people.[2] The Baptizer says to the crowds who have come to him at the Jordan to be baptized: "You brood of vipers! Who warned you to flee from the wrath to come? Bear fruits worthy of repentance. Do not begin to say to yourselves, 'We have Abraham as our ancestor'; for I tell you, God is able from these stones to raise up children to Abraham" (Luke 3:7-8).

This says cuttingly that descent from Abraham, that is, belonging to the people Israel, cannot rescue from the approaching judgment. Probably the Baptizer goes much further than that: not only is ethnic membership of no avail, but belonging to Abraham's faith does not help. Even being part of the history of God with his people will fail to rescue them. The text continues: "Even now the axe is lying at the root of the trees; every tree that does not bear good fruit [will be] cut down and thrown into the fire" (Luke 3:9). This urgent warning is also directed to Israel, because its background is a familiar comparison in the Old Testament tradition: Israel is "God's planting," firmly rooted in the Land. In the Psalms of Solomon, an apocryphal writing from the first century BCE, that line of tradition is drawn out still more: there Israel appears as God's planting that cannot be rooted out for all eternity.[3]

And that is precisely what John the Baptizer denies. He turns most sharply against any kind of collective certainty of salvation. Israel has become a collective disaster, and therefore judgment has come on the whole people of God. The axe is already at the root of the trees God has planted, and if Israel does not turn back even the root stock will be dug up. God will place Israel under judgment precisely because it is *God's* planting. Every tree in the orchard Israel that bears no fruit will be cut down. And "bearing fruit" is no longer possible without the radical repentance that is offered the people now, with baptism in the Jordan.

Israel needs a new exodus and at the same time a new entry into the Promised Land. Therefore John does not go into the cities and towns, and therefore he does not baptize just anywhere, but where Israel had once crossed the Jordan to enter the Promised Land. The history between God and his people is thus pressing toward a final crisis. Judgment on Israel is about to happen immediately. But that judgment can be transformed into salvation if Israel turns back and bears fruit after all.

Lest there be misunderstanding, let me say here that when I speak again and again of Israel I mean the Israel to which John the Baptizer was then preaching. He was a prophet of Israel—and Israel's prophets since Amos had all spoken just as severely and without compromise. They had to speak that way. But the Baptizer's words were received into the New Testament, and therefore they apply also to every Christian and to the church, just as they applied to Israel at that time. If the church does not repent and turn back, the judgment of which the Baptizer once spoke will come on it even today.

John the Baptizer had a multitude of images for God's hard judgment on his people. One of them is the axe. The judge has already measured for the blow about to fall, and now his arm is swinging back. The axe is about to fall. Another image is winnowing with a shovel, when the cut-up straw and chaff are separated from the wheat. The grain falls directly to the ground while the straw is tossed a little farther away and the chaff is swept away by the wind. The judge already has the full shovel in his hand (Matt 3:12). A third image is that of a firestorm that consumes everything (cf. Luke 3:16). Major fires create storms. All those who experienced the night bombings in World War II know about those. The Baptizer says: Israel will be baptized with "storm and fire," that is, in a horrible firestorm.[4]

It cannot be clearly determined whether this fiery judgment of which the Baptizer spoke was identified with the general judgment of the world. In any case it is a judgment on Israel. Repentance and baptism in the water of the Jordan were the sealing, the protection, the only rescue from the judgment by fire.

That makes it clear that the judgment announced by the Baptizer is not a pure imposition of punishment that offers no hope. The Baptizer's concern, in his preaching of judgment, was precisely for the eschatological gathering of Israel, its repentance, its purification and sanctification, that is, its eschatological renewal. Israel is to bring "fruits" worthy of its repentance (Luke 3:8). And while the chaff is carried away by the wind, the wheat that remains will be gathered into a great granary (Luke 3:17).

And when will all that happen? Right away. The fiery judge already has the shovel in his hand, the axe is already laid to the root of the tree. This is about *this* generation in Israel.

So John the Baptizer's eschatology is not only shaped by a worldview; it is decidedly about the people of God. And it is allied with an extreme expectation that it will follow immediately. The judgment is not coming someday, in future times. Nor is it coming in such a way that there is still time to delay anything. It is so near that there is no time left. The people of God must turn back immediately, and that means concretely that every individual must go to the Jordan, confess her or his sins publicly, be baptized in the Jordan, bear fruits of repentance, and so enter into the eschatological Israel.

Jesus and the Baptizer's Preaching

This whole background must be considered if we are to understand Jesus' eschatology,[5] because Jesus obeyed the Baptizer's preaching: he let himself be baptized by John in the Jordan. He may even have been the Baptizer's disciple for a time (cf. John 3:22-30).[6] We may assume, then, that he did not subtract anything from the Baptizer's preaching of judgment. Nor did Jesus deviate from John the Baptizer's expectation of the nearness of the end. He adopted the Baptizer's overall eschatological horizon: there is no time left to wait or turn aside; now, today, every individual in Israel must act because God himself is acting now. Characteristic of Jesus' expectation of the immediacy of the crisis are the beatitudes in the Sermon on the Plain:

> Blessed are you who are poor,
> for yours is the reign of God!
>
> Blessed are you who are hungry now,
> for you will be filled.
>
> Blessed are you who weep now,
> for you will laugh! (Luke 6:20-21)

This is about the poor, the hungry, the weeping in Israel, with whom Jesus was confronted every day. It is about the hopeless, the oppressed, the despairing among the people of God who followed Jesus. Jesus calls them blessed—not because their weeping, hunger, and poverty were of any value in themselves, but because God's intervention is about to take place and because it is especially the hopeless who will experience God's hope and salvation in a measure beyond all telling.

Jesus is not promising the miserable and the poor a better life after death, which certainly would have been possible within the overall framework of Jewish eschatology in his time. Instead he directs their eyes to the eschatological turning point that is now coming, that will affect all and change everything. He promises the poor and the beaten-down in particular that they will participate in the reign of God.

So Jesus is quite sure: this turning point is at hand. It will gather Israel anew, it will make possible a new society in which the poor have a share in the wealth of the land and the sorrowing participate in the rejoicing of the people of God.

So also with the imminent expectation—an expectation that reaches out toward the true, eschatological Israel under the rule of God. If the beatitudes had only been about consolation to be had after death Jesus

would have emptied history of all value and made it nothing but a preliminary stage before the real thing. Then earthly history itself would no
longer be the place where God's salvation takes place.

However, the beatitudes also reveal a characteristic difference between
Jesus and the Baptizer. The latter preached *judgment*—in the hope that
a new Israel would arise, as if out of the fire. Jesus, in contrast, preached
God's *salvation*, the superfluity of the reign of God, which would only
become judgment if Israel rejected it. The Baptizer relied on the weight
of judgment, on terror of destruction. Jesus counts on the fascination of
salvation, the joy of the reign of God. That is not an objection to John or
a devaluing of the Baptizer. He was, according to Jesus, the greatest
"among those born of woman" (Matt 11:11), that is, the "greatest human
being of all." And yet the very next thing Jesus says is that "the least in
the kingdom of heaven is greater than he." With this paradox Jesus marks
the breathtaking newness of what is now coming in him. And with this
newness of the reign of God, Jesus' concept of time has also shifted.

The Baptizer's message is purely one of imminent expectation of the
end. The axe is raised but has not yet fallen. But Jesus can say: salvation
is here. So he really crossed a threshold that neither the Baptizer nor the
whole of the Old Testament could or would cross.

The Proclamation in Mark 1:15

The gospels illustrate this especially in Jesus' first appearance. That
beginning is marked by the proclamation with which Mark summarizes
Jesus' preaching in the first chapter of his gospel: "The time is fulfilled,
and the reign of God has come near; [therefore] repent, and believe in
the good news!" (Mark 1:15).

First of all: what the evangelist summarizes here is proclamation. Jesus
is not just talking *about* the reign of God. He is announcing it. He proclaims it, and later he has his disciples proclaim it in Israel (Matt 10:7).
A proclamation always has a public character. What Jesus says about the
reign of God is not apocalyptic secret knowledge but a public address
to all Israel.

Furthermore, the beginning of this proclamation is precisely *not* a call
to Israel to repent and believe the Gospel. Rather, repentance, turning
back, is a consequence of the salvation that is already present: the time
is fulfilled and the reign of God has come near. At the beginning, then,
as throughout the Bible, is God's action, not human action. God has taken

the initiative. He alone gives the reign of God. It is the business of the people of God to respond. God's action makes human action possible.

But the structure of Mark 1:15 shows us still more: biblical scholars have rethought many times what exactly "has come near" could mean. Is it that the reign of God is now closer than it was before in the dimension of linear time? That would inevitably mean that it is still not here. In that case the threshold to the new has not been crossed, and Jesus would have been no different, at least as far as his proclamation about the time of the reign of God was concerned, from the others who had preached "imminent expectation" in Israel.

The problem is solved if we take the first part of the proclamation seriously: "the time is fulfilled." This opening clause gives the accent and clarifies the question of time. "The time is fulfilled," of course, appears in the garments of solemn biblical language. But it means nothing different from our expression, "the time has come." The biblical clothing of the expression indicates that this is about the promises of the prophets: now they are being fulfilled. Paul means the same thing when he writes: "See, now is the acceptable time; see, now is the day of salvation" (2 Cor 6:2). The second clause, "the reign of God has come near," following the groundbreaking opening statement, cannot mean that the time of fulfillment has not yet really arrived.

It is true that "has come near" contains a "not yet," but it is not about God's action; it is about Israel's response. The people of God, at this moment, has not yet turned back. It is still in the moment of decision for or against the Gospel. Therefore, the reign of God is near but not yet present. It is being offered to the people of God. It is laid at their feet. They are within reach of it; they can reach out and touch it. But as long as it is not accepted it is only near, and people must still pray: "Your kingdom come!" (Matt 6:10).

In the Synagogue at Nazareth

There is no scene in the Gospel that more clearly illustrates this tension between "already" and "not yet" than Jesus' preaching in the synagogue at Nazareth, as narrated in Luke 4:16-30. Jesus has returned to Nazareth for a short time, and on the Sabbath he goes into the synagogue, is installed as lector, reads a text from the book of Isaiah describing the eschatological restoration of Israel by the Anointed One appointed by God (Isa 61:1-2), and then says, interpreting the prophetic text: "Today this scripture has been fulfilled in your hearing" (Luke 4:21).

What does that mean? Luke means to say that in Jesus' appearance, his preaching, and his saving deeds the book of Isaiah is now fulfilled, and with it all of Scripture. Now, with the appearance of Jesus, the promised future is beginning. Now is the time of fulfillment!

And who brings this fulfillment? Who is the grammatical subject of the fulfillment, concealed in the passive voice? In the first place it is God himself. God takes the initiative. God fulfills. But at the same time Jesus is the "actant" to be supplied. He too, who is entirely surrendered to the will of God, now through his preaching and his mighty deeds is fulfilling the ancient promises.

But then the story goes on and in doing so betrays more and more clearly that—from Luke's point of view—it summarizes Jesus' whole public life and actions. First Jesus meets happy agreement. But then the wind shifts. Suddenly the inhabitants of Nazareth take offense at Jesus. The offense lies in the concreteness of the preacher: "Is not this Joseph's son?" (Luke 4:22). That is: it is true that everyone prays for and dreams about God's eschatological action, but in the hour when it actually happens it is evident that people had not imagined it quite this way. Not like this! not so concretely! not right here in Nazareth, and above all, not at this moment!

So Jesus' hearers prefer to push everything off into the future, and the story comes to no good end. The reign of God announced by Jesus is not accepted. The "today" offered by God is denied. And that, that alone, is why "already" becomes "not yet."

That Nasty "Today"

It was not only in Nazareth that the "today" of the Gospel was not accepted. Later also, in the course of the church's history, it has again and again been denied or rendered toothless. The reason was the same as in Nazareth: apparently it goes against the human grain for God to become concrete in our lives. Then people's desires and favorite notions are in danger, and so are their ideas about time. It can't be *today*, because that would mean that our lives have to change *today* already. Therefore God's salvation is better delayed into the future. There it can lie, hygienically and snugly packed, at rest, inconsequential.

This process of suppression often intensifies the hope for another world. But it can also turn against the concrete church. There is a particular form of contempt for the church that arises directly out of the delay of Jesus' "today." I refer not to skepticism or the hatred of outsiders, but to a contempt for the church that comes from the inmost circles in the church itself and is so destructive because baptized people who were, in fact, called to be witnesses to the presence of God no longer believe that God wants to give his salvation in the here and now of the concrete, offensive church.

What went on in the synagogue at Nazareth continues in the church. Therefore it is necessary to engage constantly with Jesus' "today," not only because otherwise what is new about Jesus and the New Testament remains unclear, but also for the sake of the renewal of the church. It cannot be renewed if it does not finally accept the "today" that has come to it. For the New Testament people of God everything depends on whether it can believe again that the promises are meant to be fulfilled already, now, and that God is acting *today*.

For Jesus, God's "today" was the center of his existence. There had been imminent expectations in Israel long before Jesus, but the "today" in Jesus' preaching explodes every kind of such expectation. Jesus knows with the utmost certainty that the promised, longed-for, prayed-for future is here, that the reign of God is breaking forth. That is the only way to understand Jesus' unbending assurance of fulfillment. That is the only way to comprehend his beatitude addressed to his disciples: "Blessed are the eyes that see what you see! For I tell you that many prophets and kings desired to see what you see, but did not see it, and to hear what you hear, but did not hear it" (Luke 10:23-24).

It was not only in Nazareth that people took offense at this "today" in Jesus' preaching. Many other people shook their heads at what they heard, and said, "the world goes on just as ever; nothing has changed, so the reign of God can't have come!" Jesus answered them: oh yes, something has changed: "if it is by the finger of God that I cast out the demons, then the [reign] of God has come to you" (Luke 11:20).

Demons come in many forms. Maybe we can translate this saying of Jesus as: if people who cannot escape their state of possession, their obsessions, the destructive compulsions that have built up in them and around them because of the evils in society and the history of disaster within which they stand, even in the midst of the people of God—if such people are able to breathe again through the power of Jesus, become free and able to trust, then the reign of evil is already broken, and the reign of God is already palpably present.

For the reign of God does not come as lightning throughout the world, not as a universal spectacle from heaven; it comes into the world like a grain of wheat that grows. In Jesus' deeds of healing the "today" of the reign of God is already visible and tangible.

The Ultimate Ground for the "Now Already"

Ultimately Jesus' present eschatology is about who God is. Jesus lives to God in a revolutionary new relationship. For him God is so powerful in his goodness and so present in his power that from God's point of view there is nothing left to happen. Because Jesus lives in full union with the will of his heavenly Father he knows that when God comes he does not come halfway but entirely. And God does not come at just any time, even in the immediate future; God comes today.

We simply do not do justice to Jesus' message if we talk as if God gives his *basileia*, but not entirely at the moment; as if he caused it to dawn, but only bit by bit; as if he revealed it, but only in anticipation. We cannot say all that, any more than we could say that God revealed himself in Jesus, but only in preliminary fashion, only in pieces, and absolutely not wholly and with finality.

We can only do justice to the New Testament if we insist that God spoke himself fully in Jesus. Jesus is the definitive presence of God in the world. Who sees him, sees the Father (John 14:9). He is "the Son" in a sense that cannot be said of any human being. Ultimately the unconditional "today" Jesus proclaims is grounded in his unrestricted participation in the eternal "today" of God.

Those who subtract from Jesus' present eschatology are therefore in great danger of minimizing the mystery of Jesus' person. It is no accident that it is John's gospel, which contains the statement "I and the Father are one" (10:30)—note: it does not say "I and the Father are identical," but "I and the Father are one"—that represents the clearest and most unconditional present eschatology in the New Testament. Thus the "not yet" of the reign of God is brought about not by God's hesitation but by the hesitance of human beings to turn their lives around. People prefer not to let God get too close. They would rather dance at their own weddings than at the one to which God is inviting them.

Honorable Excuses

So Jesus had to tell in a parable (Luke 14:15-24) how a man prepared a banquet, taking care to provide a fine meal and doing everything to make his guests happy. Finally it was ready—and the guests did not come, even though they had long since been invited. Instead, one excuse after another arrived: I have bought a farm, please excuse me. I have bought five yoke of oxen, please excuse me. I have just gotten married; alas, I cannot come.

The parable is neither about the salvation of individuals nor about joy beyond this world. It is about God's feast with his people, which is to happen now, in the hour of Jesus' appearing. That feast is as much in question today as it was then. Those invited continue to find new excuses to shield themselves from the God who is near and from the gathering of the people of God.

For the most part the excuses are honorable. They almost always end with: "I would like to. But at the moment it is not possible!" But Jesus' "today" says: you have no more time, because the world is burning down. You have to act now, for you have encountered God's cause. You have to put your whole existence in play, right now—now, because you have received God's invitation.

Not a Kantian Ethics of Duty

But—when we put it this way, we see immediately that this "you must!" cannot stand in isolation, or it will fall short of Jesus' proclamation. In such a case Jesus would be nothing but the holiest of all moralists. Jesus' aim, with his "today," is not primarily duty, the imperative, the moral "must," but the jubilee over the feast that is offered, the joy at the treasure and the pearl we can find already.

The parable of the treasure in the field and the pearl of great price (Matt 13:44-46) will be treated at length later in this book (cf. chap. 14). Here I want only to point out the uncompromising present eschatology of the parable. It does not say: "It is with the reign of God as with a treasure someone found. He buried it again, went home rejoicing, and lived afterward with the happy thought that the treasure existed and at some time in the future he would hold it in his hand." No, the parable tells how the man obtains the treasure, on the spot: "in his joy he goes and sells all that he has and buys that field" (Matt 13:44).

So the hidden treasure of the reign of God is already dug up, and the pearl of great value has already been acquired. The feast is ready to begin, and everything depends now only on whether those invited will come.

Theological Avoidance Maneuvers

This chapter has been about Jesus' proclamation of the reign of God. The focus was quite clearly on the present aspect of the reign of God as proclaimed by Jesus. There is a reason for that: it is just this present aspect in Jesus' preaching that is repeatedly softened, both in theology and in teaching and preaching.

It is true that biblical scholars constantly emphasize that in the interpretation of the reign-of-God texts surrounding Jesus the tension between present and future, or between "already" and "not yet," cannot be resolved in favor of either pole. But this insight, correct in itself, is then for the most part not maintained. The principle has scarcely been established when the present character of the reign of God is soft-pedaled again. This means, for example, that the reign of God is only present in Jesus' own person, or it is only present in Jesus' symbolic actions, or it is only present in Jesus' words, or it is dynamic, proleptic, anticipative, punctually-situationally present, or—here the analysis is highly refined—it is present in the mode of its expression. I can't help it: the real result of such restrictions after the fact is that the reign of God is forced farther into the future. One need have no respect for such linguistic artistry; we can simply regard it as a set of classic avoidance maneuvers.

Not only Protestant theology but Roman Catholic as well has been laden with such evasive maneuvering for centuries now. Neoscholasticism made of Jesus' eschatology a tract on "the last things." Paul's theology of the Spirit suffered a similar fate. In Paul's writing, Jesus' present eschatology is contained in the theology of the Holy Spirit, who has taken up residence in the baptized and is changing the world through them. But what has happened to Paul's talk about the presence of the Spirit? All this is why it is the present aspect of Jesus' proclamation that has to be kept in the foreground if we want to speak adequately about his idea of the reign of God.

The Humble Form of the Reign of God

Certainly this chapter has omitted another aspect of Jesus' appearance that must be included here; otherwise all that he said about the reign of God in his preaching would have been one-sided and even distorted. Everyone who reads the gospels and lets them affect him or her has the impression that a marvelous glow lay on the beginning of Jesus' work, a kind of bright morning light. Think, for example, of the Baptizer's question in Matthew 11, the one Jesus answered with the jubilant cry: "The blind receive their sight, the lame walk, the lepers are cleansed, the deaf hear, the dead are raised, and the poor have good news brought to them" (Matt 11:5). Or consider the wedding at Cana, which the Fourth Evangelist concludes with the statement: "Jesus did this, the first of his signs, in Cana of Galilee, and revealed his glory; and his disciples believed in him" (John 2:11).

Jesus must have received an amazing amount of attention in Israel. People ran after him. They brought their sick. They came with their cares and concerns. They hoped for the messianic turning of events. They sensed the new thing, something enormous, something that would surpass everything else. They said: "A new teaching out of sovereign power!" (Mark 1:27).[7]

Jesus found disciples who followed him. They, too, were fascinated by his message and awaited the great overturning of things. Some biblical scholars speak of this as Jesus' "Galilean springtime."

There was much that was right in the way people in Israel reacted to Jesus, and much that was false. Jesus did, in fact, proclaim an overturning, a revolution. He spoke of an action of God that changed everything. But he did not have a political revolution in mind, one that would drive the Romans from the land, nor was he thinking of a messianic fairytale time in which roasted doves flew onto people's plates. The turning of which he spoke was something different. It presupposed faith, joy in God, becoming his followers, discipleship, a radical understanding of Torah, a new community, new family. Still more, the turning of which he spoke presupposed surrender to the will of God, unto death.

The whole of Mark's gospel has a substructure whose purpose is to show this "other," strange, alienating, resistant aspect of Jesus' message. In Mark the corresponding instructions to the disciples are, in fact, central—and, of course, so are the misunderstandings on the part of the disciples that precede each of them. The whole of Mark's gospel progresses with a terrible goal-directedness toward Jesus' passion. And it is not very different in the other gospels.

"Galilean springtime"—if that expression is at all justified, it has a heavy counterweight in the gospels: the disciples' lack of understanding, the hatred shown by Jesus' enemies from the very beginning (Mark 3:6), and at the end his helpless, horrible hanging on the cross. We cannot separate Jesus' end from his message about the reign of God. We must not think that the proclamation of the *basileia* and the cross are two completely different things that have nothing to do with one another.

Jesus' death on the cross again modifies his message about the reign of God. Whether it did so for Jesus is something we can leave open at this point. But in any case it did so for the hearers of the Gospel after

Good Friday. It was only in Jesus' death that this message achieved its proper profundity.

Jesus' death did not revoke his proclamation of the reign of God; it did not put paid to the good news of the beginning. Instead, it demonstrated the reality contained in that proclamation. It definitively revealed the hidden and humbled[8] shape of the reign of God. What does that mean? It means that the reign of God does not come without persecution, without sacrifice. Indeed, it does not come without daily dying. It cannot come any other way.

What was contained in Jesus' preaching from the very beginning was fully illuminated by his death: the reign of God demands a change of rulership that human beings must carry out. It demands letting go and self-surrender. The reign of God does not come without pure receiving, and that receiving is also always an acceptance of suffering. In his passion Jesus was by no means far from the reign of God; instead, the reign of God comes precisely in the "hour" in which Jesus himself can do no more but hands himself over and surrenders to God's truth. This is the basic thread of John's gospel. The "hour" of deepest "humiliation" is the hour of his "glorification," the hour in which the glory of God encompasses Jesus' whole "work."

So Jesus' announcement of the reign of God achieves in his death, once again, a final precision and focus: the concept "reign of God" cannot be used from here on unless at the same time one speaks of Jesus' surrender even unto death. For Jesus' disciples this means that they cannot live in the realm where God reigns without obedience to what this reign of God brings with it. And that, in the midst of a resistant society and resistant church, does not happen without suffering, without sacrifice, without passion stories.

Ultimately, Jesus' death lays bare all human self-glorification and thereby also every superficial and presumptuous notion of the reign of God. God's realm can happen only where human beings collide with their own limits, where they do not know how to go on, where they hand themselves over and give space to God alone so that God can act. Only there, in the zone of constant dying and rising, the reign of God begins.

Chapter 3

The Reign of God
and the People of God

The preceding chapter showed that for Jesus the coming of the reign of God was no longer something in the distant or near future but something that was happening already, now, in the present hour. Rescue, liberation, salvation—for Jesus it had all irrevocably begun. "If it is by the finger of God that I cast out the demons, then the reign of God has come to you" (Luke 11:20). But at the same time Jesus' disciples are supposed to pray daily: "your kingdom come" (Luke 11:2). For the reign of God has not come everywhere, not by a long sight, because it has not yet been accepted everywhere—not even by the disciples themselves, who according to the gospels were still dreaming about their own reign (Mark 9:34).

We have seen that in today's biblical scholarship this tension between the "already" and the "not yet" of the reign of God is much emphasized, though with the greatest variety of nuances. There are scarcely any exegetes left who see the reign of God as beginning in an utterly distant future.

But in contrast, another aspect of Jesus' proclamation is not yet clear in exegesis in general. The explosive power of the reign of God is not only defused by pushing it into the distant future or into a time beyond time. It can also be handed over to impotence by being made homeless.

For Jesus the reign of God not only has its own time, it also has its own place in which to be made visible and tangible. That place is the people of God.

To say the same thing in two Greek words: as the reign of God has its *kairos*, its proper time, it also has its own *topos*, its place. It is not a u-topia, which means "no place, nowhere." The island of Utopia invented by the brilliant English Lord Chancellor and humanist Thomas More (1478–1535) to illustrate his critique of society did not exist and he did not mean for it to do so (cf. chap. 21). In contrast, for Jesus the reign of God is, despite all opposition and persecution, an event whose realization begins in history. Therefore it can be grasped and seen: first in Jesus himself but then necessarily also in the eschatological Israel that Jesus is gathering around himself.

So we must not talk only about the *time* of the reign of God; we must apply the same intensity and clarity to the search for its relationship to the *people of God*. Is that being adequately pursued? That is the subject of this chapter. Despite a number of brief excursions into the history of theology, this will not lead us away from Jesus but will bring us closer to him.

Is It Addressed to "Humanity"?

In professional exegetical literature there are long chapters and treatments of Jesus' idea of the reign of God in which the question of time is shoved back and forth. But the explicit question of its *place*, that is, of the relationship between the reign of God and the people of God, is lacking in many cases, or else it appears only indirectly. This is demonstrated in almost exemplary fashion by Andreas Lindemann in a long article, "Herrschaft Gottes/Reich Gottes" ["Reign of God/Kingdom of God"] in the *Theologische Realenzyklopädie*.[1] Obviously much of what Lindemann writes is quite correct, but nowhere does he reflect on the theological relationship between Jesus' preaching of the reign of God and Israel. Instead, he speaks emphatically and repeatedly of "human beings" or "people" in general. God pursues the human being. A person's sins are forgiven. The reign of God has consequences for human behavior; God's forgiveness must be matched by human forgiveness. Human beings must be responsible before God. God makes demands on people. The inbreaking reign of God establishes new and definitive standards for human action.

A reader cannot entirely avoid the impression that Jesus apparently had nothing to say to Israel in his preaching. Instead, as a citizen of the world, he wanted to address all humanity. His message about the reign of God was directed to all people of good will throughout the world. The fact that it had its beginning and crucial situation in Israel was probably just an accident.

All this is the more strange in that Erich Zenger, in the Old Testament section of the same article, insistently emphasizes the connection between the sovereign rule of God and the people of God, Israel.[2] Apparently the connection is still not sufficiently present in New Testament exegesis. Therefore, it seems good at this point to consider at least *one* Old Testament passage at greater length. Many such texts could be used, but in some of them the dimension of the reign of God is especially prominent.

The Beasts and the Son of Man (the Human One)

My choice is the great apocalyptic vision in the seventh chapter of Daniel.[3] It not only has the advantage of speaking explicitly about the connection between the reign of God and the people of God; as regards the time of its composition, the book of Daniel, as one of the last books in the Hebrew Bible—it was created in the second century BCE—comes relatively close to the time of Jesus. Here is the vision in Daniel 7, slightly shortened:

> I, Daniel, saw in my vision by night the four winds of heaven stirring up the great sea, and four great beasts came up out of the sea, different from one another. The first was like a lion and had eagles' wings. . . . Another beast appeared, a second one, that looked like a bear. It was raised up on one side, had three tusks in its mouth among its teeth and was told, "Arise, devour many bodies!" After this, as I watched, another appeared, like a leopard. The beast had four wings of a bird on its back and four heads; and dominion was given to it.
>
> After this I saw in the visions by night a fourth beast, terrifying and dreadful and exceedingly strong. It had great iron teeth and was devouring, breaking in pieces, and stamping what was left with its feet. It was different from all the beasts that preceded it, and it had ten horns. I was considering the horns, when another horn appeared, a little one coming up among them; to make room for it, three of the earlier horns were plucked up by the roots. There were eyes like human eyes in this horn, and a mouth speaking arrogantly.

As I watched,
    thrones were set in place,
    and an Ancient One took his throne,
his clothing was white as snow,
    and the hair of his head like pure wool;
his throne was fiery flames,
    and its wheels were burning fire.
A stream of fire issued
    and flowed out from his presence.
A thousand thousands served him,
    and ten thousand times ten thousand stood attending him.
The court sat in judgment,
    and the books were opened.

I watched then because of the noise of the arrogant words that the horn was speaking. And as I watched, the beast was put to death, and its body destroyed and given over to be burned with fire. As for the rest of the beasts, their dominion was taken away. . . .

As I watched in the night visions,
    I saw one like a human being [lit.: son of man]
        coming with the clouds of heaven.
And he came to the Ancient One
    and was presented before him.
To him was given dominion
    and glory and kingship,
that all peoples, nations, and languages
    should serve him.
His dominion is an everlasting dominion
    that shall not pass away,
and his kingship is one
    that shall never be destroyed. (Dan 7:2-14)

This symbolic text was written in Israel during a period of great crisis. Daniel is the pseudonym of a theologian and prophet whose real name is no longer known. He lived in the second century before Christ under Antiochus III and then Antiochus IV, the Syrian rulers notorious in Jewish history. Antiochus IV ruled from 175–164 BCE. His plan was to Hellenize Israel. He plundered the Jerusalem temple and entered the holy of holies—a sacrilege to Jews who followed the Law. He established a cult of Zeus Olympios in the temple precincts. Jews were forbidden to practice their own worship or to celebrate the Sabbath. That is the immediate historical background for the book of Daniel and its hopes for the end time.

Because this was a time when faith was in crisis and persecution was rampant, the text says it is night. The four winds are the four compass directions and are an image representing the fact that this text is about the whole world, not only Israel. This is about world history. And the great sea spoken of in the night visions is not a body of water that can be geographically located. It is the world ocean, the primeval sea, and thus an image of chaos. For ancient people the sea was chaotic and perilous.

Thus the four beasts emerge from the chaos, and they themselves represent social chaos. They stand for four world empires, or we could say four societies, each more bestial and evil than the one before it. The lion, for the author of the book of Daniel, was the great power Babylon. The bear was the empire of the Medes, the leopard that of the Persians.

Then the prophet sees the fourth beast, and here the imagery almost gets away from him, so horrible is it. This is *the* beast itself. It is the world power that was most dangerous to Israel's faith: the Hellenistic empire of the Seleucids, a successor to Alexander's. The ten horns are ten Hellenistic rulers. The last horn, the "little one," is Antiochus IV. As the arrogance of the last horn reaches its climax, an ancient one appears: this is God himself. He alone, and not the bestial world empires, is master of the world and of history. They have only been assigned the right to rule in a limited and transferred fashion (Dan 7:6, 12). That God is the true Lord of history is evident in what follows.

A heavenly court is assembled to judge all the world empires, but especially the beasts. The sentence is carried out immediately. Then a fifth empire appears before the world court, a fifth society. As previously the symbols were lion, bear, leopard, beast, now the corresponding symbol is the human being. For "son of man" simply means "human being." The whole series—lion, bear, leopard, beast, human being—thus represents successive societies. The fifth society is, of course, very carefully dissociated from those that precede it. It is no longer brutal, no longer bestial, but finally a human society. Therefore it is symbolized not by beasts but by a human being.

We must see what a sharp distinction the text makes at this point: the fifth society does not arise out of the sea of chaos but comes from heaven. It comes "with the clouds of heaven" (Dan 7:13). Thus the new, eschatological society comes from above. It cannot be made by human beings. It is God's gift to the world. It is the end of all violent rule.

And yet, even though this ultimate and final empire, this rule without end, comes from above, it does not float above the world. Despite its heavenly origin it is altogether earthly and worldly. It is the longed-for true, eschatological Israel, for in the subsequent interpretation of the vision it is identified absolutely with the "holy ones of the Most High." An interpreting angel says to Daniel:

> "As for these four great beasts, four kings shall arise out of the earth. But the holy ones of the Most High shall receive the kingdom and possess the kingdom forever—forever and ever. . . . The kingship and dominion and the greatness of the kingdoms under the whole heaven shall be given to the people of the holy ones of the Most High; their kingdom shall be an everlasting kingdom, and all dominions shall serve and obey them." (Dan 7:17-18, 27)

Thus not only the vision itself but its context makes clear that this is about empires, societies—and the one society represented by the "human being" is Israel. But it is not simply the Israel of the present. It is the hoped-for eschatological Israel. It is a counter-reality over against all social constructions of history thus far, which either relied on brutal violence or could not survive without it.

The human being/son of man is thus a symbol for the ultimate and final royal rule of God, but at the same time a figure for the true Israel that serves God the Father alone. The two cannot be separated, for the royal rule is "given" (Dan 7:14) forever to this true, eschatological Israel. And that royal rule comes from God; it is God's own rule, now revealed in all its purity and without blemish—in a finite human society.

Daniel 7 only shows in a carefully developed form what appears in many other late Old Testament texts: the reign of God and the people of God belong together. The "field" within which the reign of God appears is first of all and primarily Israel. It is true that God reigns as king over the whole world, but that royal rule is revealed in Israel. It never manifests itself to the nations independently of Israel but always in connection with Israel and through Israel.

The Abraham Principle

Why is that? Why is there this unending fixation on Israel in the Old Testament? Is this the inferiority complex of a little nation that had to fear for its existence all the time and therefore almost of necessity developed a theological megalomania? Most certainly not. If we read the Old Testament from beginning to end—from Abraham to Daniel, so to speak—then looking back, considering the *whole* of it and at the same time incorporating the great revolutions in world history, we could say:[4] The God of the Bible, like all revolutionaries, desires a complete overturning, the radical alteration of the whole of the world's society. For in this the revolutionaries are right: what is at stake is the whole world, and the change must be radical, simply because the misery of the world cries to heaven and because it begins deep within the human heart. But how can God change society at its roots without taking away its freedom and its humanity?

It can only be that God "starts out small," beginning at a single place in the world. There must be a place—visible, comprehensible, subject to examination—where liberation and healing begin, that is, where the world can become what it is meant to be according to God's plan. Starting from this place, then, the new thing can spread abroad. But it most certainly cannot happen through indoctrination or violence. Human beings must have the opportunity to view the new thing and test it. Then if they want to they can allow themselves to be drawn into the history of salvation and the story of peace that God is bringing into being. Only in this way can the freedom of the individual and of the nations be preserved. What drives one toward the new thing cannot be compulsion, not even moral pressure, but only the fascination of a world transformed.

So God has to start small, with a small nation. More precisely, God cannot even begin with a nation. God must start with an individual, because only the individual is the point where God can build on *change undertaken freely*.

That is precisely what the stories of the patriarchs in Genesis tell about. The first pages of the Bible had told of the creation of the world, the development of the story of humankind, and—in a few hints—the growth of human civilization and culture. But along with all that the Bible also spoke immediately of disobedience to God and thus of the growth of destructive rivalries and brutal violence.

But then Genesis 12 starts over with something new. It suddenly ceases to look at humanity as a whole and begins to talk about an individual: Abraham. God begins to transform the world by starting anew, at a particular place in the world, with a single individual:

> Now the LORD said to Abram, "Go from your country and your kindred and your father's house to the land that I will show you. I will make of you a great nation, and I will bless you, and make your name great, so that you will be a blessing. I will bless those who bless you, and the one who curses you I will curse; and in you all the families of the earth shall be blessed." (Gen 12:1-3)

So God makes a new beginning with an individual. However, he will not remain a lone individual. He will become a great nation. That is unavoidable, since an individual could not show what God wants: *a new society*. So the individual has to be there at the beginning, but in the end the result must be a new society because redemption, salvation, peace, blessing always have also—and indeed, primarily—a social dimension. At the very end of the Bible we will find the image of the "holy city," the "new Jerusalem" (Rev 21)—and the city, the *polis*, was in antiquity the proper image of society.

Nevertheless, the indispensable role of the *individual* remains integral to the people God wants to create. The people of God can never be a pure collectivity, never simply a mass; it must always also be "Abraham," that is, a people in which every individual is constantly called by God to perform her or his duty. We may call the whole thing the "Abraham principle."

For the Sake of the Nations

From all this we can already see that the people God chooses and creates cannot rest within itself. It is not self-enclosed, existing for its own sake. It is chosen out of the mass of the nations *for the sake of those nations*. Abraham was, after all, dragged out of his family and his homeland so that he could be a blessing for many others. In the people that came from him was to be made visible and tangible what God wants for the whole world: nonviolence, freedom, peace, salvation.

Because God desires the salvation of the world, that salvation has to be tangibly present in the experimental field of a small nation, precisely so that the other nations can see that there really can be justice and peace in the world, so they can see that justice and peace are not utopia, not "nowhere," and so they can freely take on this new social order. Of course that puts a shocking burden on this nation: the burden of election. Because if the people of God does not do justice to its task, if instead of peace in its midst there is conflict, instead of nonviolence it works violence, instead of showing forth salvation it spreads disaster, it cannot be a blessing for the nations. Then it falls short of the meaning of its existence; then it will not only be a laughingstock for the nations but will do great harm.

A Basic Biblical Constant

That, or something like it, is the description one must give of the meaning of Israel's election, looking back especially at the stories of the patriarchs in Genesis but also at any number of other key biblical texts such as Exodus 19:5-6 or Isaiah 2:1-5. At any rate, this election and its function for the world form a basic constant in the Old Testament. According to the Old Testament, salvation and the reign of God cannot otherwise exist in the world.

But then the question arises: is this basic constant of the Old Testament abandoned in the New Testament? Is it no longer valid there? Has it given way to a vague and placeless universalism? Anyone who says or even hints at such a thing will have to prove it. He or she will have to prove that for Jesus, Israel was indeed no longer the sign of blessing (or of judgment) for all nations but that he had separated himself internally from Israel and preached an absolute salvation, that is, one divorced from Israel—with "people in general" as the immediate audience for his message.

It would then have to be proved explicitly and in detail that Jesus only appeared in Israel because that was his place of origin, because he was naturally shaped in some way, like every human being, by the history of his people, but that otherwise he had set himself apart from Israel's history of election. And yet there is not the faintest evidence of such a thing. It simply cannot be produced. Precisely where Jesus (like John the Baptizer before him) calls into question the participation of Israel, or part of Israel, in ultimate and definitive salvation (cf. Matt 8:11-12) he presumes Israel's salvation-historical function. But above all there is an overabundance of texts to show that Jesus did not abandon the fundamental constant we have described. I will speak of those texts at length in the following chapters. Most important of these is the choice of the Twelve—a demonstrative sign-action showing that Jesus cared about the twelve tribes of Israel. The Twelve are a visible sign and, of course, also an "instrument" of his will to gather all Israel. And why? for the sake of Israel? No, for the sake of the world!

The principle behind this is pointedly formulated in James's speech in Acts 15, aided by a mixed quotation based on Amos 9:11-12:

> After this I [the Lord] will return, and I will rebuild the tent of David, which has fallen; from its ruins I will rebuild it, and I will set it [the tent] up, so that [!] all other people may seek the Lord—even all the Gentiles over whom my name has been called. Thus says the Lord, who has been making these things known from long ago. (Acts 15:16-18)

The sense of this combined quotation is that the fallen Israel must be rebuilt *precisely in order that* the Gentile nations, over whom the name of the Lord has long been called out, may seek and find God. They cannot perceive him otherwise. The ultimate goal of the rebuilding of Israel is the coming of the Gentiles. Jesus thought no differently.

Obviously this resolute will of Jesus to gather all Israel (for the sake of the nations) had everything to do with his proclamation of the reign of God. The two are inseparable. There is no text that better summarizes Jesus' praxis and his innermost intention than the Our Father. As we will see (cf. chap. 4), the very first petition of this direction-giving prayer is about the sanctification and gathering of Israel. The background is the theology of the book of Ezekiel, especially Ezekiel 36. This "petition for gathering" is followed immediately—in the same breath, so to speak—by the petition for the coming of the reign of God. These two petitions are the most important ones Jesus entrusted to his disciples, and they belong inextricably together. The reign of God must have a people.

How is it that such clear truths, which so obviously spring to our attention even on the basis of the Old Testament, have not been a matter of course in the history of New Testament exegesis? The reason must be a widespread framework of ideas that is deeply anchored in Christians' heads.

God and the Soul

The religious subjectivism and individualism that have always threatened Christian theology left profound traces especially in the theology of the nineteenth century and the early years of the twentieth. The depth of this can be observed in the work of Adolf von Harnack, one of the most influential theologians and scholars of his time. Harnack lived from 1851 to 1930. In the winter semester of 1899–1900 he gave sixteen lectures for students from all departments of the University of Berlin, entitled *Das Wesen des Christentums* [*The Essence of Christianity*]. More than six hundred students heard them. The book Harnack published a few months later, based on his lecture manuscripts and bearing the same title, was an even greater public event; it went through numerous editions and its ongoing influence was extraordinary.[5]

In *What Is Christianity*, Harnack used the concepts of individualism and subjectivism without any shadow of criticism. He was convinced that those two concepts rightly and substantively described Jesus' preaching.[6] Of course, Harnack knew that Jesus worked "within his own people" and that his preaching about the coming of the reign of God was eschatological. But he separated "what is traditional and what is peculiar" in Jesus' preaching and so distinguished the "kernel from the husk."[7] Once one peels off the Jewish husk one finds something very simple: "the Gospel in the Gospel."[8] At the end of his third lecture Harnack spoke the now-famous sentences:

> If anyone wants to know what the kingdom of God and the coming of it meant in Jesus' message, he must read and study his parables. He will then see what it is that is meant. The kingdom of God comes by coming to the individual, by entering into his soul and laying hold of it. True, the kingdom of God is the rule of God; but it is the rule of the holy God in the hearts of individuals; *it is God Himself in His power.* From this point of view everything that is dramatic in the external and historical sense has vanished; and gone, too, are all the external hopes for the future. Take whatever parable you will, the parable of the sower, of the pearl of great price, of the treasure buried in the field—the word of God, God Himself, is the kingdom. It is not a question of angels and devils, thrones and principalities, but of God and the soul, the soul and its God.[9]

With this Harnack had produced a radical reduction of Jesus' preaching. He says without any concern at all:

> In the combination of these ideas—God the Father, Providence, the position of men as God's children, the infinite value of the human soul—the whole Gospel is expressed.[10]

> The individual is called upon to listen to the glad message of mercy and the Fatherhood of God, and to make up his mind whether he will be on God's side and the Eternal's, or on the side of the world and of time.[11]

> Here for the first time everything that is external and merely future is abandoned: it is the individual, not the nation or the state, which is redeemed.[12]

> The Gospel is above all questions of mundane development; it is concerned, not with material things but with the souls of men.[13]

> Jesus never had anyone but the individual in mind.[14]

"The individual" and "the inner" are key words that appear repeatedly throughout the sixteen lectures. Harnack repeats the expression drawn from Augustine, "God and the soul, the soul and its God," almost like a mantra. It is evident on its face that a message of Jesus like the one that is here—supposedly—brought out of its shell has nothing to do with the people of God and does not intend to. Harnack reveals that already, in anticipation, in the first lecture: "Jesus Christ's teaching will at once bring us by steps which, if few, will be great, to a height where its connexion with Judaism is seen to be only a loose one."[15] Finally, in the tenth lecture, Paul will definitively "deliver" the "Christian religion from Judaism,"[16] for Paul, with his knowledge, confidence, and strength, set this "new religion" "in competition with the Israelitish religion."[17]

The degree to which such idiotic notions are complicit in the calamitous history of the twentieth century need not be discussed here. In any case, it is highly dangerous to separate Christianity from Israel and commit oneself to theological individualism.

Harnack was by no means alone in his narrowing of the message of Jesus to the individual. He was, in fact, representative of a broad current of liberal theology at the end of the nineteenth century and the beginning of the twentieth. The idea that the reign of God has to do only with individuals and is something profoundly internal was widely accepted at the time, especially in segments of Protestant theology. There were corresponding phenomena in Catholic theology and piety. The motto of countless parish missions, "save your soul!" is very familiar.

The Reign of God Within

There is a saying of Jesus in the gospels that appears to support the internal nature of the reign of God invoked by Harnack and many others. Harnack quotes it several times in his lectures. It is in Luke's gospel, at the end of a short narrative that prepares us for the saying itself:

> Once he was asked by the Pharisees when the reign of God was coming, and he answered, "The reign of God is not coming with things that can be observed; nor will they say, 'Look, here it is!' or 'There it is!' For, in fact, the reign of God is [already] among you [*entos hymōn*]." (Luke 17:20-21)

Most translations today render *entos hymōn* as "among you" or "in your midst." The question is whether this does justice to the Greek text. But first a brief word on the form of the whole pericope: in terms of narrative technique the two verses constitute a "chreia," that is, a genre that creates the necessary narrative framework for an important and decisive saying.

The saying, which is the heart of the matter, is placed at the end. Here the saying itself is: "the reign of God is [already] *entos hymōn*."

But there is no point in pursuing the structure preceding the saying too intensively here. In Luke's sense of things the Pharisees are apparently asking for signs (portents) of the reign of God, as the disciples in Mark 13:4 ask about signs foretelling the end of the world. Jesus answers that there are no such (visible) signs ahead of time. Why? Simply because the reign of God is already present. Because it already exists there is no point in looking for it "here" or "there" (cf. Mark 13:21).

Of course, the crucial question is *how* the reign of God is present. The precise meaning of Luke's Greek phrase in 17:21, *entos hymōn*, is disputed. It could mean "with you" or "between you" or (in view of the textual context) "among you," "in your midst." But it can also mean "within your sphere of influence," "within your power," "available to you," "at your disposal." These latter meanings of *entos* are found, at any rate, in several passages of the Greek classics, but particularly in a number of ancient papyri.[18] This has a superb application here. Besides, elsewhere Luke always writes "in the midst of" or "among" as *en meso*. But however we decide this, the point is that Luke wants to say that the reign of God is already here. It has already come. That is why searching for portents is pointless.

But Martin Luther—and this is what makes Luke 17:21 so explosive—translated *entos hymōn* as "The reign of God is within you." That is also a possible meaning of the words. In that case the text would say: "From outside there is nothing to be seen. But within, in the soul, in human hearts, the reign of God is already present."

As I have said: that is a possible translation of the Greek. But it fits badly in the context, because then the passage would say that the Pharisees already have the reign of God within them. Above all, that kind of invisibility and internal character in no way matches the manner in which Jesus speaks about the reign of God elsewhere. The realm of which he speaks is precisely *not* a purely internal, altogether spiritual sphere that is hidden and inaccessible, for "the blind receive their sight, the lame walk, the lepers are cleansed, the deaf hear, the dead are raised, and the poor have good news brought to them" (Matt 11:5). All that is happening before everyone's eyes. The reign of God is breaking forth in the midst of the world and not only within people. Every dimension of reality is to be placed within the realm of God: soul and body, health and sickness, wealth and poverty, adults and children, family and society. That makes Luther's translation altogether improbable. It neither matches the close context of the text nor fits in the broader context of Jesus' message and practice. For that reason Luther's translation is generally rejected today.

But it created, or at least accelerated, a fateful and continuing impact. Harnack and many others used this translation as support for assigning the reign of God to the invisible realm of the soul. This apparently solved a whole list of problems, almost as if incidentally. For example, there was the so-called imminent expectation of the end of things. If the place for the reign of God is only in the soul it can certainly be present already. The reign of God within the soul is not disturbing to anybody and can be asserted at any time. The problem of "the reign of God and society" was also resolved. If the reign of God is only within, a clean and simple separation can be made between external conditions and the hidden realm.

In reality, of course, the separation cannot be maintained. It is not only individuals and their inner lives that need redeeming but also the situations within which they live—for example, the lack of freedom, the structures of injustice, and the mechanisms of manipulation that have eaten their way into society.

Jesus was not just concerned with souls. He wanted a changed society. That is precisely why he begins the new thing within a community of disciples whom he orders to quit acting as if they are superior, to forgive one another seventy-seven times a day, and to turn the other cheek when someone strikes them.

Even Origen

Of course, it was not Adolf von Harnack who first located the reign of God "within." We have seen that Martin Luther had already understood it as an "inner kingdom." But Luther was not the first to interpret the text in that way either. Throughout the history of theology, but especially in the history of mysticism, we find a long line of related interpretations that go back as far as Origen, the great theologian of Alexandria (185–ca. 255). Origen wrote a work "On Prayer" in about the year 233, and within it he gives an interpretation of the Our Father. Speaking of the third petition, he says:

> [Whoever] prays for the coming of the kingdom of God prays with good reason for rising and fruit bearing and perfecting of God's kingdom within him. . . . The Father is present with him, and Christ rules together with the Father in the perfected Soul, according to the

saying . . . We will come unto him and make abode with him. By
God's kingdom I understand the blessed condition of the mind and
the settled order of wise reflection.[19]

For Origen, then, the "coming" of the reign is the "coming" of the Father
and Son into the soul of the one who truly prays. They take up their
dwelling in the inmost being of that person. That is a very beautiful and
also an altogether biblical thought (cf. John 14:23). But does it really cover
what Jesus meant by the coming of the reign of God?

Purely Religious?

We are seeking reasons why exegetes today find it so difficult to connect the reign of God and the people of God in any meaningful way. One
of the most important reasons was treated at length because it played a
central role in the epochal forgetfulness regarding the people of God in
the last several centuries, namely, individualism or subjectivism. Adolf
von Harnack was swimming with a powerful tide here. But there were
many other reasons for the absence of the idea of the people of God from
discussions about the reign of God: these, for example:

1. In twentieth-century exegetical literature we repeatedly encounter,
even among serious exegetes, the assertion that the reign of God announced by Jesus, and the salvation he promised, were "a purely religious matter."[20] We can understand this formulation if we know what
it was supposed to mean. Mainly it was a matter of distinguishing Jesus'
reign of God from Jewish expectations of the reestablishment of the
nation and political action against the Roman occupying power. But
more than that: the expression "purely religious" was meant to separate
it from the expectation of a glorious messianic kingdom.

All these distinctions were justified. The question is only whether the
label "purely religious" did not open the gates to new misunderstandings. What do we mean by "purely religious"? If the words are meant
to exclude the world and society, they are meaningless and have nothing
to do with the Bible.

2. A further reason why today's exegesis has such a hard time considering the reign of God and the people of God together is that in the
twentieth century people no longer spoke only of the "purely religious"
character of the reign of God; they also said that it is "supernatural,"
"otherworldly," a "simply unworldly thing." That, at any rate, is how

Rudolf Bultmann formulated it in his book on Jesus that appeared in 1926:

> [The reign of God] is not a good toward which the will and action of men is directed, not an ideal which is in any sense realized through human conduct, which in any sense requires *men* to bring it into existence. Being eschatological, it is wholly supernatural.[21]

> Whoever seeks it must realize that he cuts himself off from the world, otherwise he belongs to those who are not fit, who put their hand to the plow and look back.[22]

> ["Entering into" the reign of God] does not imply any possibility of conceiving the Kingdom as something which either is or can be realized in any organization of world fellowship.[23]

We can also have some understanding for this eloquent language, with its measured formulations. It is typical of the "dialectical theology" emerging out of the critical experiences of World War I. These theologians rightly wanted to separate themselves from a broad current in nineteenth-century Protestantism that was convinced that the reign of God was developing in the growth of culture and intellect. Dialectical theology was right to oppose that.

But this opposition was in part presented in a dangerously one-sided language, as can be seen very clearly in the quotations from Bultmann. Does the reign of God really have nothing to do with human activity? A whole series of Jesus' parables flagrantly contradicts that thesis. I will have more to say about that in chapter 7. And does the reign of God really have nothing to do with "world fellowship"? Then the reign of God would truly be a kind of cosmic cloud somewhere in the universe. It would have nothing to do with this world. And can we say that the reign of God is "supernatural" or somehow "cut off from the world"? Then there would be no chance for a bridge to the Old Testament and Judaism. The Jewish religious historian Gershom Scholem (1897–1982), a great scholar of Judaism and Christianity, wrote in one of his essays:

> Judaism, in all its forms and shapes, has always held fast to a concept of redemption, which it has seen as a process taking place in public, on the stage of history and in the medium of community, in short, decisively occurring in the visible world and impossible to be conceived without such a visible appearance. In contrast, Christianity has an idea that redemption takes place in the "spiritual" realm and is invisible, playing itself out in the soul, in the world of each indi-

vidual, and effecting a secret transformation that need not correspond to anything in the world outside.[24]

Scholem is right in many respects. In these sentences he formulates one
of the most dangerous constrictions in Christianity, and especially in
Christian theology. But he is also wrong. From the beginning the church
concerned itself with the world and society. Even those Christians who
have lived the monastic life have transformed and cultivated the world
to an extraordinary degree. But when Bultmann calls the reign of God
"wholly supernatural," something that cannot be realized within secular
society, he affirms Gershom Scholem's verdict against Christianity.

3. Finally, there is one more reason why today's exegetes have a hard
time thinking of the reign of God and the people of God together. In the
Middle Ages (alongside some quite different positions) there was a line
of theological thinking that identified the reign of God with the church.
Berthold of Regensburg, one of the greatest popular preachers in the
Middle Ages (ca. 1210–1272), repeatedly equated the kingdom of heaven
with "holy Christendom" in his sermons. For him the two are identical.
And that line of interpretation appears repeatedly throughout the medieval period. Basically, we find it already in the work of Gregory the
Great (540–604). For him Jesus' parables of the reign of God mean nothing
but the church. In the background, as so often in the Middle Ages, we
find Augustine, but a coarsened and simplified Augustine.

The real Augustine was much more cautious here. He worked with a
twofold concept of the reign of God. While he said that the church was
already the kingdom of God, he asserted that it is not yet the "kingdom
of perfect peace."[25] And since Augustine had an extraordinary influence
on theology and preaching (and was not always read very carefully), it
is no wonder that the church was repeatedly equated with the reign of
God over the centuries.

But then at some point there came a time when people no longer believed in that equation. In 1892 appeared the famous book by Johannes
Weiss (1863–1914), *Jesus' Proclamation of the Kingdom of God*, and in it—
against the trends of Enlightenment theology and rationalism, but also
those of German idealism—the eschatological character of the reign of
God in Jesus' understanding was worked out in detail.[26] In the wake of
Weiss's insight, the identification of the reign of God with the church
was increasingly rejected. Since then we hear again and again that obviously one cannot equate the two. The reign of God and the church must
be clearly distinguished. The reign of God is not the same thing as the

church, and the church is something different from the reign of God. This runs like a *basso continuo* through today's exegetical and dogmatic literature.

And that is quite right. Obviously the church is not identical with the reign of God. But when we constantly hear this ground bass playing we are no longer in a position to ask the right questions about the relationship between the reign of God and the church, or between the reign of God and the people of God. The theme has become taboo, so to speak. And that is a shame. It is not only a shame, it is fateful. It once again affirms Gershom Scholem's verdict.

But what really is the relationship between the reign of God and the people of God, or between the reign of God and the church? It is high time this chapter produced an answer. It should be clear by now that we have to speak of *correlation*, not *identity*. But how could such a correlation be described?

The Church and the Reign of God

There could be a great many different ways to do it, but Vatican II pointed out an especially meaningful path, namely to understand the church as a basic sacrament prior to all the individual sacraments.[27] This suggests the possibility of describing the relationship between the reign of God and the people of God also in terms of sacrament. So we can say that the people of God, or the church, is the sacrament of the reign of God in the process of becoming reality. Probably that is by far the best way to compare the two realities.

The classic definition of the church's sacraments is very familiar: "The sacraments are visible signs of invisible realities." That definition had already been used by Augustine. If we apply it to the relationship between the reign of God and the church we would say that the "invisible reality" is the reign of God, which is humanly unimaginable. It is greater and more glorious than anything we can think of. It encompasses all creation. It will encompass world society. God is making it a reality within history and will perfect and complete it in the resurrection to everlasting life.

The "visible sign" of this unimaginable reign of God, however, is the people of God, or the church. The "sign" would thus be a people—and hence a visible, tangible, graspable, definable, identifiable reality. This sign-character remains, as it does with all sacramental actions. The signs designate and indicate; they point to something greater than themselves.

Thus the signs do not exist in and for themselves; in themselves they are nothing. All that they have comes from that to which they refer.

On the other hand, these sacramental signs are visible and perceptible. As at baptism we can see and feel the flowing water, in anointing the stroking with oil, at the ordination of a priest the imposition of hands, in the Eucharist the meal, and in every sacrament we can hear the crucial words—so also the people of God is visible and perceptible in the world. We can hear the Gospel; we can see the people of God living together. And as one can not only see and hear but also receive a sacrament, so one can participate in the life of the people of God. It is communicable.

Every sacrament is also a sign that *points to something*. It indicates the existence of a deeper and greater reality. The people of God is also an indicative sacrament, precisely in this sense: it points to the reign of God insofar as it is still hidden and incomplete, yet at the same time it reveals essential features of what is to come.

But a sacrament is not only a sign that points to something. It is also an *effective* sign. It effects participation in Christ himself and thus in his work and his destiny. In the same way the people of God is also more than a mere pointer. It makes present the reign of God as "already and not yet." It gives a share already in the reign of God. It makes its members already companions at table in the reign of God. It allows them to experience the power of the reign of God even now, through the Holy Spirit. And as church it links its members already to the risen Christ, in whom the reign of God has already become a perfected reality.

Thus the concept of sacrament seems to be a meaningful possibility for defining the correlation between the reign of God and the people of God more precisely. It secures the visibility of the reign of God and prevents it from drifting without a location. We can, for example, with the help of this model, interpret something like Luke 11:20 without incurring the usual problems: "If it is by the finger of God that I cast out the demons, then the reign of God has come to you." As we can see, Jesus' exorcisms of demons liberate deeply disturbed people from diseased compulsions that bind them and deprive them of freedom. Such liberation is a tangible and perceptible reality, not only for the sick people themselves, but also for their environment. A bit of the world has been changed.

What we can see is the reign of God itself. In the process of healing it remains hidden, but it is already present in the *sign*: the sign is the healing of mentally ill people. Those signs are so powerful that they attract attention. People are talking throughout the country about Jesus' mighty deeds. The signs thus create space for the reign of God and allow it to come.

Nevertheless, the reign of God preserves its incognito status. It has to be believed, just as the hidden grace of the sacraments must be believed. One can take the sacraments to be empty signs with nothing behind them, and in the same way it was possible to regard Jesus' exorcisms as trickery or the work of the devil. That is just what Jesus' enemies did (cf. Mark 3:22).

So what is the reign of God? In New Testament exegesis it often remains remarkably ambivalent. It has no real place in the world. It is true that it was visible for a short while in Jesus, in his words and his deeds, but after that it apparently remains suspended like mist in the air. No one can grasp it. This book takes a different tack. It is meant, among other things, to show the deep connection between the reign of God and the people of God. That is the primary purpose of the next chapter.

Chapter 4

The Gathering of Israel

In the preceding chapters I have already spoken more than once about Jesus' "gathering of Israel." It is high time to take a closer look at that idea, because it is not at all clear what it means. "The gathering of Israel" is not one of the classic theological concepts. You can still search theological dictionaries in vain for it. The closest you will come is "collection."

The Concept of Gathering

Still, "gathering" is a word that appears frequently in the Bible. From the time of the exile onward, the gathering of the scattered people of God was one of the fundamental ideas in Israel's theology.[1] Deuteronomy 30:1-5 reads:

> When all these things have happened to you, the blessings and the curses that I have set before you, if you call them to mind among all the nations where the LORD your God has driven you, and return to the LORD your God, and you and your children obey him with all your heart and with all your soul, just as I am commanding you today, then the LORD your God will restore your fortunes and have compassion on you, gathering you again from all the peoples among whom the LORD your God has scattered you. Even if you are exiled to the ends of the world, from there the LORD your God will gather

> you, and from there he will bring you back. The LORD your God will
> bring you into the land that your ancestors possessed, and you will
> possess it; he will make you more prosperous and numerous than
> your ancestors.

We see in this text that the idea of the gathering of the people of God
presumes that it is scattered among the nations. Among the prophets, in
particular, the "gathering of what is scattered," that is, those in the
Diaspora, plays a major role—and always with great theological significance. "Gathering" in many cases becomes almost a soteriological *ter-
minus technicus*, that is, a fixed concept representing the bringing of
salvation. "Gathering" Israel is often parallel to "liberating," "saving,"
"healing," and "redeeming" Israel. Thus the term acquires a certain
independent quality of representing the coming of salvation, even though
"gathering from the Diaspora" remains controlling.

It is always God who gathers the people. It is never said that the people
will gather themselves. The background is the image of the shepherd
who gathers his or her flock and leads them home—and scattered sheep,
as we know, cannot gather themselves. The goal of the gathering is a
renewed dwelling in the Land. It is true that the gathering of the people
of God means more than simply bringing them together. It always means
as well that the people will find unity among themselves:

> [The LORD] will raise a signal for the nations,
>   and will assemble the outcasts of Israel,
> and gather the dispersed of Judah
>   from the four corners of the earth.
> The jealousy of Ephraim shall depart,
>   the hostility of Judah shall be cut off;
> Ephraim shall not be jealous of Judah,
>   and Judah shall not be hostile towards Ephraim. (Isa 11:12-13)

Ephraim here represents the Northern Kingdom, Judah the Southern
Kingdom. The division between the northern and southern realms will
be healed by the gathering of the people of God. The rivalry of the tribes
will come to an end. Gathering from the exile is thus not only being led
back into the Land but also the overcoming of the mortal divisions within
the people of God itself.

In the postexilic period the gathering of Israel gradually became a
central part of the promise of salvation, comparable to the exodus from

Egypt, Israel's primal confession. "With a mighty hand and an out-stretched arm" God will lead Israel out from among the nations—as once before out of Egypt. In Jeremiah 23:7-8 we even read:

> Therefore the days are surely coming, says the LORD, when it shall no longer be said, "As the LORD lives who brought the people of Israel up out of the land of Egypt," but "As the LORD lives who brought out and led the offspring of the house of Israel out of the land of the north and out of all the lands where he had driven them!"

Thus the bringing back of the people from the Diaspora more and more clearly becomes a fundamental statement about God, God's nature, and the way God acts. This is evident in the relative clausal construction in Isaiah 56:8: "Thus says the Lord GOD, who gathers the outcasts of Israel." Here we already find prayer language, a praise of God's action that has become a fixed formula. In fact, the "gathering of Israel" enters more and more into the inventory of prayer formulae. In Psalm 106:47, Israel prays: "Save us, O LORD our God, and gather us from among the nations." And in the final Hallel, the great conclusion to the book of Psalms, Psalm 147:2-3 reads:

> The LORD builds up Jerusalem [anew];
>   he gathers the outcasts of Israel.
> He heals the brokenhearted,
>   and binds up their wounds.

In the Shemoneh Esrei, Israel's daily prayer, which very probably was composed in the first century CE, that development then came to its conclusion. The tenth petition is: "Sound the great shofar for our freedom and raise a banner to gather our exiles and unite us together from the four corners of the earth. Blessed are You, LORD, who regathers the scattered of His people Israel."

Thus the petition for an eschatological gathering is among Israel's fixed prayer formulae. In the time of Jesus the petition had long been in circulation. So it was almost a matter of course for him to adopt the idea of "gathering." He did not need to think directly of gathering out of the Diaspora, because the idea had already acquired its own quality. It stood for the eschatological union, rescue, and redemption of Israel. But Jesus not only made verbal use of the idea; in his own matter-of-fact way he brought into being exactly what the idea meant.

John the Baptizer

The Baptizer must have given Jesus a critical impetus. It is true that John preached the immediately approaching judgment, but this expectation of the judgment soon to come did not make the gathering of Israel somehow superfluous. On the contrary: it made it all the more urgent. Precisely because the time still remaining for Israel is so limited, the Baptizer had to bring the people together and equip them for what was about to happen. The one who judges with fire will then bring this gathering process to an end: he will fill the granary with wheat and burn the chaff in unquenchable fire (Matt 3:12).

We have already seen[2] that the Baptizer addresses not humanity in general or all sinners throughout the world but the people of God. The baptism he confers is not intended to inaugurate a special community or to rescue individuals as such from judgment (though it is meant to do that too); it is an "eschatological sacrament" for Israel.[3]

What is important for the Baptizer is that there must always be true children of Abraham, always the true Israel (Matt 3:9). The repentance and baptism now offered by God is the last chance for Israel to become this people of God, for Israel is now in the deepest crisis of its history. It can repent and allow itself to be gathered like wheat, or it can refuse to repent. In that case there will be a separation, just as the chaff is separated from the wheat (Matt 3:12). So for the Baptizer, as far as Israel is concerned, there is gathering and there is separation. Jesus, in his own way, will accomplish both.

"Whoever Does Not Gather with Me"

Jesus too wanted nothing else but to gather Israel in the face of the reign of God now coming to pass. But his point of view is different: the impulse is not the impending judgment but the joy of the reign of God. Judgment is not suppressed or ignored; it remains in the background. If Israel refuses, it will bring judgment on itself. So Jesus can say: "Whoever is not with me is against me, and whoever does not gather with me scatters" (Matt 12:30 // Luke 11:23). This saying of Jesus has rightly been dubbed a "call to decision."[4] There can be no neutrality toward Jesus, only for or against. Whoever does not decide *for him* has already decided *against him*.

But what makes this saying of Jesus even weightier is that it is not just about a decision for or against Jesus. Since this is about the eschatological gathering of Israel, the choice for or against Jesus is also a decision for or against the salvation of Israel.[5] Anyone who does not gather with Jesus now, in this crucial eschatological situation, stands in the way of the salvation and redemption of the people of God.

Besides this radical call to decision there is another saying in which Jesus also speaks of the gathering of Israel. It must have been uttered in a late phase of his work because he is already looking back at a good many refusals: "Jerusalem, Jerusalem, the city that kills the prophets and stones those who are sent to it! How often have I desired to gather your children together as a hen gathers her brood under her wings, and you were not willing!" (Matt 23:37 // Luke 13:34). On the surface this means that Jesus often wanted to gather the inhabitants of Jerusalem, that is, to make it the center of the eschatological Israel. But that would presume that he had appeared in Jerusalem a number of times. We cannot exclude that, although it contradicts the way things are presented in the Synoptic Gospels.[6] But we can also understand Jesus' words differently if we suppose that Jerusalem stands for all Israel.

Thus, for example, in the biblical book of Lamentations the words "Jerusalem," "daughter Zion," "daughter Judah," "daughter of my people," and "Jacob" are repeatedly exchanged for one another. "Jacob" means all Israel. In and of themselves Lamentations 1, 2, and 4 refer to the city of Jerusalem. It is addressed in the same way that Jesus addresses Jerusalem in our text. But the three songs constantly look beyond the city itself to encompass the whole land. For every reader or hearer of Lamentations it was clear that here Jerusalem represents Israel. The lamentation over the destroyed capital is at the same time a lamentation over the people of God, sunk so deep in misery. Jesus quite certainly knew these language conventions. Therefore he could have understood all Israel as included among the "children of Jerusalem." The capital city is responsible for the land and also representative of it.

But however that may be, these words were probably spoken in Jerusalem, and in them Jesus summarizes his whole activity in retrospect—as his effort to bring about the eschatological gathering of Israel.

The image of the bird (in the Greek text) is, as so often with Jesus, taken from everyday observation. The reference is not to the eagle that spreads its wings but to the hen who repeatedly invites her scattered chicks to gather around her, clucking at them in a low tone; sometimes she also tucks them under her wings. But the true point of comparison in the image is not the protection of the young ones under her wings but the gathering of them.

The Petition for Gathering in the Our Father

At this point we must certainly take a look at the Our Father, for this prayer that Jesus formulated for his disciples summarizes his whole will in one work of genius. For that very reason we find an irritating state of things in the Our Father: here Israel, the people of God, apparently does not appear. There does not seem to be anything said about the gathering of the people of God either. Does that not refute everything we have said to this point? The objection is justified, but it misses the point, because the Our Father itself is shaped by the theme of the gathering of Israel. Its very first petition is: "Hallowed be Thy name!" (Matt 6:9 // Luke 11:2). Exegetes are united in saying that this is not only and not even primarily about the hallowing of the Name of God *by Israel*. Rather, what is in the foreground is that God is to hallow his own Name, just as he is to bring about his royal reign (second petition) and accomplish his plan of salvation (third petition). But what does it mean for God to hallow his Name?

We can simply not understand this first petition without its Old Testament background. At its base is the theology of the book of Ezekiel, especially chapters 20 and 36. Ezekiel speaks repeatedly of the holy Name of God, and this book contains the single passage in the Hebrew Bible in which the statement that the Name of God will be hallowed has God himself as the acting subject (Ezek 36:23).

In and of itself the hallowing of the Name (*qiddush hashem*) is a widely attested Old Testament and Jewish theme. But the subject is always the human being or the people Israel, and the reference is primarily to keeping the commandments. This is clear in the basic text, Leviticus 22:31-32: "Thus you shall keep my commandments and observe them: I am the LORD. You shall not profane my holy name, that I may be sanctified among the people of Israel." So Israel is to hallow the Name of God. That is the normal usage. The statement that God himself hallows his Name, however, points clearly to Ezekiel. In that book, at Ezekiel 36:19-28, we read:

> I scattered them [the Israelites] among the nations, and they were dispersed through the countries; in accordance with their conduct and their deeds I judged them. But when they came to the nations, wherever they came, they profaned my holy name, in that it was said of them, "These are the people of the LORD, and yet they had to go out of his land." But I had concern for my holy name, which

the house of Israel had profaned among the nations to which they came.

Therefore say to the house of Israel, Thus says the Lord GOD: It is not for your sake, O house of Israel, that I am about to act, but for the sake of my holy name, which you have profaned among the nations to which you came. I will sanctify my great name, which has been profaned among the nations, and which you have profaned among them; and the nations shall know that I am the LORD, says the Lord GOD, when through you I display my holiness before their eyes. I will take you from the nations, and gather you from all the countries, and bring you into your own land. I will sprinkle clean water upon you, and you shall be clean from all your uncleannesses, and from all your idols I will cleanse you. A new heart I will give you, and a new spirit I will put within you; and I will remove from your body the heart of stone and give you a heart of flesh. I will put my spirit within you, and make you follow my statutes and be careful to observe my ordinances. Then you shall live in the land that I gave to your ancestors; and you shall be my people, and I will be your God.

In this text, which summarizes the expectation of salvation throughout the whole book of Ezekiel, there are five series of statements:

First series: Israel dwelt in the Land God had given it. But it did not live according to Torah, the social order given by God. It did not serve the God who had chosen it but other gods. Thus it despised the Land and profaned the Name of God. It filled the Land with envy, hatred, and rivalry. So it spoiled the Land and destroyed the brilliance that ought to emanate from it.

Second series: God could not endure this profanation and despising of the Land. He had to drive Israel out of the Land and disperse it among the pagan nations. But why did God have to drive out his people? People today resist such an image of God. Must God punish? Must God deport people? What the Bible means is more obvious if we formulate such statements consistently in human terms: a society that constantly lives contrary to God's order of creation destroys itself. That is true in particular of the people of God with its special calling for the sake of the other nations. If it stubbornly acts contrary to its calling, it destroys the ground on which it stands. It destroys its basis. It deprives itself of its land and of its very existence.

Third series: The scattering of Israel among the nations, which it has brought on itself, makes things still worse, since the result of this dispersion is that the Name of God is profaned still further. Now all the world ridicules Israel and its God. The nations say: what a miserable, powerless god this YHWH is! He is a god who does not care for his own people. He is a god without a people. He is a god without a country.

Fourth series: God has to put an end to this profanation of his Name. He cannot allow his Name to continue to be made a laughingstock because of Israel's dispersal among the nations. Therefore God himself will now hallow his Name before all the nations. The fact that he intervenes is not at all due to Israel's deserving.

Fifth series: How does God put an end to this unbearable state of things? How does he hallow his Name? He does so by gathering his people from the dispersion and bringing them back into the Land. He hallows his Name by freeing the Israelites from their idols and giving them a new heart and a new spirit. He takes the hearts of stone out of their breasts and gives them hearts of flesh. So it becomes possible for Israel to live according to the social order God has ordained.

The first petition of the Our Father summarizes this whole text from Ezekiel 36 in a single sentence. The petition "hallowed be Thy Name" begs God to gather his people from the dispersion, to make them one people again, give them a new heart, and fill them with the Holy Spirit. To put it another way: the first petition of the Our Father implores that there once again be a place in the world where the glory and honor of God are visible—a place because of which God's name can be honored, and also called upon, even by the nations.

But it is true that the Our Father does not speak of the people of God in the same way as, for example, the Shemoneh Esrei does. Nothing is said about the house of David. The city of Jerusalem is not mentioned, nor are Zion and the temple, because in the time of Jesus all that could have been misunderstood as political, and particularly by the Zealot movement with which Jesus was constantly confronted, and by many others as well. Jesus' whole concern is with the honor of God, with God's good name. God's only honor is his people, but not a people understood in nationalistic terms; instead, this people is an Israel such as Ezekiel had in mind.

Result: the first petition of the Our Father, which, because it is placed first of all, Jesus apparently regarded as the most important and most urgent in the prayer of his disciples, has a precise meaning, its content clearly outlined: it is a plea for the eschatological gathering and restoration of the people of God. That is exactly the way in which the Name of God will be hallowed.

The Choice of the Twelve

Thus Jesus has his disciples pray in the Our Father for the eschatological gathering of Israel. But he not only asks them to pray for it. He acts. Jesus chooses for himself—probably from out of a larger group of disciples—twelve whom he will send out in pairs to proclaim the reign of God throughout the land. They represent the gathering of Israel:

> [And he goes] up the mountain and [calls] to him those whom he wanted, and they came to him. And he [created] twelve to be with him, and to be sent out to proclaim the message, and to have authority to cast out demons. [And he created] the Twelve: Simon (to whom he gave the name Peter); James son of Zebedee and John the brother of James (to whom he gave the name Boanerges, that is, Sons of Thunder); and Andrew, and Philip, and Bartholomew, and Matthew, and Thomas, and James son of Alphaeus, and Thaddaeus, and Simon the Cananaean, and Judas Iscariot, who betrayed him. (Mark 3:13-19)

"He created" points to a unique event at a particular place and a particular time. Jesus, with a demonstrative gesture that must have impressed, constituted a circle of twelve disciples. The number twelve can only refer to the twelve tribes of Israel.

But reference to the twelve tribes touches a central point of Israel's eschatological hope, for although the system of twelve tribes had long ceased to exist, people hoped that in the eschatological time of salvation the people of the twelve tribes would be fully restored. The end of the book of Ezekiel describes, in broad strokes, how the twelve tribes, brought back to life in the end time, will receive their definitive shares in the Land (Ezek 47–48). Against the background of this living hope Jesus' creation of the Twelve can only be seen as a deliberate sign of eschatological fulfillment. The Twelve exemplify the gathering and restoration of Israel as the eschatological people of the twelve tribes that is now beginning with Jesus. They thus embody the growth center of eschatological Israel.

Places of Jesus' Activity

The theological program revealed in the call to decision in Matthew 12:30 ("whoever is not with me"), then in the lament in Matthew 23:37 ("Jerusalem, Jerusalem"), then in the first petition of the Our Father, but above all in the creation of the Twelve, corresponds precisely to Jesus' actual presence on the scene. He restricted his activity to Jewish territory. Nazareth, Nain, Cana, Capernaum, Chorazin, Magdala, and Bethsaida were places long occupied by a Jewish population.

There is not a single reason to believe that Jesus ever left Jewish territory to teach in the presence of Gentiles. When it happened that he entered Gentile territory (Mark 5:1; 7:24, 31; 8:27) the reason may have been in part that he sought out marginal Jewish groups in boundary zones. The relevant texts, strikingly enough, do *not* say that he entered Gerasa, Tyre, or Caesarea Philippi. They speak, instead, of the rural surroundings of each of these ancient cities.

Obviously Jesus could meet Gentiles everywhere, even in primarily Jewish territory. In several such encounters he also healed Gentiles. But such healings were consciously related in the Synoptic tradition as exceptions. In the story of the centurion at Capernaum (Luke 7:1-10) the relationship to Israel is explicitly established: "I tell you, not even in Israel have I found such faith" (Luke 7:9). The same is true of the story of the Syrophoenician woman and her sick daughter (Mark 7:24-30). When the woman asks Jesus to heal her daughter, Jesus at first refuses: "Let the children be fed first, for it is not fair to take the children's food and throw it to the dogs" (Mark 7:27). Obviously the purpose of this image is not to show that Gentiles are dogs. Instead, it is about the Bible's principle of salvation history: first Israel must be saved, and only then can the Gentiles also be convinced of God's salvation.

It is still the time when salvation must transform Israel. The hour in which the Gentiles' hunger can be satisfied has not yet come. That Jesus then, nevertheless, allows himself to be persuaded by the quick-witted woman—she simply turns his saying back on him—shows his openness and respect for the Gentile world. Jesus does not let himself be bound by rigid strategies, but fundamentally his concern is with Israel.

Therefore he does not enter Gentile cities with his proclamation. Very close to the places where Jesus worked lay any number of cities of the Hellenistic type with a predominantly Gentile population, or at least strong Gentile minorities—for example, Sepphoris, Scythopolis, Hippos, Gadara, Gerasa, Tiberias, and Caesarea Philippi. Jesus does not seem ever to have worked in any of these cities. It may be that he deliberately avoided them during his public activity. Instead, he goes up to Jerusalem, to the place that summarizes and represents Israel. Anyone who wanted to address all Israel had to do so in Jerusalem.

Naturally all of that is no accident. It would have been very easy for Jesus to appear among the Gentiles, and he might even have been highly successful. But Jesus concentrated on Israel.

The Pilgrimage of the Nations

Thus Jesus does not have an active mission to the Gentiles in view. He holds to the rule enunciated in Matthew 10:6: "Go [only] to the lost sheep of the house of Israel." But how shall salvation reach the Gentiles? Israel's theology had long since found a solution to that in the motif-complex of the "pilgrimage of the nations."

This pilgrimage of the nations will take place in the future, "in days to come" (Isa 2:2) or "in the last days." It is thus an eschatological event put in motion by God, because it exceeds all human expectations and abilities. Nevertheless, in this as in all things God acts through people, concrete history, and a concrete place, namely, Israel. The motif-complex of the pilgrimage of the nations says that God acts on the peoples of the world through the people of God, who in the last days will become a new society. The image for that new society is the eschatological city of Jerusalem, or simply Mount Zion. It draws the nations. It shines out above all the mountains of the world (Isa 2:2), for a city set high on a hill cannot remain hidden (Matt 5:14).

The reason why the peoples will be drawn to Zion is important: a fascination exceeding all others will emanate from eschatological Israel. This fascination can be described in various ways. Ultimately it is God himself who shines forth in the power of his actions and the peaceful quality of his social order.

What the nations experience on Zion, or in Israel, they will take for themselves, so that it will spread throughout the whole world—for example, nonviolence. They will beat their swords into plowshares (Isa 2:4).

It is true that the pilgrimage of the nations is an eschatological event, but Israel is called now, already, to make a way for what is to come. Characteristic of this appeal is the cry in Isaiah 2:5, immediately after the description of the future pilgrimage of the nations: "O house of Jacob, come, let us walk in the light of the LORD!" To that extent the Old Testament itself is aware of a "self-realizing eschatology," or the dialectic of "already and not yet." The pilgrimage of the nations to Zion is being prepared already in Israel's turning back.

Thus the vision of the pilgrimage of the nations answers the question of what God intends with the peoples of the world. Jesus' concentration on the people of God takes place against a universal horizon. It is not an egoistic view fixed on Israel; it is about the nations. It is about the world.

However, Israel's theology contains not only the motif-complex of the pilgrimage of the nations or the idea that the blessing of God that lies on Israel will extend from there to encompass other nations (cf., e.g., Isa 19:23-25). There are also quite different positions, such as the many threats uttered by the prophets against the nations.[7] These announce destruction. There is also the idea of a hostile attack of the nations against the city of God, which will not succeed but will be broken against Zion.

In Isaiah 8:9-10 the Gentile peoples are even ridiculed. Let them come against Jerusalem, if they will! Let them arm themselves for the decisive battle! Let them, by all means, make plans and forge alliances! Nothing will help them: they will be shattered against Zion. When the first line of this threat reads "Smash!" it presupposes that the hostile armies are already devastating the land around Jerusalem.

> Smash, you peoples! for you will be crushed.
> Listen, all you far countries!
> Arm yourselves! for you will be crushed.
> Gird yourselves! for you will be shattered.
> Make a plan! for it will be thwarted.
> Forge an alliance: it will not come about.
> For God is with us. (Isa 8:9-10)[8]

Jesus knew his Bible, and obviously he also knew the ideas about the attack of the nations, their hostility to Israel, and their ultimate destruction. But it is striking that all that plays no role in his preaching. He does, of course, take it as given that there will be a judgment of the world, but in that judgment it will go better with Tyre and Sidon than with unbelieving Israel (Matt 11:21-22).

It seems that, as far as the fate of the Gentile nations is concerned, Jesus read the Old Testament critically, in the sense that he adopted particular aspects of Old Testament eschatology and let others fall into the background. He made choices. He says nothing about the destruction of the nations, but he does seem to have adopted the idea of the pilgrimage of the nations and used it against Israel.

The word of warning in Matthew 8:11-12 // Luke 13:28-29 is crucial. Jesus must have spoken it as the hardening of Israel as a whole began to show itself. It comes from the Sayings Source and has to be reconstructed out of its varying forms in Matthew and Luke. It would have been something like: "Many will come from the rising and the setting and recline at table in the reign of God—together with Abraham, Isaac, and Jacob. But you will be cast out into the outermost darkness, where there will be weeping and gnashing of teeth."

The saying looks to the future. Abraham, Isaac, and Jacob, the ancestors of Israel, have risen from the dead. Obviously they are only named as important representatives of the people of God. With them all the righteous of Israel have risen. The reign of God is coming to its fulfillment, portrayed in the image of the eschatological meal taken from Isaiah 25:6-8. The meal is here an image of fullness, of festival, of a fulfilled life that will never again be brought to an end. In this situation, then, the "many" come from the rising and the setting, that is, from the east and from the west.

The "many" in the saying are contrasted with Jesus' Jewish audience. So he is speaking of the Gentiles. "Many" is a Semitic formulation and means a great, incalculable number. An unimaginable number of Gentiles are participating in the banquet of fulfillment. But the Israel that rejects Jesus will not be present, of all things, at this eternal banquet for whom everyone hopes. The unbelieving part of Israel will be thrown out into the uttermost darkness.

We can scarcely imagine a greater provocation. But that very provocation shows that Jesus was concerned first and foremost about the eschatological gathering of Israel. Matthew 8:11-12 is a last attempt by Jesus, carried to the limits, to shake up his audience and achieve their repentance after all.

So the word of warning is directed at Israel. Its real theme is not the fate of the Gentiles, but it makes clear, indirectly, how Jesus thought: He knows the vision of the pilgrimage of the nations; he expects the coming of the Gentiles to Zion. Indeed, he presumes salvation for the Gentiles as a matter of course.

Chapter 5

The Call to Discipleship

How do the gospels picture the beginning of Jesus' work? Often the beginning discloses everything that will come after. Is the first thing a sermon that summarizes what Jesus wanted? Or a healing story? Or a symbolic action like that in the temple? Many things would be possible.

In the Gospel of Mark the first concrete narrative in Jesus' public appearance describes how he calls Simon Peter, his brother Andrew, and the sons of Zebedee, James and John, to follow him (Mark 1:16-20). The Gospel of Matthew's arrangement corresponds (Matt 4:18-22). But even the Gospel of John begins Jesus' work with the calling of disciples: here it is Andrew, Simon Peter, Philip, and Nathanael (John 1:35-51). However, the first callings are told differently in the Fourth Gospel from what we read in Mark and Matthew.

This placement at the beginning of Jesus' work need not mean much for the historical question. The fact that three evangelists begin Jesus' activity in just this way could simply be a question of compositional technique. After all, Luke did it differently. In his account Jesus begins his public appearance by serving as lector and preacher in the synagogue at Nazareth (Luke 4:16-30). One could also argue that the disciples are almost always thought of as present in the gospel narratives. Quite often they even appear as actors. So they have to be introduced at the very beginning of the narrative sequence.

All that is worth considering. But it may be that Mark, Matthew, and John did hang on to something crucial. Maybe they wanted to say that there was no activity of Jesus in Israel without a call to discipleship. In fact, discipleship is something fundamental. Without it there would be no Gospel, no gathering of Israel, and no church. It is as elementary as the proclamation of the reign of God, Jesus' preaching, and his healing miracles. The gospels show that as clearly as possible. But what does it mean to be a disciple of Jesus? That is the subject of this chapter.[1]

Discipleship Is Concrete

Here again we begin with a philological fact: "follow" (following, etc.) appears in the gospels some eighty times, mainly in a theological sense, but never as a noun, "followership" or "discipleship" (*akolouthēsis*). It is always in verb form (*akolouthein*). That is: there is no such thing in the gospels as abstract discipleship. It is not an idea or a purely inward disposition; it exists only as a concrete, visible, tangible event.

Accordingly, we must imagine Jesus' followers' "discipleship" quite concretely, as "walking behind." If you visit the Near East you can still see it: an Arab woman walks behind her husband, not alongside him. The son follows the father. The bride follows her bridegroom, the employee walks behind his employer, the student behind her teacher. And so it was, of course, in Jesus' time also. A series of texts from the later rabbinic tradition shows that the students of the teachers of the Law walked behind their teacher, their rabbi, keeping a respectful distance. They followed him. That was simply a matter of proper deportment.

Given all that, we could suppose that the historical model for the disciples' following was the rabbinic relationship of teacher and student—especially since the word "disciple" is based on the Greek word *mathetēs*, and *mathetēs* means nothing but student. The German word "Jünger" [disciple] rests on late Latin *junior*, which at the time, differently from today, also meant "student" or "pupil" or "learner."[2]

The Rabbis and Their Students

Thus—according to the gospels—Jesus called "students" to follow him. Were the students he gathered around him, then, comparable to the rabbis' students of the Law? As likely as this conclusion seems, it is inaccurate for three reasons:

First: the proper term for a rabbinic student's entry into the Jewish house of study was not "following this or that rabbi," but "studying (or learning) Torah." So it is said of Rabbi Chanina ben Dosa (first c. CE) that he went to ʾArab (in upper Galilee) "to study Torah with Rabbi Johanan ben Zakkai."[3] This is a stereotypical formula in rabbinic texts, and that in itself is remarkable. Mark says of Peter and Andrew *not* that "they came to Nazareth to study Torah with Jesus," but "As Jesus passed along the Sea of Galilee, he saw Simon and his brother Andrew casting a net into the sea—for they were fishermen. And Jesus said to them, 'Follow me and I will make you fish for people.' And immediately they left their nets and followed him" (Mark 1:16-18).

So Simon and the others do not follow Jesus in order to learn Torah but to become fishers of people with Jesus. Discipleship, following Jesus, is not their idea, their plan, their project; they are called, against their accustomed way of life, against their life-project, probably even against their idea of what a devout life should be. This was not their own will but that of a stranger—and yet they recognized, in that stranger's will, the will of God.

Jesus calls to discipleship. There is not a single story in the rabbinic traditions in which a rabbi called a student to follow him. The reason is very simple: a rabbinic student seeks his or her own teacher. We have a lovely saying by the scribe Yehoshua ben Perachia (first c. BCE): "Make for yourself a rabbi, acquire for yourself a friend; and judge every person in their favor."[4] Occasionally it is even recommended that the *talmid*, the scribal student, should change teachers in order to get to know other interpretations of Torah. This was quite consistent with the rabbinic system of teaching and thought. It is the principle of the Talmud that different opinions or traditions be set alongside one another. Such a thing is foreign to the New Testament. And change teachers? That would have been unthinkable where Jesus was concerned.

A second difference: It was repeatedly emphasized to rabbinic students that they were to "serve" their teacher. The rabbinic tradition lists forty-eight things through which knowledge of Torah is to be acquired. Besides study, careful listening, intelligence, fear of God, joy, and purity of heart, the list also includes "serving the wise." This "serving" means that the student performs for the teacher all the services that would otherwise be done by a servant or a slave. Thus he washes the rabbi's feet, serves at and clears the table, cleans the house and the courtyard, goes to the market and purchases necessities. Serving the teacher is an essential part of studying Torah. But with Jesus things were different, in a way that was unheard of in his time. The evangelist Mark repeats these words of his: "the Son of Man came not to be served but to serve, and to give his life a ransom for many" (Mark 10:45). In its Lukan variant the saying is:

"For who is greater, the one who is at the table or the one who serves? Is it not the one at the table? But I am among you as one who serves" (Luke 22:27).

Texts such as these distill what Jesus constantly inculcated in his disciples: a new way of being together. He does not allow himself to be served; instead, he is the servant at his disciples' table. Hence the washing of feet before the last meal, which the evangelist John regards as so crucial that he tells of it instead of the universally familiar words of institution (John 13:1-20).

How different from the rabbinic tradition! And yet one must not be unjust to them, for when they say again and again that a disciple must serve his rabbi their intention was not to have dummies around them to make their lives easier. Their idea, rather, was that those who serve their teacher are constantly in the teacher's presence, and that gives them the opportunity to learn the correct observance of the Law *in practice*. For as students accompany their rabbi through the whole day they see without interruption how their master observes the Torah, and so they themselves learn Torah. That is the background of the "serving of the wise," and it is a very beautiful and moving background.

But we also see here the profound difference: in the Talmudic relationship of teacher and student everything revolves around the Torah. It is to become their way of life. The text of the Torah must be learned by heart. Its interpretation by great scholars must be studied. The practice of living the Torah every day must be rehearsed and memorized down to the smallest detail.

Jesus also taught his disciples and had them practice and internalize the right way of life, and the Torah was by no means absent, as we can see from the Sermon on the Mount. There we find a collection of rules for interpretation, for a right understanding of Torah, and also any number of tangible examples of how Torah is to be grasped and lived now, at the time of its eschatological fulfillment.

And yet for Jesus the Torah has a different position: it is transformed by the message of the arrival of the reign of God.[5] Therefore Jesus does not first of all encourage the disciples he gathers around him to study the Torah; he begins instead by creating a new way of being together with them. Under the sign of the now-inbreaking reign of God, human community must also be renewed—finally to become what the Torah had always intended it to be.

And just here we find a *third difference* between Jesus' disciples and those of the scribes and rabbis: for them what was crucial was the continuous communication of the traditional teaching and an ongoing close and ever-more-accurate interpretation of Torah. That demanded not only an orderly educational system but also a *stabilitas loci*, a stability of place in an established house of study—and both the house of study and the educational system required a secure means of support. Most rabbis were craftsmen.

Jesus, on the other hand, did not conduct an established educational operation in rabbinic style; instead, being his disciple meant following him into always-changing situations. But within this constant change, accompanied by its eschatological pressure, there took place a daily exercise, a daily inculcation of the new community of discipleship—involving, for example, the rule that disciples had to forgive one another seventy-seven times a day, that is, constantly (Matt 18:21-22). They could not and must not live together any other way in the reign of God.

There was no *stabilitas loci* with Jesus. He traveled throughout Israel with his disciples in an unstable, itinerant fashion, totally surrendered to whatever the situation of the approaching reign of God demanded at any particular time. Jesus had no place to lay his head (Luke 9:58).

Our Daily Bread

And what about a secure basis for life? Anyone who wants to know what it was like for Jesus' disciples would do well to read the Our Father. It is not a prayer for everyone. It is a prayer for Jesus' disciples and followers. It is *their* prayer. It distills the whole of what moves them.

In the fourth petition the disciples (in the usual translation) ask for their "daily bread." This petition in particular seems to suggest that it is a prayer suitable for anyone. After all, people need bread, daily sustenance, always and everywhere in the world. And yet in that respect the fourth petition of the Our Father is much more concrete and situation-bound.

First, we must observe that "give us today our daily bread" is simply an attempt at translation of Matthew 6:11. Where our Bibles read "daily," the Greek has *epiousios*, a word that is not attested anywhere in pre-Christian Greek literature. So we must reconstruct what it might mean.

There is much in favor of the suggestion that *epiousios* does not mean "daily" in a general sense but much more precisely bread for the coming day, the day after this one. In that case *epiousios* would be derived from *epienai* (cf. Acts 7:26; 16:11; 20:15; 21:18). Then Jesus' disciples would be praying in the Our Father solely for bread for that evening and the next day. (In Israel the "following" day begins in the evening, when it grows dark.) Why do the disciples pray only for bread for the next day, for tomorrow?

They do so simply because they are traveling through the land with Jesus and in the morning they do not yet know whether anyone will take them in that evening and give them something to eat! Therefore they have to pray to their Father in heaven—since they have left their earthly fathers—for their bread for the next day. They cannot undertake to plan or set aside for the future. They have no time for it. But they may and should pray for bread for one day.

So nothing is prepared in advance for the long haul. The eschatological situation is so acute, the current preaching so primary that planning is impossible. The view barely extends to the next day. So we can describe the original meaning of the bread petition as follows: "Grant that today we will meet people who will take us into their houses and give us something to eat tonight so that our lives, our food are secured for one more day."

More than that is impossible, but more is not necessary, because Jesus' disciples are surrounded and sustained by the parental care of God. So their situation corresponds to that of Israel in the Old Testament wilderness narratives. With its exodus Israel abandoned the things that sustained its life in the Egyptian welfare state. A new social order of mutual solidarity was to be begun. In the extraordinary situation of the wilderness God fed his people with manna—according to Exodus 16—but the Israelites were not allowed to store up the manna. Except for the day before the Sabbath they could only gather what they needed for a single day. Exodus 16:4 speaks of the ration for the coming day. It is possible that *epiousios* is an attempt at a corresponding allusion to Exodus 16:4 in Greek.

But however things developed linguistically, we have a hard time imagining that Jesus could have formulated the petition for bread for the coming day—that is, for only one day—without having the manna story in mind. He knew that his disciples, who were now preaching the reign of God throughout the land "like sheep in the midst of wolves" (Matt 10:16) were, like Israel in the past, in a basically impossible wilderness situation. Moreover, the fourth petition of the Our Father corresponds in part to Jesus' injunction in Matthew 6:34: "So do not worry about tomorrow, for tomorrow will bring worries of its own. Today's trouble is enough for today."

Light Luggage

But it is not only the fourth petition of the Our Father that illuminates the absence of a settled school on the rabbinic model. The so-called equipment rule in Luke 9:3 // Matthew 10:9-10 // Mark 6:8-9 also reflects the itinerant existence of Jesus and his disciples. The disciples are sent out without money, a sack for provisions, a second tunic, a staff, even without sandals.

Many interpreters assert that this harsh and radical equipment rule is about the theme of "modesty of needs" or "humility." Jesus' disciples in that case, in their lack of any concern for their own needs are to surpass even the Cynic-Stoic itinerant philosophers, who did wear their philosophers' cloaks, always had a begging sack with them, and maintained an emergency ration of bread. But is that really the case?

Is not the phrase "modesty of needs" an all-too-transparent attempt to accommodate the Gospel to today's ideas? The twentieth and twenty-first centuries have a surfeit of civilization and a longing for a "simple life." It is clear that the deficient equipment of the missionary disciples is meant to be a *sign*. But was it really just about trumping even the Gentile itinerant philosophers in their poverty? Jesus' message and practice point in a completely different direction.

The light equipment of Jesus' disciples is intended to point to the new thing that is happening in Israel. Everywhere in the cities and villages the disciples, when they go there to preach the reign of God, find Jesus' adherents and sympathizers, "people of peace" (Luke 10:6), who receive them into their houses and provide everything for them.

So the disciples are not alone. Around them the true eschatological Israel is beginning to gather. They are indeed without means, but they have everything. They are indeed poor, and yet they are rich. A group of people throughout the land, all of them seized by the reign of God, trusting one another without reservation, sharing with one another, caring for one another: that is an inexhaustible reserve.

So in the disciples' equipment rule the point is not primarily poverty or lack of demands. The deficient equipment of the disciples is, instead, an *indicative sign* pointing to the eschatological-solidary mutuality within the people of God that makes Jesus' disciples free and available.

This freedom, and the associated trust in help from others, has another side, of course: Jesus' mission discourse (Matt 10:5-15 // Mark 6:7-11 // Luke 9:2-5 // Luke 10:3-12) takes into account that it could happen that in the evening Jesus' disciples might not find a house that would receive them, no "people of peace," but only rejection, hatred, and hostility: "If anyone will not welcome you or listen to your words, shake off the dust from your feet as you leave that house or town. Truly I tell you, it will be more tolerable for the land of Sodom and Gomorrah on the day of judgment than for that town" (Matt 10:14-15). So it is bitterly necessary to pray in the morning for the next day's bread. Jesus and his disciples do not know whether a meal will be set before them in the evening. Many texts in the gospels can only be understood against the background of the eschatological—constantly endangered and yet incomprehensibly blessed—existence of the disciples.

But back to our starting point! We were speaking of the orderly educational institutions of the rabbis, their *stabilitas loci*, their secure basis. It is probably clear by now that in this respect also we cannot derive discipleship of Jesus from the rabbinic relation between teacher and student. Being a disciple means sharing the fate of Jesus, who had no place to lay his head. It means uncertainty, danger, opposition. It means surrender to the new demands, every day, of the coming of the reign of God. But it also means a new community in Jesus' "new family." So Jesus' call to discipleship cannot be derived from the rabbinic relationship between teacher and student.

Discipleship among the Zealots

But where, then, did Jesus get his call to discipleship if not from the rabbis? We come much closer to the heart of the matter when we look at the charismatic-prophetic freedom fighters in the Judaism of the time. They had something like "discipleship," and they even used the term.

The revolt of the Maccabees against the Seleucids began when Mattathias, a Jewish priest, called for battle against the Hellenistic destroyers of the Jewish tradition. He assembled fighters with the cry, "Let everyone who is zealous for the law and supports the covenant come out with me!" (1 Macc 2:27). The account in 1 Maccabees continues: "Then he and his sons fled to the hills and left all that they had in the town. At that time many who were seeking righteousness and justice went down to the wilderness to live there, they, their sons, their wives, and their livestock, because troubles pressed heavily upon them" (1 Macc 2:28-30).

What follows is a typical freedom struggle against the Syrian occupation force, conducted mainly with guerilla tactics from the mountains and wadis of the Judean wilderness. And from that point on, charismatic leadership figures steadily appeared in Israel and set off popular movements. One of them was Judas the Galilean (Acts 5:37), the founder of the Zealot movement.[6] Another was called Theudas (Acts 5:36), and still another Luke simply calls "the Egyptian" (Acts 21:38). What did these guerillas or the pseudo-prophets who called the people into the wilderness have to do with Jesus?

To begin with, apparently quite a bit, because they too were about the reign of God. Josephus writes of Judas the Galilean: "Under his administration [i.e., that of the procurator Coponius], a Galilaean, named Judas, incited his countrymen to revolt, upbraiding them as cowards for consenting to pay tribute to the Romans and tolerating mortal masters, after having God for their lord."[7]

The Zealots (zealot = fanatic) were thus concerned about Israel's faith. As once the prophet Elijah, with burning zeal, had demanded a choice between YHWH and Baal, so Judas the Galilean demanded that Israel choose between the God of their ancestors and the divine Roman emperor. For the Zealots, then, the fight against Rome was a matter of faith. They passionately called people to enter into the true faith as they saw it. They could only imagine Israel as a state ruled by God alone. Therefore they called all Israel to follow them, which in the great majority of cases meant leaving home and household and removing to the wilderness. Charlatans within or alongside the Zealot movement, like Theudas and "the Egyptian," even promised their followers showy messianic miracles, eschatological miracles in the wilderness.

At first glance the correspondences with the Jesus movement are striking: the theme of the reign of God, the demand for faith, the call to discipleship to the point of endangering one's own life, the unconditional surrender of property and goods for the cause of God, and above all the eschatological horizon. Here we are much closer to the phenomenon of discipleship than with the rabbis. Above all, it is historically certain that these movements were contemporary with the Jesus movement; the rabbinic practices we spoke of before can only be derived from later sources.

But despite these parallels that seem so striking, discipleship of Jesus is something different. Jesus and his disciples were far removed in their thinking and acting from the Jewish freedom fighters. Jesus, when he was asked whether it was permissible to pay Roman taxes, emphatically affirmed that it was. When people tried to draw him into a political trap with this problem, the subject of such heated discussion in Israel at the time, he made a distinction: "Give to the emperor the things that are the emperor's, and to God the things that are God's" (Mark 12:17). "The things that are God's"—that is something different. That is not battle with weapons for a theocratic state, which is what Zealot fanaticism longed for. "The things that are God's" or "what belongs to God"—that is one's whole existence; that is faith in the "today" of the Good News; that is turning back to that message and to a nonviolent community in Israel that is now beginning.

For according to Jesus, God does not want Israel to be a people that fights, like all others, to assert itself as a nation. God wants a people in which the peace of God and God's kind of rule become reality. That is the reason for the unbelievably sharp demand for nonviolence in the Sermon on the Mount: "But I say to you, Do not resist an evildoer. But if anyone strikes you on the right cheek, turn the other also; and if anyone wants to sue you and take your coat, give your cloak as well; and if anyone forces you to go one mile, go also the second mile" (Matt 5:39-41). The Zealots demanded precisely the opposite. They said: don't take it! Fight back! Don't help the Roman soldiers (for example, by carrying their baggage for miles)! No, help us in the underground to arm against the occupation force!

When Jesus talks about nonviolence he is first of all placing a clear distance between himself and the fighters-for-God in his time. That the disciples, in accordance with the equipment rule described above, were to take no staff, no shoes, and no money with them was not only an indicative sign of the eschatological-solidary community in the people of God. It was intended, beyond that, to make visible the difference between them and the Zealot God's-army types: someone who does not even have a staff cannot protect himself. He is defenseless. And someone who has no shoes on her feet cannot even flee, given the stony soil of Palestine, if she is attacked. This is a sign of pure nonviolence that positively shouts its character. All of it goes contrary to the Zealots and their ideology of a military theocratic state.

But also the fact that the disciples were to have no money in their belts was directed against the Zealots, because they collected and extorted money for their struggle against the Romans. None of that had anything to do with modesty of demands or asceticism. Jesus simply did not want his disciples to be confused with rebels against Roman rule.

Free Discipleship

Thus nonviolence signals the fundamental difference between Jesus and the Zealots. But that difference is also indicated by the idea of freedom. What does that mean?

The Zealot movement, as well as other enthusiastic movements like those of Theudas and "the Egyptian," tried to draw as many people in Israel as possible to follow them. They wanted the people as such to rise up against the Romans, or in other words, all Israel was supposed to follow these new charismatics. The Zealots' reckless use of violence, not hesitating even at murder, was directed not only at the Roman occupiers but also against all Jews who submitted to Roman rule for the sake of peace.[8] Here again something entirely different was evident in Jesus' movement: he did not regard Israel as a uniform collective but instead respected to a sometimes off-putting degree the freedom and specific calling of every individual.

Jesus calls individuals to discipleship, each of them chosen and approached by him in person. The next chapter will explore this phenomenon in more detail. Here we may say only that for Jesus the Good News of the coming of the reign of God was directed to everyone, and the same was true for the consequences of that message: the call to repentance. But the call to discipleship was not addressed to everyone; it was only for those Jesus chose for himself. He expects of them that they share his unstable itinerant life, that they abandon their property, that they leave their families and live with him together as a community of disciples.

This is a call to a new form of life, a call to a very insecure and hard life—and for that very reason a call that presupposes freedom of decision. No one may be forced to live this way. Here again we see the profound difference between Jesus and the fanaticism of the Zealots.

Elijah and Elisha

The real model for following Jesus is found—and what else would we expect?—in the Bible itself, in the prophet Elijah's calling of Elisha. The story is told this way in 1 Kings 19:19-21:

> So he [Elijah] set out from there, and found Elisha son of Shaphat, who was plowing. There were twelve yoke of oxen ahead of him, and he was with the twelfth. Elijah passed by him and threw his mantle over him. He left the oxen, ran after Elijah, and said, "Let me kiss my father and my mother, and then I will follow you." Then Elijah said to him, "Go back again; for what have I done to you?" He returned from following him, took the yoke of oxen, and slaughtered them; using the equipment from the oxen, he boiled their flesh, and gave it to the people, and they ate. Then he set out and followed Elijah, and became his servant.

Elisha is portrayed in this text as the son of a well-to-do farmer, for he plows with twelve pairs of oxen at a time. He himself works with the last, the twelfth span, and so he can see how the eleven servants ahead of him draw their furrows.

Elijah calls Elisha by throwing his mantle over him, so Elisha is conscripted for God's business. He knows immediately what it means for him: leaving his family, breaking with his previous occupation, discipleship. The rest of the story only tells us how this wealthy heir leaves behind his family and his occupation.

First Elisha asks Elijah for permission to take leave of his parents. He knows, then, that he is no longer his own master but the servant of Elijah. Elijah permits him to take his leave; the somewhat difficult text at this point can scarcely be understood in any other way. By saying "what have I done to you?" he allows Elijah full freedom of action. The one who is called can only follow freely. But that very action makes Elisha aware of what has happened to him.

Probably the text means to say that he does not even return to his house, but improvises a farewell dinner for his farmhands in the field. He uses the yoke and equipment of a span of oxen as firewood as a sign that he is giving up his previous occupation and that God's business cannot wait. Thus this story reveals itself in many ways as a prelude to the later discipleship of those who followed Jesus' call. For example, it shows us the "immediacy" of discipleship. But it also shows that the new thing God has begun with Israel can only be handed on from person to person. There is no automatic transfer of faith to the next generation. Calling and charism must be handed on face to face. Elisha must, so to speak, feel Elijah's mantle on his own body.

But the narrative shows us still more, namely, the importance of the nonprofessional. Elisha probably never would have considered, by himself, that he might become a prophet. He had quite different things in view: his parents' farming operation, commerce, family. Probably he was called for that very reason. God does not just need ordained ministers; God also needs religious nonprofessionals experienced in their trades. God needs people who are able to plow with twelve span of oxen or to handle angle irons and levels and plumblines—and who then apply the level and the plumbline also to the condition of the people of God. That is the way it is supposed to be with many others as well, including Jesus and the fisherfolk he called to be his disciples, in the course of salvation history.

This text from the Elijah-Elisha narrative cycle in the books of Kings brings us closest to the content of Jesus' call to discipleship. There is much in favor of the idea that here, as in other cases,[9] Jesus made direct reference to his Bible. He must have had a very personal access to Torah and the prophets. That does not mean that there could not also have been other elements from the history of the tradition in play. But it is significant that the story of the calling of Elisha plays virtually no role in the rabbinic tradition.[10]

The Meaning of Discipleship

This chapter has been an attempt to work out the contours of discipleship of Jesus in contrast to the rabbinic teacher-student relationship and the Jewish revolutionary movements. Of course, in the process we have already seen some hints at why Jesus called disciples in the first place. But now, at the end of the chapter, we need to ask the question again, and bluntly.

Obviously Jesus did not gather disciples around him because he needed a kind of "court." It would also be perverse to suppose that he only gathered disciples at the point when resistance began to stiffen against him. The notion here would be that in such a situation he withdrew to a protected circle of likeminded people in order to be able to communicate his idea of the reign of God at least to them.

Anyone who wants to construct the scene this way has the whole breadth of the gospels to contend with. The calling of disciples who would leave everything behind and follow Jesus was not an emergency measure, a retreat, a substitute for action. For Jesus it was, from the very beginning, part of the proclamation of the reign of God.

This is clear from the mission of the disciples mentioned above. There can be no doubt of that historically. It is true that the oral material that is part of the story of the disciples' mission played an important role for the early Christian itinerant missionaries after Easter. It has been handed down and updated in terms of their mission—for example, in the prohibition of transferring from one house to another (Luke 10:7). But the existence of the later itinerant missionaries in itself confirms that Jesus had already sent out disciples.

And why did he send them? His mission discourse says it as clearly as possible: the disciples are to proclaim the reign of God, heal, and expel demons.[11] That is, they are to do exactly what Jesus does. They share his fate, his duties, his joys and sorrows. They have been taken into service; they are laborers for the reign of God. This is shown very clearly in a saying placed at the beginning of the mission discourse in the Sayings Source: "The harvest is plentiful, but the laborers are few; therefore ask the Lord of the harvest to send out laborers into his harvest" (Matt 9:37-

38; Luke 10:2). In biblical language the harvest, when used as an image, almost always means the judgment at the end of time.[12] The metaphor "harvest" is thus eschatologically colored throughout the Bible. The same is true of the saying about the plentiful harvest just quoted. It means to say that the "last times" are now here. The reign of God is dawning and the gathering of Israel for the reign of God is beginning. "The fields are ripe for harvesting," the Gospel of John would later say (John 4:35).

So the call to discipleship is inseparable from the coming of the reign of God and Jesus' eschatological gathering of Israel. The great work now at hand requires many laborers. This is evident also in the scene in Mark in which the first disciples are called. The meaning of the call to discipleship is explicitly formulated there: "Jesus called to him: 'Follow me and I will make you fish for people'" (Mark 1:17). Jesus refers to the "calling" of those he summons. He has no hesitation in speaking of "fishing for people," even though the expression "fish for people" or "catch people" is used in a negative way throughout the Bible.[13] We can see here again that it is part of Jesus' way of speaking to use expressions that are unusual, exciting, demanding, or even inflammatory or provocative. In any case, the saying about fishing for people makes it clear that the calling of Peter and Andrew and all the other disciples means that they will work with Jesus in gathering people for the reign of God. Obviously, this is about the gathering of Israel.

Chapter 6

The Many Faces of Being Called

Jesus called people from Israel to follow him. He gathered disciples around him. The call to these disciples to follow after him and to place everything, without reserve, in the service of the reign of God must have accompanied his preaching from the very beginning. But does that mean he wanted to call all Israel to discipleship? Was it his goal that gradually everyone in Israel would become a disciple?

A Nation of Disciples?

There are indications in the text of the New Testament that point in just that direction. The Acts of the Apostles often speaks simply of "the disciples." The series of these references begins in Acts 6:1-2: "Now during those days, when the disciples were increasing in number, the Hellenists [the Greek-speaking Jews in the community] complained against the Hebrews [the Aramaic-speaking Jews] because their widows were being neglected in the daily distribution of food. And the twelve called together the whole community of the disciples."

"The disciples" here refers to the whole community. This unique usage, which may go back to the time of the earliest Jerusalem community, appears elsewhere in Acts as well. In that book "disciple" can simply mean "Christian" or "member of the community," and "the disciples" often means nothing but the community in Jerusalem or in some other place.[1]

Add to this that the gospels, which refer constantly to Jesus' disciples, are not only looking back to the past but also making the time of Jesus transparent to the later time of the church. When the evangelists speak of Jesus and his disciples, they are also speaking of their own ecclesial present. Therefore it seems altogether likely that we should see discipleship as a comprehensive and essential characteristic of the church.[2] Favoring this is also the command to mission at the end of Matthew's gospel: "Go therefore and make disciples of all nations!" (Matt 28:19).

We could set up an equation: church = discipleship. But is that right? If we read the New Testament more closely, things look different. The language of the gospels and Acts does show unmistakably that without discipleship there can be no New Testament–style church. But that usage remains unique within the New Testament. The epistolary literature avoids the word "disciple." The usage in Acts and corresponding redactional layers in the gospels may ultimately stem from the breakthrough situation of the young post-Easter church. At that early period distinctions were not yet necessary. Those came later, but the foundations were already laid in the gospel tradition.

For according to the gospels one can only become a disciple by being chosen by Jesus—usually with the cry, "Come, follow me!" or "Follow me!"[3] And Jesus does not call everyone to follow him. According to Mark 1:15 the proclamation of the reign of God culminates in the call, "repent and believe in the good news!" but not, "follow me and become my disciple!" There is no text in which Jesus calls all Israel to discipleship or to following him. But above all, he nowhere makes being a disciple a requirement for participation in the reign of God.

So we have to suppose that life toward the reign of God—in sociological terms, participation in the Jesus movement—allowed for some very different ways of life. This chapter is about those various ways of living. It is significant that they did not arise out of the needs of the later great church but are grounded already in the gospels, even in the pre-Easter reign-of-God praxis of Jesus. In what follows I will go through these various ways of life in the order in which they appear in the gospels themselves. But I will rely primarily on the Gospel of Mark.

The Disciples

As we have seen, Jesus used a striking and clearly defined symbolic action in choosing twelve from a larger group of disciples, making them an eloquent sign of the gathering of the eschatological people of the

twelve tribes. He "created" them (Mark 3:14). They represent eschatological Israel, which begins with the group of twelve and centers on Jesus
and the Twelve.

Alongside the Twelve, however, there were a larger number of disciples. The Twelve live and act in the midst of this larger circle of disciples. Therefore we must say that the Twelve are disciples, but not all
disciples are part of the group of the Twelve. That needs to be explicitly
emphasized, because in Matthew's gospel it could seem that the Twelve
and the group of disciples were identical. Matthew speaks a number of
times very clearly of "the twelve disciples" (10:1; 11:1; 20:17; cf. 28:16).
Did he mean to restrict the group of disciples to the Twelve? Possibly,
but it is not clear what his intent was.

In contrast, the situation is very obvious in Mark. For him the group
of disciples extends beyond the Twelve. Mark 2:13-14 reports how Jesus
called the toll collector Levi to be his disciple. Thereupon, Levi made a
great banquet in his house and invited his professional colleagues and
many of his friends and acquaintances. Mark then remarks in this connection: "And as he sat at dinner in Levi's house, many tax collectors
and sinners were also sitting with Jesus and his disciples—for there were
many who followed him" (Mark 2:15).[4] This note makes clear how Mark
imagined the situation. First: there is a larger group of disciples from
among whom later (Mark 3:13-14) the Twelve are drawn. Second: one
becomes a disciple by "following" Jesus.

Luke formulates still more clearly. After he has told how Jesus, on the
mountain, has called the Twelve out of a larger crowd of disciples (Luke
6:12-13), he introduces the Sermon on the Plain (corresponding to Matthew's Sermon on the Mount) as follows: "He came down with them
and stood on a level place, with a great crowd of his disciples and a great
multitude of people from all Judea, Jerusalem, and the coast of Tyre and
Sidon. They had come to hear him and to be healed of their diseases"
(Luke 6:17-18). The theological scenery resembles the arrangement of
the audience of Matthew's Sermon on the Mount (Matt 4:23–5:1), but
Luke allots space to Jesus' listeners even more carefully than Matthew
does: first, there is the group of the Twelve, just chosen, then around
them "the great crowd" of the other disciples, and finally, in a still
broader circle, the whole multitude of people. Luke thus thinks there
was a large crowd of disciples.

This is clear also from the fact that, besides the mission of the Twelve
in 9:1-2, Luke a little later, in 10:1, tells of still another mission of seventy-
two disciples.[5] This mission could, of course, rest on a misunderstanding

on the part of Luke.[6] But it may be that with the number seventy-two he was not so far from the actual size of the group of disciples.

Moreover, there is, of course, much to commend the idea that the boundaries of the group of disciples were fluid. The number of the Twelve was fixed, but the number of disciples shifted. The Fourth Gospel tells how one day a large number of disciples took offense at Jesus and left him (John 6:60-71).

We are in the fortunate position of having at least a few names of disciples who were not part of the Twelve but seem to have belonged to the broader group of disciples: Joseph Barsabbas (Acts 1:23); Cleopas (Luke 24:18); Nathanael (John 1:45; 21:2); Mary of Magdala (Mark 15:40-41); Mary, the [daughter?/mother?] of James the Younger (Mark 15:40); Mary, the mother of Joses (Mark 15:40); Salome (Mark 15:40-41); Joanna, the wife of Chuza (Luke 8:1-3); Susanna (Luke 8:1-3); and for a time also Matthias, who then was taken into the group of the Twelve in place of Judas Iscariot (Acts 1:23, 26). The list shows that Jesus' group of disciples also included women. That was remarkable in an Eastern context and was anything but ordinary. It appears that here Jesus deliberately violated social standards of behavior.

So much, then, about the existence of a broader circle of disciples around the Twelve! In our context it is important to note that Jesus apparently did not attempt to gain disciples at any cost. Instead, he issued warnings: "As they were going along the road, someone said to him, 'I will follow you wherever you go.' And Jesus said to him, 'Foxes have holes, and birds of the air have nests; but the Son of Man has nowhere to lay his head' " (Luke 9:57-58).

Other observations point in the same direction: Jesus by no means called everyone who met him openly and in faith to be his disciple. He went to the home of the toll collector Zacchaeus (Luke 19:1-10) as well as that of the toll collector Levi (Mark 2:14-17). But Zacchaeus did not receive an invitation to discipleship as Levi did. Zacchaeus vows to change his life; in the future he will give half of his wealth to the poor of Israel and return wrongfully obtained money fourfold.[7] But he will stay in Jericho and continue to practice his usual calling as a toll collector. Apparently there existed alongside the disciples a broad spectrum of people who opened themselves to the Gospel and took Jesus' call to repentance to heart but who did not enter into his immediate circle of disciples.

Why was the group of disciples so important to Jesus? Obviously his disciples helped him in many ways: they found lodging (Mark 14:13-16; Luke 9:52), took care of meals and other things (Mark 6:37). It is said explicitly that the women who followed Jesus supported him and the whole group of disciples financially (Luke 8:3). But as indispensable as those things were, they were not the main reason. As Mark 3:14 says of the Twelve, the disciples were to be always "with him."

The coming of the reign of God was not a theory, an abstract dogma, a mere teaching; it was the beginning of a dramatic history. The reign of God requires a dedicated community, a form of life into which it can enter and be made visible. The circle of men and women who followed Jesus, their solidary community, their being-together with one another, was to show that now, in the midst of Israel, a bit of "new society" had begun. In this way above all the disciples are Jesus' "witnesses" of the reign of God now coming to be. They are, certainly, supposed to witness to the reign of God through their words, but not only in words; they witness also by their believing life together. That is why there are also so many "instructions for disciples" handed on to us in the gospels.

Participants in Jesus' Story

If we look through the gospels we see that the Twelve and the group of disciples surrounding them play a crucial role. For example, the relatively short Gospel of Mark speaks of Jesus' "disciples" forty-four times. But we have already come across the fact that the Twelve and the other disciples are by no means all those who were on Jesus' side and played a role in the Jesus movement. Mark gives us an important example in the story of the blind beggar Bartimaeus (10:46-52).

This story takes place at the gate leading out of Jericho in the direction of Jerusalem. The blind man is sitting precisely where the Galilean pilgrims would set out on the last stage of their journey to the holy city. He hears Jesus passing by with a crowd of disciples and festival pilgrims, and he cries loudly, "Jesus, Son of David, have mercy on me!" His cry for help is thus a messianic confession as well. Those around him are angry and order him to be quiet, but the blind man shouts still louder. Jesus notices him and heals him with the words, "Go; your faith has made you well." So Jesus does not call the healed man to join his disciples. He does not tell him, "Come, follow me!" In fact, he releases him. But Bartimaeus, who can see again, is filled with so much gratitude that he follows Jesus. Mark says literally that he "followed him on the way" (10:52).

In the context that can only mean he accompanies Jesus to Jerusalem. He does not follow Jesus as a disciple but apparently as someone who goes part of the way with him. And he does not go just anywhere but walks with Jesus on the last part of his way, the part that will end at the cross. So the healed man becomes a participant in Jesus' story—and that is a great, great thing.

Another example: Mark tells a story about the healing of a possessed man in the region of Gerasa (5:1-20). When Jesus has freed the man from his demons, the man begs him "that he might be with him" (Mark 5:18). That is exactly the expression Mark uses to describe a function of the Twelve, namely, "that they would be with Jesus" (cf. 3:14). So the healed man is, in fact, asking to be allowed to remain as close as possible to Jesus, as a disciple. "But he refused, and said to him, 'Go home to your friends, and tell them how much the Lord has done for you, and what mercy he has shown you.' And he went away and began to proclaim in the Decapolis how much Jesus had done for him; and everyone was amazed" (Mark 5:19-20).

Many interpreters suppose that this conclusion to the narrative reflects the post-Easter mission in the cities of the Decapolis. The narrative, they say, presumes that the man was a Gentile, and he is now depicted as the first Christian missionary to the Gentile Decapolis. Therefore, following the logic of the narrative, he could not become a disciple in the direct sense, because the disciples of the pre-Easter Jesus were attentive only to Israel.

We may leave open the question whether the man was really a Gentile. In any case, the narrative shows that not everyone was called to be part of the group of disciples. The gospels take account of the possibility that someone, even though he or she wanted to be a disciple, could be sent back to his or her family. But that does not in any way mean that such a person was unimportant to the Jesus movement. The healed man of Gerasa will become a proclaimer of Jesus precisely in *his* circle and even perhaps prepare for the later mission. He will become a participant in the story of Jesus.

Apparently there were—like the healed Bartimaeus and the possessed man from the region of Gerasa—a good many other temporary companions around Jesus, those who "went with" or sympathized with him. They were not disciples in the strict sense. Nothing is said about their receiving a formal call to discipleship of Jesus. And yet they were important for the new thing beginning in Israel with Jesus.

Resident Members of the Jesus Movement

Bartimaeus accompanied Jesus from Jericho to Jerusalem. But there were many others who were never on the road with him and yet were indispensable for Jesus' work: for example, the Lazarus household. According to the Gospel of John there was a very affectionate relationship between Jesus and the family of Lazarus: Jesus and Lazarus were friends (John 11:3). When Lazarus died, Jesus wept on the way to his tomb (John 11:35). The household of Lazarus, which was in Bethany, must have been a kind of support station for Jesus on the road to Jerusalem. But nowhere is it said that Lazarus belonged among Jesus' disciples or followers.

Obviously Jesus' circle included families of friends like that of Lazarus and his sisters whose houses were always at Jesus' disposal. There were many men and women in Israel who listened to Jesus and placed their hopes in him, supported him and sympathized with him. But they were not among the disciples in the strict sense. They did not follow Jesus in his unstable itinerant life but remained at home. We can therefore call them "resident" adherents of Jesus. Foremost among them were those who took Jesus and his disciples into their houses overnight. As we have already seen, Jesus often did not know during the day where he would be staying at night.

This situation is illuminated strikingly by a little scene taking place on the road to Jerusalem. Jesus has sent out messengers to seek lodging for himself and his disciples in a Samaritan village, but Jesus is not received there because he is on the way to Jerusalem (Luke 9:51-56). That was by no means an innocuous thing. Josephus tells how, during the time of the Procurator Ventidius Cumanus (48–52 CE), Galilean pilgrims were traveling through Samaritan territory on their way to Jerusalem for a festival. They were attacked by the Samaritans, and one of the pilgrims was murdered.[8]

The danger to which Jesus and his disciples were constantly exposed is also reflected in the mission discourse.[9] As we have already seen, the disciples, sent out deliberately without means or weapons, are meant to be distinguished from the armed Zealots. For that very reason, after they have been on the road all day, they need hosts for the evening. They need people who will provide meals for them and give them shelter and protection for the night.

But entry into strangers' houses is not only about a roof over the head and security for their own lives; it is equally, in fact more, about gaining new people for Jesus' message. The houses into which the disciples enter should become bases for the gathering of Israel. A network of houses into which eschatological peace has entered is to spread over the whole land. In this way a living basis comes into existence, one that will sustain the disciples' work of proclamation. Jesus' immediate followers, those who travel with him throughout Israel, and those among his adherents, friends, and sympathizers who remain tied to their own homes augment and sustain each other, offer mutual support and help, and so constitute an inseparable, organic whole.

Concretely: Jesus' resident adherents urgently need the new thing Jesus has begun if they are to change anything about their urgent physical and spiritual needs. The families that remain at home derive their life from the "new family" that is visible in the group of disciples. On the other hand, the disciples who are traveling through the land urgently need the support of established houses. Thus here there are constant radiant auras, reciprocal effects, overlappings. The disciples no longer live for themselves alone but for the people of God, and the resident supporters no longer live only for themselves and their children.

Occasional Helpers

The houses of those who receive Jesus and his disciples for the night thus become bases for the Jesus movement. But there was another type of relationship to the new thing in Israel. It was sporadic, momentary, less firm, and yet of great importance. Mark describes this kind of relationship in a short, meaningful word of promise directed to Jesus' disciples. It may, at least in its outlines, go back to Jesus himself: "whoever gives you a cup of water to drink because you bear the name of Christ will by no means lose the reward" (Mark 9:41).

We have to imagine the situation this describes: the heat of a long day without shade, the thirst known only to those who have been in the lands of the south, and then the cup of water, offered because someone wants to help Jesus' disciples. Perhaps the man or woman who gives the water will never encounter the disciples again and never again be able to help them. But it has happened this one time, it was necessary to their lives, and God will respond to it with eternal reward.

Another example of "occasional help" that comes to mind is the deed of Joseph of Arimathea:

> When evening had come, and since it was the day of Preparation, that is, the day before the sabbath, Joseph of Arimathea, a respected member of the council, who was also himself waiting expectantly for the kingdom of God, went boldly to Pilate and asked for the body of Jesus. Then Pilate wondered if he were already dead; and summoning the centurion, he asked him whether he had been dead for some time. When he learned from the centurion that he was dead, he granted the body to Joseph. Then Joseph bought a linen cloth, and taking down the body, wrapped it in the linen cloth, and laid it in a tomb that had been hewn out of the rock. (Mark 15:42-46)

We can only understand this narrative if we know that crucifixion in antiquity was normally made more cruel by the fact that those crucified were denied burial. Concretely that meant that the corpses of those executed remained on the crosses until they had been torn apart and devoured by raptors and wild beasts. Only then were the remains put in the ground somewhere.

We also need to know that for the people of the ancient world the refusal of burial was a much more terrible thing than it is for people today. Those who had been executed were thus shamed still further after the fact. They were denied the honor due to the dead. Their afterlife was destroyed forever. For Jewish sensibilities, the refusal of a grave was not only a horrible degradation of the dead but also a cultic desecration of the Land. Joseph of Arimathea's deed has to be understood against that background.

Who was this Joseph? He was a councilor, probably a member of the Sanhedrin in Jerusalem. He was highly regarded and influential. Otherwise he would not have been admitted to Pilate's presence. But was he a disciple of Jesus? Matthew 27:57 and John 19:38 present him as such. Mark and Luke, in contrast, simply say that he "was waiting expectantly for the kingdom of God" (Mark 15:43; Luke 23:51). If we consider that the Fourth Evangelist had a much broader concept of discipleship than Mark did, we will probably conclude that Joseph, while he was Jesus' silent sympathizer, had never been a disciple in the proper sense of the word.[10]

Joseph was precisely what I have called an "occasional helper." Only a single situation is described in which he came to the aid of Jesus and his cause. But in that situation he acted not only correctly and without fear but also generously and with full commitment. God's cause needs such people. Their single action is as important as constant discipleship.

The Beneficiaries of the New Thing

If we consider the social structure of today's parishes it is obvious that they contain not only the so-called core congregation, the group of those who participate in congregational life regularly and with greater or lesser personal engagement. Every parish also contains a considerable number of those less engaged, outsiders, occasional visitors, guests, and beneficiaries. What is interesting is that there were already such people around Jesus. We have thus, sociologically speaking, arrived at the periphery of the "Jesus movement," a marginal zone that is by no means unimportant. We can use the text of Mark's gospel to make this clear as well.

Mark 9:38-40 tells of an unusual occurrence, in our Bibles usually given the title "another exorcist" or "a stranger working miracles," or something like that. The disciples see a man exorcising demons. John, the son of Zebedee, who with his brother James was dubbed a "Son of Thunder" by Jesus (Mark 3:17), tells Jesus disapprovingly about this. In and of itself such a thing would not bother the disciples. At that time, just as now, there were many kinds of diseases that verged on the psychosomatic. These very illnesses were often ascribed to demonic influences, and in Israel, as throughout the whole ancient world, there were healers and exorcists who attempted to master such illnesses (cf. chap. 9, "Jesus' Miracles").

Jesus' disciples encountered one such "healer." They probably would not have taken any notice of him if they had not heard him driving out the demons of illness "in the name of Jesus." Apparently the man was so impressed with Jesus' deeds that he said to himself, "There is a power at work that I can make use of." And so he invoked the spirits of illness "in the name of Jesus," but without accepting the consequences that should have been obvious to him. He was not a disciple; he did not follow Jesus; he traveled around the country by himself and healed people. He used the name of Jesus, which he perceived as embodying power, but he worked for himself and his own ends.

That is precisely what got the disciples so excited and annoyed. They tried to forbid the strange exorcist from using the name of Jesus, with the argument that he was not a follower of Jesus (Mark 9:38), but they had no success. So they came to Jesus and asked him to speak a word of power and intervene. And in this situation Jesus said something altogether astonishing: "Do not stop him; for no one who does a deed of power in my name will be able soon afterward to speak evil of me. Whoever is not against us is for us" (Mark 9:39-40). This saying betrays the fact that Jesus and his disciples were surrounded by a cloud of rumors and calumnies, mean gossip and accusations. Jesus was apparently convinced that if someone remained apart, that is, did not belong with him and his followers but still drew some benefit from the new thing that was happening, that person would not join in such slanders—and so he or she would already be on the side of the new.

So it is possible to belong to Jesus and his disciples by standing for the truth and not talking about things one knows nothing about. That is, so to speak, the most distant style of encounter with the cause of Jesus. The strange exorcist is outside. He even uses the salvation that has come with Jesus for his own purposes. He becomes a benefactor of the new thing. That is not so bad, Jesus says. That too is a possibility. It is even something good, if in this way someone is brought to say good things about the work of God and not slander it.

The saying "whoever is not against us is for us" thus has a very particular "Sitz im Leben." It is said about people who are outside the new thing Jesus has begun in Israel. It is true of them, but only of them. It is not true of those who have learned about Jesus, heard his words, and are familiar with his Gospel. Another saying of Jesus, spoken on another occasion, applies to them: "Whoever is not with me is against me, and whoever does not gather with me scatters" (Matt 12:30 // Luke 11:23).

A Complex Pattern

In summary, we may say that the gospels, especially Mark, are aware of a great variety of forms of participation in Jesus' cause. There were the Twelve. There was the broader circle of disciples. There were those who participated in Jesus' life. There were the localized, resident adherents who made their houses available. There were people who helped in particular situations, if only by offering a cup of water. Finally, there were the pure beneficiaries who profited from Jesus' cause and for that very reason did not speak against it.

These structural lines that run through the gospels are not accidental. They express something that is essential for the eschatological people of God, as Jesus sees it, and therefore an indispensable part of the church. In today's church, because it is not a shapeless mass, we can find all these forms expressed. It is a complex pattern, as complex as the human body. The openness of the gospels, the openness of Jesus must warn us against regarding people as lacking in faith if they are unable to adopt a disciple's way of life or if it is something completely alien to them. In any event, Jesus never did.

On the other hand, of course, no one may reject the specific call that comes to her or him. It is not only that in such a case one fails to enter into the broad space God wants to open for that person. Rejecting the call also closes the space to others and places obstacles in the way of possibilities of growth for the people of God.

Certainly it is also true that one may not usurp a calling. Not every disciple of Jesus could be one of the Twelve. They are in the first place a pure sign, created by Jesus, to make visible God's will for an eschatological renewal of the people of the twelve tribes. At the same time, the Twelve are sent to Israel and therefore are clothed with an eschatological office that will continue in the church. That is why they are rightly called "apostles" (those who are sent) even in the gospels.[11]

It is also true that not everyone can be a disciple, since discipleship also presupposes a special call from Jesus. It does not depend on the will of the individual. It can be that someone wants to follow Jesus but is not made his disciple. Thus, not belonging to the circle of disciples as such is by no means an indication of lack of faith or a sign that someone is marginal. Nowhere does Jesus describe those of his adherents he has not called to follow him as undecided or half-hearted.[12] Each person who accepts Jesus' message about the reign of God has his or her own calling. Each can, in her own way and to his own capacity, contribute to the building up of the whole. No one is second class. The healed man of Gerasa is as important for Jesus' cause as the disciples who travel with Jesus through the land.

The Question of the More Radical Way of Life

Is a disciple's existence the more radical way of life? Here again we need to be careful.[13] The ethos of discipleship is certainly a radical one. Is there anything harder and more ruthless than to be called by Jesus to discipleship, to answer him that first one must bury one's father—perhaps recently dead, perhaps lying on his deathbed, perhaps old and ill—and be told, "Let the dead bury their own dead; but as for you, go and proclaim the kingdom of God" (Luke 9:60)? And yet the ethos of the Sermon on the Mount, which is not just for the disciples but for everyone in the eschatological people of God, is just as radical, because it demands that one abandon not only evil deeds but every hurtful word directed at a brother or sister in faith (Matt 5:22). It demands regarding someone else's marriage (and of course one's own) as so holy that one may not even look with desire at another's spouse (Matt 5:27-28). It demands that married couples no longer divorce but remain faithful until death (Matt 5:31-32). It commands that there be no twisting and manipulation of language any more but only absolute clarity (Matt 5:37) and that one give to anyone who asks for anything (Matt 5:42).

For a man's lustful glance at someone else's wife to be equated with the act of adultery is just as drastic as the demand that disciples leave their families. Jesus demands of the one group an absolute and unbreakable fidelity to their spouses (Matt 5:31-32) and of the others absolute and unbreakable fidelity to their task of proclamation (Luke 9:62). This means that Jesus regards the concrete way of life, whether marriage or discipleship for preaching, as sacred. Both ways of life are only possible in their radical form in light of the brilliance and fascination that emanate from the reign of God. But above all, neither way of life exists in isolation and independent of the other. The disciples, as they travel, are sustained by the aid of the families that open their houses to them in the evening, and the families live from and within the new family that began in the circle of disciples.

Two-Level Ethos?

Thus there is no two-level ethos, one of perfection for the apostles and disciples and a less perfect one for the rest of the people of God. We must admit, certainly, that there is one text in the gospels that seems to presume such a two-level ethos: the story of the rich man who came to Jesus with the question of how he could "inherit eternal life" (Mark 10:17-22). Jesus points him to the Ten Commandments. The man responds: "I have kept all these since my youth." Jesus looks at him, embraces him, and says, " 'You lack one thing; go, sell what you own, and give the money to the poor, and you will have treasure in heaven; then come, follow me.' When he heard this, he was shocked and went away grieving, for he had many possessions" (Mark 10:21-22).

Matthew has reworked the Markan text. The phrase "you lack one thing" has been rewritten to "if you wish to be perfect" (Matt 19:21). The gospel story of the rich young man has had an extraordinary influence throughout the history of the church: again and again it has given men and women the strength to abandon their bourgeois existence and begin an alternative life of discipleship in community. The history of the founding of many religious orders began with this text. The Matthean phrase, "if you wish to be perfect," however, has also given rise to the idea that there have to be two orders of life in the church: that of the perfect, who live the life of discipleship, and that of the less-than-perfect, to whom only the Ten Commandments and the love commandment apply.

But that kind of two-level ethos does not do justice to the text. Neither Mark nor Matthew is formulating norms for the people of God here. The story is about a concrete case. Jesus says "sell what you own" to a particular person who has come to him searching and dissatisfied. Jesus' demand is addressed to him personally. It is a call to discipleship. Obviously, in the minds of the evangelists this text is also transparent for the later church: there will be many callings to follow, to discipleship, to radical abandonment of possessions. But these calls will also always be specific callings for individuals and not a law for everyone.

This becomes still clearer if we consider the closing words of Matthew's interpretation. Behind the word "perfect" stands the Hebrew adjective *tāmim*, which means "entire," "undivided," "complete," "intact." Being perfect in the biblical sense, when applied to persons, thus means living wholly and entirely in the presence of God. The rich man in the story had kept his wealth separate from his relationship to God, and therefore something "more" was required of him. Jesus wants his "whole [self]."[14]

And "wholeness" or "integrity" of the self is again not a privilege of disciples alone. The poor widow who puts in two copper coins, in contrast to the rich who give only part of their excess to the temple, gives away everything she has. She gives "what is hers" entirely (Mark 12:41-44).

This "wholeness" is different for everyone. For one it can mean abandoning everything. For others it can mean remaining at home and making one's house available to Jesus' messengers. Perhaps for a third it can even mean only giving a cup of fresh water to the disciples as they pass by. Everyone who lives her or his specific calling "entirely" lives "perfectly."

The more closely we read the gospels, the clearer it constantly appears that the various ways of life under the reign of God do not arise out of accidental circumstances but are essential to the Gospel. They spring not only from the practical-functional point of view that Jesus could not possibly have traveled through Israel with thousands of followers, and they did not derive solely from the fact that only a relative few in Israel became his disciples. We have to look deeper. Ultimately, the variety of callings is a precondition for the freedom of every individual within the people of God.

Every individual has her or his own history, with an individual ability or inability to see, an individual freedom or lack of freedom. This individual history corresponds to the calling of each person. Only those who see are called. And no one is called to something that is completely outside his or her sphere of possibilities. Not everyone can be called to everything, but the various callings can work together to form the whole of the people of God.

The division of the church into perfect and less-than-perfect, into better and normal, into radical ethos and less radical ethos, ignores the unity of the people of God and the organization of all its members toward the same goal.

Chapter 7

Jesus' Parables

It is impossible to talk about Jesus without mentioning his language—not whether he spoke Aramaic, and also Hebrew or Greek. *That* question can be quickly answered: in Galilee, that is, where Jesus grew up, people spoke a West-Aramaic dialect. It was no different in Jerusalem, apart from a somewhat different accent. Aramaic was the common language, and it was also Jesus' everyday language. The gospel tradition gives us only a few of the Aramaic words Jesus used: for example, *ʾabbaʾ* = my father (Mark 14:36), *gehinnam* = hell (Mark 9:43), *ʾelohi* = my God (Mark 15:34), *ʾippetach* = open! (Mark 7:34), *kepaʾ* = rock (John 1:42), *qorban* = sacrificial offering (Mark 7:11), *mamonaʾ* = property (Matt 6:24), *pashaʾ* = Passover (Mark 14:1), *rabbuni* = my lord (Mark 10:51), *reqaʾ* = fool (Matt 5:22), *telitaʾ qum* = little girl, get up! (Mark 5:41).

Jesus heard Hebrew in the synagogue when the Sacred Scriptures were read. Probably he knew long passages from the Hebrew Bible by heart. And fragmentary knowledge of Greek was probably indispensable for him as a worker in the building trades. It is possible that Jesus worked for years in Sepphoris, which was only about four miles from Nazareth. That city had been completely destroyed after an insurrection; this was done by the Roman legate Publius Quintilius Varus, the later loser of the so-called Varus battle in Germania. In the time of Jesus, Sepphoris was rebuilt on Herod Antipas's orders.

Creative Language

But none of that is what we mean by Jesus' "language." We are referring to his speaking style, his way of putting the reality of the reign of God into words. It would be revealing if Jesus had used an imprecise, vague, or bombastic style. In that case we would simply say, "Your speech betrays you." But the case is exactly the opposite. Jesus' language was accurate. It was specific and precise. It was concise and pointed. There was not an ounce of extra fat in it. For example, one day while he was speaking, a woman in the crowd interrupted and shouted at him: "Blessed the womb that bore you, and the breasts that nursed you" (Luke 11:27). In many translations and commentaries this shout is entitled "benediction of Jesus' mother." But that simply misses the point of what the woman was saying, because it is *Jesus himself* who is being called blessed here; this is done by exalting his mother. That is good oriental style (and not unknown in Greek culture, either). In the East one praises someone by praising his or her mother and abuses someone by slandering her or his mother.[1] But how does Jesus respond to this shout of "blessed the womb that bore you"? He answers: "Rather: blessed are those who hear the word of God and keep it" (Luke 11:28).

What is that all about? An official correction of what the woman had said? Certainly not! The woman had paid Jesus a compliment. As a polite oriental gentleman, Jesus offers a compliment in return. The woman, after all, had been listening to him. Therefore, she herself is being called blessed.

But at the same time Jesus' answer contains a very tactful clarification. He does not praise this woman alone as blessed but includes all the listeners in his reciprocal compliment. Certainly he could not say, "Rather: blessed are you who hear the word of God and keep it," because Jesus cannot tell whether everyone in the crowd is keeping God's word. Therefore the indirect "blessed are those" is altogether appropriate here. And yet that by no means exhausts what Jesus' clarification contains, for he not only opens the reciprocal compliment to a larger group of people, ultimately the "new family" now coming to be in Israel (cf. Mark 3:35). No, he also indicates that "hearing" alone is insufficient. "Doing" has to follow. Ultimately he even says: it is not a matter of admiring me as a person but of doing the word of God.

How many words have I just used, and had to use, to explicate Luke 11:27-28! Jesus was better. He said it all in a single brief statement that could scarcely have been formulated more succinctly. A polite return compliment—and yet at the same time a whole block of theology, for this little statement made it clear to everyone that the listeners, when they heard Jesus, were hearing the word of God itself.

Obviously such brevity and exactness are also connected to the catechetical aims of the later gospel tradition: Jesus' words and parables were used for preaching and baptismal instruction after Easter. For that purpose they had to be compressed and divided and shaped in such a way that they could be easily remembered. The strict form of many of these texts thus rests on the necessities of the later tradition.

But that by no means explains everything. Jesus himself must have had an extraordinary command of language; it comes through everywhere. It was so powerful that it also shaped the language of his disciples and those who handed on his tradition. Masters of language like G. K. Chesterton and Dorothy L. Sayers point explicitly to this unique quality of Jesus.

A Precise Observer

The degree to which the language of the historical Jesus continues to permeate the tradition is shown by a phenomenon that runs throughout the whole gospel tradition: Jesus' words and parables betray a deep love for reality. They reveal a careful observation of things and people. And beyond all that they are richly imaginative and inventive. How unforgettable are the words, "It is easier for a camel to go through the eye of a needle than for someone who is rich to enter the reign of God" (Matt 19:24). Anyone who has heard this saying about the proverbially largest animal and the proverbially smallest hole will never forget it—not only because it is so terribly vivid, but also because of its illusionless severity. Obviously it does not mean to say that in principle there is no salvation for rich people—one hundred percent of them. This kind of language is not interested in statistical accuracy. Its intention is to disturb, to shake us awake, to make us uneasy, to break through the icy armor of human indifference. We can see how uncomfortable it is from the fact that medieval theologians asserted that there was a narrow gate in Jerusalem that was called "the needle's eye." That drew all the sting from Jesus' words. But that gate was an invention. It never existed. It was the offspring of the imagination of an Irish monk in the eighth century.[2] Jesus wants to disturb his listeners. Therefore he loves paradox and has no hesitation in saying, "how can you say to your [sister or brother in faith], 'Let me take the speck out of your eye,' while the log is in your own eye? You hypocrite, first take the log out of your own eye, and then you will see clearly to take the speck out of your neighbor's eye" (Matt 7:4-5).

Another example of the vividness, brevity, and keenness of Jesus' language: in 1945 the complete "Gospel of Thomas" was discovered at Nag Hammadi in Egypt. Its existence was already known from individual quotations in the church fathers. It was probably written around the middle of the second century. Because of its gnosticizing tendencies, it was rightly excluded by the church from the canon of Sacred Scripture from the start. It contains a saying about the Pharisees: "They are like a dog sleeping in the cattle manger: the dog neither eats nor [lets] the cattle eat" (*GThom* 102). A Greek proverb is at the root of this. It speaks of unbearable people who can neither enjoy anything themselves nor let anyone else have enjoyment. Jesus, who apparently was much more educated than many exegetes allow, adopted the proverb and put it in a new context, for there is parallel content in Matthew 23:13 // Luke 11:52. Jesus was using similar familiar words when he said, "let the dead bury their own dead" (Matt 8:22) or "doctor, cure yourself!" (Luke 4:23).

So Jesus quotes. But how pointedly and disturbingly he quotes! If the subject were not so serious one could almost hear in the image of the dog in the manger a trace of Jesus' humor: we only have to imagine how the cattle try to feed and cannot because the dog will not leave his comfortable spot in the manger. That, says Jesus, is just how the people's theological teachers lie on the sources of knowledge. But they themselves do not live out of those sources and they prevent others from reaching that knowledge. Jesus apparently was a close observer.

And so it is with all his images and parables. It is astonishing how much "world" we find in Jesus' parables and similitudes. Here is the world of rulers and politicians, businesspeople and great landowners, just as we also find the world of housewives and poor day laborers, fisherfolk and farmers. One must simply read the text against the grain. It is necessary to probe the sentences to see what realities they contain in order to see, behind the text, the narrator Jesus, deeply participant and carefully observant.

Here we have a story about a rich man's banquet (Luke 14:16-24), and there one about how a poor woman looks for a lost coin (Luke 15:8-10). Here we read how a great mustard bush grows out of a little mustard seed (Mark 4:30-32) and how a small amount of sourdough leavens a huge quantity of dough (Matt 13:33). Here is a description of how a victim of assault lies in his blood, and a priest and a Levite pass by and simply look away (Luke 10:30-35). Here a terrorist prepares for his attack (*GThom* 98), and there a manager who has been fired for good cause secures his living for coming years with a clever trick (Luke 16:1-7).

The Corrupt Manager

The parable in Luke 16:1-7 is especially revealing because it shows that the early church already had problems with Jesus' parable material. A whole series of commentaries has been attached to the parable (Luke 16:8-13), all of them relating to the keyword "mammon." Their purpose is to explain the parable, protect it against misunderstandings, and draw the right conclusions from it. But Jesus does not "protect" his challenging language. He uses daring images for the reign of God. And he tells stories that do not sound at all pious. For example, this one about the corrupt manager:

> There was a rich man who had a manager, and charges were brought to him that this man was squandering his property. So he summoned him and said to him, "What is this that I hear about you? Give me an accounting of your management, because you cannot be my manager any longer."
>
> Then the manager said to himself, "What will I do, now that my master is taking the position away from me? I am not strong enough to dig, and I am ashamed to beg. I have decided what to do so that, when I am dismissed as manager, people may welcome me into their homes."
>
> So, summoning his master's debtors one by one, he asked the first, "How much do you owe my master?" He answered, "A hundred jugs of olive oil." He said to him, "Take your bill, sit down quickly, and make it fifty." Then he asked another, "And how much do you owe?" He replied, "A hundred containers of wheat." He said to him, "Take your bill and make it eighty." (Luke 16:1–7)

A pious story? No, this is a story of a crime. It tells of a double betrayal. It takes place in the Palestine of the time. There, in Jesus' time, the rich land in the valleys belonged to the "state" or a few very rich owners of large estates. Most of the latter lived elsewhere—in Antioch, Alexandria, or Rome—and had managers to take care of their property.

The manager in Luke 16 embezzles the goods entrusted to him. He manages the money right into his own pocket. The owner apparently has no way of inspecting the books. He is exploited by his manager by every dishonest art in the book. But then, one day, someone fingers the manager. Who, the story does not say. The manager is then given a date by which he must lay all his accounts on the table.

The manager knows that he cannot conceal his embezzlement. He also knows that he is going to lose his position and has no chance of finding another. His future looks ruined.

Therefore he undertakes a new betrayal, and now more audaciously than before: he calls in his master's various debtors and has them rewrite their bills in their own favor and against the interests of his employer. In this way he lays obligations on people who will support him later. He creates "the right of hospitality" for himself. Obligations of this sort played an extraordinary role in antiquity. There was no such thing as insurance, and there was no social welfare system like ours. Obviously, the deceitful manager has the debtors come to him one at a time; there must not be any witnesses to such business. The amounts are extraordinarily high: a hundred jugs of oil are about 3,600 liters, the yield of some 145 olive trees. The quantity of wheat is similarly high.

How does the story end? We might ask instead: how would it end today? Probably on a high moral note. For example: the second embezzlement is also discovered, the crook loses everything and goes to prison. Moral: crime does not pay! At any rate, that is how the story was told in the eighteenth and nineteenth centuries. In recent decades, however, it would probably have been given a social touch, criticized the unscrupulous nature of the exploitative landowner, described the behavior of the manager and the indebted tenants as a bitterly necessary defense, and so made a story of social heroes out of the crime tale. In that case also the story would have turned out to be highly moral.

But what is so baffling is that Jesus' story does not end morally at all—neither according to bourgeois or antibourgeois morality. We can see how little the story was aimed at moral teaching in Jesus' mind by the fact that he does not even tell the end. That remains open; it is not interesting.

Apparently this story of a swindler is about something else entirely. The first commentary added to the tale is still aware of this: Jesus praises the criminal manager—"the Lord" is obviously Jesus and not the injured landowner—but what he applauds is not his crime but the consistency and initiative with which he rescues his own existence.

In his own terms the manager acted very consistently. He had no illusions. He considered his opportunities quite soberly. He used his mind. He engaged his whole imagination and, after calculating everything, he proceeded quickly and as efficiently as possible.

That—Jesus wants to tell his listeners—is just how you must act in the face of the reign of God. It is offered to you, now, today. But it will only come to you if you engage your mind, your imagination, your passion, your whole existence. By far the best explanation of the parable is given in the last of the commentaries: "No slave can serve two masters; for a slave will either hate the one and love the other, or be devoted to the one and despise the other. You cannot serve God and wealth" (Luke 16:13).

That is: those who want to live in the reign of God can only have God as their master. Only God may they serve—with their whole will, all their strength, their whole lives. If they have other masters besides God they are divided, pulled here and there, have no drive. Then they do not really engage, they risk nothing, they do things only halfway. Then their lives lack all inner strength and all the brilliance that belongs to the reign of God.

The swindling manager did nothing halfway. He went all the way. He risked everything and invested everything. For that, and only for that, Jesus admires him and says: if only my disciples—on their own terms— would act as sensibly as this manager!

So Jesus in his parables not only depicts the world of the good and respectable but also that of the shady and the hypocritical, the swindlers and the tricksters. He does not depict a holy and intact world. Not even the world of children is polished up. In the parable of the "children playing" Jesus tells how a group of children cannot agree what to play. There are a bunch of spoilsports who are not happy with any suggestion. They don't want to play wedding, but they don't want to play funeral either. Nothing pleases them. There is a loud argument, and in the end no game is played at all. The spoilsports have succeeded. Those who wanted to play say to them: "We played the flute for you, and you did not dance; we wailed, and you did not mourn" (Matt 11:17). The following commentary is then given: they didn't like John the Baptizer with his asceticism and preaching of repentance. Then came Jesus. He ate and drank with the sinners, but they didn't want him either and called him "a glutton and a drunkard!" (Matt 11:18-19). The parable of the children at play shows how closely Jesus observed everything. He knew that children already practice the bigger quarrels of adults. And he must have had painful experience of the disunity in the people of God, the rivalries among the various groups in Israel and the strife over his own person.

The Parable of the Sower

Jesus observed his surroundings carefully and lovingly. In the so-called parable of the sower (Mark 4:3-9)[3] the enemies of the seed are first depicted: the birds who peck up part of the seed; then the rocky ground bearing only a thin, quickly drying layer of soil; then the thistles that grow tall and smother the sprouting wheat so that it cannot develop grain. And yet: "other seed fell into good soil and brought forth grain, growing up and increasing and yielding thirty and sixty and a hundred-fold" (Mark 4:8).

This parable has created great difficulties for modern interpreters. These are connected in the first place with the notoriously incorrect translation of the parable's ending. The Greek does not have "thirtyfold, sixtyfold and a hundredfold," but rather "a part [of the grain sown on good ground] yielded thirty, part sixty, part a hundred."

A hundredfold yield? That seemed to many interpreters very far from reality, well outside any ordinary experience. Jesus was exaggerating, pushing the soil's yield into the realm of fantasy because he wanted to say that the reign of God, with its abundance, surpasses all human experience.

But did Jesus really inflate his parables, or similitudes, in that way? His audience were altogether familiar with this subject. Most of them were small farmers, tenants, and day laborers in agriculture. If Jesus had told unrealistic stories about their own realm of activity he would have deprived his parables of any persuasive power. In fact, the parable of the sower achieves the pinnacle of its realism at the end, with the series thirty, sixty, one hundred, for this series incorporates the biological phenomenon of "stocking." What is that?

Grain, as it germinates, first produces only a single shoot. But at a very early stage the lowermost nodes, far beneath the earth's surface (the so-called stock nodes), push out side shoots that cause the main stem to branch out beneath the earth. Thus in normal cases a single grain produces an entire "stock" of two to five stems or even more. As far as the number of stems in a "stock" is concerned, Jesus remains in a realistic average realm. Because he has to schematize within the narrative he works with a top figure of three stems, reckoning a yield of thirty grains per stem. That too is normal and close to reality. Before the intensively hybridized types of wheat grown today came into general use the *average* number of grains per ear even in Europe was not much more than thirty to thirty-five.

In this similitude Jesus describes the situation of a farmer who had sown a field, a part of the stony ground of the Galilean hill country. Many of the grains thus sown yielded nothing. Flocks of birds following the sower, ground interspersed with rocks, and tenacious weeds were at fault. But part of the seed sown fell on good soil. Of that, part produced thirty grains per seed sown—that is, there was no stocking. Another part produced sixty grains per seed sown—a stocking of two stems. Still another part produced around a hundred grains per seed sown—here there was a stocking of three stems.

In this way the unusual sequence thirty, sixty, a hundred (one hundred for ninety) is immediately obvious. There is no question of a rupturing of reality. Quite the contrary! Jesus was a very sober observer who allowed himself no flights of imagination, but told stories with a love for detail and a positively biological exactness. The same could be demonstrated in many other parables.

And what did Jesus mean by the parable of the sower? What did he want to tell his listeners? As in many of his parables, here again he speaks of the reign of God, which is coming. It has already been sown. In fact, the wheat is already growing. The reign of God has many enemies, however, and they seem overwhelming. And yet, despite all these enemies and opponents, the reign of God will come to pass. The work of God will succeed. It will bear fruit. In the end a rich harvest will be produced.

Why So Many Parables about Growing?

At this point it is time for a reflection. Why did Jesus tell so many parables about seeds and growing? The gospels contain not only the parable of the sower but also the ones about the weeds among the wheat (Matt 13:24-30), the mustard seed (Mark 4:30-32), the leaven (Matt 13:33), and the seed growing secretly (Mark 4:26-29). Apparently with the aid of this material Jesus was able to clarify some aspects of the reign of God now becoming reality that seemed crucial to him. This narrative material gave him the opportunity to depict not only the unstoppable growth of the reign of God but also the shockingly minute and hidden character of its beginning, and even more: the superior power of the opponents who threaten the work of God from beginning to end.

Thus Jesus deftly avoided the path opened by Jewish apocalyptic. The latter was also deeply touched by Israel's miserable situation and the power of God's opponents in history. Most apocalypticists, however, drew a different conclusion. For them it was no longer imaginable that God could still succeed in a world so depraved. Therefore they said that God's promises could no longer be fulfilled "in this world," "in this age." God would have to intervene with visible power in history, destroy the old world, and create a new one, the "new age." Only there could God's promises finally become reality.[4]

Jesus is no apocalypticist. He can, of course, make use of apocalyptic images, but he does not teach an apocalyptic system. Above all, he never succumbs to the dualism of many apocalypticists, the system of two worlds succeeding one another and sharply distinct one from the other. One can see that especially in the material of his parables of growth. This is everyday material. For example, in Mark 4:30-32, Jesus speaks not simply of the world tree (as in Matt 13:32 // Luke 13:18-19) but instead about a common mustard bush. He takes his imagery from the vegetable garden. And he talks about what a housewife in Israel did every day: grinding meal, kneading in leaven, and baking bread. He tells also about the paltry fields of ordinary people in the hill country of Israel where the soil is thin, there are almost no fenced-off paths, and thorns and thistles are nearly ineradicable.

With the aid of a world that lay before his hearers' eyes every day he depicts the coming of the reign of God and in doing so makes clear something about its very nature: the reign of God is happening already in the midst of people's ordinary, familiar, everyday surroundings. It does not arrive in apocalyptic thunder and lightning, not in a grand act of God that no one can resist, but in the same way as a mustard bush grows.

The reign of God grows in secret, in what is little, in what is inconspicuous, because God wants the old world to transform itself freely into God's reign. In his parables about seed Jesus portrays a silent revolution, and the best symbol for it is growth. It happens in silence. Growing things make no noise.

Sowing People

But let us return to the parable of the sower.[5] It was explained *allegorically*, even in the early church, that is, each individual part of the parable was applied to a piece of current reality. We can read that already in Mark 4:13-20. The wheat that is sown became the word of the Gospel placed in the hearts of the hearers. That was a lovely and appropriate interpretation.

Of course, if we look to the Old Testament to find what could have been meant there by the metaphor "God's sowing," we discover not the sowing of the divine word but the sowing of people—with the reference always being to Israel. This is particularly clear (apart from Zech 10:9 and Hos 2:25) in Jeremiah 31:27: "The days are surely coming, says the LORD, when I will sow the house of Israel and the house of Judah with the seed of humans and the seed of animals." God has indeed scattered the people of God among the nations but now is sowing them again in the land of Israel in the time of salvation that is to come, so that they may once more become the true people of God. Against this biblical background the parable of the sower probably did not speak originally of the sowing of the word, even though it was later so interpreted, but much more likely of the sowing and growth of the true, eschatological Israel.

This is also abundantly clear in the later allegorical interpretation of the parable, that is, in Mark 4:13-20. It is true that there the seed is first interpreted as the word of God: "The sower sows the word." But from then on the text suddenly begins to speak quite differently. To see that, of course, one must not follow one of the smoothing and harmonizing translations of this passage. The Greek text, literally translated, says in verses 16, 18, and 20:

> These are those who are sown on the rocky ground . . .
> Others are those who are sown amid thorns . . .
> Those are they who are sown on good ground . . .

But this means that the early church's reading of Jesus' parable first interprets the seed as the word of God, then turns around and suddenly reads the seed as a sowing of people. Two fields of imagery are mixed together. Thus the early church's interpretation still had a feeling for the idea that the original background for the parable of the sower was the sowing of human beings.

Thus the parable corresponds exactly to what we have already seen in chapters 2 and 3. For Jesus the reign of God has not only its own *time* but also its own *place* to become visible and tangible. It is first perceptible in Jesus himself but then also in Israel, which Jesus gathers as a new community around himself. So also the parable of the sower looks to Israel, which is now being confronted with the reign of God.

The Workers in the Vineyard

The parable of the sower speaks of the new sowing, the growth, and the abundance of a new society within Israel, and so do other parables, for example, the workers in the vineyard (Matt 20:1-16):

> It is with the kingdom of heaven as with a landowner who went out early in the morning to hire laborers for his vineyard. After agreeing with the laborers for a denarius for the day, he sent them into his vineyard. When he went out about the third hour he saw others standing idle in the marketplace; and he said to them, "You also go

into the vineyard, and I will pay you whatever is right." So they went. When he went out again at the sixth and ninth hours he did the same. And at the eleventh hour he went out and found others standing around, and he said to them, "Why are you standing here idle all day?" They said to him, "Because no one has hired us." He said to them, "You also go into the vineyard." When evening came, the owner of the vineyard said to his manager, "Call the laborers and give them their pay, beginning with the last and then going to the first." When those hired at the eleventh hour came, each of them received a denarius. Now when the first came, they thought they would receive more; but each of them also received a denarius. And when they received it, they grumbled against the landowner, saying, "These last worked only one hour, and you have made them equal to us who have borne the burden of the [whole] day and the scorching heat." But he replied to one of them, "Friend, I am doing you no wrong; did you not agree with me for a denarius? Take what belongs to you and go; I choose to give to this last the same as I give to you. Am I not allowed to do what I choose with what belongs to me? Or is your view evil because I am good?" (Matt 20:1-15)

Here Jesus tells a story weighed down with joylessness. It apparently takes place at the time of the grape crush. The grapes are ripe and must be harvested as quickly as possible. Otherwise it would be hard to explain why the landowner would seek workers all day long. We cannot sense in this parable the least bit of the happiness that filled the days of the crush in ancient Israel. Here are none of the glad shouts that rang out over the vineyards, none of the greetings and blessings exchanged by passersby with the vineyard workers (Ps 129:8). The parable presupposes a grey and sober world of work in which labor is only a grind.

The reason should be clear: Jesus' parables offer us an astonishingly vivid picture of the social conditions in Palestine in the first century. The times when free farmers in Israel harvested their own vineyards with joy were long past. Most had long since lost their land to large landowners. The Romans demanded such enormous sums that every operation had to produce a high added value and thus was forced to economize. This meant that agricultural operations had to be large and required cheap labor, either slaves or wage workers. Very few family farms could maintain themselves. So the majority of former farmers now worked as day laborers. They were hired in the marketplace in the morning and paid in the evening. Work went on from sunup to sundown, from daybreak to first dark.

An agricultural worker earned just enough in such a day's labor to be able to feed his or her family the next day. If the worker was not hired in the morning, that family's children would go hungry the next day. These conditions are reflected in the parable: a joyless work world. And to that extent Jesus' story is completely realistic.

There is thus no reason to look askance at the "workers of the first hour" who demanded a just system of payment. From their point of view they were quite right. A denarius was certainly not a bad day's wage. But if the last, who have worked only a single hour in the cool of early evening, receive just as much as they themselves who have toiled many hours in blazing heat, that is not only unjust but also inhuman. It degrades their labor. That is the logic of the "workers of the first hour." Are they right?

Every society, even the worst slaveholding regime, depends on the fact that at least a certain degree of justice is preserved. Otherwise, the society will collapse. To that extent we can understand the wrathful protest of the one who makes himself the spokesman for the others, and to that extent the ending of the parable is in the first place "impossible." Only when we have made ourselves aware of all that do we acquire access to the real meaning of the story, because here two worlds—or two different forms of society—collide.

On the one hand the parable describes the old society soberly and realistically, the society that repeatedly gains the upper hand even where Jesus is attempting to gather the people of God anew. There it is every person for himself or herself. There everyone struggles for her or his own existence. There people are envious when someone has more. There we find unending conflict between those "above" and those "below." But rivalry exists in the same way—perhaps even more—between those who belong to the same social class. Their comparing of themselves to one another leads to constant mistrust and ongoing power struggles.

Law, one of the most valuable achievements of humanity, exists to hold these struggles somewhat in check. It is quite right that workers living in such a society struggle for their rights. In a world built on rivalry they have no other choice. The masterful art of the parable consists precisely in the way it shows, with the greatest possible economy of words and images, how God's new world suddenly erupts into this world of the old society. For the story ends differently from what the hearers expect. They expect the last workers, who were idle almost all day, to receive only a couple of copper coins. That they receive exactly as much as the first must have been a great shock to Jesus' listeners. The ground was ripped from under their feet. All previous standards were removed.

But if they open themselves to the parable they do not fall into nothingness but find their feet standing on the ground of the reign of God, God's new society.

In the reign of God, different rules apply. It is true that people work from morning to night here too. God's world is not a land of the lotus eaters. But here work has dignity, and no one need go home in the evening filled with worry and anxiety. No one is alone. Above all: it is possible to live without rivalry because there is now something greater and more expansive than all one's own desires: work for God's cause. Precisely this common cause desired by everyone creates a solidarity that makes it possible to suffer with the suffering of others and to join in others' joy.

Of course, in the world of the parable this new society has not yet come to fruition. It is proleptically visible only in the landowner, who—contrary to all experience in the old society—is "good" (20:15). The Greek text uses *agathos* for "good." The word is usually translated "generous" here: "Are you envious because I am generous?" That is how the NRSV has the landowner speak to one of the resentful workers. But the Greek text, when literally translated, has "is your eye evil because I am good?" That is not quite the same, because in its basic meaning *agathos* means "good" in the sense of "usable," "suitable," "appropriate," "proper." When the landowner gives the last just as much as the first he acts properly, reasonably, and therefore well. He is, of course, not "reasonable" according to the standards of a society shaped by struggles to divide things but reasonable by the standards of the reign of God. Jesus was the first to fully grasp the reasonableness of the reign of God. It is reflected, for example, in his demands in the Sermon on the Mount. Renunciation of violence (Matt 5:38-42) is the only possible way to bring about genuine peace. Jesus rejected all violence in principle and thus set in motion a sequence of effects that could not have been foreseen. Therefore he is the suitable, the appropriate, person.

Yet again: at the moment when Jesus tells the story, the new thing has not yet begun to spread. It is proleptically visible only in him, the most suitable person for the reign of God. But it is also already visible in his disciples and sympathizers: namely, at the moment when they abandon their own rivalries and assist one another in solidarity.

All this has probably made it clear that we miss the meaning of the parable if we designate its theme simply as the overflowing generosity of God. Obviously, it ultimately speaks of God's limitless and undeserved generosity, but if the parable was about only that it would be completely devoid of obligatory character. Every believer speaks today of God's generosity; such talk costs nothing and changes nothing. If Jesus had talked only about the generous God he would not have been crucified.

The grumbling of the workers hired at the first hour reflects the grumbling of those contemporaries of Jesus who were outraged by the new thing he was beginning with his disciples: a common life growing out of constant forgiveness and solidarity and in which, therefore, latecomers and sinners who had not offered any service found their place. Jesus was reproached again and again for eating with tax collectors and sinners.

Thus Matthew 20:1-15 is not about some abstract characteristic of God. Jesus speaks of the boundless generosity of God solely from the point of view that this generosity is now reality since his own appearance and is so in the form of a new society that is beginning to grow around him and through him. The parable speaks of how this new reality is breaking into the weariness and hopelessness of the people of God. It is an outrageous process. It makes the lowest into the highest; it awakens deep anxieties; it causes scandal. But it also allows hope to bloom and bestows deep joy.

In the parable of the hired workers Jesus depicts what is now happening, at this very hour: the coming of the reign of God. He interprets what is already taking place before his hearers' eyes, its impact still hidden and yet visible. The parable does not provide a timeless teaching. It reveals things that are already happening and by revealing them sets them free. A new possibility for living becomes plausible.

The hearers can depend on the parable's import. They can enter into the story the parable tells and allow Jesus' words to give them a new foundation on which to stand. They can ask Jesus to make them part of his group of disciples where the new thing is already beginning to grow. Or they can become sympathizers with the Jesus movement and thus support the new world that is beginning there.

Thus, Jesus' words are effective. They create reality. In the parable of the workers in the vineyard, which so exactly describes the gloomy social conditions of his time, Jesus was also surely thinking that the time of harvest in Israel must again become what, in God's eyes, it should always have been: a time of jubilation and shouts of joy.

The Seed Growing Secretly

It is surely clear by now that Jesus' parables illuminate the reign of God from all sides; still more, they entice us to enter into it. And because the reign of God cannot be reduced to simple formulae, Jesus' parables often seem to contradict each other. We can show this through three examples.

The first of these is the parable of the seed growing secretly (Mark 4:26-29). It is one of Jesus' loveliest parables: short, compact, positively functional in its direct and virtually unadorned style, and yet imbued with a marvelous hope:

> The kingdom of God is as if someone would scatter seed on the ground, and would sleep and rise night and day, and the seed would sprout and grow, he does not know how. The earth produces of itself, first the stalk, then the head, then the full grain in the head. But when the grain is ripe, at once he goes in with his sickle, because the harvest has come.

This parable tells of the coming of the reign of God in the image of a field that produces seed and allows it to grow steadily until harvest. The accent is not on the sowing. The farmer who sowed the seed is part of the plan of the parable. Nor is the accent on the harvest. It too is simply part of the frame that holds together the central and focal part of the parable. What is crucial is only the description of how the wheat grows while the farmer does nothing. Only here, in the central part of the parable, is there a description of "phases." Only here does the narrative become detailed.

That is very strange to people today. As biologically enlightened moderns they know *how* the seed grows and *why* it grows and what one can do to make it grow faster or slower, taller or shorter, and above all pest-resistant. The work of today's agricultural engineers is by no means finished when the seed is sown. At the least, there is still spraying to be done.

At that time in Galilee or Judea it was quite different. The parable depicts the impossibility of intervening in the growth of the seed. The farmers had to wait. They slept and rose, day and night, and the earth produced its yield "of itself." Human beings could not understand or influence the miracle of growth. They only knew that God's creative power was at work and in the end gave the harvest.

From beginning to end the parable is about the coming of the reign of God. It is not about the fact that the reign of God will only come if first the seed is sown. It is certainly not about the idea that the reign of God comes slowly, as grain gradually ripens. Its point is solely that human beings cannot bring about or force the coming of God's reign, most certainly not by violence, as the Zealots thought possible. They can only wait. They may sleep quietly at night. God brings the reign of God. God alone.

The parable shows the creative power and historical might of God. No one will prevent God from working and bringing God's salvation.

The human response to this knowledge of God can only be a deep, calm trust in God.

The Other Aspect of the Matter

And yet that is only one side of the story. For on the other hand the same Jesus calls his hearers to absolute decisiveness and a marshaling of all their strength in light of the reign of God. In the Coptic Gospel of Thomas, mentioned above, we find a parable that points in that very direction. It portrays a resistance fighter who plans a political murder and prepares himself at home to the last detail. Again and again he draws his sword and thrusts it into the mud wall of his house. When he is sure that he is quick enough and strong enough, he goes out to impale the man who is to be eliminated.

That parable resembles in many respects the similitude about the deceitful manager (Luke 16:1-7). The story itself is just as immoral, the event is described with the same soberness and precision, and the real message points in the same direction. Therefore, we may regard the parable of the terrorist as an authentic Jesus parable. It reads: "The Father's reign is like a person who wanted to kill someone powerful. While still at home he drew his sword and thrust it into the wall to find out whether his hand would go in. Then he killed the powerful one" (*GThom* 98).

Here again we should note the catechetical brevity. Obviously a good storyteller would develop the parable in more detail. But a good storyteller like Jesus would place the emphasis in his depiction of events on the preparatory self-reassurance or training of the terrorist because that, and not the carrying out of the murder, is the crucial point. The murder can be taken care of with a short statement, because what the storyteller means to say is something different: the reign of God demands a person's whole commitment. One may not go to sleep but must engage passionately, do everything one can in order to obtain a share in the reign of God. Only "the violent bear it away" (Matt 11:12).

The Parable of the Talents

Thus the reign of God requires people who go for broke. That is exactly the point of the parable of the talents or, as it is often called, the parable of the "money given in trust":

> [With the heavenly reign] it is as if a man, going on a journey, summoned his slaves and entrusted his property to them; to one he gave

five talents, to another two, to another one, to each according to his ability. Then he went away.

The one who had received the five talents went off at once and traded with them, and made five more talents. In the same way, the one who had the two talents made two more talents. But the one who had received the one talent went off and dug a hole in the ground and hid his master's money.

After a long time the master of those slaves came and settled accounts with them. Then the one who had received the five talents came forward, bringing five more talents, saying, "Master, you handed over to me five talents; see, I have made five more talents." His master said to him, "Well done, good and trustworthy slave; you have been trustworthy in a few things, I will put you in charge of many things; enter into the joy of your master."

And the one with the two talents also came forward, saying, "Master, you handed over to me two talents; see, I have made two more talents." His master said to him, "Well done, good and trustworthy slave; you have been trustworthy in a few things, I will put you in charge of many things; enter into the joy of your master."

Then the one who had received the one talent also came forward, saying, "Master, I knew that you were a harsh man, reaping where you did not sow, and gathering where you did not scatter seed; so I was afraid, and I went and hid your talent in the ground. Here you have what is yours."

But his master replied, "You wicked and lazy slave! You knew, did you, that I reap where I did not sow, and gather where I did not scatter? Then you ought to have invested my money with the bankers, and on my return I would have received what was my own with interest.

"So take the talent from him, and give it to the one with the ten talents. For to all those who have, more will be given, and they will have an abundance; but from those who have nothing, even what they have will be taken away. As for this worthless slave, throw him into the outer darkness, where there will be weeping and gnashing of teeth." (Matt 25:14-30)

At first glance it seems that everything about this parable is clear. Apparently it means to say that God has given each person different abilities and expects that each will apply the abilities given to her or him. At any rate, that is how the parable is commonly interpreted. God requires much of those to whom God has given much; from those to whom less has been given, less is accordingly required.

But was that all Jesus wanted to say? Did he only mean that "you should apply the abilities God has given you"? Jesus was executed for what he said and did. Let me repeat: nobody is executed for teaching nothing more than bourgeois morality.

But there are other problems with the parable. In Matthew's gospel it is included in a larger composition of parables about the return of the Son of Man, that is, the Christ of the Parousia. It is quite clear that Matthew (and the early church with him) understood the parable in that light. The master who goes away is now the exalted Christ. When he returns he will demand a reckoning from each according to her or his abilities. The accounting given by the slaves is thus the judgment of the world. Whoever withstands the judgment receives a share in the eternal banquet of joy ("enter into the joy of your master"). But those, like the third slave, who do not withstand the judgment will lose everything and will be thrown into the outermost darkness.

Thus Matthew interpreted the traditional Jesus parable, in light of the early church's expectation of the return of Christ, as being about the judgment of the world, and apparently in doing so he also made changes in the text of the parable. In using it for his own teaching he updated it. That is the right of every Christian teacher. Every preacher today also does something similar in interpreting the Sunday gospel: she or he brings it up to date. Luke did something similar with parallel material in the parable of the pounds (Luke 19:11-27).

None of that should prevent us from inquiring about the meaning Jesus intended in the parable. Was Jesus really talking about his own return in the parable of the talents? What was this parable about originally?

A Millionaire on a Business Trip

We can most readily enter into the imagery of the parable if we begin with the figure of the man who hands out the talents to his slaves. This is another of those immoral figures we encounter rather often, as we have seen, in Jesus' parables. This "master" is one of the very wealthy, because he hands out enormous sums of money to his "slaves" or "servants"—that is, highly placed slaves or employees with significant responsibilities. In addition, this man is a boaster because he calls these huge sums "a few things," or "a little," that is, minor matters. That is, of course, an obvious understatement. Bankers nowadays talk casually of "peanuts" in much the same way. This boaster confirms quite candidly in his dialogue with the third slave that he conducts his business in immoral ways: "You knew, did you, that I reap where I did not sow, and gather where I did not scatter?" (Matt 25:26 // Luke 19:22). That is, the man uses evil methods in his business. He exploits other people. He lends money at usurious rates. He collects harshly; he sucks up everything. Probably he speculates habitually in high-risk ventures. Now he goes abroad for a while, perhaps to exploit new financial sources or to collect money.

In any case, this reconstruction of the original story in the parable is partly hypothetical. It could also be that the sums entrusted were elevated so enormously by Matthew himself, since the Lukan parallel speaks of "minas" (Luke 19:13), which are considerably less valuable than talents. In that case "trustworthy in a few things" (Luke 19:17) would not be ironic but intended seriously. But even if the original parable went that way, what follows must in any case have been part of it: slaves one and two are worthy reflections of their master. While he is abroad they each increase the capital entrusted to them by a hundred percent. That, obviously, could not have been done with solid buying and selling but only by methods executed behind closed doors, by daring acts outside the realm of legality that, of course, corresponded exactly to those of the master.

The third slave is afraid to run such risks. He dares nothing, not even depositing the money given to him in a "private bank." After all, even a bank could go bankrupt. He hides his master's money in the storehouse most commonly used in antiquity: he buries it. In this way he loses nothing, but he makes not a cent of profit.

And precisely in that way he loses everything. He belongs to a company that values lightning-fast action, initiative, pleasure in risk, and— high returns. When his master returns from abroad, the third slave is kicked out. His professional existence is destroyed.

Thus in telling his parable, as he sometimes does, Jesus makes use of unusual, tension-building material. The stuff of the story he tells is neither religious nor moral. Jesus places his listeners in a world that is harsh and reckless. People there who do not risk everything cannot last. They will be fired.

What a bold move, to make a statement about the reign of God in terms of immoral material, a story from the world of speculators and players! And what a demand lies behind this parable! For what it means to say should be clear in the context of the other parables we have already discussed. Jesus is talking about the plan God has for the world. He speaks of the new thing God wants to create in the midst of the old society. This, God's cause, Jesus says, will not succeed with cowards, with people who are immovable, who are constantly trying to make themselves secure, who would rather delay than act. God's new society only succeeds with people who are ready to risk, who put everything on the table, who go for broke and become "perpetrators" with ultimate decisiveness.

A Paradox

Thus in his parables Jesus can say that the reign of God comes as a pure miracle "of itself" (recall the parable of the seed growing secretly), but he can also say that it must be seized with ultimate decision if it is to come. Is that a contradiction? Not necessarily, but it *is* a paradox. Apparently both things need to be said if one wants to speak accurately about the reign of God. The paradox must not be resolved, any more than the tension between the present and future natures of the reign of God may be relaxed.

Jesus was a master of brief, striking sayings and skilled at telling stories in images and parables. Obviously, he did not invent the parable form, which had long existed both in the ancient world and in Israel. But Jesus took old, existing forms to a new level. The number of parables we have from him is also outside the norm. If we exclude the similitudes and images in the Gospel of John, which have an entirely different character, we come to a total of about forty parables in the Synoptic Gospels. That is unique in antiquity.

But it is not simply a matter of quantity. Jesus' parables and images have never been equaled in quality either. With them he leads his listeners into a world with which they are already familiar or at least one they have heard about, a world he describes with accurate realism. But at the same time he makes that world alien and thus blows up the well-worn paths of customary pious thinking. Jesus wants to show that the reign of God has its own logic. It does not fit in the usual molds of religious talk about God. Jesus' saying also applies to his own language: "no one puts new wine into old wineskins; otherwise, the wine will burst the skins, and the wine is lost, and so are the skins; but one puts new wine into fresh wineskins" (Mark 2:22).

Chapter 8

Jesus and the World of Signs

Jesus didn't just talk. He didn't just announce the reign of God. He acted not only through words but just as intensively through gestures, symbols, and signs. Obviously, language itself is a system of signs, but this chapter is about Jesus' physical conduct, which surprisingly often was concentrated in formal "symbolic acts."

The Bodily Sphere

Jesus embraced children when they were brought to him, laid his hands on them and blessed them (Mark 10:16). He embraced[1] the rich man who asked him about eternal life (Mark 10:21). He sat at table with toll collectors and sinners (Mark 2:15). He washed his disciples' feet and dried them (John 13:3-5). He healed sick people, not through mere words, but usually by touching them as well. He laid his hands on them (Mark 6:5). He took Peter's mother-in-law by the hand and lifted her up (Mark 1:31), just as he did the daughter of Jairus, the head of the synagogue (Mark 5:41). He touched a leper to heal him (Mark 1:41). He put his fingers into the ears of a deaf man with a speech impediment and touched his tongue with his saliva (Mark 7:33). He spat[2] in a blind man's eyes and laid hands on him (Mark 8:23). For another blind person he made a paste of dirt and saliva, spread it on his eyes, and ordered him to wash in the pool of Siloam (John 9:6-7).

Of course many of these physical actions were simply part of ancient culture: before a formal meal one had to wash one's feet; people embraced each other in greeting; laying on of hands was part of healing, and saliva was used therapeutically on the eyes. All that may be quite usual and a matter of course.

And yet there is more here, as is clear in the healing of the leper as told in Mark 1:40-45. Jesus touches the leper, and that was not common. It was, in fact, forbidden and shunned. According to Leviticus 13:45-46 lepers had to wear torn clothing and leave their hair unkempt, men had to cover their beards, and they must call attention to themselves by shouting "unclean! unclean!" No one was to come near them. Jesus' touching of the leper was a gesture that overcame a deep social rift in antiquity. It is a helping, healing, community-creating deed.

Just as people were supposed to stay away from lepers, they were also supposed to keep their distance from public sinners. In the Israel of Jesus' time it was simply not "the thing" to eat with "toll collectors and sinners." The view of Jesus' contemporaries in Judaism was that the tax and toll collectors made their money in dishonorable ways. They were looked on as thieves and robbers. One who followed the Torah would never, ever eat with them.

It was customary as well to wash one's feet before a banquet, but it was certainly not customary for the one called master and lord to wash the feet of his table companions. That was something for servants or slaves to do. Thus, many of Jesus' little gestures and signs broke through what was customary, even though they were still embedded in the culture of the world of the time.

But above all we must see that, for Jesus, behind the gestures and attitudes that were otherwise well-established in antiquity stood a *biblical* awareness of the human being. For in all this he was always also making a statement about the bodily nature of the human and thus about a crucial dimension of human existence. The human is dust and earth, but earth into which God has breathed his own breath (Gen 2:7), and therefore Jesus can make a paste of earth and spread it on a blind man's eyes. This act is more than an instance of natural healing, and it has not the least thing to do with magical practices. It makes it clear that healing and liberation are not something purely spiritual or merely internal. Earth comes to the aid of humanity (Rev 12:16), and the body is to be redeemed just as is the soul.

It seems to me that the fact that Jesus had a deep relationship with physical attitudes, the language of the body, and the world of signs is of great significance, because precisely in this it becomes clear that he lived in an unbroken relationship to human physicality. Jesus is not alien, helpless, or disturbed in his relation to the body; for him, body and bodiliness are indispensable aspects of humanity.

Jesus takes the body and its needs seriously. No one could have said of him what antiquity said of the pagan philosopher Plotinus and what Athanasius reported of the Christian hermit Antony: Plotinus "lived like someone who was ashamed to have been born into a human body,"[3] and Antony "blushed" when he ate in the presence of others.[4]

The story of Plotinus reveals the absolutizing of the spiritual that was possible in the world of Greek culture, and in reading the description of Antony's life we need to be aware that anti-bodily tendencies from late antiquity had penetrated Christianity so that the language of its legends distorted the reality of the saints' lives. But supposing that Antony really did regard eating as something slightly indecent: what would he have thought if he had seen Jesus at a banquet with toll collectors and sinners that most certainly was not as silent and respectable as depicted in the paintings of the Last Supper in Christian art? And what kind of confusion would have overcome him if he had been involved in what Luke relates in chapter 7 of his gospel?

> One of the Pharisees asked Jesus to eat with him, and he went into the Pharisee's house and took his place at the table. And a woman in the city, who was a sinner, having learned that he was eating in the Pharisee's house, brought an alabaster jar of ointment. She stood behind him at his feet, weeping, and began to bathe his feet with her tears and to dry them with her hair. Then she continued kissing his feet and anointing them with the ointment. (Luke 7:36-38)

Jesus is not upset in this story. He defends the woman against the criticism that begins immediately to be hurled at her. He interprets her action as a sign of her faith. The uninhibited behavior of the woman and that of Jesus are a match. Jesus understands. He knows what the woman's signs mean. He has no fear of physical behavior.

The incarnational nature of Jesus' work is obvious in his deeds of healing but also in all his signs and gestures: God's salvation must enter into the world and penetrate every facet of its reality. It is not just a matter of changing minds. It is just as much about matter. Nothing can be left out. Redemption is meant for the whole of creation. The history of revelation has not been a progressive dissolution of the worldly but a

more and more comprehensive incarnation, a deeper and deeper satura-
tion of the world with the Spirit of God.[5] God has "moved in on us" to
do us good.

A Demonstrative Healing

Surprisingly often Jesus' behavior concentrates into a formal symbolic
act. The meaning of that will be clearer from the following example. I will
begin with an incident that is related in Mark 3:1-6:

> Again he entered the synagogue, and a man was there who had a
> withered hand. They watched him to see whether he would cure
> him on the sabbath, so that they might accuse him. And he said to
> the man who had the withered hand, "Come forward." Then he said
> to them, "Is it lawful to do good or to do harm on the sabbath, to
> save life or to kill?" But they were silent. He looked around at them
> with anger; he was grieved at their hardness of heart and said to the
> man, "Stretch out your hand." He stretched it out, and his hand was
> restored. The Pharisees went out and immediately conspired with
> the Herodians against him, how to destroy him.

No question: it is not only a person's illness that is being healed here.
This is more: the healing becomes a demonstration, provoked by Jesus'
opponents who are watching his every move, even lurking about in the
hope that they can put the law on him. That very attitude forces Jesus
to react quite clearly. He calls the crippled man forward. This healing is
meant to be a provocation. It is to show that the Torah is to be interpreted
in light of what God really wants: in this case, to save life or give back
life that has been lost or diminished, whatever the circumstances.

The healing becomes a symbolic act that says something fundamental
about Jesus' attitude toward the Torah. What really should happen pri-
vately and quietly, namely, the healing of a person, becomes in the face
of the hardening of his opponents a public, provocative sign that extends
far beyond the pure act of healing.

New Family

Mark 3:20-35 brings us a step further. We could title this part of the
text "The Founding of a New Family."[6] The three-part story first presents
us with the kind of enmity Jesus encounters when he begins to gather

Israel for the reign of God. The resistance comes from two quarters: Jesus' own relatives, who simply call him "crazy" (3:21), and the Jerusalem authorities, who have sent scribes to Galilee to observe Jesus. They, in turn, demonize Jesus by saying he is possessed by an evil spirit and does his miracles with the aid of the supreme evil spirit (3:22). Jesus warns the scribes with a saying about sin against the Holy Spirit, but he dismisses his relatives, who have come to put him under house arrest, with the curt question, "Who are my mother and my brothers?" (3:33).

But the narrative intends more than simply to illustrate the resistance to Jesus. It only gets to its real point when Jesus constitutes a "new family," the family of those who do the will of God: "And looking at those who sat around him, he said, 'Here are my mother and my brothers! Whoever does the will of God is my brother and sister and mother'" (3:34-35).

In Israel, "doing the will of God" in and of itself meant following the Torah. But that cannot be what is intended in this situation, because Jesus' family and relatives certainly kept the Torah. The common formula has acquired a new meaning. Here "doing the will of God" can only mean learning from Jesus what the living will of God is for "today," the today that has broken upon Israel with Jesus' appearing, and then responding obediently to this "today." Whoever does that becomes Jesus' brother, sister, and mother, and so belongs to Jesus' new family.

As important as it is to rightly understand what "the will of God" has to mean in this passage, it is equally important to take the form of the saying seriously. Jesus is formulating his words here not merely in high rhetorical style, but even in juridical terms.[7] Looking at the people seated around him, he speaks a declaratory formula analogous to one that was used at marriages in Israel (and also in divorces):[8] "This is my mother, and these are my brothers!" The whole scene—like the healing of the man with the withered hand—is a kind of demonstration or illustration. We could also say that it is a definitive statement of intent. And yet such terminology is not adequate to what is happening here. Jesus wants to do more than merely declare or illustrate, just as the symbolic actions of the Old Testament prophets were more than illustrations or demonstrative declarations of intent. There is something creative in a symbolic action; it establishes a new reality. In our case it even has a formal-juridical dimension: Jesus releases himself from his physical relations and establishes a "new family."

So what is related in Mark 3:20-35 is not a mere incident, and what he says about those who now follow the will of God is not simply rhetoric.

Anyone who knows what clan and family mean in the Middle East can only see in Jesus' distancing himself from his own family an event that cuts deeply into social relationships, something that is anything but innocuous.

The Installation of the Twelve

Finally, the installation of the Twelve in Mark 3:13-19 has a juridical-institutional dimension. I have already mentioned these texts in chapter 4, but only in regard to the fact that it is one of the clearest pieces of evidence for the "gathering of Israel" Jesus intended. Here my concern is with the institutional dimension of the event.

Both the carefully preserved list of the Twelve, with Simon Peter as the first, and the verb *epoiēsen* (= "he created" or "he installed," from Greek *poiein*) show that this is a symbolic action that creates a new reality within Israel and also has institutional character, for there is no other comparable *complete* list of names in the early church, except for the Seven in Acts 6:5. In the Old Testament, "create" can be used for installation in office, for example, of judges or priests,[9] and such a public-official action is likewise intended here. Both the list and the verb indicate that this is something special, deeply embedded in memory.

When Jesus called the Twelve out of a larger group of disciples and set them before the others as a precisely defined group, it was in the first place a vivid illustration, a demonstration of his will to gather all Israel. But here again we would underestimate the depth dimension of the symbolic action if we saw it only as that. It is also an initiation of the future, of something that is already proleptically realized in a prophetic sign. In the beginning of realization the future is already projected in advance.

Jesus' symbolic actions open up a new reality, institute meaning, put in place a reality into which one can enter. To that extent they have a basic sacramental structure and are the preliminary stages of the church's later sacraments. With the establishment of the Twelve and their preaching of the reign of God the existence of eschatological Israel has already begun.

"He created the Twelve"—anyone familiar with the Bible hears the fixed formula "God created" from the creation account in Genesis 1:1–2:4 in the background here. But there is also an echo of Deutero-Isaiah, who says again and again that God "has created" his people (e.g., Isa 43:1, 21) and "will create" new things for his people (Isa 43:19). With Jesus' institution of the Twelve, the promises from the book of Isaiah begin to be fulfilled definitively. The new creation of Israel is beginning.

If Jesus did anything in the way of creating institutions, it was primarily in the creation of the Twelve. This symbolic action has a juridical dimension. However, it was not for the sake of a church about to be newly founded that would take Israel's place in the history of salvation; it was for the sake of the eschatological Israel that was to be gathered. It was out of that eschatological Israel that Jesus instituted and founded that the church came into being after Easter.[10]

The Constitution of a New Reality

The first section of this chapter spoke of Jesus' gestures and attitudes, the next three about a demonstrative healing (Mark 3:1-6), the institution of a new family (Mark 3:34-35), and the installation of the Twelve (Mark 3:13-19). The number of symbolic actions that accompanied Jesus' appearance was certainly much, much greater. We must also say something about Jesus' solemn entry into the city of Jerusalem (Mark 11:1-11), the subsequent action in the Temple (Mark 11:15-19), and Jesus' gesture with the bread and wine at the Last Supper (Mark 14:22-25). But those three symbolic actions are closely related to one another: they begin Jesus' passion. Therefore they need to be treated in this book at a later time, namely, in chapter 15 ("Decision in Jerusalem").

But by now it should already be clear that Jesus did not only act through his words. He also acted in gestures and signs that often concentrated themselves into symbolic actions. In this way much of his life acquired a symbolic dimension: for example, his celibacy, which we will also need to discuss (chaps. 13 and 14). But none of it is symbolic in the pale, watered-down sense in which people today, surrounded as they are by traffic signs, pictograms, and computer symbols, think of signs and symbols. The symbols and signs in the life of Jesus create meaning. They constitute new reality. In everything he did—and above all in his symbolic actions—Jesus was creating the beginning of the eschatological Israel.

Chapter 9

Jesus' Miracles

Human words have enormous power. They can tear down or build up. They can gather and scatter. Words can thrust the world into deep distress, and they can give rise to an unending sequence of events. Once the concept of human rights was put into words it could no longer be banished from history. Since the Sermon on the Mount was composed, it has not ceased to incite silent revolutions. Nevertheless, it would be a fundamental mistake to think that the world is governed only by words and that only words set history in motion.

For Jesus the word did indeed play a major role: he instructed and taught, he corrected and warned, he interpreted events prophetically, he preached the Gospel of the reign of God, and more than that: he proclaimed it publicly. And yet Jesus did not just talk. He not only announced the reign of God. His work was not merely a "word event." His whole public activity from beginning to end was shot through with action the evangelists call "deeds of power" (*dynameis*) and "signs" (*sēmeia*).[1] For centuries the church has called these "miracles." Anyone who wants to say anything about Jesus cannot avoid engaging with his miracles. This chapter will have to show what that word can mean.

Testimonies

Even if the gospels had not contained a single miracle story we would have known that miracles were an integral part of Jesus' activity. For

128

example, the Jewish historian Josephus (first c. CE) includes in his *Antiquities of the Jews* a note about Jesus (*Ant.* 18.63-64) that speaks of his miracles. This note was previously suspected of being a Christian interpolation from start to finish, but today most scholars believe that Josephus really did speak about Jesus at this point, though his statement received some Christian editing. There is much to favor this redactional hypothesis. It is true that we can scarcely reconstruct the whole of the original wording, but the substance of the note probably included the words, "He was a doer of startling deeds [*paradoxōn ergōn poiētēs*]." Josephus was referring to Jesus' miracles.[2]

Luke 13:31-33 also speaks of Jesus' deeds. In this little composition Luke takes up some of the oldest pieces of tradition. We can see this in the fact that here Jesus—contrary to post-Easter Christology—is called a "prophet." What is it about? Pharisees are warning Jesus about Herod Antipas, suggesting he leave the region because Herod wants to kill him. In his response Jesus describes Herod with sharp irony as a "fox." In antiquity the fox was regarded as sly but also as a creature that constantly overestimated its own cunning.[3] Besides that, it smelled bad. We have to read Jesus' answer to the Pharisees against that background:

> Go and tell that fox for me, "Listen, I am casting out demons and performing cures today and tomorrow, and on the third day I finish my work. Yet today, tomorrow, and the next day I must be on my way, because it is impossible for a prophet to be killed outside of Jerusalem." (Luke 13:31-33)

This saying shows how realistically Jesus viewed his own situation, but at the same time it illustrates his determination. He will go on doing as he has done. Someone like Herod will by no means turn him aside from his path. For our context, what is important is that the discourse names Jesus' central activities as driving out demons and healing. Both were the reason why news about Jesus spread rapidly and people ran after him.

We have other sayings in which Jesus speaks of his miracles, for example, the "woe" on the Galilean towns: "Woe to you, Chorazin! Woe to you, Bethsaida! For if the deeds of power done in you had been done in Tyre and Sidon, they would have repented long ago, sitting in sackcloth and ashes" (Luke 10:13). In this connection we should also refer to the beatitude Jesus spoke over his disciples, cited earlier: "Blessed are the eyes that see what you see! For I tell you that many prophets and kings desired to see what you see, but did not see it, and to hear what you hear, but did not hear it" (Luke 10:23-24). What do the disciples see? Obviously, the mighty deeds now being done for the sick and the possessed, the outcasts and the socially isolated. But it was not only the disciples who saw all that. Jesus' opponents did too. They were in no position to deny Jesus' healings and exorcisms of demons. They had no recourse except to reinterpret them, which they did, with perverse results: "And the scribes who came down from Jerusalem said, 'He has Beelzebul, and by the ruler of the demons he casts out demons'" (Mark 3:22).

Who is Beelzebul? We find the name in the second book of Kings (2 Kgs 1:2), where it is the name of the god of the Phoenician city of Ekron.[4] The word is made up of Ba'al and *zebul* (= ruler). So this is the pagan god Ba'al, who is given an honorific epithet, *zebul*. Obviously, this Beelzebul was a horror to the Jews, like all pagan gods. For them he was a demon, and evidently they regarded him as the chief demon.

It is only against this background that it becomes clear what is going on here. Scribes—that is, theologians—explain that Jesus is not driving out demons with the aid of the God of Israel but with that of a foreign god who himself is nothing but a demon. This officially charges Jesus with apostasy from the faith of Israel. Indeed, as the Markan text correctly interprets, he is charged with being possessed himself. There could be no more effective slander of Jesus in Israel, especially in the eyes of simple, pious people. He was thus branded as an idolater and seducer of the people. But this compromising slander itself makes it clear that Jesus' opponents could not deny that he drove out demons. All they could do was twist the facts and in doing so demonize Jesus.[5]

So the fact remains: even if the New Testament contained not a single concrete miracle story it would be evident that Jesus healed sick and possessed people. In addition, we have to conclude from the same evidence that healings and other miracles were frequent after Easter, in the early communities. Apparently something began with Jesus that continued seamlessly into the early church.

Miracle Stories

Now, of course, it is true that the gospels not only give indirect evidence of Jesus' miracles. They describe them as well. In fact, they relate an unusually large number of miracles. Mark's gospel in particular is positively stuffed with accounts of miracles.

The phenomenon of the numerous miracles in the gospels is quite often downplayed by saying that such things were simply the rule in antiquity. It is said that in that time stories of miracles were constantly being told, belief in miracles had grown greatly, and people told of miracles by many "divine people." The miraculous was somehow "in the air," and even in the Judaism of Jesus' time things were not much different.

But it is not quite so simple.[6] Obviously in antiquity people, especially simple people, believed in miracles. But there was also a strong skepticism about and a critique of miracles. There were indeed sanctuaries—the most famous being Epidauros, with its cult of Asclepius—to which people went in droves to be instructed by the god during their "temple sleep" as to the nature of their illness and the therapy to be applied. In Epidauros and other sanctuaries there was also a particular "temple medicine" that apparently evinced many successes. But major personalities who not only imparted therapies but actually performed miraculous healings were extremely rare in antiquity, and well-attested "miracles" were even more uncommon.

It is against this background that we have to read the gospels, especially Mark's, which may ultimately rest on the witness and tradition of Simon Peter. Mark relates the following healings and exorcisms:[7]

> The possessed man in the synagogue (1:23-26)
>
> Peter's mother-in-law (1:30-31)
>
> The leper (1:40-45)
>
> The lame man (2:1-12)
>
> The man with the withered hand (3:1-6)
>
> The possessed man of Gerasa (5:1-20)
>
> The woman with the hemorrhage (5:25-34)
>
> The daughter of the Syrophoenician woman (7:24-30)
>
> The deaf man with the speech impediment (7:31-37)
>
> The blind man at Bethsaida (8:22-26)
>
> The possessed son (9:14-29)
>
> Blind Bartimaeus (10:46-52)

But Mark's gospel contains other miracles that cannot simply be summarized under "healings and exorcisms":

The stilling of the storm (4:35-41)

The raising of Jairus's daughter (5:21-43)

The feeding of the five thousand (6:35-44)

Walking on the lake (6:45-52)

The feeding of the four thousand (8:1-9)

The withered fig tree (11:12-14, 20-25)

Add to these some ten miracle stories in Matthew's and Luke's special material, as well as seven miracle narratives in John. Thus Jesus is depicted as definitely a miracle worker, and a great many miracles are attributed to him, something that is unique in antiquity.

Biblical scholarship has long regarded these miracles analytically. As early as the Enlightenment a distinction was made between "healing miracles" and "nature miracles"; the latter included, for example, the stilling of the storm on Lake Gennesareth. Today, a still more careful distinction is made between "healings" and "exorcisms" on the one hand and "raising the dead," "epiphany miracles" (walking on the lake), "gift miracles" (multiplication of the loaves), "rescue miracles" (stilling of the storm), "normative miracles" (Sabbath healings), and "punishment miracles" (the withered fig tree) on the other.

Nothing can be said against such distinctions in themselves. Cataloging is part of scholarship, and it is the joy of many exegetes to create more and more subtle and difficult classifications. But there are also problems with the sharp classification of gospel miracles, for it is unmistakable that this classification in New Testament exegesis was created also, and perhaps primarily, in order to be able to evaluate the miracles *historically*. It goes like this: there *were* healings and exorcisms; there were *no* raisings of the dead, epiphany miracles, gift miracles, or rescue miracles. Thus the cataloging of the miracles very obviously serves the purpose of historically disqualifying a number of the miracle stories.

But there is a second problem as well: the various genres of miracles thus created are much more closely related than at first appears:

1. Should we classify the story about Jairus's little daughter (Mark 5:21-43) as a healing or a raising of the dead? Christian tradition has always regarded it as the latter, but the narrative itself is ambivalent—in contrast to the story of the raising of the young man at Nain (Luke 7:11-17). Her relatives consider the girl to be dead, but Jesus apparently does not. The text leaves it all in the air. Here we can see how fluid things are in such stories.

2. Healings and exorcisms cannot be sharply distinguished. In Judaism, and in antiquity as a whole, "normal" illnesses were often attributed to demonic influence.[8]

- Luke 13:10-17 speaks of the healing of a woman who has been bent over for many years. Jesus interprets her illness as Satan's binding (13:16).

- Matthew 12:22 speaks of a person who is blind and has a speech impediment. His blindness and inability to speak are explained in demonological terms. Jesus heals him, and he can once again speak and see.

- The servant of the Gentile centurion "is lying at home paralyzed, in terrible distress" (Matt 8:6). The Greek expression for being "in terrible distress," *deinōs basanizomenos*, is the language of antiquity, and we must expand it: he is being distressed by the demons of sickness. When, in the course of the narrative, the centurion tells Jesus that his soldiers obey him to the letter and expects the same from Jesus he is obviously referring to the demons that cause illness. The centurion is convinced that the demons must also obey Jesus to the letter.

- Within the narrative about the healing of Peter's mother-in-law Luke alters his Markan model. While Mark had written "he came and took her by the hand and lifted her up" (Mark 1:31), Luke instead has: "then he stood over her and rebuked the fever, and it left her" (Luke 4:39). Thus Jesus shouts at the fever as if it were a demon. He speaks a word of power, as in an exorcism. He yells at the illness as once God had yelled at the powers of chaos (Pss 17:16; 67:31; 75:7; 103:7; 105:9, LXX).

- Paul too attributes his illness, which apparently was accompanied by painful distortions of vision (Gal 4:13-15), to a "messenger of Satan" who repeatedly beats him with its fists (2 Cor 12:7-9).

3. It makes very good sense to distinguish the stilling of the storm on the lake (Mark 4:35-41) from the healing of demoniacs, and yet we must see that in this narrative Jesus acts like an exorcist. He "shouts at the wind" and commands it as if it were a demon: "Peace! Be still!" (cf. Mark 1:25). And then the lake becomes calm, just as possessed people become quiet, even comatose, immediately after their healing (cf. Mark 9:26). Jesus' action was altogether plausible to people in antiquity: water, especially deep water, was regarded as the residence of demons, just as the desert was. Therefore, in Mark

4:35-41, the narrative types of "rescue miracle" and "exorcism" are intermingled.

It could not be otherwise. For people in Israel, as for people everywhere in antiquity, chaos threatened from all sides. It revealed itself in a variety of illnesses, in lameness, in disfigurement, in wounds, in social isolation, in the powers of nature, and above all in death. People in ancient Israel would have said that the underworld threatens us everywhere. In Jesus' time people were convinced that demonic powers were a constant danger. The most horrible power of all was death—and it too was occupied by demons. Hebrews 2:14 says that the devil has the power of death.

When Jesus heals sick people, drives out demons, calms the waters, and raises the dead, the basic happening is the same in all cases: he confronts the powers of chaos, conquers demons, heals the damaged and distorted world, so that the reign of God may become visible and creation attain to the integrity and beauty God intends for it.

We are already—it was pretty much inevitable—involved in the history of how people have dealt with Jesus' miracles. That is a broad field, but it cannot be altogether avoided. Precisely from the way in which people have dealt with the miracle stories in the four gospels over the last three hundred years we can learn a great deal about how to approach these miracles in appropriate fashion. How have people treated Jesus' miracles?

Enlightenment

Biblical miracles have lived a hard life since the European Enlightenment. While before that they were almost a matter of course, something that illuminated Jesus' divinity, afterward they became an embarrassment. Nowadays they are sometimes simply disputed. The principle of analogy is applied; it can be formulated, somewhat simplified, as: "What does not happen now did not happen then either. If no one today can walk on a lake, Jesus did not walk on water."

The theologians of the Enlightenment period found the matter somewhat more difficult, of course. Since they did not want to frivolously deny the miracle stories found in the Bible, some of them undertook to explain those stories "rationally" and make them "understandable" for enlightened people. With authors such as K. F. Bahrdt (1740–1792), K. H. G. Venturini (1768–1849), or H. E. G. Paulus (1761–1851), this could take abstruse forms.[9] Since "secret orders" had been growing in Europe since the eighteenth century, it seemed plausible that there were such "secret orders" in Jesus' time as well. And who might have belonged to such a society? Obviously, the mysterious Essenes. So Jesus belonged to the Essenes and shared their goal: bringing the superstitious people to a genuine religion of reason.

Of course, in doing so Jesus had to use some slick means in order to reach the people to begin with. Therefore, even though he only wanted to be a wise enlightener, he appeared in the role of Messiah and worked with well-organized and skillfully applied staging. For the multiplication of the loaves, for example, bread had already been collected in a cave; it was then handed to Jesus out of the darkness by Essene assistants and distributed by the disciples. The Syrophoenician woman's daughter received medicine from a disciple who took it from Jesus' portable medicine chest while Jesus himself engaged the mother in conversation. To walk on the lake Jesus used floating planks. And so on.

We smile at this, and yet the rationalizations of Jesus' miracles have continued until today. How often do we still hear that the miraculous multiplication of loaves consisted in the fact that, after Jesus' table prayer, some of those assembled reached into their pockets, took out some bread, and shared it with their neighbors. That was infectious. Because eventually all shared their bread with one another, everyone was satisfied. Or we read with astonishment that the calming of the storm was nothing more than that after Jesus' word of command the storm simply subsided, not in nature, but in the perception of the disciples. Jesus took away their fear.

As much as all that falls short of the essence of Jesus' miracles, the attempts at explanation are right about one thing: reason may not be dismissed when we are faced with miracles. Rationality must also have access to Jesus' miracles.

History of Religions

Does this rational access consist in the application of the techniques of comparative religion? Yes and no! Obviously, Jesus' miracles must be compared to all those reported in the Old Testament, in Judaism, and in antiquity. As a result we see that, in fact, there are a few well-attested miracles there as well, and their historicity cannot be doubted. These include, for example, the healing of two men by Vespasian (9–79 CE), recounted for us by Tacitus and Suetonius.[10] According to Tacitus (ca. 58–120 CE) this happened in the year 70.

Vespasian had just been named emperor, but his rule was not yet secured. While he waited in Alexandria for favorable weather in order to be able to sail for Rome he was badgered by two sick men who wanted him to heal them. One was blind and the other scarcely had the use of one of his hands any longer. The blind man begged Vespasian to spread the imperial saliva on his eyes and eyeballs. The other asked the emperor to touch his crippled hand with the sole of his foot. At first Vespasian found the idea ridiculous, but as the two sick men continued to bother him he began to like the idea. Of course, he did not want to embarrass himself, so first he obtained a medical opinion. The doctors were ambivalent. A healing might be possible, and it could be brought about by natural causes. But it might also be that the gods wanted to help Vespasian. Ultimately, the emperor attempted the healing in the presence of the assembled crowd. "He was convinced," Tacitus writes, "that there were no limits to his destiny: nothing now seemed incredible." And behold: the hand was healed and the blind man could see again.

There can be no doubt about this event. The charism of healing was expected of a new emperor or king, and not only then. The idea endured in Europe beyond the Middle Ages and into the nineteenth century: in France and England it was part of the ritual that a newly anointed king should touch sick people. Apparently, from time to time, the special circumstances and the sick person's expectations released healing powers.

Josephus tells another story in his *Jewish Antiquities*.[11] He has just been speaking of the wisdom of Solomon and his power to banish demons. Then he continues:

> [A]nd this method of cure is of great force unto this day; for I have seen a certain man of my own country whose name was Eleazar, releasing people that were demoniacal in the presence of Vespasian, and his sons, and his captains, and the whole multitude of his soldiers. The manner of the cure was this: He put a ring that had a root of one of those sorts mentioned by Solomon to the nostrils of the demoniac, after which he drew out the demon through his nostrils; and when the man fell down immediately, he abjured him to return into him no more, making still mention of Solomon, and reciting the incantations which he composed. And when Eleazar would persuade and demonstrate to the spectators that he had such a power, he set a little way off a cup or basin full of water, and commanded the demon, as he went out of the man, to overturn it, and thereby to let the specta-

tors know that he had left the man; and when this was done, the skill
and wisdom of Solomon was shown very manifestly.

Josephus explicitly emphasizes his own status as eyewitness (*historēsa*)
at the beginning of the story. We have no reason to doubt it. Apparently
there were quite a few Jewish exorcists in the first century. This is, in fact,
confirmed by Jesus himself when he defends himself against the accusation that he is driving out demons with the aid of the prince of demons:
"If I cast out demons by Beelzebul, by whom do your own exorcists
[Greek: sons] cast them out? Therefore they will be your judges" (Matt
12:27; Luke 11:19).

So Josephus tells of demons being driven out by a Jewish exorcist.
What is most revealing in this is the way he proceeds: by calling on the
name of Solomon, with magical formulae that supposedly come from
Solomon, and by causing the victim to smell a magical root. That draws
the demon out of the possessed person. Finally, the demons are also
adjured not to return. We know from Luke 9:49 that another Jewish
exorcist used the name "Jesus" in his treatment of possessed persons—
further proof of the activity of Jewish exorcists! Apparently they too were
successful.

But the difference between them and Jesus is striking: in his exorcisms
Jesus never made use of a "name." He acted on his own authority. Above
all: he never employed magical practices. Finally, he did not stage any
demonstrations as Eleazar did in causing the expelled demon to upset
a basin.

Besides Eleazar we can mention two other Jewish names: Honi the
Circle-Drawer (first c. BCE) and Chanina ben Dosa (first c. CE). Both
were charismatics, wonder workers, and people who healed by prayer.
Honi was famous for his prayer for rain. It is said that during a period
of severe drought he drew a circle, placed himself within it, and said
that he would not leave that circle until God caused it to rain. Thereupon
it rained so heavily that he had to beg God for a suitable amount of rain
(*m. Ta'anit* 3.8). Both these men worked their miracles through insistent
prayer—and that in itself is completely atypical of Jesus.[12]

So if we look at Jesus' environment we see that it did indeed contain
healers and miracle workers. We even find a certain number of well-
attested accounts of miracles. But they are clearly different from the
stories about Jesus' miracles. Moreover, there was no miracle worker in
antiquity besides Jesus from whom we have such a large number of
plausibly attested miracles handed down to us.

Structural Matters

This fact is not changed by the way New Testament exegesis, since the introduction of the so-called form-critical method, has demanded a comparison among New Testament, Old Testament, Jewish, and Hellenistic miracle narratives. Not only have the structures of all the texts in question been investigated; their motifs have also been compared in detail. This has revealed a large number of common motifs and has shown that the basic structure of miracle stories is frequently repeated.

To make it clear to the reader what we are talking about I will quote from the influential book by Rudolf Bultmann, *The History of the Synoptic Tradition*, where he gives a list of typical and frequently recurring motifs in miracle stories.[13] The list given here is only partial and is much more refined in Bultmann's work.

> Information on the length of the illness
>
> Dangerous character of the illness
>
> Ineffective treatment by doctors
>
> Doubts about the miracle worker
>
> Approach of the miracle worker to the sick person
>
> Removal of the onlookers
>
> Touching the sick person with the hand
>
> A miracle-working word
>
> Description of the success
>
> Demonstration of the success
>
> Dismissal of the healed person
>
> Impression of the miracle on those present

Of course, the motifs vary among individual texts. Sometimes there are more, sometimes fewer, and sometimes they are accompanied by additional motifs. This is therefore an *ideal* list divorced from all the particularities of a given text. Further work has been done on the motifs in New Testament miracle stories since Bultmann. Gerd Theissen and Annette Merz have materially refined and expanded the list.[14]

What should we say about the whole matter? Making such lists is a good thing. Abstracting the typical features of a text can help us better understand individual texts. In addition, the process reveals the "international" form-language of the time that was used to tell about miracles. But as helpful as such lists can be, they are also deceptive because they promote the impression that the gospels' miracle texts are freely composed fantasies based on an inventory of motifs that was available at the time. In addition, we should consider that this inventory of motifs, composed two thousand years after the fact, has been cobbled together out of all possible literary directions and angles. These lists are made up on the basis of texts that are fundamentally different in their form and intent. They include temple inscriptions, magical texts, fairy tales, ancient novels—and also historical works.[15]

We should also consider that the motif complex "miracle story" is to a degree simply a given on the basis of the thing itself. The healer must approach the sick person or the sick person the healer. Otherwise the two would not encounter one another. Normally (except in the case of healings at a distance) the healer will also touch the sick person and speak a powerful word. Could the healer keep silence and remain at a distance? Likewise, the success of the healing must be marked in some way. Otherwise there would be no need to tell the story in the first place. The fact that those present then react in some way to the miracle is also typically human. It could not be otherwise, and it is an integral part of the miracle.

Add one other thing: language is always socially shaped. That is its nature. Our speech is much more strongly affected than we suspect by existing forms and structures. We write our letters according to models of which we are scarcely aware. Politicians' statements are stereotypical to the point of banality. Even declarations of love are usually preformed down to the last detail. Those who think they speak in a form they themselves have created independently, one that has never existed before and owes its shape only to the particular situation, deceive themselves mightily. New types of forms succeed but rarely. And scarcely have they begun to exist before they become common property. Because all that is so, we can conclude nothing about the historicity of an event solely from the form in which it is related—neither that what is told is historical nor that it is unhistorical.

Therefore, the crucial question about Jesus' miracles is not about their form. Ultimately, the issue is always a decision: are miracles possible? And what is a miracle, after all? I will now address this question.

The Concept of Miracles

The biblical concept of miracle is not equivalent to the apologetically colored notion of miracles in the neoscholasticism of the nineteenth and early twentieth centuries. As we have already seen, the gospels speak of

Jesus' "deeds of power" and "signs." Obviously these refer to miracles. But in the Old and New Testaments, the concept of miracle was still wide open. It was not about "natural laws" in the modern sense and most certainly not about breaking them. For the Bible a miracle is something unusual, inexplicable, incomprehensible, disturbing, unexpected, shocking, something that amazes and that explodes the ordinary, something by which God plucks people out of their indifference and causes them to look to him. But—in precisely the opposite direction—miracles could also appear in the midst of the everyday: for example, in the experience that God continually supports and sustains the created order (Ps 136:4-9). For biblical people God is constantly speaking to his people, and therefore every happy result, every story of rescue, even the glory of creation can be experienced as a miracle.

Since the appearance of modern thought, however, miracles have fallen into the slipstream of enlightened criticism. The world is to be explained in *secular* terms, that is, with respect for its own laws and processes. In view of this paradigm shift, theology sought to protect miracles and in the course of its apologetic defense it defined them more clearly, as "events contrary to nature." So this means that God breaks natural laws. From time to time he intervenes directly in the world's causal connections in order to demonstrate his power in a plausible way.

But the Bible spoke of things that were unusual, amazing, having sign-character, and not of a rupture of natural laws at certain points in time. This openness of the original biblical concept of miracle makes room for today's theology to formulate the uniqueness of miracles more appropriately, that is, more in accordance with the nature of creation.

If we are better to understand the nature of miracles, we have to consistently apply what theology has discovered regarding the notion of "grace" to the question of miracles. It often happens that theological problems attached to a particular point have long since been resolved in other parts of theology. What has today's theology of grace to say in this regard?[16] It says that when a person receives grace from God two freedoms encounter one another: the freedom of God and that of the human being. God never intervenes in the world by avoiding human freedom and independence. God does not replace by his own action what human beings ought to do. God does not put *divine* freedom in place of *human* freedom. Divine grace does not destroy human action but makes it possible and builds it up.

At the same time the theology of grace insists, as a consequence of the theology of creation, that God does not act as an "intra-worldly cause" (*causa secunda*). That is, God does not intervene directly in the world, going around the lawful course of creation. It is true that God is constantly and unceasingly at work, but in his own way. He acts as the world-transcending cause outside and beyond the world (*causa prima*). So the doctrine of grace arrives at the formula: God must do everything, and the human being must do everything. Where God's work happens in history it is entirely and completely the work of God—but at the same time it is entirely and completely human work.[17]

These insights from the doctrine of grace must now be applied to miracles, for a miracle, as we have said, is only a special case of God's constant work in the world. If we see a miracle as part of what God has always been graciously bringing about in the world, we must say that a genuine miracle is done by God, but precisely not in such a way that God sets aside human action and the laws of nature. Rather, every miracle is at the same time always a bringing to the fore what human and nature are able to do. Natural laws are thus not broken but elevated to a higher level. The miracle exalts nature; it does not bore holes in it. It does not destroy the natural order of things but brings it to its fulfillment.[18]

This view of miracles has the advantage, in any case, that natural scientists are not deprived from the outset of any opportunity to consider the theological concept of miracles possible. Indeed, they cannot do otherwise than proceed as they do, since they have to speak of natural laws that—at least statistically—are not broken. Their scientific presuppositions and premises obligate them to reckon with a homogeneous field of physical causes.[19] Theology has no right to try to talk them out of that position.

The view of miracles presented here is favored above all, however, by the fact that it can take seriously the independence of nature and the human. This is immediately apparent in Jesus' healing miracles: in the gospels they occur only when someone "believes." Jesus says to the woman with the hemorrhage, "Daughter, your faith has made you well: go in peace, and be healed of your disease" (Mark 5:34). So it was her faith that healed the woman, her belief in Jesus as the savior. But it was *her* faith, and if she had not had such faith she would not have been healed of the "scourging blows" (thus the underlying Greek word) of her illness. Here we find a fully independent meaning of "faith" in the context of miracle stories. It appears nowhere else in antiquity. Ancient miracle stories were always about whether or not the witnesses or recipients of the action are persuaded of the reality of the miracle. Here, in contrast, the sick person herself must believe; otherwise, she will not be healed.

We find many similar passages in the gospels.[20] Again and again faith in God is demanded—in God, who is now acting in Jesus. This is about God's creative power, but also about Jesus, who in every miracle stands in God's stead. If that faith is not present, the miracle cannot happen. In Nazareth, Mark says quite explicitly, Jesus could not work any miracles because they did not believe in him there (Mark 6:5-6). So Jesus is elementally dependent on faith if he is to heal. In Mark 11:23 Jesus dares a radically pointed statement: "Truly I tell you, if you say to this mountain, 'Be taken up and thrown into the sea,' and if you do not doubt in your heart, but believe that what you say will come to pass, it will be done for you." Human action in miracles cannot be more sharply emphasized: without faith, nothing happens. This is the proper context for the observation that Jesus healed only individuals. He did not perform any group healings. It was only the apocryphal Acts of apostles that began to tell of mass healings. This again shows that the inbreaking of the reign of God is not a spectacle. God's action is tied to the faith of concrete people. The reign of God needs believers who freely open themselves to it.

What is true of people is also true of so-called nature. It too must "share" in the action, must participate, must play its part. Natural laws are not broken; they are put in service of a new and greater whole. No ordinary human action, certainly not one undertaken in freedom, puts the corresponding natural laws (such as the principle of inertia) out of effect. When a human being acts by free decision, then spirit, person, freedom, or whatever we call it interferes with the material world—but not as if human freedom eliminated natural laws; it does not abrogate but "elevates" them. In this connection we can speak of the "plasticity," the "malleability," of matter or nature.[21] Analogously to the synergy between spirit and matter, God's action, when it enters the world through the faith of a human being, does not destroy the laws of matter but raises them to a new level.

Therefore I have no problem, in the case of Jesus' miracles, with taking into account all the "natural" forces that can otherwise be observed in great physicians and healers or experienced educators. As the acts of human freedom do not abrogate the physical laws but put them at their service, so in the case of Jesus his existence altogether in harmony with the will of God called upon the powers of the world, extending into a profound depth that is impenetrable to us even today. To set aside these natural abilities of Jesus would mean denying him his real humanity.

No one can define where the limits of "nature" in this sphere lie, unless one would lay claim to having an absolutely complete and comprehensive knowledge of all the powers at work in nature. Who would dare to make such an assertion? Professional medicine is aware that, for example, in some malignant carcinomas, there can be "spontaneous healings" that cannot be explained but may have to do with holistic phenomena such as "inner attitude" and "unconditional will to heal." We also know about the so-called placebo effect, the observation that the *expectation* of being healed can activate the body's powers of self-healing, even if the treatment has not involved the application of any effective pharmacological means. Apparently every person has powers of self-healing, but they require the *kairos*, the right moment, the right constellation, and often the right person to set them in motion—the person of the healer.

In summary, we need not defend ourselves against the *natural* dimensions of biblical miracles. That is no denial of their *divine* dimension. Here again the old scholastic axiom applies: "grace presupposes nature and perfects it." The biblical miracles would lose their strangeness or embarrassing character if, finally, what the theology of grace has long since worked out were applied to them. Let me again emphasize that taking seriously the "natural" dimensions of a miracle by no means excludes the action of God. God always acts in and through the world's autonomy.

Demons

The view of miracles described here is also compatible with Jesus' exorcisms. I have already pointed out that in antiquity in general, and also in Judaism, all that is chaotic and destructive could be attributed to demonic powers. This was true in particular of psychoses and mental illness in general. If a sick person's identity was disturbed, or if she or he had lost all self-control, it was all too easy to assume that the person was possessed by a demon.

Beyond that, it is important to keep in mind that at the time it was simply assumed that there was such a thing as "possession" in this sense and also that someone who was possessed could be freed from his or her demons through exorcisms. This made it easy for sick people, the handicapped, the oppressed, people in hopeless situations—in short, all those who were socially stigmatized—to slip into the role of a possessed person. Normally this was a completely unconscious move. Those who were pushed to the edges of society thus had a "social construct" at their disposal that made it possible for them to give expression to their socially hopeless situation "in a language of symptoms which is publicly accept-able."[22] They thus succeeded in being noticed, having people pay atten-tion to them and "treat" them. Cécile Ernst, in a study on the driving out of devils in the sixteenth and seventeenth centuries, for which—in con-trast to the biblical exorcisms—we have extensive biographical material at our disposal, has demonstrated precisely this phenomenon.[23]

Today's biblical scholars frequently remark that obviously we can no longer share that era's belief in demons.[24] Superficially that is correct, and yet it is fundamentally false. Of course we would ask today what underlies phenomena of possession from a medical, psychological, and social-psychological point of view, and we will have no hesitation in regarding exorcisms as a prescientific method of (often successful) "psychotherapy." But that, certainly, is by no means a real explanation of the explosion of the phenomena of possession in particular times and cultural groups, for we must suppose that some kind of deep crisis is revealed in these phenomena—a crisis resulting from guilt, namely, from the self-betrayal, lies, egoisms, recklessness, meanness, and heartlessness of society.

These things not only happen again and again; they settle themselves in the world in the form of a damaged and distorted state of things that no individual can overcome. The New Testament is therefore quite right to speak of the "powers." In such a connection one must indeed talk about the demons of society—and also, of course, of their victims. For there are particularly sensitive people in whom the chaos and guilt of whole generations, their obsessions and compulsions, concentrate and express themselves physically. Evil in history and society can gather itself to a "potency," and it very often takes hold precisely of the weakest and objectifies itself in them in the symptoms that are common in the particular society. The illnesses thus produced can be so powerful that the sick persons require help from outside themselves—possibly through a word of power that transposes them into a new situation.

Jesus must have had a profound power to bring such crises to light, to take the form of their expression seriously, and still more, to force them to take objective form and so to heal them. In this he showed him-self to be the stronger one, the one who cannot be led astray by the wounds that evil can inflict but through his truthfulness and lack of ambiguity can banish the demons of society. It would be naïve to think that we can leave Jesus' exorcisms behind us as constructs conditioned by time. Rather, they are his confrontations with the power of evil and everything in the world that stands in opposition to God.[25] It is true that in the first place Jesus' exorcisms were conducted "naturally." The possessed people were sick, and Jesus offered healing. But behind their illnesses lurk the sicknesses of society, and the one who heals them stands in the place of God, who cannot permit God's good creation to be distorted and destroyed.

All these considerations extend well beyond purely historical questions. They touch a nerve center of theology, but they could not be avoided here because, as I have said, the question whether or not particular miracles (including the so-called nature miracles) took place is not usually determined by historical means but by prior decisions that are located in an entirely different sphere. When Rudolf Bultmann repeatedly dismissed the biblical wonders as "Mirakel,"[26] his estimation was not the result of historical insight but, as harsh as this may sound, rested on a bad dogmatics and an unenlightened theology.

Now we must address the theology of Jesus' miracles. It is essential, because only through it can we clearly see how Jesus' miracles differ from all the extrabiblical miracles.

The Specific Character of Jesus' Miracles

Something about this has already been said: namely, that Jesus did not work with magical arts as did the exorcist Eleazar whom Josephus writes about. He did not use amulets, magical roots, or abracadabra. In driving out demons he did not call upon powerful "names." Even his "commands" to the demons had nothing to do with magic. Jesus rules the demons in the same way that, according to the psalms, God rules the forces opposed to God. Even when he stuck his fingers into the ears of a deaf man or used saliva to heal the blind he was not employing magical practices; he was simply making use of the therapeutic means common in his time. Incidentally, these cases show very clearly that he counted on nature to help him.

We have also touched on another point that is important for the theology of Jesus' miracles, namely, the faith Jesus requires in each instance. Such demands for faith do not appear in miracle stories outside the Bible. The ancient world did not even have a concept of faith, at any rate not faith as the Bible understands it.

But there is another characteristic that is important for Jesus' miracles, one we have not yet addressed: his miracles are always for other people, never for himself. Jesus' miracles are pure acts of concern for people in need. This applies not only to the healing miracles and exorcisms but also to the raising of the dead, the stilling of the storm, and the multi-plication of the loaves. Jesus never did anything to help himself.[27]

It is very revealing that later, in the apocryphal Infancy Gospels and novelistic Acts of apostles people, even Christians, had no hesitation in relating self-help miracles performed by Jesus and the apostles.[28] The fact that the canonical gospels are altogether devoid of these shows that they retain something specific to Jesus. In antiquity, and even in Judaism, it was apparently a matter of course that one should expect a great miracle worker to perform miracles on his or her own behalf. According to Mark, the spectators at Jesus' execution mocked him by saying, "He saved others; he cannot save himself. Let the Messiah, the King of Israel, come down from the cross now, so that we may see and believe" (Mark 15:31-32).

Of course, we must see that this mockery is not only suggesting a miracle in aid of Jesus. It is also, and even primarily, about a demonstration. The idea that the Messiah or the bringer of salvation must *prove* himself to be such, and by means of a specific miracle that reveals his power and legitimacy, was widely accepted. Josephus reports that before the Jewish war messianic pretenders and pseudo-prophets appeared and aroused the people against the Romans. As legitimation for their actions they promised spectacular miracles:

> These works, that were done by the robbers [= Zealots], filled the city [Jerusalem] with all sorts of impiety. And now these impostors and deceivers persuaded the multitude to follow them into the wilderness, and pretended that they would exhibit manifest wonders and signs, that would be performed by the providence of God.
>
> . . . Moreover, there came out of Egypt about this time to Jerusalem, one that said he was a prophet, and advised the multitude of the common people to go along with him to the Mount of Olives, as it was called, which lay over against the city, and at the distance of five furlongs. He said farther, that he would show them from hence, how, at his command, the walls of Jerusalem would fall down; and he promised that he would procure them an entrance into the city through those walls, when they were fallen down.[29]

Apparently these pseudo-prophets found many followers. They promised the people kinds of miraculous events they called "signs of redemption" but all of which had something excessive and bombastic about them. Similar demands for signs were directed at Jesus. According to Mark 8:11-13, this happened one day:

> The Pharisees came and began to argue with him, asking him for a
> sign from heaven, to test him. And he sighed deeply in his spirit and
> said, "Why does this generation ask for a sign? Truly I tell you, no
> sign will be given to this generation." And he left them.

Jesus' "spirit" was deeply disturbed by this demand for a sign, which
was in direct contradiction to his understanding of miracles. Similar
demands for signs appear in the Gospel of John (2:18; 6:30-31). Jesus
rejects them all severely, even harshly. For him the dimension of faith is
part of any miracle. He demanded faith before any miracle could take
place, and he presupposed that a deepened faith and repentance would
follow the miraculous event. He must have sensed that the signs asked
of him simply as legitimation had nothing to do with the longing to be
able to believe. There was something Sophistic and seductive about them.
Therefore he refused to let himself be legitimated by God (which is what
"a sign from heaven" in Mark 8:11 means). He rejected every kind of
authenticating miracle and any wonder performed for show. Apparently
he regarded such things as idolatrous posing.

So Jesus did not regard the saving deeds he performed as isolated
authenticating miracles. His deeds of power had a different origin and
goal. They arose out of the crisis, the need he encountered on all sides,
and they are the beginning of the new world God is giving. They are
signs of the inbreaking reign of God. They are signs that now the Old
Testament prophecies are being fulfilled. Hence Jesus' mighty deeds
stand within a referential context that itself makes them what they are.
There is absolutely no comparable framework for the miracles otherwise
reported in antiquity.

At this point it is worthwhile taking a closer look at the story of the
raising of a dead girl by Apollonius of Tyana. This will make it obvious
what I mean by a "referential context." Apollonius, an itinerant philosopher, lived between 40 and 120 CE. He was regarded in antiquity as a
preacher and a miracle worker. He is supposed to have forged amulets
that protected against earthquake, wind, water, mosquitoes, and mice.
We have scarcely any truly reliable sources regarding his teaching and
life. Over a hundred years later Philostratus was encouraged by the
Roman empress Julia Domna to write a novelistic description of his life
that in many respects reads like an "anti-gospel."[30] As part of this *Vita*,
Philostratus tells the following story:

> A girl had died just in the hour of her marriage, and the bridegroom
> was following her bier lamenting as was natural his marriage left

unfulfilled, and the whole of Rome was mourning with him, for the maiden belonged to a consular family. Apollonius then witnessing their grief, said: "Put down the bier, for I will stay the tears that you are shedding for this maiden."

And withal he asked what was her name. The crowd accordingly thought that he was about to deliver such an oration as is commonly delivered to grace the funeral as to stir up lamentation; but he did nothing of the kind, but merely touching her and whispering in secret some spell over her, at once woke up the maiden from her seeming death; and the girl spoke out loud, and returned to her father's house, just as Alcestis did when she was brought back to life by Heracles. And the relations of the maiden wanted to present him with the sum of 150,000 sesterces, but he said that he would freely present the money to the young lady by way of dowry.

Now whether he detected some spark of life in her, which those who were nursing her had not noticed—for it is said that although it was raining at the time, a vapor went up from her face—or whether her life was really extinct, and he restored it by the warmth of his touch, is a mysterious problem which neither I myself nor those who were present could decide.[31]

It seems almost required of us to compare this story with that of the raising of the young man of Nain:

Soon afterwards he went to a town called Nain, and his disciples and a large crowd went with him. As he approached the gate of the town, a man who had died was being carried out. He was his mother's only son, and she was a widow; and with her was a large crowd from the town. When the Lord saw her, he had compassion for her and said to her, "Do not weep." Then he came forward and touched the bier, and the bearers stood still. And he said, "Young man, I say to you, rise!" The dead man sat up and began to speak, and Jesus gave him to his mother. Fear seized all of them; and they glorified God, saying, "A great prophet has risen among us!" and "God has looked favorably on his people!" This word about him spread throughout Judea and all the surrounding country. (Luke 7:11-17)

If we compare the two stories—setting aside all historical questions!—we see that they have much in common. In both the bringer of benefit encounters a funeral procession and causes the bier to halt. The dead person is young in both cases: in the first, a young woman about to be married; in the second, a "young man." In the one it is the bridegroom who is mourning, in the other a mother who now has no one left to care for her. In the Hellenistic story the city of Rome shares in the bridegroom's sorrow, and in the biblical tale many people are accompanying the funeral procession out of the city of Nain. Apollonius is depicted as a sympathetic and selfless benefactor: he wants to put an end to the tears being shed for the dead girl, and he gives his honorarium to the girl as her dowry. Jesus is seized by pity for the widow and tells her, "Do not weep." Apollonius touches the dead girl, Jesus the bier. Apollonius heals by his word, and so does Jesus. But what is especially striking is that the Hellenistic storyteller recalls the raising of Alcestis by the demigod Heracles, while the biblical narrator uses a literary reference to recall the raising of the son of the widow of Zarephath by the prophet Elijah: "He gave him to his mother" (1 Kgs 17:23).

But now for the differences: Apollonius's miracle-working words are magical. Philostratus does not want to say it too directly, but that is the precise background. Jesus, in contrast, does not utter any words of wizardry but speaks a very brief command: "Rise!" Further, Philostratus insinuates that the girl only appeared to be dead. In doing so he intends to show that he is a critical and objective narrator. Luke, in contrast, leaves no doubt: the man was dead. A further difference in the story as a whole is the role of God. F. C. Conybeare's English translation of the Apollonius story omits a detail in the original that is still reflected in German versions: namely, that in the third paragraph instead of "it was raining at the time," the text reads "Zeus caused dew to fall on her." But why did Zeus do that? To sustain a spark of life in her? Or was the dew only a signal for the wonder worker that the girl was not really dead? Here again Philostratus maintains an ambivalence that is typical of him. There is no such ambiguity in Luke. For him it is clear that God himself was acting through Jesus: "God has looked favorably on his people."

But the *decisive* difference is that Philostratus portrays Apollonius as an effective and humane miracle worker. The real character of this humanity is revealed by the horrifying story in which Apollonius has a supposed plague demon stoned.[32] That need not, however, concern us here. In any case, Philostratus wants to celebrate Apollonius as a humane wonder worker. It is true that Zeus is permitted to peek through the curtain a bit, but in reality it is all about Apollonius, and the whole event, despite the sorrow of the city of Rome over the young woman, remains a private matter.

It is just the reverse in Luke: here it is all about Israel. A prophet like Elijah has "risen among us" [or: been raised up among us], and "God has looked favorably on [lit.: visited] his people." Luke is quoting from Zechariah's canticle:

> Blessed be the Lord God of Israel,
>   for he has looked favorably on his people and redeemed them.
> He has raised up a mighty savior for us
>   in the house of his servant David,
> as he spoke through the mouths of his holy prophets from of old.
> (Luke 1:68-70)

Thus a whole fabric of relationships is made visible. It is not only that God himself has acted in Jesus to raise up the young man of Nain! Still more, God has acted in Israel, his people. This theological interpretation of the event is breathtaking. It is anything but obvious. What has happened in the little village of Nain, and for one widow, is applied to all Israel. The miracle story opens a vista onto a long history of God's promises and mighty deeds in Israel. Therefore Jesus' mercy shown to the widow is not mere human sympathy as with Apollonius, but a reflection of God's mercy on his people (Luke 1:54, 72). And therefore the witnesses of the miracle are seized with fear that issues in praise of God.

Thus the mighty deed on behalf of the young man of Nain is part of a long history—the history of God's mighty deeds in his own special people. There is no comparable history in Apollonius, and so his miracle is ultimately "private." With Jesus nothing is "private."

The whole is still clearer when we consider, for example, miraculous phenomena known in Hinduism.[33] Here the divine is present as "power" in every living thing. Therefore everyone, through religious practice and appropriate application, can acquire superhuman abilities that are regarded as miraculous, becoming a yogi. Then one can supposedly make oneself tiny or enormous, heavy or weightless, present in many places at the same time and having control over everything—in short, such a person acquires an irresistible will. That too is "private" in an exalted sense.

The contrast to the biblical miracles hits you in the eye. The latter happen in and for Israel and are part of a long history of rescue, of salvation. That is what I mean by the phrases "referential context" and "frame of reference." Jesus' miracles cannot be understood outside this referential context. "Reference" is the inmost center of his mighty deeds. His miracles point to the reign of God, now breaking forth: "if it is by the finger of God that I cast out the demons, then the kingdom of God has come to you" (Luke 11:20). But they also point to the new creation of the people of God now coming to pass. They are in service of the gathering of Israel, and in them the world to come is already shining forth, a world in which everything will be made whole by God—not only human beings but all creation. Every miracle of Jesus reveals a bit of the new heaven and the new earth.[34]

Without this reference there is no such thing as a miracle in the Christian sense. It is therefore no accident that in the theological language of the gospels Jesus' miracles are not only called "mighty deeds" but also "signs." Apparently this word intends precisely what I have here called a "referential context."[35] If the gospels, in their description of Jesus' miracles, had been concerned only with what ruptures the norm they could have spoken of Jesus' *paradoxa erga* or his *thaumasia*. But, apart from Matthew 21:15, they do not do so, for the unusual and marvelous is not what makes Jesus' miracles. Otherwise, the healings achieved by the emperor Vespasian would also have been real miracles. But they lacked the sign-context we find here. Vespasian's healings point only to the god-given luck of Vespasian, his *fortuna*.

In every New Testament miracle the referential context of the inbreaking reign of God and the eschatological new creation of Israel is present. The wonder worker believes in that context, and the recipients of the miracle believe in him. We see this very beautifully in the Gentile woman who begs Jesus to heal her sick daughter:

> From there he set out and went away to the region of Tyre. He entered a house and did not want anyone to know he was there. Yet he could not escape notice, but a woman whose little daughter had an unclean spirit immediately heard about him, and she came and bowed down at his feet. Now the woman was a Gentile, of Syrophoenician origin. She begged him to cast the demon out of her daughter. He said to her, "Let the children be fed first, for it is not fair to take the children's food and throw it to the dogs." But she answered him, "Sir, even the dogs under the table eat the children's crumbs." Then he said to her, "For saying that, you may go—the demon has [already] left your daughter." So she went home, found the child lying on the bed, and the demon gone. (Mark 7:24-30)

Jesus does not want to heal the daughter of the Gentile woman. When he at first refuses the woman it is not, of course, because he does not care about Gentiles. On the contrary: precisely *because* he cares for the Gentiles he must concentrate on Israel, for if God's new world does not shine forth in Israel it will not be manifest to the world of the nations either. That is why Israel has the primacy. It is a primacy *for the sake of the world*.

Certainly Jesus says all that in an image that comes close to being offensive: children sit at table, and one must not take the bread from them to feed the household dogs. But this woman is quick-witted. She counters Jesus with his own weapons: even the dogs get a share of the little crumbs that fall under the table when children are eating. In this the woman reveals her faith, and still more: she puts herself in Jesus' frame of reference.

That context must exist both for the wonder worker and for the recipient of the miracle. If it is present in both, will the miracle happen? No. Not always. It can happen, but it need not, for as with the gift of grace, so it is with every genuine miracle. Two freedoms encounter each other: human freedom and the freedom of God.

Chapter 10

Warning about Judgment

To this point in the book we have spoken almost exclusively about the holiness of the reign of God that transforms the world. In the words of Jesus, in his parables, and above all in his deeds of power, this new and self-transforming world is presented again and again to our eyes. Those who speak of Jesus must talk first and last of this side of his appearing. But to leave it at that would yield an incomplete and somewhat unfocused image, for besides his preaching of salvation—or better, in the midst of it—Jesus also addressed the theme of judgment.

Repressed and Downplayed

Certainly a great many interpreters excise this theme. There are even books about Jesus in which it is simply not there. Catechesis and religious instruction avoid it, and it is almost never preached. The reason, repeated almost to the point of exhaustion, is "Jesus preached the good news, not the grim news."

Now, that is not altogether wrong. Jesus did not come to threaten. When he speaks of the reign of God he talks first of all about the treasure a day laborer stumbles upon, about the precious pearl a merchant finds, about the tiny mustard seed that grows into a mighty shrub, about the overabundant harvest produced by a field of wheat, about the days of the marriage feast during which no one can fast.

Nevertheless, the formula "good news, not grim news" is a trivialization, because it muffles the theme of judgment by downplaying it as "grim news." It fits wonderfully, of course, into the image of a Jesus scrubbed clean of every offensive feature and adored by the current spirit of the times, but it has little to do with the realism of his preaching.

Another comforting saying is, "Jesus announced that God is our merciful Father who forgives everything. A preaching of judgment had no place at all in such proclamation."[1] But this reasoning is also hasty and trivial. It is unable to sustain tensions. It softens the evil in the world in the name of an oversweetened compassion. It does precisely what Franz Kafka ridicules in his story "Up in the Gallery":

> If some frail, consumptive equestrienne on a reeling horse in the ring, in front of a tireless audience, were uninterruptedly driven around in a circle for months on end by a ruthless, whip-cracking ringmaster, whirring on the horse, blowing kisses, swaying at the waist, and if this performance under the incessant roar of the orchestra and the ventilators were to continue into the ever-widening dreary future, accompanied by applause that kept waning and swelling up again, from hands that are actually steam hammers—then perhaps a young gallery visitor might hurry down the long stairway through all the tiers, plunge into the ring, and shout "Halt!" over the fanfares of the ever-adjusting orchestra.
>
> But since it is not like that—since a beautiful lady, in white and red, comes soaring in through the curtains that the proud liveried footmen open before her; since the ringmaster, devotedly seeking her eyes, breathing toward her in an animal stance; since he lovingly hands her up on the dapple-gray horse as if she were his utterly beloved granddaughter taking off on a dangerous journey; since he cannot make up his mind to signal with the whip; but finally pulls himself together and cracks it smartly; runs alongside the horse, his mouth open; follows the rider's leap with sharp eyes; scarcely believes her skill; tries to warn her by shouting in English; furiously admonishes the grooms, who clutch hoops, to be very attentive; since before the great breakneck leap he raises his hands, beseeching the orchestra to hush; since he finally lifts the girl down from the trembling horse, kisses her on both cheeks, and considers no tribute from the public satisfactory enough; while she herself, supported by him, high on the tips of her toes, in a whirl of dust, her arms outspread, her head thrown back, tries to share her bliss with the entire circus—since this is so, the gallery visitor puts his face on the railing and, sinking into the concluding march as into a heavy dream, he weeps without realizing it.[2]

The first part of this text depicts the world as it is: its misery, its eternal circling, its brutality, its mercilessness. That is reality. But it does not appear that way and is not perceived that way: therefore the twofold "if" and the consistently maintained subjunctive mood. The second part of the text depicts exactly the same world but now staged as a no-longer-transparent world of appearances.

In summary: the audience have the truth concealed from them. They are helplessly handed over to a manipulated reality. Therefore they can no longer rebel. They can no longer rush down the long stairway and shout "stop!" Only their unconscious continues to resist: the young visitor in the gallery weeps without knowing it.

Jesus saw through the polished world of appearances that others raise up around us and the self-deceptions we constantly build up in ourselves. He did not let himself be euthanized. He sees injustice in its destructive power. He knows what manipulation, lies, and violence incessantly bring about in the world. Therefore he is in a position to cry "stop!" His words about the threatened judgment are a shout, a revolt against society's self-deceptions and unreal pseudo-worlds. Had he spoken only of divine mercy he would have made himself complicit and helped to conceal the real situation in Israel.

Judgment Preached from the Outset

Judgment is a theme in every layer of gospel tradition. It appears in Mark, in the Sayings Source, in the special material of Matthew and Luke, and in the Johannine tradition. In his book on Jesus' preaching of judgment Marius Reiser took the trouble to calculate the percentage of discourse material on the theme of "judgment" within the Synoptic Gospels.[3] The result is astonishing: sayings and parables about judgment comprise seventy-six verses in the Sayings Source (= 35 percent of the discourse material), thirty-seven verses in Mark's gospel (= 22 percent of the discourse material), sixty verses in Matthew's special material (= 64 percent of the discourse material), and thirty-seven verses in Luke's special material (= 28 percent of the discourse material).

Of course, such statistics have ragged edges. It is not always possible to decide clearly what ought to be counted and what should be omitted. Nevertheless, a clear contour emerges: even the apparent truth that Matthew favored the theme of judgment does not change the fact that at least a quarter of the discourse material transmitted as having come from Jesus concerns itself with the theme of "judgment." The unavoidable conclusion is that Jesus must have spoken about it often.

Certainly the question remains: did he do that from the beginning, or did the theme appear in only a later phase of his preaching? We cannot overlook the fact that Jesus was not simply surrounded by sympathizers and disciples. He had increasing numbers of determined opponents, especially among the theologians. They deliberately sought to slander him. They called him a glutton and a drunkard, a friend of sinners, a eunuch and a demoniac, a possessed Samaritan, an apostate from the faith, an impostor, and a deceiver of the people.[4] But Jesus did not encounter total acceptance among the ordinary people either. We can see that in the reaction of his hometown, Nazareth (Mark 6:1-6). Could it be that, after an initial period of success, a "Galilean spring," Jesus encountered increasing opposition and that it was only from that point on that he began to speak of judgment as well?

As attractive as that view is, it has its problems. Certainly we can expect that as Jesus encountered increasing opposition the theme of "judgment" came more to the fore. But it must have been there from the beginning, because it is an integral part of the theme of the reign of God. We see this clearly in the complex of tradition relating to the mission of the disciples. Within the second mission discourse in Luke, based on the Sayings Source, we read:

> Whenever you enter a town and its people welcome you, eat what is set before you; cure the sick who are there, and say to them, "The kingdom of God has come near to you." But whenever you enter a town and they do not welcome you, go out into its streets and say, "Even the dust of your town that clings to our feet, we wipe off in protest against you. Yet know this: the kingdom of God has come near." I tell you, on that day it will be more tolerable for Sodom than for that town. (Luke 10:8-12)

This text makes it clear that salvation is being proclaimed, and not only proclaimed but becoming reality: the sick are healed, and in just that way the coming of the reign of God appears. But if Jesus' messengers are not received, the salvation they wanted to bring is reversed into condemnation: the reign of God becomes judgment. It turns into a self-evoked distress. The prophetic sign-actions of Jesus' messengers reveal the fact as they publicly shake the dust of the city from their feet. In doing so they mean to say, "We are breaking off all connection with you. We are even purifying ourselves of the dust of your town so that in the coming day of judgment it will not cling to us and incriminate us." The sign-action presupposes that Jesus' messengers will appear at the coming final judgment to witness against the city in question (cf. Mark 6:11).

So the proclamation of the reign of God and the (possible) announcement of judgment are internally connected, and therefore they belong together from the beginning. The reason for this is that the reign of God that Jesus proclaims and has his disciples proclaim sets every hearer face-to-face with an ultimate decision: for or against God, for or against Jesus, in whom and through whom God himself is now definitively acting. This radical decision does not happen only at the end of Jesus' public activity. It is happening from the beginning onward. And for that very reason the proclamation of the reign of God brings about a *krisis* from the outset, that is, division, separation, judgment. This appears in a Jesus saying that applies to his whole activity: "Do not think that I have come to bring peace to the earth; I have not come to bring peace, but a sword" (Matt 10:34).

I will address this saying at length later on (see chap. 19). At this point let me say only that the "sword" here has nothing at all to do with a call for violence. It is a sign of the division Jesus brings to the world. Those who hear his words and see his mighty deeds are brought, willy-nilly, into a situation in which they have to decide. Their decision will become for them either salvation or judgment; it leads to the reign of God or to a state of opposition to God that is pure destruction. As John the Baptizer had said before, so Jesus says now: Israel is in a final crisis, and therefore the whole nation and every individual within it is like someone being led before a judge:

> Come to terms quickly with your accuser while you are on the way to court with him, or your accuser may hand you over to the judge, and the judge to the guard, and you will be thrown into prison. Truly I tell you, you will never get out until you have paid the last penny [*quadrans*: the smallest copper coin]. (Matt 5:25-26)

The metaphor presumes the institution of imprisonment for debt: someone who owes money will be held in prison (sometimes with his or her whole family) until the whole debt is paid. There is thus a distant similarity to today's practice of imprisoning people to obtain their cooperation. We know from ancient sources that, once someone fell into the machinery of this system of justice, the procedure was rigorously carried out. The metaphoric saying advises that one should avoid getting involved in it, but instead come to an agreement with the opponent beforehand, if necessary at the last minute, on the way to the judge.

Matthew interpreted the metaphor in terms of reconciliation with the brother or sister in faith, which is a possible and meaningful actualization. But Jesus himself intended something far more fundamental. He wanted to say that now every individual in Israel is like someone on the way to appear before a judge. Each is in a situation that will decide his or her whole life. Therefore, it is important to act decisively and wisely in this eschatological hour—and to do so immediately. Once one stands before the judge, it is too late.

Marius Reiser considers it possible that in this image Jesus—indirectly and ironically—saw himself as the accuser.[5] That would certainly fit with his skillful use of images and parables and with the concealed presence he repeatedly adopts in his parables. He would have taken up the Old Testament motif of the legal case God has against his people, and he himself would then be standing in the place of God—in a legal case against Israel. There is still time to accept his words and turn around, but the time is short. Soon it will be too late.

God's Banquet

So from the beginning there is a close connection in Jesus' proclamation between the reign of God and judgment. But there must have been a time when the theme of judgment emerged more sharply and urgently for him. This was the period when resistance formed against him and it became evident that even his mighty deeds effected very little repentance among the people. The invitation to Israel had long since been issued—would it in the end be refused? Jesus interprets this situation in a parable that still leaves everything open but expresses an emphatic warning and is formulated as pointedly as possible:

> Someone gave a great dinner and invited many. At the time for the dinner he sent his slave to say to those who had been invited, "Come; for everything is ready now." But they all alike began to make excuses. The first said to him, "I have bought a piece of land, and I must go out and see it; please accept my regrets." Another said, "I have bought five yoke of oxen, and I am going to try them out; please accept my regrets." Another said, "I have just been married, and therefore I cannot come." So the slave returned and reported this to his master. Then the owner of the house became angry and said to his slave, "Go out at once into the streets and lanes of the town and bring in the poor, the crippled, the blind, and the lame."

> And the slave said, "Sir, what you ordered has been done, and there is still room." Then the master said to the slave, "Go out into the roads and lanes, and compel people to come in, so that my house may be filled. For I tell you, none of those who were invited will taste my dinner." (Luke 14:16-24)

The parable relates a crazy, scarcely imaginable tale: all those invited to a banquet send regrets, all of them without exception. That is grotesque, even eerie. But the host knows what to do: he brings in other guests. As off-putting as is the refusal of all those invited, the gathering of the substitute guests is just as bizarre: they are hauled in from every corner and cranny. Indeed, they have to be begged to come in, because obviously they are embarrassed at being totally unprepared.

Most interpreters of the parable consider the double gathering of substitute guests to be secondary. Here Luke is said to have been thinking of various phases of the later mission.[6] The latter may well be true of Luke, but Jesus could have intended the doubling to emphasize the unusual character of the situation. The hall must really be full. If those invited do not want to come, then God invites others, and he brings them together from every direction.

For Jesus' audience it was clear that he was speaking of God's eschatological banquet. That is the indispensable presupposition behind the parable. It was also clear to them that this eternal banquet was laid for Israel. The parable presumes all that and it is from these presuppositions that it derives its shocking force: those invited and chosen by God will not come. Their places remain empty. But God can invite others. The banquet will take place in any event. But it becomes a judgment on Israel: none of those originally invited will taste of the meal.[7]

No one should ever have doubted that Jesus already (and not the evangelists later) had the Gentiles in view in this parable. Those first invited are not a particular group in Israel, but the whole people of God. That in the first place only the leaders of Israel or the righteous or wealthy within the people should be invited to the meal in the reign of God, and only after their refusal the poor and sinners, would contradict Jesus' message and practice in every way. Therefore, those first invited can only be all Israel. But in that case those invited later are the Gentiles. That this is the case is evident from Jesus' saying in Matthew 8:11-12 // Luke 13:28-29, which we have already discussed (chap. 4). It can be reconstructed as follows from the Sayings Source: "Many will come from the rising and the setting and recline at table in the reign of God—together with Abraham, Isaac, and Jacob. But you will be cast out into the outermost darkness, where there will be weeping and gnashing of teeth." Those who come from East and West, that is, from a great distance, can only be Gentiles. But those first invited, who are meant to recline at table with the ancestors of Israel, are cast out. Here the language is much more direct than in the parable. Therefore the provocation is likewise much greater. But the goal is the same: this is about the repentance, the turning back, of Israel.

Witnesses against Israel

There are also judgment sayings from Jesus' lips in which witnesses appear against Israel. These include first of all a saying directed to the Twelve whom Jesus had appointed. They are to be not only a sign of the gathering of the eschatological Israel. In addition, they will function as witnesses at the final judgment: "You . . . will . . . sit on twelve thrones, judging the twelve tribes of Israel" (Matt 19:28; cf. Luke 22:30). The twelve are here probably to be regarded as observers at the judgment. The background is Daniel 7:9. That vision in Daniel 7 played a major role for Jesus, and it is the only passage in which thrones for a committee of judges are set up at the last judgment.[8] But that is not so important. More significant is the question: how will the Twelve judge their own people? They will do so simply by following Jesus and remaining with him (Matt 19:27; cf. Luke 22:28). Their discipleship and fidelity become a counter-witness to all the lack of faith and all the infidelity in the people of God. In other words, there is no further need for a solemn final sentence from a judge: the discipleship of some becomes the judgment of others.

The same is true of the double saying about the queen of the South and the Ninevites, which can easily be reconstructed from the Sayings Source:

> The queen of the South will rise up at the judgment together with this generation and condemn it. For she came from the ends of the earth to hear Solomon's wisdom—and behold, here is something greater than Solomon.

> The men of Nineveh will rise up at the judgment together with this generation and condemn it. For they repented at the preaching of Jonah—and behold, here is something greater than Jonah. (cf. Luke 11:31-32 // Matt 12:41-42)

The two parts of the double saying are precisely matched and so strictly planned that later tradents were able to remember it easily. Here again Jesus took his illustrative material from Sacred Scripture: the first book of Kings (1 Kgs 5:14 [English, 4:34]; 10:1-13) tells of the Queen of Sheba, and the book of Jonah (chap. 3) has the story of the Ninevites. Despite the almost complete agreement of the two parts of the saying, there is an escalation present as well: the queen of the South only listens to Solomon, but the Ninevites repent.

But the issue in our context is something different. We have here a clear scene of judgment. The judgment of the world has begun. The accused stand before the judge. Those accused are "this generation," that is, the generation that has heard Jesus' preaching and seen his miracles. During the judicial process witnesses arise from their places. The queen of Sheba stands up and testifies against Israel with her longing for Solomon's wisdom; then the Ninevites get up and witness against Israel with their repentance.

There is a shocking provocation in this double saying as well. It consists in the fact that the witnesses against Israel in both cases are Gentiles. Here we have come upon something that is characteristic of Jesus: he is amazed at the faith of the Gentile centurion (Matt 8:10). He heals the daughter of the Syrophoenician woman (Mark 7:29). He makes a man of Samaria the positive protagonist of a parable (Luke 10:25-37). He says that it will be better for the Gentile cities of Tyre and Sidon at the judgment than for the Jewish villages of Chorazin and Bethsaida (Matt 11:22), and adds that if the mighty deeds done in Capernaum had occurred in Sodom, that city would still be standing (Matt 11:23).

This is precisely the place for the observation that Jesus' proclamations of judgment are all directed against Israel. There are no words of judgment against the Gentiles. That is crucial, for in the Old Testament nearly all the prophetic books contain speeches about God's judgment on the nations. Simply read in Ezekiel 25–32 the threatening discourses against Ammon, Moab, Edom, Egypt, the Philistines, and especially Tyre and Sidon. There is nothing like these in Jesus' words. How should we evaluate this phenomenon?

In my opinion it is inadequate to answer that Jesus had a special openness to and lack of prejudice about Gentiles. He may well have had such an astonishing openness. But the fact that his judgment discourses are all directed to Israel can be explained only by the fact that Jesus concentrated his whole proclamation and work on Israel. Obviously, he was familiar with the promises of the pilgrimage of the nations to Zion. But those very promises presuppose that Israel will open itself to God's eschatological action and return to God. Therefore the path of the nations ultimately depends on the faith of Israel. And that faith is what is crucial for Jesus now, in this hour of decision.

The Presence of Judgment

Jesus' appearance in Israel marks the decisive crisis in its history. Nothing is yet final. There is still, for Jesus, a last hope that his audience will grasp the "signs of the times" and understand their own situation (Luke 12:54-57). That is why his judgment sayings have such power. That is why he speaks so sharply. Even if Jesus in the end formulated the judgment on Israel as a settled fact, his discourse was still "conditioned," still a warning, still the unremitting attempt to achieve repentance.

The history of the subsequent few decades validated Jesus' warnings. Whole sections of the people did not take his call to repentance and nonviolence seriously. The Zealots were able to set loose a war against Rome that took an immense number of victims and at the end of which the city of Jerusalem and the temple were a field of ruins. Previously the different Jewish groups had fought among themselves within the city itself and killed one another off.

We simply have to read these horrible eruptions of violence, which Josephus tells about in his *Jewish War*, in light of Jesus' judgment sayings. His warnings were not something we can simply erase from his preaching. Jesus was realistic to the utmost, and he wanted to preserve Israel from the catastrophe into which it was maneuvering itself. When he speaks of the threatening judgment he is not merely referring to the judgment of the world at the end of time. He always means also the judgment that is already taking place in history and is caused by unbelief itself. The coming judgment about which Jesus speaks extends just as much into the present as the coming reign of God. Here too the axiom of "already and not yet" applies. Jesus' judgment sayings are absolutely intended to provoke and shock. That is how they hope to bring people to repentance and change the course of history.

Is it allowable for Jesus to provoke, to drive fear into people? I say yes. He was allowed to do it just as were all Israel's prophets, because the warning of judgment is always aimed to bring it about that the poor and the oppressed, who have no one to stand with and for them, should be helped *now*, that society's structures of injustice should be changed *now*, that Israel should *now* struggle for peace and reconciliation.

The crisis in society by which it is bringing itself down cried out to heaven at that time just as it cries to heaven today. Jesus saw that misery clearly. He had the oppression and rape of the poor before his eyes. Should he have remained silent? Should he have said, "Oh well, it isn't so bad"? In light of the catastrophe toward which Israel was plummeting, which he clearly saw coming, should he have simply spoken of divine mercy that covers everything? A Jesus without a preaching of judgment, one who never shook things up, never shocked, never warned, never spoke of consequences would, for me, be absolutely unworthy of belief.

Judgment as Salvation

As regards the theme of "judgment," today so well suppressed and rendered toothless, we should also consider, however, that at some point an hour must come when history's lies and manipulations, meannesses and hidden acts of violence will all be revealed—the endless, twisted, matted tangle of human guilt and human innocence. A world that would not be judged in this sense would be a world without hope, without purpose, and without dignity. A world history in which the murderers triumph over their innocent victims, in which the ruthless are justified and the betrayed remain so forever would be absurd in the extreme.

Human courts are helpless in face of the immeasurable potential for injustice in the world; they are even involved in the injustice themselves. Ultimately, it is only God who can clarify guilt and responsibility. But judgment does not mean that in the end God will require satisfaction, that he punishes, that he demands reparation, but first and foremost that he makes history clear—or, to put it in better words, that in light of the absolute truth that God essentially is, history will reveal its own meaning. The masks will fall; the veils will be torn away; the self-deceptions will be removed. In this sense we can positively hope for judgment, judgment even for oneself and one's own life with all its confusions. Clarity in light of God's truth is salvation—and it may be precisely in such clarification that God's mercy is revealed.

There is a short text in the book of Hosea that introduces a long, wrathful discourse against Israel in which the voice of God alternates with the author's commentary. That discourse begins with chapter 4 and extends to the end of chapter 11. The introductory text reads:

> Hear the word of the LORD, O people of Israel! for the LORD has an indictment against the inhabitants of the land. There is no faithfulness or loyalty, and no knowledge of God in the land. No: swearing, lying, and murder, and stealing and adultery break out; bloodshed follows bloodshed. Therefore the land mourns, and all who live in it languish; together with the wild animals and the birds of the air, even the fish of the sea are perishing. (Hos 4:1-3)

There could be no harsher judgment on the true situation of the people of God. These three verses are "a true summary of divine wrath."[9] It affects not only the people in Israel but even the animals. The fish are perishing with all the rest.

But in Hosea the wrath of God does not have the last word. At the beginning of chapter 11 that wrath has been transformed into lament. God cannot forget his first love. And in Hosea 11:8-9 everything is reversed in God; his burning wrath collapses and is transformed into love. God puts an end to the judgment that is already in progress. The cosmic catastrophe threatened in Hosea 4:3 does not come to pass:

> How can I give you up, Ephraim? How can I hand you over, O Israel?
> . . . My heart recoils within me; my compassion grows warm and tender. I will not execute my fierce anger; I will not again destroy Ephraim; for I am God and no mortal, the Holy One in your midst, and I will not come in wrath. (Hos 11:8-9)

This transformation of wrath into compassion, of judgment into salvation, is not something we find only in Hosea. There are similar texts in other prophetic books and throughout the whole of the Old Testament. God responds to his people with faithfulness despite their own unfaithfulness and rejection. God's heart beats for Israel, and he must have mercy on it. So we read in Isaiah 54:6-8:

> For the LORD has called you like a wife forsaken and grieved in spirit, like the wife of a man's youth when she is cast off, says your God. For a brief moment I abandoned you, but with great compassion I will gather you. In overflowing wrath for a moment I hid my face from you, but with everlasting love I will have compassion on you, says the LORD, your Redeemer.

Certainly, in citing such texts one should not fall into the error of separating them from their contexts. We cannot deny that in the Bible such love is spoken of mainly in the context of judgment and catastrophe. The Old Testament texts portray not a God of cheap love who accepts everything but rather the "nevertheless" of divine fidelity in view of the infidelity of the people of God.

The love of God appears in the book of Hosea in the collapse of God's wrath. The prophet can only speak of it in view of Israel's unfaithfulness and in the context of the fearful losses brought about by that unfaithfulness. God's fidelity averts the ultimate destruction of the people, which is nothing other than self-destruction. But it does not give salvation apart from judgment. The consequences of sin cannot be left aside.

Jesus knew all these texts. His preaching of judgment presumed them. In the parable of the lost son he himself spoke of the fathomless compassion of God (Luke 15:11-32). But he also spoke of judgment. He could not do otherwise. It is precisely in the tension between salvation and judgment that runs through his whole proclamation that his deep rootedness in the Torah and the prophets is evident. That will be our next topic.

Chapter 11

Jesus and the Old Testament

The title of this chapter conceals some problems. First of all, at the time of Jesus the Bible was not defined in the same way as it was later, through the definitive Jewish and Christian delimitations of the canon. The Pharisaic canon of sacred writings did play a decisive role already, but there was also the Sadducees' canon of Scripture and that of the Samaritans, both of which recognized only the Torah, and there was the much more open idea of Scripture in the Qumran community.[1]

And, of course, Jesus never called his Bible "the Old Testament." The title of this chapter already presupposes the much later perspective of the church. We would have to speak differently if we take Jesus' point of view. In his time what Christians today call the "Old Testament" was simply called "Scripture," or "the Torah," or "the Torah and the prophets," or more precisely "the Torah, the prophets, and the other books."

That, at any rate, is how the foreword to the book of Jesus Sirach formulates it. That book, originally written in Hebrew, was composed around 190 BCE. The prologue is later and is by the Greek translator of the book, a grandson of the author. It begins: "Many great teachings have been given to us through the Law and the Prophets and the other [books of the ancestors] that followed them, and for these we should praise Israel for instruction and wisdom."

"Written on Your Heart"

So we really should ask: what was Jesus' relationship to the Torah, the prophets, and the writings? Or, more simply: how did he live with "Scripture"? What significance did it have for him? How did he deal with it? The answer, before anything else we have to say, must be: probably, on the basis of Deuteronomy 6:6-7, he knew central texts of Sacred Scripture by heart. Deuteronomy demands, "These words that I am commanding you today must be written on your heart. You shall cause your children to repeat them."[2] "They must be written on your heart" in the first place means nothing but "you must learn them by heart." This a fixed formula. And when the text continues, "You shall cause your children to repeat them," it means, "you must recite the Torah [the book of Deuteronomy] over and over again to your children" ("sons" in the original is understood to include daughters) "until they know the text by heart." And concretely that probably meant that the children heard, day after day, how their parents prayed and meditated on Scripture out loud, and so they also learned the texts, almost automatically, until they were fixed in their memory. So this is not about a way of dealing with Scripture that only Jesus practiced but about the practice of many families in Israel.

Thus we can take it as given that Jesus would have known crucial passages from the Torah and the prophets by heart, and probably all the psalms and some parts of the Wisdom literature as well. Most frequently quoted in the New Testament canon are[3] the Torah (35 percent of all direct quotations), the Psalms (24 percent), Isaiah (22.5 percent), and the Book of the Twelve [Prophets] (10 percent). Quotations from other biblical writings make up 8.5 percent. It is true that these numbers already reflect a specifically Christian perspective, but at the same time they reveal the relative values of the different parts of the canon of Scripture in the Judaism of the time. The Torah is, of course, in the foreground; then come the psalms for daily prayer and then the prophets, Isaiah above all.

How was it possible for a Jew of that time to know so many texts by heart? We can by no means judge this phenomenon in terms of the quantity of text we ourselves can recite from memory today. At that time people not only had a universally practiced mnemonic technique at their disposal. The texts themselves were shaped in such a way that they could be more easily remembered. But above all, people's heads were not crammed with our media garbage.

When Jesus withdrew and prayed for many hours alone (cf. Mark 1:35), he would have recited the Psalms and through them have entered into a deep, wordless conversation with his Father. And when the Torah was recited in the synagogue worship service, followed by sections of the prophetic books as commentary, he heard in public what he had already learned by heart as a child.

The Major Biblical Materials

And what did Jesus learn when he heard Scripture recited or spoke its verses for himself? He learned what Israel had experienced of its God over the centuries, what his great teachers and preachers had understood, formulated, and collected, what they had thought through, corrected, expanded, deepened, arranged, written down, and continued to write, namely, that there was but one God who made heaven and earth. That he had created the world with its multiplicity and its wealth but was not himself the world. That he gave existence to all things, sustained all things, contained all things, gave meaning to all things. That the gods humans created for themselves were idols, nothing but deception and nullity.

He learned that this one God had chosen little Israel out of the many nations because he wanted to have a people in the world that belonged entirely to him with its whole heart and soul and existence. That he had rescued the Israelites from the nation of Egypt, where they were oppressed and violated, in order to bring them together as a people that lived differently from the other nations, in justice and peace with one another and in holiness before its God.

He then learned that God had led Israel through the desert, fed the people, and, at Sinai, gave them a way of life that was both a just order of society and instruction for hallowing all of life. That this Torah was meant to help Israel to give witness before the eyes of the nations to its God: to God's glory, justice, and concern for the world. That God had made a covenant with Israel, to be their God and to make this people his very own.

And he learned that Israel began to grumble, even as it was being rescued from Egypt, and that the grumbling kept breaking out again and again. That Israel took a dim view of the land God wanted to give them and even slandered it. That it was frightened by the nearness of God, that it broke its covenant with God, that it wanted to be like the other nations. That God nevertheless sustained his people, with great endurance and unwearying patience, that he forgave them again and again, that he created the temple for them in Jerusalem as a place of atonement so that the horrible consequences of sin were broken asunder and the people could always begin anew.

He learned that God had given Israel festivals that divided the year, so that one could live from feast to feast. That at these festivals Israel gathered to remember its history and join in a holy community to praise God. That God raised up prophets for his people to snatch them out of their hard-heartedness and blindness. That Israel did not listen to its prophets, did not live according to its social order, sought out the gods of the nations, and so became like the Gentiles. That God therefore had to scatter it among the nations in order to bring it to repentance and reflection.

And he learned that, even in this most profound crisis of Israel's history, God never forgot his people. That he promised to gather them again, renew the fertility of the land of Israel for them, and one day to raise up a king for them who, after all the many kings who had so miserably failed them, would be the true Anointed, the true Ruler, the true God-fearer.

And finally, he learned that God had begun a history with his people that was crucial for the whole world because it brought it to the moment of decision. That this God who had resisted every name and certainly every image was the absolute Lord of history. That he would bring all history to its goal without damaging human freedom: as its Creator, its Judge, but also its Lover. Then God would be all in all and the world would breathe a sigh in God, and God himself would take away the shroud of sorrow that still covers the nations.

All that and much more the young Jesus heard, recited it daily like every faithful Jew, and took it into his heart.[4] It is impossible to measure the depth to which it penetrated, because that was a secret between him and his heavenly Father. The reader of the gospels can only dimly perceive it, for example, when the evangelist Luke tells his interpretive story of how the twelve-year-old Jesus, during his first pilgrimage to Jerusalem, remained in the temple and explained to his parents, who had sought him with great anxiety, that he had to be in what belonged to his Father (Luke 2:41-52).

Jesus, a Scribe?

All that had to be said at the outset if we are going to talk about Jesus and the Old Testament. But we have not yet come to the real topic of this chapter. We are interested not in how Jesus, as a pious Jew, lived his life on the basis of Scripture but in what role Scripture played in his preaching and his public activity. How did he deal with it as a teacher, a preacher, a prophet, and someone who was more than any prophet?

There is some indication in the very existence of his disciples (cf. chap. 5 above) that Jesus did not work with Scripture as a scribe would: the disciples did not come to Jesus to "learn Torah" but to "follow" him. Moreover, at the time of Jesus the scribes had already located themselves deliberately within the existing tradition of interpretation and relied on authorities for doing so. To ground an opinion on the Law, they appealed either to one or more passages in Scripture or to a respected teacher. Sequences of tradition handed down under the names of great scribes were of the greatest significance for rabbinic theology, for they build bridges to the *oral* Torah, which—according to the rabbinic view—had been given at Sinai in addition to the *written* Torah.[5]

But this very scribal technique apparently played no part in Jesus' thinking. The gospels do not contain a single text in which he mentions acknowledged scribal experts by name and quotes them. He does use scriptural references, but they differ from those of the later rabbis.

So what was his way of drawing on Sacred Scripture? That subject would really require a whole book. In this chapter I will merely offer three samples; we might compare them to test shafts. They are meant to show how Jesus worked with his Bible. The samples touch on three themes: first, and once again, the subject of Jesus and the reign of God (cf. chap. 2 above), then that of Jesus and the state, and finally Jesus and nonviolence.

Jesus and the Reign of God

Biblical scholars have long since agreed that the concept of the reign of God was central to Jesus' preaching. Paul scarcely used it at all, and in John's gospel, in contrast to the Synoptics, it disappears altogether. Things continued that way in the early church: the concept of the "reign of God" or "kingdom of heaven" acquired a new content or else played only a secondary role in theology.

That is in itself astonishing, for in ancient Judaism God's kingship played a very significant role indeed. But a finer distinction needs to be made. It was taken as a matter of course that God is already king and, as such, is ruler of the whole world and is Lord of Israel in a special sense, as the YHWH-is-king hymns themselves (Pss 93; 96–99) make abundantly clear. In the worship at the temple but also in synagogue worship

God was addressed as king,[6] enthroned in the midst of his people Israel. God effects justice and righteousness, protects the lives of those devoted to him, is master of all the powerful and mighty, and everything must bow to his rule. Still more, future salvation is already a reality in heaven, where the eschatological temple, the new Jerusalem, the heavenly city are already prepared. There the angels are already celebrating the reign of God around the divine throne. Biblical scholarship has called this notion of God's kingship "theocratic."

This is to be distinguished from another point of view that developed more and more clearly after the collapse of the Davidic kingdom and is rightly called "eschatological." It expects the kingship of God as a manifestation, an event that breaks into history, a powerful eschatological and thus final revelation of God's eternal kingship.

Of course, these two points of view, the theocratic and the eschatological, do not exist in complete isolation from one another. Combinations and overlappings appear again and again.[7] In Jesus' time both the theocratic and the eschatological notions of God's kingship were in circulation. The Kaddish, a very ancient Jewish prayer, may stand as an example of the eschatological type. Its core was probably prayed as early as the first century CE.[8] Originally it concluded the synagogal reading of Scripture. Today it begins:

> May His great name be exalted and sanctified in the world which He created according to His will! May He establish His kingdom and may His salvation blossom and His anointed be near during your lifetime and during your days and during the lifetimes of all the House of Israel, speedily and very soon!

So the text does not speak simply of God's eternal kingship, which is assumed. Its petition is that this kingship become a reality in Israel, that it be "established." God is asked to establish it in Israel in this very generation, to reveal his lordship in the world as quickly as possible.

We do not really know with certainty whether the Kaddish was being prayed in Jesus' time, but we cannot exclude the possibility because the Our Father has a certain kinship to the Kaddish. Both prayers ask first that the divine Name be sanctified and then in the second place that the reign of God may come. Given this striking agreement, it could well be that the Kaddish already existed in Jesus' time and that, together with other prayers, it contributed to Jesus' ability to assume that his listeners took the reign of God as a given. We may take it for granted that the concept of God's *malkutha*, the royal rule of God, was commonly known and that Jesus himself was familiar with it from his youth.

And yet there must have been something more in Jesus' view, because the way he then went on to speak about the reign of God had a unique contour. The very fact that for him the reign of God was absolutely central and imbued everything he said and did is unique to him. This phenomenon can only be explained by a very personal reference to Scripture, more precisely to the book of Isaiah. That is the only way to grasp the *specific* way he talked about the reign of God. Isaiah contains a text that was apparently of the highest significance for Jesus' thinking and doing, namely, Isaiah 52:7-9:

> How beautiful upon the mountains are the feet of the messenger who announces peace, who brings good news, who announces salvation, who says to Zion, "Your God reigns."
>
> Listen! Your sentinels lift up their voices, together they sing for joy; for in plain sight they see the return of the LORD to Zion.
>
> Break forth together into singing, you ruins of Jerusalem; for the LORD has comforted his people, he has redeemed Jerusalem.

These verses are part of the larger text complex of Isaiah 40–55, which biblical scholars call "Deutero-Isaiah," that is, "Second Isaiah." This is because these chapters presuppose a situation that does not fit the time of the historical Isaiah, namely, the crisis of the Babylonian exile and the misery of those who remained behind in Jerusalem and Judea. In this situation a prophet arose who deliberately linked to the tradition of the historical Isaiah and even assumed his character and his voice. We do not know the name of the prophet because this person simply continued the prophetic words of Isaiah, writing against the danger that Israel would assimilate to Babylon and be sucked into the worship of the gods of Babylon. But the prophet also writes against the danger of resignation, radicalizing faith in the one, unique God (the "worship of YHWH alone" thus became "monotheism") and announcing a new exodus. The deported will return to Zion in a solemn festival procession, and in that way the God of Israel will show himself to be the lord of all the nations.

Isaiah 40–55 is constructed as a great dramatic poem. Voices are interwoven: here the voice of God, there the voice of the prophet. Israel, the suffering servant of God in Babylon, is addressed; in other scenes the addressees are those who have remained behind in Jerusalem and Judea.

The text we have quoted, Isaiah 52:7-9, has those still in Jerusalem in view. For them the future is brought into the present: the new Exodus from the land between the rivers into the motherland is already happening. Those remaining in Jerusalem already see how the procession of those formerly deported is approaching the city. They see the messengers of joy who run ahead of the caravans. They hear the jubilation of the watchers on the city walls. A shout of joy breaks forth over the ruins of Jerusalem.

What is so special about this text? What does it have to do with the origins of Jesus' specific message? We may offer five observations:

1. A messenger of good news appears, in Hebrew a *mebassêr*, in Greek an *euaggelizomenos*. There is much to favor the idea that here in this passage, and in Isaiah 61:1-2, we find the *theological* source of the word *evangelium*, "Gospel." It is true that there were in the Hellenistic world of the time a good many *euaggelia*, messages of good news, as, for example, in the announcement of a new ruler's ascent to the throne. But the *one* Gospel of God that speaks of *God*'s action in history has its origin here, in this text.

Evidently Jesus recognized himself in the messenger of good news in Isaiah 52. He was convinced that *now*, with his appearance, Isaiah's message of salvation was being fulfilled. *Now* the promises of Isaiah, that "the blind receive their sight, the lame walk, the lepers are cleansed, the deaf hear, the dead are raised, and the poor have *good news* brought to them," are coming to pass.[9] So what Jesus brings is *the* good news, and he himself is its messenger.

2. In accordance with our text, the content of the good news is *called out*, *proclaimed* by the messenger. Jesus did exactly that. He not only taught like the scribes but announced his message of the reign of God in all of Israel, or caused it to be announced by the disciples he sent out. That is something different from mere teaching.

3. What, according to Isaiah, is the content of this message? In itself it is the return of the exiles to Jerusalem and thus the rescue and restoration of Israel. But that is *not* how it is formulated. Instead, Isaiah speaks of God's return to Zion. So behind the return of the deportees stands God himself; it is God who has brought about this return, God who leads it, God who is coming back. God identifies once again with his people.

4. And the direct content of the proclamation? It is: "Your God has become king." That is, God becomes king precisely in gathering, leading

back, and restoring Israel. So the proclamation does not speak primarily about God's eternal kingship, something it simply presumes. Nor does the proclamation say that God's royal reign will break forth *soon* after the return of the exiles. What it really says is that in the very moment in which the exiles return, God *becomes* king. That is, God's eternal lordship is now revealed as an event within history. With the return of the exiles God's royal rule is definitively realized in the world. God now *reveals* himself conclusively and ultimately as king; God *manifests* himself decisively as king. The watchers are already beginning their rejoicing.

This is the precise point to which Jesus linked. He applied Isaiah 52:7-9, and the theology of the book of Isaiah as a whole, to his own present in a wholly personal way unique to him: he himself is the messenger of the good news; he himself proclaims it. And this message says that God's royal reign is happening *now*, is coming *now*. This eschatological event that God is setting in motion and that is manifest in Jesus' actions will gather and restore Israel. That Jesus simply applied to himself a text that spoke of God's messenger of good news and the royal reign of God now manifesting itself assumes a breathtaking boldness.

5. One final observation about Isaiah 52:7-9: it is not a marginal text in Scripture to which Jesus refers and on the basis of which he speaks and acts. This is a central text because the creed that "God rules as king" constitutes the center of the Torah. After all, what is this solemn formula "God rules as king" all about? It is a clear reference to the first commandment of the Decalogue. What does that commandment say? "You shall have no other gods before me" (Exod 20:3 // Deut 5:7). And the commentary on this commandment in Deuteronomy, the *shemaʿ Israel*, says, "Hear, O Israel: The LORD is our God, the LORD alone. You shall love the LORD your God with all your heart, and with all your soul, and with all your might" (Deut 6:4-5).

And now comes the crucial point: the announcement of the present coming of the reign of God is the *eschatological historicization and making present* of what the first commandment of the Decalogue and its commentary in Deuteronomy 6 say. To put it another way: the proclamation of the reign of God coming now is the definitive historical realization of what has always been before Israel's eyes and what it sought to live in the Torah: for Israel there can be only this *one* God and he must become Lord of one's whole life, of every hour of the day, of all spheres of life.

How closely the royal reign of God and the great commandment (with its motif of God's unity) belong together in the Old Testament is evident from the parallelism in Zechariah 14:9: "And the LORD will become king over all the earth; on that day the LORD will be one and his name one." So Jesus, with his proclamation of the reign of God, makes the center of the Torah the center of his preaching. What Jesus proclaims is thus nothing other than the center of the Torah—an insight that is of the utmost importance for Christian-Jewish dialogue. It is, of course, true that this center of Torah is found in Jesus in a new, eschatological sense that overthrows everything else.

In Mark's gospel this association between the first commandment and God's reign is unmistakably set before our eyes: after a scribe has called the first commandment (together with the love commandment from Lev 19:18) the greatest of all commandments, Jesus says to him, "You are not far from the reign of God" (Mark 12:34).

Jesus must have had a sense, for us almost shocking, of who God is and what is the center of God's will. It is a historical will: it is manifested in God's actions in his people in the midst of this history. And Israel is called now to surrender itself totally to this will manifested in Jesus.

So what has our first sample shown us? It suggests that Jesus had a unique and genuine access to the Sacred Scriptures. He applies Isaiah 52:7-9 to himself and develops his proclamation of the reign of God out of this text. This in no way excludes the possibility that he also linked to the existing abstract term *malkutha*. It does not even deny that people in Israel had otherwise made use of Isaiah 52:7-9.[10] But beyond all these caveats, Jesus was apparently in a position to read Scripture with new eyes and on the basis of a breathtaking claim.

Jesus and the State

The second sampling relates to the Our Father.[11] This prayer, which Jesus gave to his disciples as their very own, is one of the shortest and at the same time one of the most profound prayers in Christianity. It discloses, as does no other text, who Jesus was. Every petition in the Our Father is deeply grounded in the Old Testament. We have already seen that in the fourth chapter of this book, where we spoke of the first petition in the prayer, the so-called gathering petition. That plea draws on the theology of the book of Ezekiel.

But we should not merely ask what the Our Father says and what it asks; we should also ask what it does not say and what it does not ask for. Then we see that the Our Father speaks neither of Zion nor of Jerusalem nor of the land of Israel nor of Israel as a nation. It does speak of the gathering of the people of God, but *not* of Israel as a national entity.

That is by no means a matter of course, for in the *Amida*, the Eighteen Benedictions, one of the most important prayers of Judaism and one whose early stages may go back to the time of Jesus,[12] things are altogether different. The seventh petition reads, "Look upon our affliction and plead our cause, and redeem us speedily for Your name's sake; for You are a mighty Redeemer. Blessed art thou, O L-rd, the Redeemer of Israel." The fourteenth petition is still clearer: "And Jerusalem, Your city, return in mercy, and dwell therein as You have spoken; rebuild it soon in our days as an everlasting building, and speedily set up therein the throne of David. Blessed art thou, O L-rd, who rebuilds Jerusalem." Neither the struggle Israel is here conducting with God's help nor the eschatological rebuilding of Jerusalem nor the coming of the Messiah need be interpreted in the Eighteen Benedictions in a national sense. But one *could* read the quoted passages from the prayer in that way, and the Zealots *did* most certainly interpret the prayer just so. In the Our Father, Jesus consistently excludes all the corresponding terms. Apparently he did not want his gathering of the people of God to be misunderstood in the sense of reconstructing a nation-state.

It is true that we do not know exactly when the Eighteen Benedictions were formulated, but we have solid ground under our feet in the Psalms of Solomon, mentioned above. They were created in the first century BCE.[13] The seventeenth psalm in the collection speaks of the coming Messiah, who will purify Jerusalem of Gentile peoples and destroy all the lawless nations. He will gather for God a holy people and will not permit Israel ever again to give a place to injustice. Foreigners and strangers will no longer be allowed to dwell in the Land. Then the Gentile nations will all be subjected to Israel and be required to serve the people of God under the yoke of the Messiah.

Here, clearly, the author is drawing a picture of an eschatological state belonging to God. It has a center in Jerusalem. It has an authority who acts in the name of God: the Messiah. It has fixed boundaries: those separating Israel from the Gentile nations. It is a "pure community" and in this sense a homogeneous and uniform society: there are no sinners in it, and it no longer contains anything unclean. All that can appeal to individual passages in the Old Testament, perhaps even whole strata of Old Testament texts: compare, for example, Psalm 2; Isaiah 52:1; Joel 4:9-17.

The Hasmoneans attempted to reestablish a Jewish state in the wake of the catastrophe of the royal period. John Hyrcanus I (reigned 134–104 BCE) reconquered parts of Samaria and the land east of the Jordan. He forced the Idumeans in the south to accept male circumcision and incor-

Jesus and the Old Testament

porated them into the worshiping community of Jerusalem. Aristobulus I (104–103 BCE) reconquered Galilee and joined it once again with Judea. He forced the Itureans in the north to accept male circumcision and assumed the title of king. Alexander Jannaeus (103–76 BCE) brought all of Palestine under his rule, as well as further parts of the land east of the Jordan and the coastal plain. But then came the Romans under Pompey (106–48 BCE) and destroyed all these efforts to re-create a Jewish territorial state. In 63 BCE Pompey entered Jerusalem, seized the temple precincts, and carried out a horrifying bloodbath there. From that time on, Israel was divided and lay under the rule of Rome.

Jesus himself was directly confronted with the attempt to construct a new Jewish state in the Zealots' dreams of revolt. This time it was supposed to be a real state subject to God. The Zealots longed to revolt against Rome not only because of the profound misery in Jewish society but even more because they were convinced that if God alone were to be the Lord of Israel, then the Romans could not rule in the Land.

Jesus opposed this. He intended something fundamentally different by his gathering of Israel. His idea was the establishment not of a God-state but of a new society under the rule of God. Those are not the same thing. His new society began in his community of disciples, which rested on pure acceptance. Its center was the community of his disciples. So the people of God is not meant to have a state or pseudo-state structure.

Certainly Jesus did not reject the state as an institution, but he did not believe that one could serve the Gospel through the state and with the state's aid, or by imitating political forms of rule. When he was asked the tricky and at the time highly dangerous question whether a Jew was permitted to pay taxes to the emperor, he answered, "Give to the emperor the things that are the emperor's, and to God the things that are God's" (Mark 12:17). The emperor's right as a guarantor of order is acknowledged, but in this antithetical parallelism he by no means has rights equal to God's. What most translations give as "and" is in Greek an *adversative kai*; the correct translation would be: "Give [indeed] to the emperor the things that are the emperor's, *but* give to God the things that are God's" (Mark 12:17).

Jesus knows that the state, with its own structures of rule, is necessary. But the people of God is not a state. Therefore Jesus had no regard for the Zealots, who counted on violence and terror to make of Israel a state in the sense of the Psalms of Solomon. Of course, he probably did not think much of the Roman emperor and his ilk either. He was rather skeptical in their regard. According to Mark 10:42-45, Jesus said:

> You know that among the Gentiles those whom they recognize as their rulers lord it over them, and their great ones are tyrants over them. But it is not so among you; but whoever wishes to become great among you must be your servant, and whoever wishes to be first among you must be slave of all. For the Son of Man came not to be served but to serve, and to give his life a ransom for many.

These words show that Jesus regarded contemporary "world politics" realistically and soberly. He saw through the arrogance of the powerful and the manipulative mechanisms of their political propaganda (cf. Luke 22:25). They derived their self-satisfaction from the exploitation of those under them. "You know that this is so," he says. But at the same time, Mark 10:42-45 shows how Jesus imagined the transformation: it has to come as a silent revolution from below, from a completely different perspective, from an attitude that does not seek its own benefit but that of others. This is the attitude Christian tradition calls "humility."

What is unique in the small discourse composition in Mark 10:42-45 is that in it the disciples are set in direct contrast to the nations and their rulers. But let me say again that the purpose of this is not to condemn all human forms of government. Power is not denounced here as something evil in itself. Jesus by no means questions the necessity of the state, but his interest is not in improving confidence in the government. It is only in God's new society, which is beginning something unheard of, something altogether new, in the midst of the old world.

This new thing extends to the utmost depths out of which society constantly recreates itself. Mark 10:42-45 summarizes it in the simple call no longer to seek to rule but instead to serve. "Serve" here should not be read in a bland and colorless sense. In its original meaning the word signified nothing other than waiting on tables. It was based on daily table service, which in the ancient world was the burden of slaves, servants, or free women. It was above all at table that the contrast between those more highly placed, who reclined comfortably, and the slaves or women who had to serve was most keenly felt. In Greek and Roman culture serving in the house was regarded as menial. It was by no means seldom at ancient banquets that the guests would wipe their greasy fingers on the hair of the slaves serving them.[14] "How could a human being be happy while having to serve anyone at all?" asked the Sophist Callicles in the Platonic dialogue *Gorgias* (491c). So it is no accident that Jesus shapes the new society he is beginning with his disciples at table. This is the starting point for the true revolution; here begins the genuinely classless society.

So Jesus does not fight for the correct politics or the right form of the state but instead for fraternity and sorority in the people of God. He struggles not for power and for freedom from Rome but for the overturning and remaking of what power is. And that is certainly a political agenda. He knows that peace and justice, feeding on true fear of God, must grow from below.

Jesus certainly desires the revolution—he wants "new wine in new wineskins" (Mark 2:22)—but a completely different kind of revolution. The usual sort of revolution requires masses of people and must happen quickly. Jesus counts on the leaven that, almost unnoticeably, raises the whole mass of dough (Matt 13:33), and he compares the coming of the reign of God to a mustard seed, which is very tiny and yet grows into a great shrub (Mark 4:30-32), in the version in the Sayings Source even into a World Tree (Matt 13:31-32 // Luke 13:18-19).

And for this particular point of view, which no longer counts on the state or expects salvation from kings, Jesus had a monumental share of the Old Testament behind him: namely, the Torah, the first five books of Moses. The Torah had grown out of the history of the failure of the kingship in Israel and the experience of the catastrophe of exile. In order to give a true evaluation of the significance of the Torah in the context we are talking about here I must broaden the perspective somewhat.

To begin with, the structure of the Hebrew Bible does not follow the model of a continuing "biblical history." Older readers, remembering the so-called School Bibles or Bible History books of an earlier time, may still be familiar with the image of an ongoing biblical narrative. It began with the creation of the world, continued with Adam and Eve, Cain and Abel, and their children, through Abraham, Moses, the judges, David, Solomon, until finally it reached the Maccabees. This all took place in as homogeneous a narrative as possible incorporating everything to be found in the Old Testament. Prophets such as Amos, Isaiah, or Jeremiah were introduced at appropriate places. Where the Old Testament itself revealed some holes in the story they were filled in, at least as far as possible.

But that picture in no way does justice to the structure of the Hebrew Bible. The real Old Testament does not offer a continuous history of events. Taken as a whole, it is not history at all. Its first and most important part is the "Torah," followed by the "Nebiim," the prophets. The books of Joshua, Judges, 1 Samuel, 2 Samuel, 1 Kings, and 2 Kings were also counted among the prophets—because of the fact that the prophets Nathan, Ahijah, Micah ben Imlah, Elijah, Elisha, Isaiah, and Huldah play an important part in them.[15] Finally, the third block is made up of the

"Kethubim," the "writings." The reason for mentioning all this is that the Torah, in Jewish understanding—an understanding that was being shaped already in Old Testament times—is the foundation, the basis of all Sacred Scripture. The "prophets" and the "writings" are by no means sections with equal weight; they exist with reference to the Torah and are understood to be a kind of commentary on the Torah. The fact that this is really so is indicated by the synagogal liturgy, in which the Torah is always recited first and as the reading that determines all the rest.

The Torah *in its present form* originated, at the earliest, toward the end of the Babylonian exile, but more probably soon after the end of the exile. It was intended to secure Israel's identity and rescue it from a total rupture of continuity. This is true, of course, only of the Torah "in its present form," for many texts of the Torah are older than that. It contains songs, narratives, and collections of laws that belong to older strands of tradition. But in the context of our question we are not concerned about those ancient traditions that were worked into the Torah; we are considering the overall composition, that is, the final form we know today. The *Sitz im Leben* of the Torah as a whole composition is the crisis, indeed catastrophe, of the exile. And the Torah is not simply a collection of laws; rather, its law collections are framed by and interwoven with stories.

An important question for us is: when does the story end, the one that constitutes the frame for Israel's history and repeatedly interrupts it? The answer is amazing.[16] The frame of the story is not extended to the entry into the Promised Land under Joshua, much less to David's kingship, and certainly not as far as the Maccabees. Rather, the Torah ends with the death of Moses (Deut 34). He sees the land of promise from a distance, but he is not allowed to enter it. And with him Israel also stands on the borders of the land, but it may not enter. When the annual recitation of the Torah reaches this point it stops and begins again from the beginning.

Christians for the most part do not perceive this break in the text because they have a wrong idea about the Hebrew Bible. They still have something like the "Bible history" of the old school Bibles in their heads, and those simply continued the story without interruption after the death of Moses.

Of course, we have to ask why the basic text for Israel's identity ends with the death of Moses. Why doesn't it end after the people have entered the Promised Land? Or with the building of Solomon's temple? Or with the reforms under King Josiah? Why is Israel's history interrupted? Why does Israel's fundamental text accept an open ending? A border situation? An unfinished narrative?

The answer can only be: because the ongoing history of Israel, especially that of its period as a nation-state, was not regarded as a time that lent Israel its identity. The final redactors of the Torah were of the opinion that what Israel was in its innermost self, what constituted it, what it was for, was revealed not under David and Solomon but under Moses, and, more precisely, it revealed itself in Israel's liberation from Egypt and the covenant with its God at Sinai.[17]

It only becomes clear what that ultimately means when we keep in mind that, at the time when the Torah was created as a unit, the royal period was already in the past. People could look back at that period in its entirety, and in the eyes of the final redactors of the Torah, who were seeking God's true will in and for history, the royal period was not only an unlucky era but a theological catastrophe. That period could in no way be one that created identity. It could only be a time of warning against going that way again. Therefore it was not included in Israel's basic text. Instead, the identity of the people of God was sought in Israel's early period, in the time of the "patriarchs," the time when a covenant was made with God, the time when Israel was still on its way, the time of its testing in the wilderness.

Consequently, the Torah shows little interest in an earthly king. The covenant God forges with Israel makes every worldly king a spectator, and so the legal materials in the Torah for the most part say nothing about a king or a state. If we sift through the concrete law in the Torah we see immediately that the king plays an insignificant role; in most of the law collections he does not appear at all. There are cultic laws, social laws, family law, but scarcely any law applying to political institutions. The only partial exception is Deuteronomy 17:14-20, a law concerning the king:[18]

> When you have come into the land that the LORD your God is giving you, and have taken possession of it and settled in it, and you say, "I will set a king over me, like all the nations that are around me," you may indeed set over you a king whom the LORD your God will choose. One of your own community you may set as king over you; you are not permitted to put a foreigner over you, who is not of your own community.
>
> Even so, he must not acquire many horses for himself, or return the people to Egypt in order to acquire more horses, since the LORD has said to you, "You must never return that way again."
>
> And he must not acquire many wives for himself, or else his heart will turn away; also silver and gold he must not acquire in great quantity for himself. When he has taken the throne of his kingdom,

he shall have a copy of this law written for him in the presence of
the levitical priests. It shall remain with him and he shall read in it
all the days of his life, so that he may learn to fear the LORD his God,
diligently observing all the words of this law and these statutes,
neither exalting himself above other members of the community nor
turning aside from the commandment, either to the right or to the
left, so that he and his descendants may reign long over his kingdom
in Israel.

This text shows that Israel need not have a king at all. That in itself is
something revolutionary against the horizon of ancient Near Eastern
societies. But if Israel really wants a king it should install him itself—and
in terms of constitutional law that means there is to be no absolutism
but only a constitutional monarchy. The constitutional nature of the idea
is also apparent in the fact that the Torah is above the king. He is to read
it daily and keep it with him at all times.

Besides, the king's power is limited: he is not to lead the army in war
(cf. Deut 20:9, where the king does not appear). He has nothing to do
with the observance of the laws (cf. Deut 17:8-13, where the king is also
absent). And he is not the final instance for appeal (Deut 19:17). If we
look at the matter closely we find that there is to be a division of authority in Israel: independent judges, independent priests, a prophet from
time to time, always one chosen by God (Deut 18:18). The king is also to
be distinguished from the other Oriental potentates in that he keeps his
chariots, his harem, and his treasury within limits. Thus in the projected
constitution in Deuteronomy 17 he plays only a marginal role. He is not
central. Compared with the usual custom in the ancient Near East, his
status was entirely relative. To put it in a nutshell: his main task was to
study the Torah every day.

But the most crucial statement is in Deuteronomy 17:20: the king is
not to "exalt himself above other members of the community [lit.: his
brothers]." That is, the king is an Israelite like all the rest, a brother within
a whole people of brothers and sisters. This is particularly emphasized
in Deuteronomy, the last book of the Torah. At least during the festivals
at the central sanctuary all class differences are eliminated. The ideals
of the original people of the twelve tribes then reappear:

Rejoice before the LORD your God—you and your sons and your
daughters, your male and female slaves, the Levites resident in your
towns, as well as the strangers, the orphans, and the widows who
are among you—at the place that the LORD your God will choose as

a dwelling for his name. Remember that you were a slave in Egypt,
and diligently observe these statutes. (Deut 16:11-12)

However, the deuteronomic project corresponds to the Torah as a whole:
the primary figure is not the king as such, nor is it David, who does not
directly appear in the Torah. The major figure in the Torah is clearly
Moses. But Moses is anything but a king. He is presented as Israel's great
prophet, and that in turn corresponds to the fact that the focus of the
whole Torah is the rescue of the people from Egypt, that is, their rescue
from a theocracy.

Conclusion: the Torah, the basic text for Israel's identity, develops a
counter-proposal after the catastrophe of the kingship and the state. The
people of God are certainly described in this counter-proposal as a society but not as a state. Israel is to be a "holy people," that is, separated
for God and elected on behalf of the other peoples (Exod 19:6)—and for
that very reason it cannot live like the other nations. It should never
forget that it was led out of Egypt and may never return to Egypt. Egypt
was a closed system: the complete amalgamation of state, culture,
cosmos, religion, rule, and salvation. The unity of all these spheres was
visible in the person of the Pharaoh, the god-king. Israel is led out of this
"total state": at Sinai it receives a new, alternative order for its society:
hence the major space devoted to the laws within its basic text. Those
laws lack any mention of a state. Where it does appear it is relativized
to such an extent that it is unrecognizable.

The law collections in the Torah show that Israel is meant to be a people
of sisters and brothers. If there is a king in it at all, he can only be a brother
among siblings. He is no longer the dominant figure; at the center of
Israel, instead, stands God's instruction given at Sinai. Even the land,
the territorial basis for any state, is in some sense relativized: it is indeed
promised—and how emphatically is it promised!—but within the Torah
it is not taken into Israel's possession. Israel's basic text leaves the people
of God on the boundary; it keeps them standing on the border of the
land that has been promised and dedicated to them. The Jordan has not
yet been crossed.

Is that all accidental, or is it not instead a theology of genius that opens
the gates to a people of God that will live in the midst of the other nations
and, as a people God has taken as his own, can show how a community
can look if God alone is its lord? And is it an accident that Jesus, in the
midst of his disciples and an Israel to be gathered anew, adopts and tries
to put into practice these fundamental social outlines in the Torah? His

"it will not be so among you" corresponds exactly to the prophetic rejection of the words "we want to be like other nations" (cf. 1 Sam 8:5, 20). Apparently Jesus was profoundly aware of what Israel's basic text intends. It was his own unique power of discovery that enabled him to read the Torah in that way, in the midst of a Zealot movement that was assembling, having learned nothing from Israel's history. The Zealots desired to make the reign of God identical with the state and as a result they thrust Israel into the most profound possible misery. In the year 70 Jerusalem, including the temple, was destroyed by the Romans.

Jesus and Nonviolence

With all that has been said, the theme of Jesus' nonviolence has already come clearly into view; consequently, the samplings can proceed more quickly.

There is a great deal of violence in the Old Testament; we find shocking scenes of destructive exercise of power there, and we often get the impression that the image of God and violence are inextricably connected. To take only a single example from among the many we could possibly choose, we find Psalm 58 saying of the wicked:

> O God, break the teeth in their mouths;
>   tear out the fangs of the young lions, O LORD!
> Let them vanish like water that runs away;
>   like grass let them be trodden down and wither.
> Let them be like the snail that dissolves into slime;
>   like the untimely birth that never sees the sun. (Ps 58:7-9)

That is certainly a harsh text. Still, it was not a very enlightened move when, not long ago, the lectors in a city parish in Germany refused, after reading the Old Testament text at Mass, to utter the concluding formula, "The word of the living God." They gave as their reason the "horrible, violent texts" in the Old Testament, which could not have anything to do with God. Apparently it was not clear to these lectors that the Bible is always and without exception "the word of God *in human words.*" In this, Jewish and Christian theology differ fundamentally from the untenable construction of Islam, which understands the Qu'ran to be a text directly dictated by God. Apparently it had never occurred to the lectors how liberating it can be if we are permitted, for once, to express all our wrath and misery in words. The Old Testament dares to do it in many places, and very often, in the context of the passage, the lament and wrath are corrected and overcome.[19]

We should also note that, in the text just quoted, the petitioners themselves by no means resort to violence. They appeal to God and leave their cause to God. What God then does is another matter. It seems that the Old Testament knows more about human beings than a watered-down humanism can decree. Many texts of the Bible, by calling violence what it is, function precisely to reveal the violence in society that is normally *covered up*, and to disclose its reality as merciless injustice.

Finally: one of the magnificent features of the Old Testament is that its readers continually encounter texts in which violence is shattered. The prophets have the vision of an Israel that, by its example, teaches the nations how people can live together in peace and without violence. The most important and meaty text of this vision is in Isaiah 2 and Micah 4. I am quoting here from the wording in Micah:

> In days to come the mountain of the LORD's house shall be established as the highest of the mountains, and shall be raised up above the hills. Peoples shall stream to it, and many nations shall come and say: "Come, let us go up to the mountain of the LORD, to the house of the God of Jacob; that he may teach us his ways and that we may walk in his paths." For out of Zion shall go forth instruction [Torah], and the word of the LORD from Jerusalem. He shall judge between many peoples, and shall arbitrate between strong nations far away; they shall beat their swords into plowshares, and their spears into pruning hooks; nation shall not lift up sword against nation, neither shall they learn war any more; but they shall all sit under their own vines and under their own fig trees, and no one shall make them afraid; for the mouth of the LORD of hosts has spoken. For all the peoples walk, each in the name of its god, but we will walk in the name of the LORD our God forever and ever. (Mic 4:1-5)

It is absolutely necessary to notice that this prophetic poem projects a vision of the end time, but at the same time it emphasizes that the realization of the vision is already beginning now, today. The challenge at the end is crucial: "all the peoples walk, each in the name of its god, but we will walk in the name of the LORD our God forever and ever."

The corresponding passage in Isaiah reads, "O house of Jacob, come, let us walk in the light of the LORD!" (Isa 2:5). So Israel is to walk already, today, the way of the Torah, the way of peace, the way that corresponds to the name of the Lord. Then, one day, the miracle will happen: the river will run backward, the nations will learn peace from Israel and will beat their swords into plowshares. That too is in the Old Testament!

But even with that we have not said everything by far: in Deutero-Isaiah the Old Testament goes a step further. Can one live in peace and show others what peace is like "if it doesn't please one's wicked neighbors"? That is the fundamental problem of world peace. And precisely here Israel gave an answer (comparable to Socrates' principle that "suffering injustice is better than doing injustice") that overthrows everything: it is better to be a victim than a violent victor.[20]

This is the insight that true peace can only come from the victims, never from the victors. But this peace cannot be accomplished by human beings; it comes from God's initiative. This new insight on the part of Israel, which was, like Micah 4:1-5, gained from the exile, was compressed by Isaiah into the so-called fourth Servant Song. The servant is Israel itself. "Against this servant of God, according to the servant songs, the nations have conspired together. They beat and torture, even kill him. But like those who cry out in Lamentations, he takes refuge in his God. He accepts the violence that falls upon him, does not strike back, and does not avoid it. And God receives him. Suddenly, in the fourth song, we hear a confession from the other kings and nations of the world.[21] They acknowledge what God has done with this outcast."[22] And ultimately, as a result of this knowledge that overturns everything, they confess: "we accounted him stricken, struck down by God, and afflicted. But he was wounded for our transgressions, crushed for our iniquities" (Isa 53:4-5). To these prominent texts from the books of the prophets we could add others, for example Psalm 22 or Zechariah 9:9-10. All these texts show that the theme of nonviolence appears already in the Old Testament. Jesus did not invent it. He found it in his Bible; he could find it all in his Sacred Scriptures.

But things are somewhat more complicated than that. Could he find all of it? Yes. But he could also find many other things, for the Old Testament continually struggles with the theme of "violence and nonviolence." This is evident from the later history of its influence, when these key texts of nonviolence often play no part at all. There was fighting in the time of the Maccabeans and the Hasmoneans. The statements about the servant of God seemed not to exist at all. That was certainly true of the Zealots in the time of Jesus. They saw themselves as God's warriors, permitted in the name of God to use violence—brutal force, by which to establish the reign of God.

And that is not only bad intention; it is connected with the Old Testament itself, which approaches the theme of "nonviolence" like an orchestral piece with many voices. It is not easy always to hear the principal voice in the polyphony it plays, among the accompanying voices, counter-melodies, and dissonances. It is deeply moving to see the unbelievable sensitivity with which Jesus listened to the fourth Servant Song among all the many voices and used it to interpret the true rule of God and his own life. He used no violence at all. He took the sword from Peter's hand (Matt 26:52). He preferred being a victim to using violence. And by that very fact he initiated in the world an unexpected and ongoing influence. It still goes on, and no one can say where it may yet lead.

Jesus' Ability to Distinguish

What we see here in the case of nonviolence can be expanded to cover our overall theme: Jesus did not simply reproduce and repeat the Old Testament. He certainly did not insert completely new content into it. Instead, from the immense material in his Bible, from this experience of centuries, from this heaped-up mass of wisdom and history he discerned and drew out the scarlet thread of God's will—with a sensitivity and ability to distinguish that we can only marvel at.

Jesus' genius—and Jesus was a genius, if we can use such banal language of him—consisted precisely in that he brought together at its center everything Israel had already discovered, and he did so both critically and creatively. In fact, everything had long since been said in Israel, but often without the necessary weight. Or it was submerged in mountains of things said, so that it could scarcely be recognized. Sometimes it even happened that the opposite was said, leaving matters unclear. Jesus, by weighing the many voices with a critical ability to differentiate, allowed the new thing to arise out of what had already been known and hoped for.

The Our Father is itself an eloquent example of this. With each of its petitions it is bound up in Israel's great theology made up of Ezekiel, Daniel, Isaiah, and the Torah—and yet it is his very own, something that, on the basis of the proclamation of the reign of God, draws Israel's traditions together and joins them anew for today.

Or we could take the Sermon on the Mount and its rules for interpreting the Torah as another example. There is not a single statement there that does not have an Old Testament background. Nothing of the Torah is "abolished" or eliminated, "not one letter, not one stroke of a letter" (Matt 5:17-19), and yet Jesus brings everything into a new light once again: the light of his freedom and reason, his radicality and reverence for God.

First Testament or Old Testament?

This chapter began with some statements about the concept of the "Old Testament." As I said there, Jesus did not know an "Old Testament" but only the Sacred Scriptures: the Torah, the prophets, and the "writings." Is it permitted for Christians to speak of a "New Testament" and in the same breath degrade Jesus' Bible to the status of an "Old" Testament?

Probably everyone senses how easy it is to misunderstand this nomenclature and how dangerous it is to do so. It appears, in fact, that there must be a testament composed at some point that has been replaced by a *new* testament. In our legal dealings that is how it goes: a new testament (or "will") normally invalidates one that is older, written earlier.

As a consequence, the recently deceased German Old Testament scholar Erich Zenger adopted an idea from the United States and spoke no longer of an "Old Testament" but rather of the "First Testament."[23] In doing so he could even appeal to Hebrews 8:7, 13; 9:1, 15, 18. But that does not solve the problem. Since the word "testament" today calls to mind "last will and testament," even this choice of words gives many people the impression that the "First Testament" has been invalidated by a second one produced later. At the same time, "old" and "new" are terms of relationship that raise the question: to what extent is the "new" one new and the "old" one old? Besides, "old" need not necessarily be associated with "aged" or "outdated." "Old" can also be understood in the sense of "honorable" and "precious." In any case, in the ancient Near East and in antiquity "old" had positive connotations for the most part. So the problem remains, and we cannot escape the dilemma through simple renaming.

There is probably also little sense in simply tossing away respected concepts that go back to the Bible itself (cf. 2 Cor 3:14). We must keep the concepts but repeatedly clarify them anew. After all we have seen, it is obvious that "Old Testament" cannot mean something that needs improvement, or is outdated, or should be disposed of. No, the Old Testament is the basis of Christian faith, just as it was the basis for Jesus' activity, and the New Testament is nothing but the final level of interpretation, the last thorough clarification of the Bible.

Those who want to approach that clarification cannot avoid once again taking the path on which Israel was led. They believe with Abraham. They dare the Exodus from the old society. They travel with Israel through the wilderness. They stand before the fire at Sinai and receive the commandment. They must decide whether to malign the promised land or believe God's promise. They must praise, thank, petition, cry out to, and sometimes almost despair of Israel's God in the Psalms. They must accompany Israel once again on the whole of its long journey if they are in any way to arrive at the clarification that opens up and explains everything, to understand it and be able to live it.

This last, fully valid, clear interpretation took place not only in words, not only through theology, not only by means of new formulae that, we might say, set the Old Testament to rights. This clarification took place through the person of Jesus himself, his existence, his life, and his death. The words of the letter to the Hebrews are definitive and unsurpassable in this regard: "Long ago God spoke to our ancestors in many and various ways by the prophets, but in these last days he has spoken to us by a Son" (Heb 1:1-2).

Chapter 12

Jesus and the Torah

Around the year 165, the philosopher and theologian Justin was executed in Rome, by the Roman state, because of his Christian faith.[1] He came from Neapolis (today's Nablus) in Samaria, became a Christian, and was then a renowned theologian of the second century. In addition to a long *Apology*, a petition in personal law to the imperial chancery,[2] we also have the record, written in dialogue form, of his argument with Judaism, the *Dialogue with the Jew Trypho*. There Justin writes:

> For the law promulgated on Horeb is now old, and belongs to yourselves [the Jews] alone; but *this* is for all universally. Now, law placed against law has abrogated that which is before it, and a covenant which comes after in like manner has put an end to the previous one; and an eternal and final law—namely, Christ—has been given to us, and the covenant is trustworthy, after which there shall be no law, no commandment, no ordinance.[3]

This text summarizes well what Justin also says in other parts of the *Dialogue*: the Torah has lost its legal authority. In juridical terms it is abrogated. Nothing in it remains valid except what corresponds to the natural law of reason, for example, its moral demands. Also valid are its constant, often mysteriously hidden, references to Christ. But as law, the Torah has no further significance because "a new lawgiver" has come:

Jesus Christ. He has given a "new," an "eternal law." But he is not only a "lawgiver"; he himself is in person this new and eternal law.[4]

There is no question that in this theology we can already see what in time to come would be formulated more and more radically, more and more effectively, and more and more ominously: the "disowning" of Israel in salvation history. In every respect, in this view, Israel has been replaced by the church.

But it is also unquestionable that Justin tried in his own way to take the New Testament seriously. Does not Jesus appear in Matthew's Sermon on the Mount as the new Moses and thus the new lawgiver who proclaims his new Torah to the disciples and the people gathered around them? That is how it seems. After all, does the Jesus of the Sermon on the Mount not say "you have heard that it was said to those of ancient times . . . But I say to you . . ." (Matt 5:21-22, 33-34)? And does Paul not speak of the "law of Christ" in Galatians 6:2? And does Jesus not tell the disciples in the Gospel of John "I give you a new commandment" (John 13:34)? In any case, talk of the "new law of Christ" seems to have been just as common in the church of the subsequent years as the idea of the "new people of God," which was so perilously subject to misunderstanding.[5]

Therefore this chapter addresses one of the most important questions about Jesus' life: what was his attitude to the Torah? Did he come as a new lawgiver? Did he drain the Torah of its legal authority? Did he see himself as master of the Torah, or even as the one who would overthrow it? Or did he hold up the Torah precisely because he did not come to abolish it but to fulfill it? That, at any rate, is what it says in Matthew 5:17. A great deal depends on Jesus' relationship to the Torah, ultimately the relationship between the church and Israel. This chapter, therefore, is one of the most important in this book. I will proceed as I did in chapter 11 by attempting to clarify this difficult set of questions through a number of samplings.

The Twofold Commandment

According to Matthew 22:34-36, a scribe once asked Jesus which commandment in the Torah was the "greatest," that is, the primary commandment.[6] What the scribe asks is not altogether new; it was something that was commonly being asked in different ways in Jesus' time. It was the search for the center of the Torah—or the effort to summarize the Torah in brief. It was in no way about a disqualification or nonobservance of the other commandments but was primarily about didactics and the correct understanding of the whole Torah. Jesus answers the scribe's question:

> "You shall love the Lord your God with all your heart, and with all your soul, and with all your mind." This is the greatest and first commandment. And a second is like it: "You shall love your neighbor as yourself." (Matt 22:37-39)

This coupling of love of God and love of neighbor became more or less a matter of course in and through the New Testament, for Christians at any rate. But we need to pay attention to what has happened here: two commandments that in the first place have nothing to do with one another and are widely separated in the Torah have now been brought together and are, in fact, inextricably bound up with each other.

"You shall love the LORD your God" (Deut 6:4) was the second sentence in the *shema*, the "Hear, O Israel." This confession of God's unity was probably already being recited daily in Judaism in Jesus' time. It formulates the traditional center of the Torah,[7] namely, the commandment to serve YHWH alone and follow no foreign gods, indeed, not only to serve YHWH but to make YHWH the absolute center of one's life. In short, it was nothing other than a commentary on the first commandment of the Decalogue.

"You shall love your neighbor as yourself" is in the book of Leviticus within the so-called holiness code (Lev 17:1–26:46), where we read:

> You shall not hate in your heart anyone of your kin; you shall reprove your neighbor, or you will incur guilt yourself. You shall not take vengeance or bear a grudge against any of your people, but you shall love your neighbor as yourself; I am the LORD. (Lev 19:17-18)

"Anyone of your kin," "neighbor," "any of your people" here all mean the same thing. The reference is not primarily to one's physical relations but to fellow believers among the people of God.[8] One should be as intensively concerned for one's brothers and sisters in the faith of Israel and care as much for them as for one's own family. The latter, in fact, is what is meant by "as yourself," which is commonly misunderstood in an individualistic sense. The solidarity of the immediate family is thus expanded into a solidarity with every member of the people of God. This is evident again, a little later, in Leviticus 19:33-34, where that solidarity is again expanded to include resident aliens living in the land: in our terms, migrant workers or even the undocumented who work among us.

> When an alien resides with you in your land, you shall not oppress the alien. The alien who resides with you shall be to you as the citizen among you; you shall love the alien as yourself, for you were aliens in the land of Egypt: I am the LORD your God.

This, then, is what the holiness code means by "love of neighbor": practical solidarity within the people of God, a solidarity that respects and supports everyone in Israel, including aliens, just as one would do for the members of one's own family. What is absent from the holiness code is the still further expansion of the love commandment to the foreigners whom Israelites encounter as "traveling through" their land. For them the ethic is not that of love but the longstanding and very exalted "ethics of hospitality" traditional in the Near East. If necessary, one was required to protect and defend a guest with one's own life.

What was Jesus doing when he linked together the primary commandment from Deuteronomy 6 and the commandment of love of neighbor in Leviticus 19? First of all, we must be assured that in this he is acting well within the Torah. He is not proclaiming a "new commandment." He is most certainly not issuing a "new Torah." All that was already in existence. What is new with Jesus is the tight linkage between Deuteronomy 6 and Leviticus 19, the love of God and the love of neighbor. But even that linking was not altogether new. It was already beginning in Judaism at that time, it was in the air; everything was heading in that direction.[9] Of course, we cannot point to an explicit combination of quotations from Deuteronomy 6:5 and Leviticus 19:18 in the time before Jesus. We must consider the possibility that ultimately it was Jesus' deep understanding that created the linkage.

But did Jesus not understand what was already written in a completely new way, namely, as relieved of its limitations and now applying in principle to all people and not merely to all those in Israel? Here again we should take a closer look. In the letters of John, love of neighbor clearly means love for one another, that is, for sisters and brothers within the church (1 John 3:10-14; 4:20). For Paul as well, *agapē*, mutual love, has its proper place within the communities. This is quite obvious in Romans 12:9-21. As for "all people," here Paul is more inclined to speak of "keeping peace" and "doing good" (cf. Rom 12:17, 21; Gal 6:10; 1 Thess 5:15).

Did the New Testament authors misunderstand Jesus? Apparently not, for Jesus himself does not speak about love of neighbor in general, without any reference to place. We must read the texts in which he extends love of neighbor even to enemies with great attention. Then we will see that he is speaking not of those most distant, but of those who are closest, those whom his audience will encounter within Israel:

> . . . if anyone strikes you on the cheek
> . . . if anyone takes away your coat
> . . . if anyone forces you to go one mile

Offering the other cheek as well (Luke 6:29), giving one's shirt as well as the coat (Luke 6:29), carrying a Roman legionary's pack *two* miles instead of *one* (Matt 5:41)—all that assumes immediate contact. In contrast to the Stoics, Jesus never spoke of "universal love." He was interested in what happens within the people of God—corresponding precisely to Leviticus 19:17-18.

It is true that for Jesus too love has no boundaries because it must equal the love of the heavenly Father, who is gracious even to the ungrateful and the wicked (Luke 6:35 // Matt 5:45). But it has a place where it is at home and where when necessary it crosses the boundaries that may come into being. In this Jesus remains entirely in accord with the Old Testament: love is something concrete. It does not dissipate into universal love but remains tied to the real place of the "community of Israel." There it is to be made real, even toward strangers, and from there it constantly replenishes its strength.

Love of Enemies

But surely Jesus' command to love enemies went far beyond all the prescriptions for Israel and in the Torah? Let us look closely once more! The most important text for the command to love enemies in the context of what we are discussing is Luke 6:27-30:[10]

> Love your enemies, do good to those who hate you, bless those who curse you, pray for those who abuse you. If anyone strikes you on the cheek, offer the other also; and from anyone who takes away your coat do not withhold even your shirt. Give to everyone who begs from you; and if anyone takes away your goods, do not ask for them again.

Here and in the following verses we find a composition by Luke, part of the so-called Sermon on the Plain. Luke was making use of a collection of applicable sayings of Jesus that he found in the Sayings Source (cf. Matt 5:38-48). We can see from Luke 6:27-30 how categorically Jesus was capable of speaking. In the sentences quoted, he does not deal with difficulties, conditions, or particular circumstances. He speaks radically, that is, he gets to the root. Therefore the quoted sentences are not formulae to be applied like recipes. They cannot simply be reduced to an ethical system; they are an unwieldy instrument for casuistry.

So, must I give to everyone who asks of me? Jesus would have spoken that demand with an eye to the situation in Israel, where small farmers and day laborers repeatedly needed help from their neighbors or fellow believers to cope with failed harvests or in times of unemployment. For us too the words "give to everyone who begs from you" have not lost their meaning, but they cannot be applied mechanically. Should a mother going through the supermarket with her child fulfill all the wishes that are created there in the most subtle and well-thought-out ways? She would be exercising hatred for her child if she bought it everything it wants and begs its mother to give it.

The same is true of all the other statements about love of neighbor and of enemies. They cannot and must not be used as if they were operating instructions, to be applied mechanically. Rather, we need to keep in mind that biblical statements of this kind have a basis in which they are rooted, namely, the people of God. The continual parade of false interpretations of Matthew's Sermon on the Mount and/or Luke's Sermon on the Plain almost all derive from a failure to pay attention to that grounding, that basis supporting the whole.[11]

Because the biblical reality of the people of God was completely foreign to ancient religions, so also the biblical idea of love of neighbor, and certainly that of love of enemies, was equally a stranger to them.[12] In 1989 Mary W. Blundell, a professor of classical philology, published a book titled *Helping Friends and Harming Enemies*, in which she shows that "Greek popular thought is pervaded by the assumption that one should help one's friends and harm one's enemies. These fundamental principles surface continually from Homer onwards and survive well into the Roman period."[13] That states the essential. Blundell reaches her conclusions based on her outstanding knowledge of the ancient world. She brings together a multitude of textual witnesses, and these repeatedly testify that one should love one's friends, help them, lend to them. Of course, the basic principle of balanced mutuality must rule. The Greek poet Hesiod (eighth c. BCE) expresses it this way: "Be friends with the friendly, and visit him who visits you. Give to one who gives, but do not give to one who does not give."[14]

In Luke 6:32-36, the continuation of the part of the Sermon on the Plain I cited above, we find just the opposite. Here the principle of ethical mutuality that Hesiod formulates so elegantly is carried *ad absurdum*. How? Hesiod's principle completely ignores who God is and how God acts, and so it must also be ignorant of the reality of the people of God,[15] for the rule here is:

> If you love those who love you, what credit is that to you? For even sinners love those who love them. If you do good to those who do good to you, what credit is that to you? For even sinners do the same. If you lend to those from whom you hope to receive, what credit is that to you? Even sinners lend to sinners, to receive as much again. But love your enemies, do good, and lend, expecting nothing in return. Your reward will be great, and you will be children of the Most High; for he is kind to the ungrateful and the wicked. Be merciful, just as your Father is merciful. (Luke 6:32-36)

"What credit is that to you?" The translation is unhelpful. In this passage in the Greek we find *charis* three times. What it means is: if you have already mutually lent and paid back, what "reward" or "thanks" do you expect from God? But *charis* is also, and primarily, "charm," "beauty," "grace." If everything depends solely on precisely calculated mutuality, on "you help me, then I'll help you," the world is not only devoid of grace, it lacks any kind of charm or beauty. But in the company of the people of God there is supposed to be the beauty of freedom and complete undeserving. The people of God should reflect God's graciousness.

The ancient world thought differently: one was reasonably expected to give only where one received, and it was perfectly all right to hate one's enemies. In fact, one should do them harm whenever possible. So, for example, Meno, in Plato's dialogue with that name, is supposed to have been asked by Socrates about the specific virtues of a man. He replies, "This is a man's virtue: to be able to manage public business, and in doing it to help friends and hurt enemies, and to take care to keep clear of such mischief himself."[16] And one last example: the Greek poet Archilochos (seventh c. BCE) writes, "I know how to love those who love me, how to hate. My enemies I overwhelm with abuse."[17]

That is, in fact, how the majority of ancient society saw things. This was the normal, usual, commonsense attitude. Plato was one of the few who disrupted that line of thinking. In the very first book of his great work on the state, through the mouth of Socrates, he picks apart the basic premise that it is justice to do good to friends and evil to enemies, to love those who deserve it and hate those who are wicked.[18] And in the dialogue *Crito*, again through the mouth of Socrates, he proposes as a basic principle that no one may do injustice under any circumstances. It is true that most people (!) believe that someone to whom injustice has been done is entitled to do injustice in return. But no, one may not slander in return, one may not mistreat someone in return, not even when it has been done to oneself.[19]

It was not until the Roman Stoics that these basic principles proposed by Plato were again taken up—especially by Musonius, Seneca, Epictetus, and Marcus Aurelius. Seneca (d. 65 CE) warns to answer evil not with evil but instead with good. He gives as a reason: "If . . . you wish to imitate the gods, then bestow benefits upon the ungrateful as well as the grateful; for the sun rises upon the wicked as well as the good, the seas are open even to pirates."[20] Seneca is very close to the Sermon on the Mount here. But such thinking remained an exception in antiquity, and the Stoics themselves usually gave other reasons for their aversion to hatred. For example, they reflected on whether it was good for the human being to hate and to get angry. Perhaps it was contrary to the dignity of one's own person, and it could also be that it was not beneficial to the soul's tranquility.

That was certainly not stupid, but such reasoning is worlds removed from Jesus. His challenge to love of enemies was for him the consequence of the reign of God, now coming to pass. It was a consequence of the love with which God loves the world and of God's will to transform the world.

So we should not underestimate the breakthroughs regarding the thought patterns of antiquity accomplished by Plato and the Stoics. But at the same time we must see clearly what was commonplace and widely held at the time. Only then can we ask: where did Jesus get his idea about love of enemies that confronts us with such elementary force in the Sermon on the Mount? Is he not, at least in the case of love of enemies, going far beyond the Torah?

Apparently not. For the holiness code, where it speaks of love for one's "brother/sister," for one's "kin," and for one's "neighbor," includes the enemy as a matter of course. It is said that "you shall not hate in your heart anyone of your kin. . . . You shall not take vengeance or bear a grudge against any of your people" (Lev 19:17, 18). The person against whom one bears hatred in one's heart is one's enemy. And the one against whom one seeks vengeance is one's enemy. But even the enemy in Israel is a "brother/sister," is "kin," and therefore there can be no hatred against him or her. So the commandment to love one's neighbor in Leviticus 19 includes the enemy. But the Torah says it much more clearly in another place: within the still older "book of the covenant" incorporated in the book of Exodus (Exod 21:1–23:33) there is a very explicit commandment about how to behave toward one's enemies:

> When you come upon your enemy's ox or donkey going astray, you shall bring it back. When you see the donkey of one who hates you lying under its burden and you would hold back from setting it free, you must help [your enemy] to set it free. (Exod 23:4-5)

Two examples are given here, and the cases are chosen in such a way that the second is an expansion of the first. In the first case, just bringing back a strayed ox or donkey takes time and goes against the grain for the finder. One could simply let the animal go on straying and so injure one's enemy. But one is not allowed to want to hurt him or her. One must help. In the second case, there is significantly more at stake than simply bringing an animal back. Here, it is a question of cooperation: two have to work together to raise the donkey to its feet and distribute the heavy load better. And this you must do together with the person who hates you—what a task of overcoming one's own self is presented here! But it could also be a step toward reconciliation.[21]

The word "love" does not appear in this text, but in its substance it quite clearly speaks of what love means. Love in the Bible is not primarily deep feeling and upwelling emotion but effective help. When, in the parable in Luke 10:30-35, the Samaritan raises up the robbery victim, pours oil and wine on his wounds and bandages them, brings him to an inn, pays the owner and assures him that he will make good on any additional costs, Jesus is describing exactly what he thinks of as love. Exodus 23:4-5 does the same.

Even as concerns love of enemies Jesus thus thinks and speaks entirely in terms of the Torah. He interprets it. He brings its scattered parts together. He thinks through "loving God" and "loving neighbor" to their utmost consequences. Precisely on the basis of the Torah he knows who God is and how, therefore, people in Israel ought to be also.

Certainly it was not a matter of course to read the Old Testament that way, because there are other voices to be found there as well. It can indeed speak of hatred and do so with elemental rage. In Psalm 139—to take only one example—we read:

> Do I not hate those who hate you, O LORD?
> And do I not loathe those who rise up against you?
> I hate them with perfect hatred;
> I count them my enemies. (Ps 139:21-22)

We could say a great deal about this extract from a much longer psalm text. It is not about private quarrels and enmity. The one praying experiences how the people of God are being destroyed by "men of blood" (v. 19) who themselves are Israelites, and he or she wants to stand on God's side. But above all we may not overlook the "prayer dynamic" of the psalm.[22] The speaker has already asserted that she or he can never truly grasp God's thoughts (vv. 17-18) and in the end begs God to test him or her and point out the way she or he should go (vv. 23-24).

And yet, at a later time people read Psalm 139:21-22 with some justification as a call to separation from and hatred toward God's enemies. Anyone who entered the Qumran community had to swear "to love everything that [God] selects, and to hate everything that he rejects" (1 QS 1, 3-4), "to love all the [children] of light" and "to detest all the [children] of darkness" (1 QS 1, 9-10). It was forbidden to hate any member of the community (1 QS 5, 26), but one must nourish "everlasting hatred for the men of the pit" (1 QS 9, 21-22). The children of light are the members of the Qumran community, the children of darkness everyone else. That is how some people in Jesus' time interpreted the Bible.

Only against the background of these voices can we clearly see the certainty, clarity, and absolute conviction with which Jesus understood Leviticus 19:18 at its heart and uncovered the whole import of that text: love of neighbor includes the enemy and precisely in its treatment of the enemy demonstrates itself as genuine love.

But Jesus not only taught love of enemies; he lived it in his behavior toward those who in his time were excluded and socially stigmatized: in his attitude toward the "tax collectors and sinners" (Luke 7:34), the "toll collectors and prostitutes" (Matt 21:31), the "thieves, rogues, and adulterers" (Luke 18:11). People in Israel at that time felt themselves morally superior to such types. They were despised in the name of God; people avoided them and as far as possible shunned social contact with them. Jesus did the opposite and so made them his "neighbors."[23]

Anger Is Forbidden

The antitheses in the Sermon on the Mount are especially important for the question of Jesus' attitude toward the Torah; hence, our next sample will concern the first of those antitheses.[24] It begins as follows:

> You have heard that it was said to those of ancient times, "You shall not murder"; and "whoever murders shall be liable to judgment." But I say to you that if you are [merely] angry with a brother or sister, you will be liable to judgment. (Matt 5:21-22a)

The thesis that precedes the antithesis is clear. "Those of ancient times" are the Israelites who received the Torah at Sinai. To that generation, and thus to all of Israel, "it was said. . . ." The passive construction is used at this point to avoid employing the name "God." What it means is that God said to Israel, when proclaiming the Torah at Sinai, "You shall not murder." This is a word-for-word quotation of the prohibition of murder in Exodus 20:13, with the addition of "whoever murders shall be liable to judgment." There is nothing more said about what will then happen to the murderer on trial, since that is obvious. One who murders another human being is punished with death (cf., e.g., Lev 24:17). That is the thesis. Jesus is only reminding his hearers of what was known to every Jew of his time.

But now comes his antithesis: "But I say to you." This "but I" is uncanny, because if God has already spoken, then "but I" can only mean: "Now I am speaking with the same authority with which God formerly spoke. I am speaking in the role and in the place of God."

And what does Jesus say? What does he proclaim with the same authority once exercised by God at Sinai? He says that bitterness against one's brother or sister, that is, against one's fellow believer among the people of God, is the same thing as murder. Just as a murderer is brought to judgment and then punished with death, so will anyone who is merely angry at the fellow believer be brought to judgment and punished with death.

Given the way the antithesis is laid out, the anger against the fellow believer can, naturally, only be an internal emotion, anger in the heart, cold rage against the other—that is, something that would never bring anyone before the judge because it is not justiciable. Otherwise, the antithesis would not function.[25] Jesus is saying: "God has ordered that for murder one must be brought to judgment. But I am now decreeing that one must be brought to judgment even for holding anger in one's heart." It had to be clear to every hearer, at least after the initial shock, that while Jesus is formulating his words as a legal decree (if someone does such-and-such, then this and that will follow), in reality he is using that form only to uncover what it means to be angry with a fellow believer. It is like murder.

This play of language, sharpened to the utmost, is characteristic of Jesus. He can use imagery that is scarcely bearable, such as that of a beam in the eye (Matt 7:3), of tearing out one's own eye (Matt 5:29), of swallowing a camel (Matt 23:24). But he can also play with rhetorical genres to provoke or, better, to bring his hearers to insights they constantly repress. In our case this is the recognition that the deep division in the people of God that prevents them from becoming a sign for the world begins with anger against the sister or brother. No, it does not merely begin there; when anger is present, destruction is already at hand. Internal bitterness is murder of the sister or brother, murder of the people of God.

What was Jesus doing with this antithetical speech in Matthew 5:21-22? Did he abolish the Torah, or the fifth commandment of the Decalogue? By no means! Did he replace the Torah with a new commandment? Not that either! He left the fifth commandment as it stands, irreplaceable and unconditionally necessary. But he grasped it down to its roots. Murder begins in the heart and the head. It begins with anger.

And now the crucial point: this working out of the root of the fifth commandment happens already in the Torah itself. It is nothing new. When Cain was envious of his brother, when his anger boiled over and his face sank to the ground, God said to him, "If you do well, can you not look up? And if you do not do well, sin is lurking at the door; its desire is for you, but you must master it" (Gen 4:7).[26] This assumes that murder begins in the mind. Outwardly Cain had not yet done anything. But he is already on the point of murdering his brother. The evil intent is working in him. Sin is already threatening.

Human judges cannot govern thoughts; they are not justiciable. But before God the human being is a single unit, irreducible, indivisible. Therefore, one is to love God with the whole heart, soul, and strength (Deut 6:4). The trinity of "heart, soul, and strength" encompasses everything that is human: from the heart, the innermost sphere of the human, through the realm of communication ("soul" in Hebrew = "throat," "speech"), to the external, material sphere that surrounds us ("strength" in Hebrew = "ability," "property"). It is as this all-encompassing, indivisible unity that a human being is to love God.

No one can honor God externally while remaining far from God in one's heart. In essence Jesus did nothing in the first antithesis of the Sermon on the Mount but set before the eyes of his audience this basic knowledge of the Torah about the indivisibility of the human. Certainly in doing so he was being provocative and speaking with the utmost radicality. But for him it was about the Torah of Sinai.

Divorce Is Forbidden

In very similar fashion Jesus provokes his audience in the third antithesis of the Sermon on the Mount. The antithesis form is secondary here.[27] Also, the clause that permits divorce in the case of adultery was added by Matthew or the tradition before him. Originally the prohibition of divorce was probably worded something like this: "Anyone who divorces his wife causes her to commit adultery, and whoever marries a divorced woman commits adultery" (Matt 5:32).[28]

What is he saying? We can only understand it if we are familiar with divorce law in Palestinian Judaism. Divorce was permitted—for the man. He was allowed to divorce his wife by appealing to Deuteronomy 24:1, should it be that "she does not please him because he finds something objectionable about her." In light of that very loose formula it was relatively easy for a man, at least as far as the law was concerned, to dissolve his marriage to his wife. He only had to utter the formula of divorce, "You are no longer my wife, and I am no longer your husband,"[29] and hand her the writ of divorce. The marriage was at an end. But only the husband could do it. A wife could not dismiss her husband from their marriage.

Other parts of Palestinian-Jewish marriage law based on the Torah also show how unequally the wife was treated under the law. Thus a man who had intercourse with another woman by no means violated his own marriage; at most, if the other woman was married, he committed adultery against her husband. It was a different matter for the wife! In committing adultery she violated her own marriage. Here it is quite clear that the wife was not regarded as a partner but as part of her husband's property; he had an almost material right to treat her as he wanted. By committing adultery a wife diminished her husband's property; he, in contrast, by committing adultery could at most diminish the value of another man's property.

Only when we consider this social background can we understand why Jesus formulates his prohibition of divorce altogether in terms of the husband. The wife had no right in any case to divorce her husband, so Jesus speaks to the man. He puts this before his eyes: anyone who divorces his wife may force her to seek another husband because otherwise she cannot exist economically. So with the new husband she violates her first marriage, and her first husband is guilty of it because, in sending her away, he has driven her into that situation. But the new husband is also committing adultery, namely, against the first marriage from which the wife had been dismissed. To us the prohibition of divorce in its Matthean version seems extremely complicated and awkward, but Jesus had to speak that way against the background of the Palestinian-Jewish marriage law then in force. But this is by no means an adequate explanation of Jesus' harsh prohibition.

We first have to be clear about what it means for Jesus to declare that divorcing a wife or marrying a divorced woman is adultery. According to the Torah, adultery was a capital crime deserving punishment, in fact, the penalty of death (Lev 20:10; Deut 22:22-27). But that means that Jesus calls something the Torah presumes permissible a capital crime. That was, obviously, a massive provocation.

But the provocation was all the greater because Jesus clothes what he says about divorce in the form of a legal decree. There are such decrees in the Torah, with the form "Anyone who does X shall be held guilty of Y" (e.g., Lev 17:3-4; Num 35:16-21). In legal statements of this sort the first clause is the "definition of the deed" and the subsequent clause is the "determination of the legal consequences." Jesus' prohibition of divorce follows this model exactly. First, in the initial clause, the action is defined: "Anyone who divorces his wife. . . ." In the subsequent clause this action is further defined as a serious sin, namely, causing adultery: ". . . causes her to commit adultery." In this case the "determination of the legal consequences" need not be articulated because everyone knew it: if adultery was proved, the punishment was death by stoning.

So Jesus uses a legal degree as provocation. But does he really intend to establish a law? Certainly not. He is not making law here any more than he is when he says "If you are angry with a brother or sister you are liable to judgment." The intention of his words is to shake people up, to uncover the truth, to show up the falsity of the divorce practice of his time. It is true that he plays on the form of legal decrees, but *not* in order to give a new law; rather, he means to carry his contemporaries' practice *ad absurdum*.

And what is Jesus' attitude to the Torah in this instance? Is he destroying it? Is he declaring it invalid, at least on the question of divorce? Is there a concrete point at which he shows how questionable it is for him?

None of these questions does justice to Jesus' true intent. First of all, we must point out that the Torah contains no specific law that permits divorce. Deuteronomy 24:1-4 forbids any man to remarry a woman previously his wife whom he has divorced and who has then married another man. The procedure for divorce through the giving of a writ appears rather incidentally, namely, as background to the whole legal problem. The process is thus assumed as the normal course of things. So Jesus does not speak against an ordinance, certainly not a commandment in Torah, but instead against the old common law to which the Torah does not object.

Moreover, Jesus appeals, against this common law, to the true will of God—in fact, and this is crucial, to the will of God as expressed at the very beginning of the Torah. This we see in Mark 10:2-12, where Jesus refers to Genesis 1:27 and 2:24:

> But from the beginning of creation, "God made them male and female." "For this reason a man shall leave his father and mother and be joined to his wife, and the two shall become one flesh." So they are no longer two, but one flesh. Therefore what God has joined together, let no one separate. (Mark 10:6-9)

According to Mark 10, then, Jesus appeals to the Torah itself against a common law the Torah presupposes. He appeals to the creation story, which is part of the Torah. He appeals to the deep, inseparable unity there promised to the two marriage partners.

This should make it clear that Jesus' prohibition of divorce is not directed against the Torah as such but instead clarifies a particular point of Torah. With his provocative statement, clothed in legal language, he extends protection to the wife who is handed over to the man's whim and degraded to the status of a thing, and he also protects the true will of God, whose original purpose, obscured by common law, is no longer perceptible.

Jesus against the Fourth Commandment?

The next sample belongs to a completely different part of the Jesus tradition. Matthew and Luke (Matt 8:21-22 // Luke 9:59-60) both offer a saying of Jesus that calls for discipleship with the utmost harshness. In Luke's version it reads, "To another he said, 'Follow me.' But he said, 'Lord, first let me go and bury my father.' But Jesus said to him, 'Let the dead bury their own dead; but as for you, go and proclaim the [reign] of God.'" Today we can only be shocked by the irresponsibility of the saying, but at that time it must have had a far more dreadful and disgusting impact on the hearers, for throughout antiquity, and especially in Judaism, it was an obvious and positively sacred obligation of a son to bury his parents with honor. Still more, in Judaism it was not merely a pious duty; it was ordered by the fourth commandment of the Decalogue.

That commandment is addressed to adults. It commanded adult sons, in particular, to attend to their elderly parents, to treat them with respect, to see that they are properly cared for and socially secure, and in the end to bury them respectfully and honorably. Tobit 4:3-5 illuminates this very concrete content of the commandment quite well:

> [Tobit says to his son Tobias] "My son, when I die, give me a proper burial. Honor your mother and do not abandon her all the days of her life. Do whatever pleases her, and do not grieve her in anything. Remember her, my son, because she faced many dangers for you while you were in her womb. And when she dies, bury her beside me in the same grave. Revere the LORD all your days, my son, and refuse to sin or to transgress his commandments."

Evidently the fourth commandment was urgently necessary for this purpose. The Torah, and the Old Testament Wisdom literature, both reveal that it repeatedly happened that weak and vulnerable parents were taunted by their sons (Prov 30:17), cursed (Exod 21:17), beaten (Exod 21:15), robbed (Prov 28:24), mistreated (Prov 19:26), and even driven from their own property (Prov 19:26). Such excesses were, of course, also related to the fact that in Israel, as throughout the ancient Near East, the father of a family possessed a power over his children that is unimaginable to us; it could not fail to provoke a reaction. Add to this that in Israel the security given to aged parents by the cult of the ancestors was a thing of the past. For that very reason, the fourth commandment of the Decalogue fulfilled an extraordinarily important social function.[30] Its role was completely different from the one it serves nowadays, when it is mainly addressed to young children who are supposed to behave well and be obedient to their parents.

When Jesus says to someone who wants first to go home and bury his father, "let the dead bury their own dead!" it must have been very disturbing to those who heard him. It was fundamentally scandalous to them. The theologian and Judaism scholar Martin Hengel (1926–2009) remarks on Luke 9:60:

> There is hardly one logion of Jesus which more sharply runs counter to law, piety and custom than does Mt 8.22 = Lk 9.60a, the more so as here we cannot justify the overriding of these in the interests of humanitarian freedom, higher morality, greater religious intensity or even "neighbourliness." The saying is completely incompatible with the old liberal picture of Jesus and with more modern attempts to resuscitate this.[31]

So does Jesus speak "counter to" the fourth commandment in this harsh saying, and thus against the Torah? Does he override the Torah, at least on this one important point? I most certainly would not say that, for in other places, such as Mark 7:9-13, Jesus can just as emphatically and uncompromisingly defend the rights of parents against their impious children.[32]

Jesus always looks at the individual case. He sees it precisely as it is. He considers each instance for its own sake. He possesses an unimaginable feeling for what God's cause demands in each case and where God's will is being avoided and twisted into its opposite, even when that takes place under the cover of devotion to the Law.

For Jesus, that the man who first wanted to bury his father or be beside him in his last days should instead follow him immediately was more important than the fourth commandment. The reign of God, now arriving, surpasses everything in its urgency and shoves it into second place. The advancing reign of God leaves no more time for anything else. Therefore Jesus' disciples have to divest themselves of all familial considerations and ties.

Jesus' intent here is neither to offend against the Torah nor to abrogate it; he is simply concerned with the more important and urgent matter *within* the Torah. The fourth commandment is not eliminated, but in a particular concrete instance it is subordinated to the first commandment. We have already seen that for Jesus the coming of the reign of God is nothing but the eschatological historicization and making present of what the first commandment intends (cf. chap. 11 above).

Jesus against the Third Commandment?

The case is similar with regard to the Sabbath question, much discussed among scholars. The gospels offer us a whole series of texts in which Jesus appears to offend against the third commandment by healing on the Sabbath or allowing his disciples to break the Sabbath command-ment. More precisely, these appear to be offenses against the third com-mandment as it was interpreted in his time by important groups within Judaism. The following texts are relevant:

- the man with the withered hand (Mark 3:1-6)
- the bent-over woman (Luke 13:10-17)
- the man with dropsy (Luke 14:1-6)
- the lame man at the pool of Beth-zatha (John 5:1-18)
- the man born blind (John 9:1-41)
- plucking grain on the Sabbath (Mark 2:23-28)

It would not make much sense here to go into the details of how healing on the Sabbath was regarded in Jesus' time by the various groups within Israel—especially the Qumran community and the Pharisaic groups. It is evident that on particular occasions Jesus offended against the casuistic rules of these groups. The question is only whether his intention in doing so was to flout the third commandment, or even to abolish it.

Obviously not! The answer here must be exactly the same as in the case of the fourth commandment that presented itself in connection with Luke 9:59-60. For Jesus the first commandment is the absolute center of his thought and action, together with what that commandment wants to emphasize: the absolute uniqueness and preeminence of God over everything else, realized for Jesus in the reign of God now dawning. Therefore Jesus had to heal sick people even on the Sabbath, and there-fore he could not delay the healing until the next day, because the reign of God is advancing rapidly, and that people in Israel are made whole is precisely a sign of the reign of God now becoming reality. With his Sabbath healings Jesus does not abolish the third commandment, but he gives greater weight in these cases to the first commandment.

It cannot be objected against this interpretation that in the texts men-tioned Jesus never gives the approaching reign of God as a reason for his offenses against the Pharisees' interpretation of the Torah, because if we look more closely we can see that this reasoning is actually present. Luke 13:10-17 tells of the healing of a woman whose back has been bent for eighteen years, so that she can no longer stand up straight. Jesus heals the woman on the Sabbath, and in the synagogue to boot. The leader of the synagogue becomes indignant at this and says to those present, "There are six days on which work ought to be done; come on those days and be cured, and not on the sabbath day" (Luke 13:14). The fact that a bent woman has been healed is to him a minor matter compared to the offense against the Sabbath. Healing is work, and no work may be done on the Sabbath. There are six other days in the week for therapeutic actions.

How does Jesus justify himself? He calls this form of interpretation of the biblical Sabbath commandment pure hypocrisy, since, after all, those attending the synagogue untie their household animals from their stanchions on the Sabbath and lead them to water. That is, they untie knots, they release animals—and yet he should not be allowed to free a poor woman who has been fettered and tied down by Satan for many years? Thus the point of comparison is not leading to water but untying knots.[33] Jesus answers the legal casuistry that clings to words with a skillful counter-casuistry: "And ought not this woman, a daughter of Abraham whom Satan bound for eighteen long years, be set free from this bondage on the sabbath day?" (Luke 13:16).

But Jesus does more than simply reveal the contradictions in the casuistic interpretation of the Law. His own argument goes much deeper. He calls the woman "a daughter of Abraham." That is: she is part of the chosen people of God, a representative of Israel. As such she has been bound by Satan for eighteen years, and as such she is now freed from her bonds. No, she is not only freed, she "must" be set free. The phrase "reign of God" is not spoken, but it is quite obvious that it is precisely what is at stake here: the reign of God is happening now, God is becoming Lord in Israel now, Satan is being bound now, and now the people in Israel are being freed from the fetters with which they have been held bound. It is Jesus himself who forces his way into the "house of the strong man" and binds him (Matt 12:29). If we look closely we see that Jesus' Sabbath healings have a great deal to do with his proclamation of the reign of God. God will now become Lord in Israel once and for all, and the spread of the reign of God cannot be delayed for any reason.

We also need to ask ourselves why Jesus' disciples were plucking and eating ears of grain on the Sabbath, of all days. Obviously it was because they were hungry (cf. Mark 2:25). And why? Is not the background here the insecurity of Jesus' and his disciples' itinerant existence in service of the reign of God? Jesus' disciples, like himself, were dependent on people who would take them into their houses in the evenings and give them something to eat. But they did not always find houses open to them, and the labor for the Gospel did not always leave them time to think of eating at all. In this connection we need to take seriously what Mark writes,

"Then he went [into a house]; and the crowd came together again, so that they [Jesus and his disciples] could not even eat" (Mark 3:19-20). The story about plucking ears of grain presumes such a situation of completely insecure itinerant existence in which no planning was possible. The plucking of grain was not a game; it was done out of necessity, because of the hardship of existence for the reign of God. But that means that this breach of Sabbath rules is firmly connected to the proclamation of the reign of God. Here again, the first commandment has greater weight than the third as it was then interpreted.

Clean and Unclean

But there is a text that sharpens the question of Jesus' relationship to the Torah still further. In Mark 7:15 we find a saying of Jesus that really does give the impression that here an important part of the Torah, namely, the whole of the laws regarding what is clean and what is unclean, is being declared invalid. It reads, "there is nothing outside a person that by going in can defile, but the things that come out are what defile." The Lutheran theologian Ernst Käsemann (1906–1998) commented on this passage: "The man who denies that impurity from external sources can penetrate into man's essential being is striking at the presuppositions and the plain verbal sense of the Torah and at the authority of Moses himself. Over and above that, he is striking at the presuppositions of the whole classical conception of *cultus* with its sacrificial and expiatory system."[34] He concludes from this that a Jew who speaks this way "has cut himself off from the community of Judaism"—or else he is the Messiah and brings "the Messianic Torah."[35] Against this, of course, one must point out that there is no such thing as a separate "Messianic Torah" in Judaism. The Messiah is the model of fulfilling the Torah of Moses. He serves it. He interprets it. He sees to it that it is obeyed everywhere, but he does not promulgate a Torah of his own.[36] Of the alternatives Käsemann proposes, then, only one is possible: Jesus had "cut himself off from the community of Judaism." But did he really? Does what Jesus says in Mark 7:15 permit that conclusion? Let us look more closely!

Mark (or the tradition Mark used) locates the logion in this context: some Pharisees and scribes from Jerusalem observe that Jesus' disciples do not ritually wash their hands before eating and thus also make the food they eat unclean. The disciples do not obey the prescriptions regarding ritual cleanness established by the community of the Pharisees. The purpose of those prescriptions was to impose the *priestly* Torah of clean and unclean on the whole nation. All Israel is to be a "priestly kingdom and a holy nation" (Exod 19:6). It is possible that in such a situation Jesus defended his disciples with the saying found in Mark 7:15.

But we can imagine other situations in which Jesus might have spoken these words. He often ate with people who most certainly did not keep the Pharisaic rules of cleanness. Consider, for example, his eating with "toll collectors and sinners" (Mark 2:15). Probably there was little regard for ritual questions of cleanness and uncleanness in such circles. In the eyes of the Pharisees, or of people who lived according to the Pharisaic interpretation of the Law, Jesus made himself unclean by entering into such a table community and thus exposed himself to hostile attacks. The saying could come out of a context like that as well. In that case it is not a fundamental rejection of the Torah of cleanness and uncleanness but subordinates that aspect of Torah to the love commandment and the proclamation of the reign of God.

But there is a third possibility that seems to me by far the most probable.[37] We have already seen, again and again, that particular texts in the gospels are best explained in terms of the unstable itinerant lives of Jesus and his disciples. If the disciples had been traveling all day and in the evening could be happy to be received into a house and given something to eat, they would scarcely have inquired whether the food corresponded to the Pharisaic laws for cleanness. Jesus could have legitimated such an attitude on their part with the saying in Mark 7:15. In favor of that, in any case, is his saying, "eat what is set before you" in the mission discourse (Luke 10:8). We might add: "eat what is set before you without asking if it is clean or unclean." In any case, the Coptic Gospel of Thomas connected Jesus' saying about "clean and unclean" with the mission discourse (*GThom* 14). If Mark 7:15 originated in the itinerant existence of Jesus and his disciples, it is not meant to reject the Torah of clean and unclean but rather, as we have seen in the cases of the third and fourth commandments, to set the proclamation of the reign of God ahead of every other law.

Certainly we must admit that Mark 7:15, seen by itself, gives no hint of a concrete situation; it is formulated in basic terms and absolutely: what comes from without cannot make one unclean. Only what comes out of a person makes her or him unclean—the evil in the heart. But was Jesus, in fact, not abrogating the whole Torah of cleanness and uncleanness in Scripture when he said that?

We can probably make more progress on this difficult question only if we compare the way Jesus dealt with other parts of the Torah. He has no thought of eliminating the Sabbath commandment, but on occasion he subordinates it to the proclamation of the reign of God. Nor is he thinking of abrogating the fourth commandment, but when necessary he subjects it to the requirements of the reign of God. And he does not intend to abolish the temple cult, but he can subordinate it to the necessity of reconciliation (Matt 5:23-24). In the same way, we can say that Jesus was not thinking of declaring the Torah of clean and unclean false and outdated. At any rate, he commanded the leper he had made clean to show himself to the priest, in accordance with Leviticus 14, and to present the sacrifice prescribed for cleansing (Mark 1:44). Nevertheless, here again we must say that Jesus had already touched lepers without the least hesitation. Apparently he always acted with great freedom. And Mark 7:15 is really formulated in very radical and basic terms. So is this, after all, an unsolvable problem?

Probably the solution is to be sought in the same direction as in the case of the prohibition of divorce. Ultimately, Jesus appealed to God's creative will: "So they are no longer two, but one flesh. Therefore what God has joined together, let no one separate" (Mark 10:9). When Jesus asserts that nothing outside a person is unclean but all uncleanness comes from the human heart, the creation account could also be in the background. There we find, six times, "God saw that it was good." And then, when God rests on the Sabbath and creation is finished, "God saw everything that he had made, and indeed, it was very good" (Gen 1:31). If the world and everything in it is made good, and if the coming of the reign of God will restore God's original good creation, then where the reign of God is accepted nothing can be unclean. Uncleanness, then, comes about always and only through the evil that emerges from human hearts.

If Jesus thought that way, he did not simply abolish the Old Testament Torah of clean and unclean, because it too is intended to create a holy people for God in the midst of the distorted and damaged creation. In that case he placed every command regarding clean and unclean under the sign of the good creation and brought the Torah of clean and unclean into the right light by articulating the creative will of God. We might say that then he would have been clarifying the Torah through the Torah.

A New Law?

Did Jesus abolish the Torah and, as a new lawgiver, establish a new law? That is the question with which this chapter began. The philosopher and martyr Justin saw it that way. Many great theologians after him saw it that way too. But we can see how questionable that idea is from the very fact that in that case the Torah is torn apart: its moral demands have not been abrogated, only its ritual laws!

But a great deal more speaks against this position, including Matthew 5:17: "Do not think that I have come to abolish the law or the prophets. I have come not to abolish but to fulfill." Romans 3:31 likewise speaks to the contrary: "Do we then overthrow the law by this faith? By no means! On the contrary, we uphold the law." Finally, every sampling that has been made in this chapter speaks against it. Jesus does not abrogate the Torah or abolish it; he does not replace it with a new Torah; he interprets it.

But he does not interpret it as the scribes do. He does not cling to the letter. He seeks the original will of God behind the letters. He sees the Torah as a whole and therefore also reaches back to the first chapters of Torah to find there the creative will of God. He sets forth the center of the Torah: the commandment about the uniqueness and sole rule of God. And by his message of the reign of God now coming he endows that commandment with historical urgency. He places the whole Torah in the light of the reign of God and subordinates all commandments to God's reign. He combines the principal commandment with that of love of neighbor from Leviticus 19, and in doing so he gives the Torah its center or, better, he finds its center. First and last, his concern is the will of God, and he knows how easily even religious people can use external performance of the law to avoid the true will of God. And Jesus teaches all that with ultimate authority—like someone who himself stands in God's stead. "At Sinai it was said to the congregation of Israel . . . but now I say to you."

It is understandable that Jesus has repeatedly been seen as a "new lawgiver," but he was no such thing. He spoke about the one and only law of God, but he enunciated it as something fully new.

It is understandable that the Sermon on the Mount was understood to be the "new Torah" of Christians. After all, the mountain itself recalls Sinai. But in reality the Sermon on the Mount is not a new Torah. How could it be, when it does not even touch so many areas of human life? Jesus does not proclaim a new law; he brings to its fulfillment the one social project of the Torah given once for all by offering examples, in the Sermon on the Mount, that show how that social project is to be understood and lived radically, that is, in terms of its roots—and that means in terms of the true will of God.

It is understandable that people saw the love commandment, with its expansion to cover enemies, as a "new commandment." It had to seem something completely new in the world of antiquity. But it was already in the Torah.

It is understandable that people said that Jesus not only interpreted the Torah but transcended it. No, he did not transcend it; he found its center and so brought the whole Torah to its fulfillment.

And it is understandable that people have said that Jesus understood "himself" as the Torah. He did, in fact, live the Torah with his whole existence; he established it irrevocably and in unsurpassable fashion in his own person. Jesus lives in union with the will of God in the ultimate sense. And yet to say that he himself is the Torah has something danger-ous about it: the Torah is a social order, and a social order cannot be exhausted in a single person. It requires a people.

The Whole Torah

Jesus showed himself to us as the eschatological interpreter of the Torah. He comprehended the intent of the Torah as well as its dynamic. He interpreted it with an admirable sensitivity to its center. When Mark 1:22 says that he taught like one who has sovereign authority and not like the scribes, that is exactly the point. But does that mean that for Jesus, and accordingly for Christians, whole sections of the Torah have been sidelined by Jesus' centralizing interpretation, indeed, that they have basically been done away with because they have been absorbed by the twofold commandment of love of God and neighbor? Here we need to exercise extreme caution.

Obviously Jesus established a new basis for the Torah; he interpreted it definitively and thus gave it its eschatological form. But that does not mean that whole parts of the Torah were discarded like burned-out rocket stages. They were not cast off but transformed. No part of the Torah may be regarded as over and done with, certainly not as abrogated, but the whole Torah must be interpreted anew, over and over again, in light of Jesus Christ, and directed toward the will of God. Then it may certainly appear that certain parts of the Torah that at first seem strange and even comical in our eyes acquire a new meaning—or to put it in better words, they reveal the meaning intended for them from the beginning.

To give one example: the Torah contains extensive laws for what is clean and unclean (cf., e.g., Lev 11–15). These apply primarily to the house, clothing, the body, and food. There are orders for how people who are healed of skin diseases are to be declared clean. Distinctions are made between animals that confer uncleanness and those that are clean. It is established what kinds of meat may be eaten and what kinds are not to be eaten. Is all that out of date? It seems so. After all, we have learned Jesus' clear principle: "there is nothing outside a person that by going in can defile, but the things that come out are what defile" (Mark 7:15). But does that saying mean that Israel's laws for cleanness and holiness are abrogated or reduced to purely ethical norms? Christian theologians have repeatedly said, in this connection, that Jesus' distinction between "inside" and "outside" refers all external, ritual holiness from a material-prepersonal sphere to its real meaning, that is, internal, personal holiness. But we ought to be careful about such formulations, because in the New Testament even holiness separated from the external-material means decisively more than merely an inner quality of the soul or the moral person.

The whole people of God is meant to be a holy people. Thus holiness always encompasses also the community-social dimension with which the individual person is inseparably connected. Not only must the human heart be holy: so must life's conditions and relationships, the social structures and the forms of the environment in which human beings live and into which they constantly project themselves. But that is precisely what the material-ritual prescriptions of the Torah regarding cleanness and uncleanness always intended.

Belief in one God who is Lord of all must also shape the world around people. It is not enough to believe with lips and heart while despising one's own body, allowing the living space in which one is at home to deteriorate, and destroying the environment. According to the words of the prophet Zechariah, in the Israel of the end time even the horses' bells and the household utensils will be holy to the Lord: "On that day there shall be inscribed on the bells of the horses, 'Holy to the LORD.' . . . and every cooking pot in Jerusalem and Judah shall be sacred to the LORD of hosts" (Zech 14:20-21). This means that a day is coming when all Israel—not only its people, but also things and especially the conditions of life—will find themselves in the state willed by God for them and reflecting God's rulership. To the extent that they correspond to the will of God and are formed by God's nearness they will then find their identity and support life. This is precisely where the biblical concept of clean and unclean is pointing. The intent of the Torah of clean and unclean in the book of Leviticus is that faith should shape and transform the world, and as far as this real direction and goal of the Torah of clean and unclean is concerned, we are far from having fulfilled it. The laws of clean and unclean in the Old Testament deserve to be read anew, considered anew, and questioned about their original meaning.

Obviously that is not possible unless we continually make distinctions. Does the commandment of those times still match the historical dynamic in which we are placed? How could it be translated to our situation? But making precise distinctions is the Torah's purpose: it is meant to teach Israel to distinguish. To view all things in the world critically, that is, by the power of faith in the one God to differentiate among them, has indeed become a basic feature of Jewish existence. Because Israel, in light of the Torah, learned to distinguish continually—and that meant also, for example, not mixing objects and things that are different[38]—it was able to maintain its identity among the Gentiles. Assyria and Babylon, once states that stood victorious on the ruins of Israel, vanished and were absorbed into other nations, but Israel, defeated and continually persecuted, even scattered throughout the world, has remained one people.

Israel's power of distinction is part of the miracle of its identity. The church needs this constant distinguishing as urgently as does the synagogue. It must not fall into that sick condition of the spirit in which everything is the same, nothing matters more than anything else, indifference is the norm. Where no distinctions are made any longer, the old gods return.

So we may say at the end of this chapter: the Torah is the endeavor set in motion by God himself, never out of date and based on the people of God, to view all things in the world with the eyes of God, to distinguish what is right from what is false, to change what is false, and so to place everything under the rule of the one God. Frank Crüsemann, a Christian theologian, has dared to say, "The identity of the biblical God is dependent upon the connection with his Torah."[39] He is right. Therefore the church can and may not ever give up the Torah, not even parts of it. True, it must read and live the Torah in the spirit of Jesus—that is, out of the strength of the new thing that came into the world with him, out of his freedom and rationality, his radicality and reverence for God.

Chapter 13

The Life of Jesus:
Living Unconditionally

In the previous twelve chapters we were concerned primarily with "what Jesus wanted." "Who he was" was indirectly visible. From now on, the second part of this book's subtitle will be more in the foreground. Who was Jesus?

The Eye Torn Out

We repeatedly find in Jesus' words and actions a positively alarming absoluteness and lack of ambiguity. We might even have to speak of "ruthlessness." For when someone who wants to follow him asks first to be allowed to take leave of his family, Jesus says to him, "No one who puts a hand to the plow and looks back is fit for the kingdom of God" (Luke 9:62). In his clarity and exclusivity, as shown in this statement, Jesus was ruthless. He was so toward himself and could be so toward others. Many of his sayings testify to it. Here is no soothing, no calming, no pacifying, no watering down; instead, the unadorned truth is spoken—truth about human beings and the situations in which they find themselves. It is always a situation in which far-reaching, indeed, final decisions are to be made. Therefore Jesus has to say:

> If your right eye causes you to sin, tear it out and throw it away; it
> is better for you to lose one of your members than for your whole

body to be thrown into hell. And if your right hand causes you to sin, cut it off and throw it away; it is better for you to lose one of your members than for your whole body to go into hell. (Matt 5:29-30)

This text works with a point of view of that time according to which the very limbs of the body entice to sin: eyes, ears, lips, hands. The Markan parallel speaks of the foot as well (Mark 9:45). But why here in particular the right eye and the right hand? Very simply because everything "right" was considered by people of that period as better and more important. This makes the argument even more pointed: better to lose a part of the body, even if it is an especially important and precious part, such as the right hand, than with one's whole existence to go to hell.

Plucking out one's own eye, cutting off one's own hand—the double saying speaks piercingly and with a fearful severity: better to be crippled and disfigured than to be in further danger of sinning! Matthew 5:29-30 is eons removed from the Greek ideal of the harmonic person, nobly formed in all respects.

The same kind of severity and pointed meaning is found in the so-called violence saying. In this case, by way of exception, I am quoting from the easily reconstructed wording of the Sayings Source:[1] "The law and the prophets [were] until John. From then [on] the kingdom of God breaks its way violently, and the violent seize it" (cf. Matt 11:13, 12 // Luke 16:16). There are very few sayings of Jesus whose meaning has been so long disputed among exegetes. This one has often been translated and interpreted in a negative sense: "From then on the reign of God is violated, and the violent plunder it."[2] This would mean that the reign of God, as Jesus proclaims it, is being rejected and made an enemy by its opponents. They take it away from the people who listen to Jesus and who want to follow him.

From a purely grammatical point of view this negative translation is possible. But that does not say much. We need to examine the context: "the law and the prophets," which extend to the time of John the Baptizer, are, after all, something positive. What comes after them, namely, the reign of God, is still more positive. Therefore there can be no question here of a violation of the reign of God, especially since there are no parallels in Jesus' sayings for such a statement.

Moreover, if we note the provocative way Jesus constantly spoke, and if we pay special attention to the language of his parables, where any number of "immoral heroes" represent the kind of discipleship Jesus is demanding, it seems still more likely that we should interpret the "violence saying" in a positive sense, as the wording certainly allows: the reign of God is not violated; rather, it is breaking its way with power. No one can stop it, because it is God's work. But only those who dare everything and put everything in play will have a part in it. They are like violent people who do violence to themselves and their own bodies. They are ruthless with themselves.

Another Jesus saying we have received in a number of variants speaks of the same kind of unconditional attitude: "those who want to save their life will lose it, and those who lose their life for my sake will save it" (Luke 9:24).[3] The background of this saying could be a fixed form of discourse that is multiply attested in antiquity. That is how generals addressed their soldiers immediately before battle: whoever fights at complete risk of his own life and so supports those fighting at his side will be rescued. But any coward who flees will lose his life, because no one will help him.[4] If the motif of that kind of "general's pep talk" has made its way into Jesus' saying we would again have evidence that Jesus was more educated and knew more of the world than many want to allow. But quite independently of that, Luke 9:24 also reveals Jesus' radicality. Those who want to follow him have to be ready to lose their lives. That is precisely how they will save them. Obviously this saying, which Jesus addressed to others, also reflects his own attitude: he was ready to give up his life.

Luke 9:24 and its parallels are not, however, exclusively interested in the surrender of life in death. After all, human beings are also desperately engaged in "saving" their own desires and dreams, their own guiding images and plans for their lives. But these very rescue actions cause them to lose their lives—namely, the true lives that existence under the rule of God would give them. "To lose one's life" therefore refers not only to martyrdom but in given circumstances to the surrender of one's secure bourgeois existence for the sake of the reign of God.

Such radicality for the sake of God's project is not everyone's thing. Normally we want not "either-or" but "both-and." In particular, people familiar with the Gospel and desiring to serve God can be deeply conflicted here. They want to be there for God, but they also want space for themselves. They want to make a place for God in their lives, but they also want to have free segments in which they decide for themselves about their lives. They want to do the will of God, but at the same time they want to live their own dreams and longings. Jesus had in mind, with the greatest clarity of understanding possible, this internal conflict that can almost tear apart especially those who are his followers. That is the reason for the next saying, which, like so many other sayings of Jesus, uses everyday experience in its argument: "No one can serve two masters, for a slave will either hate the one and love the other, or be devoted to the one and despise the other. You cannot serve God and wealth" (Matt 6:24). That is: when it is a question of God and the reign of God, there can be nothing but undivided self-surrender. This "whole-ness" and "undividedness" appears again and again in Jesus' instructions. It is connected at its root with the unconditional way of being that he demands in relationship to God. There is probably no text in the gospel tradition that shows this more vividly than Mark 12:41-44. It is worth our while to consider it more closely.

The Widow's Sacrifice

A word in advance: the extensive temple complex in Herodian Jerusalem included the "court of the women." There, behind the colonnades, lay a hall in which visitors to the temple could leave offerings of money for the maintenance of the sanctuary and its daily sacrifices. This hall was called the "treasury." There one gave one's money to priests who served in the treasury and one named the amount and the purpose of the gift. That way everyone nearby could hear what those entering the treasury were giving for the temple and its maintenance.[5] That is the background to the logic of this text:

> He sat down opposite the treasury, and watched the crowd putting money into the treasury. Many rich people put in large sums. A poor widow came and put in two small copper coins, which are worth a penny. Then he called his disciples and said to them, "Truly I tell you, this poor widow has put in more than all those who are contributing to the treasury. For all of them have contributed out of their abundance, but she out of her poverty has put in everything she had, all she had to live on." (Mark 12:41-44)

It makes all kinds of sense to fill in the details: Jesus is very close to the treasury and hears the sums being named and their purposes. There is a constant coming and going: Jews from the homeland and the Diaspora, old and young, men and women, poor and rich. Their classes and origins can be read in their dress and often in the way they speak as well.

A woman enters the treasury. Her clothes show that she is poor, and her apparel also shows that she is a widow. So she is living in a double kind of misery. She is not only poor; she no longer has the protection of a man. Jesus sees how she gives her gift to the priest, and he hears that she is offering two copper coins. Such a coin was the smallest unit of money there was. Jesus is touched by the event. Here is a harsh contrast: just now the rich, and here the poor! Just now silver, often amounting to large sums, and now two copper coins!

Jesus also sees the background: the rich who are not in the least pained by offering a silver shekel, and the poor widow who gives everything she has. The two copper coins would have secured her food for the next day. They were literally a necessity of life. But of this utmost necessity she gives not only half—she could, after all, have handed the priest *one* coin—but everything.

Jesus sees the full implications of the event. He calls his disciples together, points to the woman who is already going away, and tells them what he has seen. He not only tells the story but interprets it, and thus the little narrative reaches the point it was heading toward from the beginning. Jesus says: the widow there has given more than all the others, for the others have given only a small part of their property, but this woman has given everything, her whole living.

Obviously, the reader of Mark's gospel is meant to see the widow's sacrifice against the background of the reign of God proclaimed by Jesus. The reign of God—that means that God turns to human beings totally and without any reservation in order to bring divine abundance to the world. This self-gift of God is a historical event: it is happening now, in Israel and in the new community life Jesus is creating. Therefore the reign of God attracts those who are able to experience God's overflowing self-gift, so that they in turn give everything they have: their whole heart, their whole existence. The poor widow who gave her two copper coins becomes a sign, a symbol of this "totality."

Mark has deliberately located this scene with the widow before the eschatological discourse (Mark 13) and the beginning of the passion account (Mark 14:1). The widow's gift already reflects for him the "wholeness" of Jesus' gift of his life. But the widow's deed also illustrates for him the scriptural saying Jesus had quoted shortly before: "you shall love the Lord your God with all your heart, and with all your soul, and with all your mind, and with all your strength" (Mark 12:30). The widow gave everything she had. She loved God with her entire "wealth."

Of course, objections immediately arise: what will the woman have to eat the next day if she has given everything away? Is this not a horrid God who demands such a "totality"?—a God who devours people totally?—a God who demands human sacrifice?—a God who even robs the poor of their last dollar and does not begrudge the lucky their good fortune?

Precisely at this point it is evident that the story of the widow's offering, like all the stories in the Bible, positively forces on us the question of the "place" of the reign of God. It is not a nebulous thing that lies in the future or is deeply hidden in the human soul. Rather, it demands a concrete "space," and that space has social dimensions (see chap. 3 above). The reign of God develops its power where people live the new common life established by God and endow that common life with everything they have. Then the poor widow is no longer alone. Then there are many who offer her protection, who share their meals with her, who comfort her in her suffering. In this common life given by God, moreover, people are not totally devoured and deprived of their freedom but instead find their freedom, good fortune, and happiness precisely there.

We might, for once, simply surrender ourselves to the little story of the widow and her offering. Apart from all historical questions, there appears in it something of what Jesus was. The "wholeness" he perceives with such admiration in the poor widow was something he himself lived. He lived it even unto death. To that extent it is no accident that Mark tells this episode shortly before Jesus' passion. As Jesus' complete clarity of focus runs through all his words, it also saturates everything he did. Jesus was a radical in his actions as in his words. That must have begun very early.

The Father's Will

Luke 2:41-52 tells how the twelve-year-old Jesus went missing from his parents in the capital city. They were already on their way home from the festival, thinking he was in another one of the groups of travelers. When they discovered their mistake, they hurried back to Jerusalem and sought him there. After three days they found him in the temple. According to the story, the young Jesus must have been driven by a deep longing to remain in the place where God was praised, to be in the place where everything was about God. To his mother's reproach that she and his father had sought him anxiously, he answers with surprise: "Why were you searching for me? Did you not know that I must be in [what belongs to my Father]?" (Luke 2:49). Let me say again that we must not approach narratives of this sort with the kind of blunt historical probing that accomplishes nothing but to raise all kinds of questions about whether it could have happened that way or not. Stories like Luke 2:41-52 are nourished by larger contexts and times. Behind them is the experience of concrete dealing with Jesus during his public life.

Luke 2:41-52 distills what became fully obvious twenty years later when Jesus appeared in public: he had left his parents behind. He had left his family. The conflict depicted in Mark 3 between him and his family had already happened (cf. chap. 8 above). It was not a mild disagreement. Jesus separated himself from his own family and gathered a group of disciples around him, people who had left their families as he had.

Jesus is now about just one thing: proclaiming the reign of God. He travels through Galilee in a restless itinerant course, totally and utterly surrendered to God's will and plan. He lives for Israel, for the eschatological gathering of the people of God. He spreads blessing and salvation around him but also the blade of decision. In word and deed he makes the reign of God present. He now lives definitively that final and radical filial obedience to God that was already glimpsed in the story about the twelve-year-old and that extends deeper than all ties to a natural family.

Apparently this sloughing off of his old ties began when, one day, he went with many others to the Jordan where John the Baptizer was preaching and baptizing. Mark recounts the decisive events that, besides his crucifixion, are among the most historically certain in Jesus' life; the account is as brief as it possibly could be: "In those days Jesus came from Nazareth of Galilee and was baptized by John in the Jordan" (Mark 1:9). This is the precise beginning of Jesus' public history. He must have heard about the Baptizer and his preaching of repentance, and he must have been deeply moved by it. He leaves his parents' house in Nazareth to be baptized by John. That created enormous difficulties for the early communities. How could he who was much greater than John have gone to the Jordan and joined the Baptizer's renewal movement? How could Jesus put himself within the crowd of those who publicly confessed that they wanted to change their lives? How could the Sinless One subject himself to a "baptism for the forgiveness of sins"? The enormity of these difficulties is evident from the fact that Matthew builds into the baptism scene a little dialogue in which John at first hesitates to admit Jesus to baptism at all (Matt 3:14-15).

The apocryphal "Gospel of the Nazarenes" (first half of the second century), which survives only in fragments, proceeds much more radically. According to that gospel, Jesus was urged by his mother and brothers to go to the Jordan with them: the whole family want to be baptized by John. But Jesus refuses, saying, "How have I sinned, that I should go there to be baptized by him?" (Jerome, *Adversus Pelagianos* III, 2). That is freely imagined, but we see in it the problem the early church had with Jesus' baptism.

How could the Son of God be baptized? In the past it was often said, in answer to this difficulty, that Jesus wanted to give the people a good example. But that kind of song and dance is woefully inadequate. Jesus went to the Baptizer because he sensed that God was acting through him. Israel was now entering the crucial phase of its history. For him that meant he had to be at the place where the fate of the people of God was being decided; he had to be on the spot where God was now acting in Israel. He had to be where the eschatological gathering and renewal of Israel was beginning. So he listened to God's appeal. The moral question of whether he considered himself a sinner is not to the point. Jesus' concern was with God's plan, with the Father's will. By being baptized he surrendered himself wholly to that plan.

Jesus' Temptations

According to the narrative sequence of the first three gospels, immediately after his baptism Jesus was driven into the desert by the Spirit of God to be tempted there (Matt 4:1; Mark 1:12-13; Luke 4:1-2). In Matthew and Luke the story of the temptations that then follows is an artistic composition. Let us be plain about it: it is a fictional story. But it was this use of fiction that presented the possibility of telling something that was full to the brim with reality: Jesus was tempted more than once.

The end of Mark's much briefer story echoes the theme of Paradise. He writes that angels served Jesus in the desert (Mark 1:13; cf. Matt 4:11). There were already Jewish legends circulating in New Testament times that told how the first humans in Paradise were served by angels. So Mark intends to say that because Jesus followed the will of God without reservation, Paradise was beginning to dawn. But in the midst of this dawning of Paradise he is tempted just as everyone else is tempted if she or he wants to serve God alone. He is tempted to will not God's plan but his own.

In Matthew's and Luke's versions the tempter approaches Jesus three times. Three times he tries to get Jesus to fall away from his assigned task. Three times Jesus answers with a saying from Scripture and thus shows that he is remaining faithful to his duty. These are not primarily temptations to which everyone is exposed, such as greed or pleasure or the arrogance of power. Instead, they are about the basic sin of the people of God, the specific temptation with which believers in particular are confronted.

The temptation of the people of God, and therefore of Jesus also, begins in the task itself—in the heart of what Israel is sent to do: to live in the world as a people that gives honor to God alone, acknowledges God as its only Lord, so that others can see and understand from this people what faith is. But if the people of God lives not for God but for itself, if it seeks not the honor of God but its own, and if in the process God is even made an instrument for the accomplishment of its own interests— then the task and the mission are perverted in their inmost heart. Then what happens is not proclamation but self-exaltation, and in place of service to others comes service to one's own interest. The story about Jesus' temptations illustrates in the most sublime form the potential sin of all those who are called.

In the first scene people make use of the new possibilities opened up by the mission of the people of God for their own interests. They get bread for themselves (Matt 4:2-4). The history of the church will show that it is possible to earn money through the Gospel.

In the second scene people serve not God but their own project by putting themselves on display. Throwing oneself down from the pinnacle of the temple is an extravagant display to test what possibilities God has to offer that one can make use of for one's own self-presentation, misusing Sacred Scripture into the bargain (Matt 4:5-7).

In the third scene everything that is going on in the depths finally comes to light: those who do not serve God alone and with all their strength, in fact, serve themselves and thus the chaotic powers of the world (Matt 4:8-10).

Only those who have understood how narrow and exposed is the path by which God is truly honored, and how quickly faith itself falls into self-help, giving oneself honor, making oneself master or mistress—only they understand the explosive point of the Matthean and Lukan temptation story: it is especially those called who can misuse their calling to serve their own persons, glorify their own deeds, and seek not to serve but to exercise religious power. And misuse of power in the name of God is the most terrible of all violations.

The stories about Jesus' temptation immediately after his baptism are intended to say that Jesus too was repeatedly tempted by all these things, in the deepest depths of his existence. But he resisted the tempter, and he did so with ultimate clarity and determination. He could do so because he held fast to the word of God. Therefore he thrice quotes Sacred Scripture, the collected wisdom of Israel about how to distinguish and decide.

What the temptation story had summarized and distilled at the beginning of the first three gospels happened again and again in the course of Jesus' public activity. To take one example: in the course of the Markan narrative Jesus asked his disciples who people said that he was. They answered that some took him for the Baptizer *redivivus*, others for the return of Elijah, and others for earlier prophets of Israel. Then Jesus asks the disciples who they themselves think he is, and Peter answers with his messianic confession. But what does the word "messiah" mean? In order not to be misunderstood, Jesus tells the disciples prophetically of his passion and execution. Then "Peter took him aside and began to rebuke him. But turning and looking at his disciples, he rebuked Peter [in turn] and said, 'Get out of my sight,[6] Satan! For you are setting your mind not on divine things but on human things'" (Mark 8:32-33).

It is out of the question that this little scene could represent a fictive narrative constructed after Easter to encourage the community to follow Jesus to the cross. Without a historical background, no one would have attached Jesus' appellation "Satan" to Peter. The historical location was probably Jesus' stated intention to go to Jerusalem for the Passover feast. Apparently it was clear to all those involved how dangerous that would be, and Peter must have reacted accordingly in the situation. We can easily picture his attempt to talk Jesus out of making the Jerusalem pilgrimage. Probably he argued quite rationally. Perhaps he said, "Not to the capital, not now! Let's stay in Galilee. We don't have to go to this particular festival. Let's hold back a little until the whole fuss has died down."

Whatever Peter may have said, Jesus reacts with unbelievable harshness. He addresses the disciple he had once called and who has followed him to this hour as "Satan," the tempter, the opponent of God, the one who confuses all people. And he does so because Peter is not thinking about what God wants but what matches his own ideas and desires.

So this profound conflict is about the will of God. That will does not mean always keeping the norms of conduct. It is not timeless. It has its moment. It has its hour, again and again, and that hour can very quickly become the moment of truth. Peter has suddenly entered into this moment of truth, just as Jesus uninterruptedly enters into it. Note: the "will of God" is not that Jesus should be killed in Jerusalem but that Israel everywhere, including in the capital city, should be confronted with the Gospel of the reign of God.

Once again Jesus acts with ultimate decisiveness. When it is a matter of the will of God, of the reign of God, everything else takes a back seat for him; he permits no compromise, even if it should cost him his life. It is true that he himself is tempted to the most profound depths of his being. The scene on the Mount of Olives shows that. And yet he possesses an inerrant consistency. Jesus went his way in an unconditional determination focused entirely on God. That unconditional attitude is revealed also in a matter that cuts deep into the life of every person: having a life partner.

Jesus' Celibacy

We spoke in the eighth chapter of this book about Jesus' sign-actions: for example, the creation of the group of the Twelve and the establishment of a new family. We set aside one fundamental sign-action in Jesus' life, namely, that he did not marry. But it must be discussed in this book, because it is an essential part of "who Jesus was." Luke 9:57-58 reports the following: "As they were going along the road, someone said to him, 'I will follow you wherever you go.' And Jesus said to him, 'Foxes have holes, and birds of the air have nests; but the Son of Man has nowhere to lay his head.'" That is: if you want to follow me you may have to live as I live. You will have no nest of your own full of comfort and safety. You will have no building in which you are sheltered and protected. You may even have your own family against you and all your relatives too.

The Son of Man has nothing on which to rest his head. We can easily think of the spouse who can embrace her husband, in whose love he can breathe, in whose understanding he can rest. Jesus had none of that. Why? Because he wasn't mature enough? Or out of hostility to the flesh? Or rejection of sexuality? Or fear of women? Or some kind of rigorism or fanaticism? Hatred of the world? The right answer is found in a saying of Jesus transmitted in Matthew 19:12:

> There are eunuchs who have been so from birth, and there are eunuchs who have been made eunuchs by others, and there are eunuchs who have made themselves eunuchs for the sake of the kingdom of heaven. Let anyone accept this who can.

This saying, typical of Jesus in its extreme sharpness and almost ironic play of language, needs an explanation of its own. The Greek text speaks of "eunuchs" and "being made eunuchs," that is, *castrati* and castration. Jesus lists three possibilities: there are men who lack sexual organs from birth, others who have been castrated against their will, and still others who have castrated themselves. We have to translate this drastic speech in order to be clear about what Jesus means. He is saying that there are people who are incapable of marriage from birth. Others are made incapable of marriage in some way by their environment. But there are also people who remain unmarried freely and by their own decision.

It sounds more genteel that way, and some modern versions translate it in this polite way.[7] But Jesus is not so genteel. His way of speaking is extraordinarily drastic, and all the more so because castration was strictly forbidden in Israel.[8] He also speaks in extreme terms in view of the fact that remaining unmarried was despised by his contemporaries. The rabbis appealed to Genesis 1:28 ("increase and multiply") to say that begetting progeny was a duty ordered by God. "He who does not engage in propagation of the race is as though he sheds blood."[9] And Rabbi Eliezer (ca. 270) said: "Any man who has no wife is no proper man; for it is said, *Male and female created He them and called their name Adam.*"[10] Where, then, does Jesus' drastic and pointed formulation come from?

There is a simple explanation.[11] We have already seen that Jesus was often attacked in scurrilous ways by his opponents. They called him a "glutton," a "drunkard," a "friend of sinners." Apparently they had also called him a "eunuch" to make his celibacy a matter of ridicule. Jesus takes up this calumny in a way characteristic of him and turns it to positive purpose. Yes indeed, he says, there are *castrati* who are mutilated from birth, and there are *castrati* who have been mutilated by other people. But there are also those who are castrated out of pure freedom, by their own free decision—for the sake of the reign of God. Let those accept it who can. What is crucial in our context is that here Jesus associates his own celibacy and the separation of his disciples from their families with the reign of God. He asserts that there is such a thing as a free choice of celibacy for the sake of God's reign. Grasping that, he says, is not for everybody. But whoever can do so has understood something essential about the reign of God.

In this way Jesus made an indirect statement about his own celibate state. Despite the drastic nature of the statement, he remains utterly discreet. But whoever wants to hear can do so: his celibacy was not blind fate, and it was certainly not accidental; nor was it a marginal phenomenon in his individual life story. It was connected with his absolute surrender to the reign of God. Celibacy is central to the person of Jesus. From that point of view it is also more profoundly understandable that

Jesus can also ask others to abandon their families, breaking off their marital ties or giving up all their links to house, profession, and home.

Nevertheless, the question remains: Does all that make any sense? What will become of someone who sets aside all natural ties? Are they not essential to human existence? What happens to someone who thinks she or he can do without marriage? These are deep questions, and very serious ones. Their virulence is evident from the way the majority of books about Jesus today are simply silent about Jesus' celibacy. Has it become an embarrassment? Not long ago a wise man, a believer, whose judgment I esteem most highly, said to me:

> I am having a harder and harder time with Jesus. The older I get and the more I reflect on him, the stranger he seems to me. And yet Jesus is a typical case of a young person who was not permitted to grow older and thus mature. After all, he did not live to be much more than thirty. But that isn't enough.

> It is only later that we acquire our real experience of life. Only when we grow older do we comprehend the fragility and limitedness of human existence. As we get older we become more tolerant, more generous, more lenient. By then we have learned that life without compromise is not possible. We see things with completely different eyes.

> But Jesus' uncompromising attitude, his radicality, his harshness, his unbending nature, this "either-or," this "all or nothing"—all that is typical of a young person who does not yet really know the reality of love and death, guilt and suffering. Jesus—no matter how great and incomparable he is—is still a typical case of a young person, and the older I get the less I know what to do with him.

At first, when I heard that judgment, I was impressed, but now I consider it simply false, because obviously not everyone grows more generous and tolerant with age. But above all, I know people who live with ulti-mate certainty and radicality for the Gospel and the church and yet are full of kindness and concern.

This interweaving of certainty and concern we find also in Jesus. We only have to consider his attitude toward the desperate, the lost, the guilty. Here Jesus is *not* rigorous, unbending, severe. In the picture of the merciful father who runs to meet his lost son, refuses to let him finish speaking his confession of guilt, and immediately restores his rights as a son (Luke 15:11-32)—in that picture Jesus portrayed himself.

Still, there remains that other picture: of the one who "recklessly" goes his way, attacks Peter and calls him Satan, and summons individuals to follow him without any condition whatsoever. So the question must be raised again: Is this not too much to demand of human beings? Is such discipleship not utterly inhuman? Wouldn't anyone who lived that way become a spiritual cripple? And where would anyone get the strength for such discipleship? Above all: How did Jesus himself come to terms with such a life? Or did he? We will pursue these questions in the next chapter.

Chapter 14

The Fascination of the Reign of God

Where does anyone get the strength for discipleship such as Jesus demands? Is someone who abandons profession, house, and family not living contrary to every measure of humanity? Can anyone live that way? How did Jesus himself deal with such a life? Or did he? Those were the questions with which we ended the previous chapter.

The Reign of God as a Lucky Find

Those who try to answer these questions cannot avoid one of Jesus' most important parables. If we want to understand it even remotely we have to listen carefully. It is the double parable of the treasure in the field and the pearl of great price:

> [It is with the kingdom of heaven as with] a treasure hidden in a field, which someone found and hid; then in his joy he goes and sells all that he has and buys that field.

> Again, [it is with the kingdom of heaven as with] a merchant in search of fine pearls; on finding one pearl of great value, he went and sold all that he had and bought it. (Matt 13:44-46)

Before delving into the content of these two parables we should first examine their form. To begin with, this is a double parable. We find a great many texts among the sayings of Jesus that are similarly structured, with double strophes. Recall the saying about tearing out one's eye and the immediately following one about cutting off one's hand (Matt 5:29-30). Apparently this kind of two-part parallel composition was not first created for the post-Easter catechesis. Jesus himself must have loved to repeat the same subject with different imagery in order to impress it on the minds of his hearers.

Of course, Jesus did not invent this technique. It was already in use, in the parallelisms in the psalms and the didactic material in the Wisdom literature. But it is striking how frequently and consistently such double strophes appear in Jesus' teaching in particular.[1] To take another example:

> I came to bring fire to the earth,[2] and how I wish it were already kindled!
>
> I have a baptism with which to be baptized, and what stress I am under until it is completed! (Luke 12:49-50)

The final clauses of this double saying ("how I wish . . ." and "what stress I am under . . .") are structured in parallel, and the two opening clauses are also related in their content: the fire in the first image corresponds to the water (of baptism) in the second. Jesus first speaks of having come to kindle a fire. That is precisely what "bring fire" means. It is the fire of his message, a fire that kindles and transforms. Certainly he himself had to sink to the depths, to the most desperate straits, as one sinks deep into water at baptism. The two-part structure of the text leaps immediately into view, and the same is true of many of Jesus' images and parables.

In Matthew 13:44-46, the text we are examining here, the parallel structure is especially obvious. Two people each come across something extremely valuable and precious, and they give up everything in order to acquire it. But just as fire and water contrast in Luke 12:49-50, so here the two actors: the first is a day laborer who has to work in a field that does not belong to him (he has to go and buy it), while the other is a wholesale merchant who has business connections everywhere. Another difference controls this double parable: the day laborer comes across the treasure by pure accident while the merchant has already been seeking precious pearls.

By making this contrast Jesus means to say that the reign of God is open to everyone, poor and rich, and one may encounter it in altogether different ways: suddenly, unexpectedly, unintentionally, or as something always longed for and sought that at a certain point one actually finds.

But something else about the form of this double parable should be considered: each of its two parts is unusually short. We quite naturally ask ourselves: Did Jesus really tell such compact stories? What is more exciting than stories about finding treasure? Why did he not draw out two such naturally absorbing stories at length, telling them in such a way that the tension steadily increased—for example, the way he did in the story of the lost son (Luke 15:11-32)? That parable is incomparably longer and more vivid than Matthew 13:44-46. Why the brevity here?

The answer could be that obviously Jesus did tell his parables at greater length, and it was the teachers and theologians of the early communities who had to compress them into a brief form and a manageable structure so that they could be handed on more easily. It could have happened that way. But it could have been completely different; it could well be that Jesus himself concluded a longer discourse on the reign of God with a brief parable the audience could remember. It would have had the function of setting an ending to the discourse and sending the hearers away with something to think about. We have to reckon with the fact that Jesus could do many different things, that he was a master of both short and long forms simply because he was a highly talented teacher. So much for the form of Matthew 13:44-46. Now for a closer examination of its content!

The parable of the treasure in the field presupposes something familiar in its day that scarcely exists among us now, namely, hiding treasure. At that time it was the order of the day. There were no savings banks, no safe-deposit boxes, and normally no houses that could not easily be broken into. It was literally possible to break into the average house in Palestine by simply digging through the mud-brick wall. The technical term for "breaking in" translates to "digging one's way through."[3]

Besides that, there were constant wars, pillagings, attacks by robbers, and fires. Hence, money and valuable objects were buried, and it could easily happen that when war swept through a locality the buried treasures were not dug up again and lay forgotten. It happened now and then that someone discovered a buried treasure in a field. There were even people who specialized in searching for forgotten treasure; in Jewish culture they were called "earth churners," "wall knockers," or "beam breakers."[4] That is the background of the first parable. We can imagine the action of the story something like this:

A day laborer is working in a field. He is a wage worker; the field does not belong to him. That he is poor is evident from the fact that he has to sell "everything" he has to be able to buy the field: his broken-down house, its furniture and utensils, a few tools, his donkey. His plowshare struck the treasure—probably a large clay jar full of silver coins—while he was plowing the field. After he has counted it and assured himself of its enormous value he hastily throws dirt back on the object he has discovered, perhaps looking furtively around to see if anyone is watching him. Then, with unspeakable joy, he turns everything he has into cash and buys the field. That way he can be sure that no one can subsequently challenge his possession of the treasure. He is not bothered by having to sell everything he has because his loss is nothing in comparison to what he has to gain.

In the second parable the milieu shifts. The actor is no longer a poor person but a wealthy merchant. This man is not described as a *kapelos*, a small shopkeeper, but as *emporos*, that is, a wholesale merchant, a man who imports and exports. The story takes place not in the country but in the city, perhaps in the course of a trading journey and probably even overseas somewhere. The merchant is apparently a specialist in pearls; he deals in them and is constantly searching for more. Pearls were highly sought after in antiquity; they were then what big diamonds are to us. Immense sums were paid for the most perfect examples.

One day the merchant comes across a pearl of unusual size and beauty. The pearl fisher or intermediate dealer is asking quite a bit for it, but the specialist knows that in the right place and at the right time he will obtain a price for this pearl that would make your head swim. So he sells all his property, everything he can turn into liquid capital, and buys the pearl. It is *the* deal of his lifetime.

What do these two parables mean to say? The introduction in each case is crucial; it does *not* say "the reign of God is like a hidden treasure" (as most translations have it) and certainly not "it is a hidden treasure," but "it *is with* the reign of God as in the following event." It is the whole event that is compared to the reign of God—from the lucky find through the selling of the property to the giant transactions the day laborer and the merchant make in the end. Hence many interpretations and translations are too narrow and one-sided when they try to find the crucial point or the central meaning of the two parables in one particular part or object.

For example, it is repeatedly said that the point of both parables is the enormous value of what is found. The reign of God is as precious as the important treasure and the shimmering pearl. Another position says no, the infinite value of the reign of God is not what is decisive here. Rather, the point is that because of the inconceivable value of the reign of God one must sacrifice everything. What is crucial is the giving, the renunciation of property, the unlimited willingness to sacrifice.[5]

No, indeed, other interpreters say. That is not the crucial point either. The day laborer has encountered a unique opportunity that will never come again in his impoverished life. Likewise the merchant: never again in his life will he see such a pearl. So those hearing the parable should recognize the unique situation in which they are placed. Now, at this hour, God is offering salvation, and now, at this hour, it must be seized.

A fourth position says that this does not really grasp the parable of the treasure in the field either. The day laborer acquires his discovery by cunning, not to say fraud. He leaves the owner of the field in the dark about what he has found. He is thus one of those "immoral heroes" in Jesus' parables, and what Jesus truly wants to bring to light here is that everything depends on a decisive seizing of the moment, an engagement that goes for broke, that quickly, recklessly, and with complete goal-directedness risks everything on one throw of the dice. The reign of God needs crooks like that.[6] There is even a fifth position that interprets the double parable to say that the real point is the overflowing joy with which the two finders sell everything. There, and nowhere else, lies the accent, and both parables must be interpreted in terms of just that.[7]

Thus two relatively brief and simple parables can create so much controversy! We have to object to the five types of interpretation so briefly sketched here that they do not take the narrative structure of parables seriously. Despite all their brevity and conciseness, they *tell stories*. And it is essential to a story that one be carried along by it and then possibly see the world and oneself in a different light—or that one for the first time catches a glimpse of what the reign of God could be about. But that means we cannot focus with Aristotelian logic on a single point in the narrative. The story does have its own internal direction, and it is by no means arbitrary. But to grasp it one has to surrender oneself to the whole story, follow it step by step, and continually discover new aspects of it.

Obviously the treasure and the pearl are of incomparable value. Obviously the occasion is unique and will never return. Obviously in such a situation one must act decisively and go for broke. Obviously one must give everything to achieve the reign of God; only those who lose their life will gain it. This dread paradox is also apparent in our double parable, just as it appears again and again throughout Jesus' whole proclamation.

And yet, all that is embedded in and must be read in light of the unimaginable joy with which the two treasure finders act. "In joy he goes" cannot be missed. In that, the fifth position is correct. The joy and fascination of the find are so great that they shape the whole event. The day laborer does not hesitate for a second, nor does the merchant. They are captivated by the brilliance of the treasure and the shimmer of the pearl. They have been seized by a joy that exceeds all measure. This does not exclude the fact that (as we see in the action of the day laborer) they act cleverly.

Jesus is here speaking a crucial truth, and what is so marvelous is that he does not formulate it as a theory but tells it as a story. To be so moved by God's cause that one gives everything for its sake is not something one can ultimately do out of a bare awareness of duty, a "thou shalt!" or certainly "you must!" That we freely will what God wills is evidently possible only when we behold bodily the beauty of God's cause, so that we take joy in and even lust after what God wants to do in the world, and so that this desire for God and God's cause is greater than all our human self-centeredness.[8]

The merchant holds to the light the pearl he has finally found, and the day laborer buries his hands in the silver coins. For Jesus, the reign of God is palpable and visible. It does not exist merely within people, and it is not hidden somewhere beyond history. Even now it can be seen, grasped, acquired, taken in exchange. That is precisely why it fascinates people and moves them to change their whole lives for the sake of the new, without in the process losing their freedom. The brilliance and joy of the reign of God are ultimately the gravity that moves us and that again and again causes the grace of God to win out in this world.

Jesus' Fundamental Choice

It seems to me that the parables of the treasure and the pearl represent a key with whose help we can understand Jesus himself more profoundly. Every really good text anyone speaks or writes is autobiographical to some degree. The same is true of this double parable. Here Jesus has told something of his own story and the basic choice in his life—perhaps entirely unconsciously, but perhaps deliberately, though with reticence and the most profound tact.

Jesus himself had, after all, given up everything else for the sake of the reign of God. He had abandoned the security of family and marriage. He had relinquished the joy of having children. He had rejected the possibility of having a house or property or other means of security. Still more profoundly, he had refused to make himself central and so exercise religious power—the most sublime and dangerous form of power. He corrects someone who calls him "good teacher": "Why do you call me good? No one is good but God alone" (Mark 10:18). Jesus does not live for himself but is totally and exclusively surrendered to the cause of God. What is crucial is that this fundamental choice did not make him an oppressed and tortured person out of whom emanates a fear of having missed out on something, or a person in whom a renunciation with which he himself has not fully come to terms is translated into aggression against others.

Jesus is a man of unheard-of freedom. He is not the type of the tortured, bitter, dissatisfied, or disappointed. Nor is he the type of the tragic or heroic. He remains to the end a free person, despite the radicality with which he goes his own way. He remains to the end a man of complete dedication and humanity.

I think the double parable of the treasure and the pearl gives us the key to Jesus' inner freedom and unbrokenness: it is true that Jesus had surrendered everything and continued to the end to give his all; in the end he had to die. But he did so like the day laborer and the merchant, who do not regret for a second the loss of their old property but instead act out of an unspeakable joy and fascination. In the blinding light of the discovery everything else pales.

It is only in this context that Jesus' celibacy is comprehensible. If Jesus remained unmarried it was not because he despised sexuality or had a false attitude toward human physicality but simply because what had happened to him was like what he tells of in the parable of the hidden treasure and the precious pearl: he was seized and overpowered by the bliss of the reign of God—and not a reign that was coming some time in the future, but one that was beginning already, that one could already gain, that one could already cash in and deal with today.

The reign of God is happening already here in this world—today. It is happening wherever people believe the Gospel, accept the reign of God, allow their lives to be changed because of their fascination with it—when they turn back from their own life plans and toward the new thing God wants to create. The parable of the treasure and the pearl is about *this* earth, now, today.

Brothers, Sisters, Houses, Fields

The new thing that comes with the reign of God is not something purely spiritual, deeply hidden in individual hearts. The new thing was as concrete for Jesus as the treasure in the field and the precious pearl.

It is the community of disciples he gathers around him. It is the "new family" of those who follow him. It is all those who hear his words and become sisters and brothers to one another. One day Peter says to Jesus:

> "Look, we have left everything and followed you." Jesus said, "Truly I tell you, there is no one who has left house or brothers or sisters or mother or father or children or fields, for my sake and for the sake of the good news, who will not receive a hundredfold now in this age—houses, brothers and sisters, mothers and children, and fields—with persecutions—and in the age to come eternal life." (Mark 10:28-30)

This paradoxical saying shows how real the promises on which Jesus and his disciples are counting truly are. They have left everything: houses, brothers, sisters, mothers, and fathers. But everything they have left they will receive back abundantly "now in this age": a hundred sisters, a hundred brothers, a hundred mothers, houses, and fields. Jesus by no means meant that symbolically. He is talking about real relationships. He means really a hundred brothers and really a hundred sisters. He means a perceptible wealth in brotherhood and sisterhood. All this takes place on the ground of the new family, the common life of the community of disciples—in which, it is true, fathers no longer have a role to play. The patriarchalism of the Near Eastern family has been destroyed. God alone will now become the measure of genuine fatherhood (cf. Matt 23:9).

With all that, Jesus kindled a fire that has never been put out. It flamed up anew on Pentecost and burned in the communities that, in an unbelievably short time, sprang up all around the Mediterranean. Those communities understood themselves not as religious groupings in which individuals came together in order to be able to live their private piety in a better way. They regarded themselves as a social body "in Jesus Christ," a new family, a new society.

Believing and allowing oneself to be baptized in the name of Jesus meant a transformation of one's whole life, a new common life in the spirit of Jesus—and, where necessary, even a counter-world against ancient society. Faith in Jesus Christ was from the beginning more than mere interiority. Where the issue is the Gospel of Jesus it is always about the world and transforms the world. The widespread notion that within the church Christians learn faith in order to apply it in the world is a perversion, to the very root, of what Jesus actually wanted. Faith is from its first second about forming and transforming the world, and the

church is the place where the material of the world is grasped and redeemed by faith.

Where the church remained true to Jesus it was always "all in"; it was
a new society.[9] It not only demanded justice; it lived justice. It not only
preached freedom but was itself a place of freedom. It saw itself not as
a place for reflection where one was armed and equipped for the building sites in the world but as the building site itself. It hoped not only for
a future life in heaven; it knew that in the common life of the baptized
heaven is already revealed and the precious treasure has already been
found. It was certain that within the space of its communities creation
was already on the way to its integrity and the form planned for it. In
short, it saw itself as the beginning of the eschatological, liberated world,
the beginning of the "new creation" as "new earth."

Now all of a sudden a book that is supposed to be about Jesus is talking about the early Christian communities! But the two are inseparable.
In the physicality of the church, in its firm insistence that redemption
must begin here and now, in its holding fast to visible community, what
Jesus began with his disciples is continuing. We cannot avoid it: anyone
who really wants to talk about Jesus must always have the church in
view as well, because we have Jesus through the church or not at all.

That is why it was so tiresome when older scholarly commentaries on
the Synoptic Gospels continually asked whether in this or that case we
were dealing with authentic sayings of Jesus or not. Obviously Jesus'
response to Peter in Mark 10:28-30 also distills the experiences of early
Christian communities, and especially the early itinerant missionaries—the persecutions they suffered as well as the experience of a new
brotherhood and sisterhood that far surpassed all physical relationships.
But all that had begun with Jesus—with the fire he had kindled.

Overflowing Abundance

In the double parable of the treasure and the pearl the two actors make
a hundredfold or even thousandfold gain. The pearl is incomparably
beautiful and the treasure in the field will fundamentally change the life
of the day laborer. The reign of God appears in an astonishing and positively overflowing abundance.

But that is not only the case in Matthew 13:44-46. The superfluity of
the reign of God is found in many other gospel texts. Jesus was continually describing it, especially in his parables. We are moved to suspect
that he described this abundance so often because he himself had ex-

perienced the reign of God that way: as brilliance, beauty, overflowing riches.

The land that was sown in the parable of the great harvest of wheat, despite all the opponents that threatened the seed from beginning to end, produced a mighty yield: one grain brought forth thirty, sixty, or a hundred more grains (Mark 4:8). From the tiny mustard seed, no bigger than the head of a pin, grows a great shrub under whose branches the birds of the air build their nests (Mark 4:30-32). On the shores of Lake Genesareth mustard bushes could achieve a height of two to three meters. In Matthew's and Luke's gospels the mustard bush even becomes a world tree (Matt 13:32 // Luke 13:19). In the parable of the leaven (Matt 13:33 // Luke 13:20-21) the small amount of leaven is contrasted with a huge amount of flour (three measures [Greek *sata*] = fifty kilograms). What is interesting is that Jesus pays no attention to the negative connotations of leaven or yeast in Israel. He illustrates the coming of the reign of God by describing how the trivial amount of yeast (or sourdough) leavens the whole quantity of flour.

A man who has wasted his inheritance and tossed away his rights as a son remembers that in his father's house even the day laborers "have bread enough and to spare" (Luke 15:17). He returns home and is immediately taken back into the family by his father, who runs to meet him. The lost son receives a signet ring and a new robe; the fatted calf is slaughtered, and a feast of joy begins (Luke 15:11-32). A king forgives a failed debtor who has wrecked his whole life by running up a debt of ten thousand talents (or a hundred million denarii). A whole day's work was required to earn even one denarius, so the king forgives a sum corresponding to the value of a hundred million working days (Matt 18:23-35). A property owner treats the day laborers he has hired at the very last hour of the afternoon to work in the harvest in his vineyard as though they had worked all day: when evening comes he pays them a full day's wage (Matt 20:1-16).

Wherever we look we see that the gospels speak of overflowing abundance, extravagance, and superfluity. And it is not only the parables that do this. In Bethany, in the house of Simon the leper, a woman breaks an alabaster jar of the costliest nard oil and pours it on Jesus' hair; some of those present are upset and speak of meaningless waste, but Jesus defends the woman (Mark 14:3-9). Peter and his companions, after having worked all night without success, put out to sea again at Jesus' command and soon draw to the shore nets filled to the point of breaking with fish (Luke 5:1-11).

The disciples of John the Baptizer and the Pharisees fasted regularly as a sign of penance and humility before God; the Pharisees went so far as to fast two days a week. Jesus was once asked why his disciples did not keep fast days, and he answered, "The [sons of the wedding banquet hall] cannot fast while the bridegroom is with them, can they?" (Mark 2:19). The "sons of the wedding banquet hall" are the friends of the bridegroom and all the guests at the wedding. So Jesus sees the time that has arrived with his preaching of the reign of God as a wedding, God's wedding with God's people—and a wedding means abundance, generosity, and superfluity. It is impossible to fast during the days of the wedding feast!

This motif of superfluity that runs throughout the gospels culminates in the stories of the wedding at Cana and the so-called miraculous multiplication of the loaves. With regard to these two narratives I follow the principle I laid down in the first chapter: the historical reality cannot be grasped independently of the interpretation. Whatever lies behind these two narratives, historically speaking, they reflect, concentrate, and interpret the extravagant fullness of the reign of God as Jesus proclaimed and lived it.[10]

A Wedding

At the very beginning of Jesus' public activity the Fourth Evangelist tells of an event that culminates in an extravagant abundance (John 2:1-12). It takes place in Cana at a wedding that threatens to end pathetically because the wine has run out. The surplus associated with Jesus' coming is shown here in a wine miracle he performs. The narrative carefully develops the fact that he gives the wedding company a huge quantity of wine, for it is not the clay jars ordinarily used to hold wine that are filled with water at Jesus' command, but six stone jars meant for ritual purification, therefore hewn from stone and unusually large. Each of these vessels, according to the evangelist, contained two to three *metretes*, or about a hundred liters. Thus in total about five to seven hundred liters of water are changed into wine. But the narrator not only states these detailed amounts; he adds very deliberately, "They filled [the jars] up to the brim."

Such details reveal the narrator's intention, which is to say that Jesus' gift is lavish. Here there is no thought of restriction, measuring, limiting, hoarding. The huge stone jars are brimful. And yet it is not enough that the abundance of wine be made evident. The narrative is just as explicit about the quality of the wine. It even introduces a separate person, the *architriklinos*—the one who supervises meals, and especially the mixing and distribution of wine. The *architriklinos* does not know where the wine in the stone jars has come from, and he is extremely offended that he is just now being told about it. The "wine rule" he pronounces (good wine is offered at the beginning and not at the end of the feast!) serves within the narrative to say modestly that the wine now being poured is a good, indeed, an outstanding vintage of the finest quality.

Thus the fullness that comes with Jesus does not remain something supersensory, internal, purely spiritual, transcendent; it is visible and tangible; it can be tasted and enjoyed.

A Banquet

Another story in the gospels speaks, similarly to the one about the wedding at Cana, of the abundance of the new thing that begins with Jesus. It is the story of the miraculous multiplication of loaves, handed down to us in the gospels no fewer than six times.[11] Let us follow the story on the basis of Mark 6:30-44.

The superscription used in almost all versions of the New Testament nowadays, "feeding of the five thousand," is not especially apt. "Feeding" is reminiscent of school lunches and charitable meals, not particularly of a feast, a banquet, a groaning board. But Mark obviously wants to tell us about a banquet, since according to Mark 6:39 Jesus tells the disciples to see to it that all those present *recline*, that is, take their places for a banquet.

People in antiquity had two different styles for eating a meal. The ordinary, everyday meal was taken sitting down, just as it is today. But when they celebrated a feast or invited guests to a festal dinner they *reclined* at table, lying on bolsters and pillows, leaning on the left arm and eating with the right. So when the disciples are to invite the people to recline on the ground it means that now a dinner is about to be served at which people will take their time; it will be a feast at which all may eat their fill. It is true that the bolsters and pillows are lacking, but they are replaced by rich, green grass, which Mark mentions specifically (6:39).

That this is actually a festive banquet is shown by the end of the story, where we are told specifically that the disciples collected the pieces that were left over. That too was a fixed ritual at a Jewish banquet: after the main course the banquet hall was "cleansed" by collecting all the fallen crumbs of bread that were larger than an olive. In Mark 6:43 the disciples collect twelve basketfuls of the remnants of the meal.

Why is there so much left over? Not because the participants in the meal did not enjoy the food or had not eaten their fill, but because it was a banquet. There are always leftovers from a banquet, as every cook knows. For a festal meal there is always more cooked, fried, and baked than is really necessary, because celebrating includes extravagance and a festal meal provides more than just enough. There can be no stinginess with such a meal; we would rather offer too much than too little. When at the end of the story of the multiplication of the loaves there are twelve baskets left over, the intention is to say that Jesus was a good host; he had presented a glorious meal and made a feast possible.

Why did the early Christian communities tell such stories? What did Jesus have to do with festal banquets, and what did groaning boards have to do with the reign of God? According to biblical theology, a great deal! In Isaiah 25:6-8 we read:

> On this mountain the LORD of hosts will make for all peoples a feast of rich food, a feast of well-aged wines, of rich food filled with marrow, of well-aged wines strained clear. And he will destroy on this mountain the shroud that is cast over all peoples, the sheet that is spread over all nations; he will swallow up death forever. Then the Lord GOD will wipe away the tears from all faces, and the disgrace of his people he will take away from all the earth, for the LORD has spoken.

This text from Isaiah presupposes that God has entered into his eschatological royal reign. This is clear from the connection to what has gone before in Isaiah 24:21-23. God's enthronement is followed by a banquet spread on Mount Zion. At this feast Israel shines with new glory. All the nations are invited to this enthronement meal, and during it the shroud of sorrow and suffering that lies over the nations is destroyed. Eschatological joy shines throughout the whole world and it will never come to an end.

For the prophets, what these images announce is still in the future. Jesus, by contrast, proclaims that the future has arrived. It is already present. The joy of the *eschaton* has begun. God's banquet with his people Israel, which is to expand into a banquet for all nations, is now beginning. Jesus is so sure that the reign of God will now become reality in the form of an abundant banquet that he calls his poor and hungry hearers blessed:

Blessed are you who are poor,
> for yours is the kingdom of God!

Blessed are you who are hungry now,
> for you will be filled!

Blessed are you who weep now,
> for you will laugh! (Luke 6:20-21)

As assurance of a reign of God that will come someday, some time, these statements in the Sermon on the Plain would have been utterly cynical, even a ridiculing of the audience. One may only promise the hungry that they will be filled if one expects that fulfillment not in the great beyond or in an uncertain future but in one that is already beginning. Jesus is altogether certain: that future is already present as an overflowing gift of God. He is already experiencing that future as a fascinating *now*.

A Basic Law of Salvation History

All the gospel texts quoted here that speak of abundance reveal a scarlet thread, a basic law of salvation history. Joseph Ratzinger, in an excursus, "Christian Structures," in his *Introduction to Christianity*, called it the "law of excess or superfluity." [12] It runs throughout the whole of that history but it finds its clearest expression in Jesus. He himself, Ratzinger says, "He is the righteousness of God, which goes far beyond what need be, which does not calculate, which really overflows; the 'notwithstanding' of his greater love, in which he infinitely surpasses the failing efforts of man." [13] This basic law of salvation history is put into words most fully in the parables of the lost son (Luke 15:11-32) and of the workers in the vineyard (Matt 20:1-16). But it also echoes in the sayings traditions in the gospels, as when Luke 6:38 says, "Give, and it will be given to you. A good measure, pressed down, shaken together, running over, will be put into your lap." It is an image from the market. The seller has filled a measure to the brim with wheat, then pressed the grains down with her hand so that there will be no empty space, shaken the whole so that the wheat is truly settled, and in the end poured a little mound on the top so that the measure overflows; finally, she pours an abundant measure of wheat into the skirt the buyer is holding open.

Superfluity, wealth, and extravagant luxury are thus the signs of the day of salvation—not skimpiness, meagerness, wretchedness, and need. Why? Because God's very self is overflowing life and because God longs to give a share in that life. God's love is without measure; God does not give to human beings according to the measure of their own good behavior or service.

Therefore the principle of superfluity is already revealed in creation. Biologists have long since observed that quantitative and qualitative extravagance plays a striking role in nature, and that evolution cannot be fully explained by a calculus of usefulness. Nature is "luxuriant." What opulence is shown just in butterflies and flowers! What an abundance of seeds is produced in order to bring forth just one living thing! What an expanse of solar systems, Milky Ways, and spiral nebulae! A whole universe is squandered just to beget more and more extravagant life forms on one tiny planet and make a place for the human spirit.[14]

Perhaps one might continue—in shock and almost stuttering—what an extravagance of human beings, of whole peoples, until at last God found the *one* people to whom he could attach the abundance of his grace in the world. In the book of Isaiah God forthrightly speaks of this squandering of nations for the sake of his own people: "I give Egypt as your ransom, Ethiopia and Saba in exchange for you. Because you are precious in my sight, and honored, and I love you, I give people in return for you, nations in exchange for your life" (Isa 43:3-4). But it also belongs to this side of divine extravagance that God—in the language of the New Testament—has given the *one*, the best and most precious of all human beings, has squandered him for the sake of the world. In light of the death of Jesus it is thus also clear that the extravagant abundance of salvation cannot be understood as a Neverland or utopia for consumers.

Overflowing grace can only reach human beings if they allow themselves to be taken into the service of God's plan. The glory that illumines Israel through Jesus is intended not to create a better life for the elect but, by way of Israel, to bring the glory of God into the world.

Finally, while the disciples were promised a hundred brothers and sisters, a hundred houses and fields, it is only "with persecutions." And the glory of Jesus that the miracle at Cana tells about will be made more explicit in the further course of the Fourth Gospel as a glory that finds its true shape only in Jesus' "hour," that is, in his suffering.[15] But in any case we may say that Jesus does not enter into that suffering for its own sake, which would be masochism. He enters into that suffering for the sake of the reign of God, which he must also proclaim in Jerusalem and from which he does not subtract an iota. He knows that the reign of God comes "with persecutions," but that does not deprive it of its brilliance and its fascinating abundance.

Chapter 15

Decision in Jerusalem

Jesus' whole existence was for the sake of the reign of God. That reign is not something vague and nebulous. Jesus was working toward the eschatological restoration of Israel, so that the reign of God might have a place. To create with and in the midst of Israel a space for the reign of God—that is what is at stake also in three sign-actions at the end of Jesus' life. The three are related; not only that, they are internally interconnected to the utmost extent: Jesus' entry into the capital city on a young donkey, his action in the temple, and the sign-action with bread and wine during his last meal. It is no accident that these particular three symbolic actions collide at the end of his life.

Jesus' Entry into the Capital

The oldest[1] account of Jesus' entry into the capital city is found in Mark 11:1-11. In this narrative a good deal of space is accorded to finding the donkey on which he is to ride: it takes up no less than two-thirds of the text. Apparently for Mark (or for the tradition available to him), the animal on whose back Jesus enters into the city is of great importance. The discovery episode is meant to emphasize that it was a young donkey and that Jesus had planned this kind of entry. That entry is then described rather briefly:

> Then they brought the colt to Jesus and threw their cloaks on it; and he sat on it. Many people spread their cloaks on the road, and others

> spread leafy branches that they had cut in the fields. Then those who
> went ahead and those who followed were shouting, "Hosanna!
> Blessed is the one who comes in the name of the Lord! Blessed is the
> coming kingdom of our ancestor David! Hosanna in the highest
> heaven!" Then he entered Jerusalem and went into the temple. (Mark
> 11:7-11)

Thus Jesus' entry is accompanied by many festival pilgrims who are on
the road to the capital with Jesus. What does their cry mean? In part it
comes from Psalm 118:25-26. Large groups of pilgrims were greeted in
Jerusalem with "blessed is the one who comes in the name of the Lord"
at the moment when they entered the space before the temple area. Here
this welcoming cry has been transformed into an acclamation addressed
exclusively to Jesus and expanded by praise of the now-inbreaking kingdom of David, that is, the messianic kingdom. In addition, the shout
now comes from the pilgrims themselves.

But we must note primarily something that is not immediately apparent
to every reader today: what Mark is describing here is nothing less than a
royal entrance. This is not the usual jubilation with which just any group
of pilgrims was received when they arrived at the temple for a festival.
Rather, the scene describes the entry of a king into his city, the arrival of
the Messiah on Zion. In a sense he is taking possession of his city.

That this is the precise intent of the narrative is shown by the presence
of the donkey, which is spoken of in the Old Testament, in Zechariah 9:9
and in Genesis 49:11, as the mount destined for the Messiah. Without
question, the use of the word "colt" is an allusion to Zechariah 9:9, which
reads, "Rejoice greatly, O daughter Zion! Shout aloud, O daughter Jerusalem! Lo, your king comes to you; [righteous] and victorious is he,
humble and riding on a donkey, on a colt, the foal of a donkey."[2]

The words "righteous," "victorious," and "humble" in Zechariah 9:9
require explanation. This king is "righteous" because he is, before God
and through God's grace, the ultimate ruler who does the will of God
entirely. He is "victorious" because God has rescued him from danger
(Hebrew *noshaʿ*). He is called "humble" because he is a lowly person,
poor before God. The external sign of this is that he rides not on a parade
horse but on a donkey, the beast of the poor. He is the longed-for king
in whom God is well pleased.

Other signals in the text also point to a *royal* entry: ancient cities received a royal ruler with branches and garments spread on the road, and

"hosanna," originally a plea ("help!"), had become a cry of homage and rejoicing. Whether or not the fact that the cry "hosanna" was originally meant for God is intended to play some role, it serves at least to introduce the subsequent homage, "blessed is the one who comes." And that is said of Jesus. So the narrative depicts a royal entrance, a "taking possession" of the city.[3]

If we look at the historical event itself there is no compelling reason to question an entrance of Jesus into Jerusalem during which he was celebrated as the Messiah. He was not only surrounded by excited festival pilgrims from Galilee who had seen his deeds of power or heard about them—most recently the healing of the blind beggar Bartimaeus in Jericho (Mark 10:46-52). There had apparently been earlier attempts in Galilee to appoint Jesus a (messianic) king (John 6:15).

The crucial question is about Jesus' own attitude to the whole business. Had the "Davidic-Messianic expectations" of the people coalesced "in the atmosphere of Jerusalem"[4] and been immediately poured out on him—against his will, so to speak? That is how many New Testament scholars see it today. They say either that Jesus did not want any of it or—still more radically—that the event was a simple arrival in Jerusalem with a crowd of pilgrims, and it was only Christian legend that, after Easter, elevated and stylized it as a royal entry.

I cannot share that skepticism. It has little to do with historical criticism and a good deal to do with the desire to create for ourselves a pleasant and modernized Jesus who fits our present ideas and offers as little resistance to the observer as possible. I am convinced that Jesus really did enter into the city on a donkey, the mount of the poor and simple people—and that he did so deliberately on the model of Zechariah 9:9.

Nowhere in the texts is there the smallest indication that Jesus distanced himself from the acclamations of the crowd around him. Apparently, in entering Jerusalem on an ass's colt Jesus was deliberately exhibiting an unmistakable sign. He wanted to come to the city as a poor, unarmed king, the messiah of peace of Zechariah 9:9 and the one who proclaimed the reign of God, as in Zechariah 14:9 ("and the Lord will become king over all the earth"). The radical rejection of all force and violence stated in Zechariah 9:10 ("He will cut off the chariot from Ephraim and the war horse from Jerusalem; and the battle bow shall be cut off, and he shall command peace to the nations") fits Jesus' self-awareness very well. Apparently he knew Zechariah 9:9 and applied the text to himself. As we saw above (chap. 11), Jesus read his Bible with an unfathomable sensitivity to what is essential.

If Jesus, when entering the city, was acting deliberately on the words of the book of Zechariah, that, of course, presumes that in that hour he made himself *publicly* known as the Messiah. We will have to speak in detail later about his messianic awareness (see chap. 19, "Jesus' Sovereign Claim"). Here, we can anticipate this much: Jesus was extremely reticent about using the word "messiah." The concept could all too easily be misunderstood in a political sense. In addition, Jesus' claim dissolved a sometimes superficial notion of the messiah. The Old Testament itself offered a sufficient basis for a deeper understanding of the concept and for transforming, purifying, and seeing it in a new light—quite apart from the fact that in the time of Jesus the expectation of a messiah was much more varied and nuanced than is often supposed. We may take it as given that when the people shouted "blessed is the [now] coming kingdom of our ancestor David," Jesus would have understood it in a deeper sense than many of those who were shouting it. He had to take all possible misunderstanding on himself.

At any rate, taking possession of the city would have been so important to him that in this instance he accepted the possibility of being misunderstood. The solemn entrance into the city was connected with his understanding of the reign of God. That reign was breaking forth. It had to be proclaimed everywhere, but especially in the capital city. And it had to be not only proclaimed but made present *in a sign* by him as representative of the reign of God. That was the reason for the action in the temple that came next and was intimately connected with his taking possession of the city.[5]

If Jesus wanted to enter Jerusalem as the humble king of Zechariah 9:9, that ultimately presumes that he was aware that everything would be decided in Jerusalem. A confrontation would ensue. Probably he had no illusions about the outcome of that confrontation, but he had to summon Jerusalem to decision because there the temple stood, there was the center of Israel, there the people of God gathered for the greatest feast of the year. There, at the Passover feast, all Israel was represented, and the proclamation of the reign of God must necessarily be as public as possible. This certainly suggested a provocative entry into the city.

I also assume that the evangelists correctly interpreted Jesus' entry into the city of Jerusalem. He wanted to establish a symbol, against the background of the book of Zechariah. The question of the extent to which the developing situation as he approached the city exerted external pressure to establish this sign, or to what degree he himself deliberately performed it, is not at all decisive, since in both cases it would be true that his entry became a vocal, resonant sign-action (cf. Luke 19:40), and he willed it to be so.[6]

The Temple Action

When Jesus entered Jerusalem as Messiah and representative of the reign of God, to proclaim that reign in the capital city as a climax to all his work in Galilee, he could not avoid the temple. The ancient principle obtained: the king, or the ruler, is responsible for the temple.[7] So the action in the temple associated with the entry into Jerusalem is no accident. The proclamation of the reign of God in Jerusalem also affected the temple and its surroundings; in fact, it applied to the temple above all. Therefore the temple action almost had to follow. In Matthew's and Luke's gospels it occurs immediately after the entry into the city, and in Mark's gospel it is closely associated with it. Mark relates it as follows:

> Then they came to Jerusalem. And he entered the temple and began to drive out those who were selling and those who were buying in the temple, and he overturned the tables of the money changers and the seats of those who sold doves; and he would not allow anyone to carry anything through the temple. He was teaching and saying, "Is it not written, 'My house shall be called a house of prayer for the nations?' But you have made it a den of robbers." And when the chief priests and the scribes heard it, they kept looking for a way to kill him; for they were afraid of him, because the whole crowd was spellbound by his teaching. (Mark 11:15-18)

Obviously all this took place neither in the priests' court nor in the courts of the men or of the women. It happened on the edges of the gigantic "court of the Gentiles" surrounding the central part of the temple. There, on the south side, in the "royal hall," stood the booths of those who sold doves and changed money. The doves were sold to the poor who could not afford a sacrificial animal; the money changers for a fee exchanged coins for Tyrian double drachmas and tetradrachmas, the only money with which one could pay the annual temple tax.[8] The extensive court of the Gentiles, however, was not only populated by those visiting the temple; it was also crossed by people looking to avoid walking the long way around. They used the temple area as a shortcut into the city or between its different quarters.

It is completely impossible that Jesus could have "cleansed" this huge area. Consequently, interpreters prefer to speak now of a "temple action" by Jesus. He must have demonstratively overturned tables and booths and scolded people carrying loads who took shortcuts over the temple mount. He could only establish a sign. And such a sign demanded also a word of interpretation. What did he say? Currently, biblical scholars are increasingly convinced that this interpretative word was Jesus' so-called temple saying. What does that mean? According to Mark, when Jesus was being interrogated by the Council, "false witnesses" came forward and asserted, "We heard him say, 'I will destroy this temple that is made with hands, and in three days I will build another, not made with hands'" (Mark 14:58). In that form it is an incredible saying. It con-trasts the gigantic temple, probably the greatest in the world at that time, with another temple not made by human hands, that is, established by God. And Jesus himself will build it. We can understand that even the authors of the gospels were alarmed by that saying. Mark attributes it to false witnesses. But they did not agree, and so their statements were use-less. Luke, in depicting the interrogation, simply omits the scene with the temple saying (Luke 22:66-69). Matthew softens it; in his gospel the false witnesses do not assert that Jesus said he *would* tear down the temple but that he *could* do it (Matt 26:61). Finally, John interprets the saying as referring to the "temple of his body," that is, to Jesus' resurrection (John 2:19-21).

Apparently, then, the early church had problems with the saying, and understandably so, since, after all, it was the Romans who destroyed the temple, and it was not rebuilt. But even the attempts to come to terms with the difficult temple saying and interpret it correctly show that there must have been such a saying. We cannot reconstruct it precisely. It must have referred to the temple of the end time. The Old Testament—and especially the book of Zechariah—had already assumed that at some time there would be such a temple in the midst of a Jerusalem gleaming with holiness.[9] It is also clear that this eschatological temple is ultimately God's creation. But Jesus must have said that the rebuilding of the final temple was already beginning with him. That, at any rate, would cor-respond exactly to his idea of the coming of the reign of God and the role he himself was to play in it. The temple action would then be an indication, a sign, in fact the initiation of this new building of the temple of the end time.[10]

Certainly Jesus would scarcely have said these things about the temple at the time of the action itself. The temple saying fits much better in a situation in which he was accosted by representatives of the Council on account of the action that had already taken place. As Mark 11:27-33 shows, there was such a situation the very next day. During the temple action itself Jesus must have spoken more directly and less enigmatically. What Mark reports as happening at that time fits much better: "Is it not written, 'My house shall be called a house of prayer for the nations?' But you have made it a den of robbers" (Mark 11:17). The words "den of robbers" are in Jeremiah's temple speech (Jer 7:1-15): the sacrifices in the temple must correspond to a just society; otherwise God can no longer dwell in this place, and the temple will be destroyed.

The phrase "house of prayer for [all] nations" is from the last ten chapters of Isaiah (specifically Isa 56:7). The immediate context speaks of the gathering of Israel (Isa 56:8), and the broader context describes the pilgrimage of the nations to the eschatological Jerusalem (Isa 60) and the glory of the city newly rebuilt by God (Isa 62). So the words with which the temple action is accompanied in Mark's gospel echo both the prophets' sharp critique of the temple and their vision of it in the end time. Then the symbolic action in the court of the Gentiles would not have been fundamentally directed against the temple as such but against everything that did not correspond to the holiness of the eschatological temple.

In connection with Jesus' proclamation of the reign of God that, of course, meant that the eschatological temple is beginning *now*. Now God is requiring holiness in his house, and it is Jesus himself through whom God is creating the new temple. Thus the temple action and the temple saying are subject to the radical "today" that shapes Jesus' whole message and practice. Because the reign of God is already breaking in and the new creation of Israel has already begun, the business of the temple in its present form cannot continue. The hour of the eschatological temple has arrived.

Did Jesus make a concrete image of this new eschatological temple for himself? We do not know; all we can be sure about is that the early Christian communities after Easter very quickly came to regard themselves as the eschatological temple, a sanctuary built of living stones.[11] They did so long before the temple was finally destroyed by the Romans in the year 70.

The Sadducaic priestly nobility that held power in Jerusalem apparently understood quite clearly the degree to which their own image of the temple was being called into question by Jesus. Just as in the case of the Torah the issue was not merely one of marginal questions about the interpretation of the Law, so here it was not simply about marginal issues regarding the temple area—for example, whether the money changers and dove sellers should not be carrying on their business in the city instead of being in the outer courts of the temple. Rather, it was about Jesus' right to see the cult in Jerusalem wholly in light of his message about the reign of God, and thus also his right to intervene. That is precisely what was so emphatically contested by the high priests, the scribes, and the elders, that is, the Council (or Sanhedrin), the highest religious authority in Israel.

The Last Meal

Luke, before describing the institution of the Eucharist, records the following words of Jesus: "I have eagerly desired to eat this Passover with you before I suffer" (Luke 22:15). The saying makes it clear that Jesus knows what is coming. He will suffer; he will be killed. For that very reason this last meal he will celebrate with the Twelve has a special significance for him. Jesus' whole longing rests on this meal. It was not just any meal, but the Passover feast. That is how Luke sees it, and so do Mark and Matthew also.

Because Jesus sees his death coming, he has to give it an interpretation.[12] The Passover meal itself gave him the opportunity to do so, because this very meal was and had been from ancient times saturated with signs, references, and interpretations. There were the bitter herbs, the unleavened bread, the lamb, and the cup of blessing (later numbered as the third cup). The meal made present the exodus from Egypt and looked forward in hope to the Messiah. An ancient Aramaic interpretive word over the unleavened bread read, "See, this is the bread of affliction that our ancestors had to eat when they came out of Egypt."[13]

Among Jesus scholars there is dispute about whether Jesus' last meal was a Passover meal at all. While the tradition of the first three evangelists clearly speaks of a Paschal meal in the night before the fifteenth of Nisan, the Fourth Gospel stresses that the day of Jesus' crucifixion was the fourteenth of Nisan, so that Jesus died at exactly the hour in which the Paschal lambs were being slaughtered in the temple.[14] But precisely that would be Johannine theology: Jesus is thus depicted as the true Paschal lamb. Consequently, John does not represent Jesus' last meal as a Passover supper.

In what follows I will give preference to the accounts of the first three gospels: Jesus' last meal was the Passover meal in the night before 15 Nisan. The counterarguments have weight, but they are in no way decisive.[15] At times they ignore the situation altogether. For example, it is argued that the Passover meal was celebrated in the family, with women and children, while Mark says that Jesus took his last meal with only the group of the Twelve.[16] Indeed, that is how Mark portrays it. And that must have been Jesus' precise intention: not to celebrate the Passover meal as it was usually done, with his natural family, but with his new family, and not with a random selection of disciples who might have been available. Instead, as Mark emphatically states, he wanted to celebrate it with the Twelve (Mark 14:17-18). His last meal had the familial intimacy that is proper to the Paschal supper, and yet the choice of participants points emphatically to Israel, to the eschatological gathering and new creation of the people of God that Jesus had begun with his circle of twelve. Here the usual ritual may not be held up against Jesus' freedom. In what follows I will rely on Mark's account for the description of the details.[17] He depicts the special character of the meal as follows:

During the meal Jesus takes the bread, speaks the usual thanksgiving prayer over it, breaks it, and hands it to the Twelve. That is the prescribed ritual. It is the table prayer before the main course, after the appetizers have been eaten and the father of the family has recalled the people's being led out of Egypt. It is true that Mark says nothing about the appetizers, the Passover liturgy, and other elements of the meal. The tradition he is following assumes all that as familiar and a matter of course. Mark and his tradition relate only what is special and unique about this one Passover meal.[18] One of those things was that Jesus interpreted the broken bread he handed to his meal companions with the words "This is my body."

"Body" should not be understood in our Western sense, in contrast to the soul. "Body" means the whole person. Jesus intends to say, "I myself am this bread, with my whole history and life. My life will be broken like this bread. I give it to you so that you may share in it."

Thus Jesus' sign-action is a prophecy of his death, which he proclaims in the sign of the broken bread. But at the same time this sign-action is more than a death prophecy, for Jesus gives the Twelve a share in his existence, in his life that will now be given over to death. Evidently his death has a depth dimension in which the Twelve, and therefore Israel, must share. Mark—in contrast to the Lukan/Pauline line of the Last Supper tradition[19]—does not yet say at this point what that dimension may be.

The Markan tradition assumes, without saying it explicitly, that the main part of the meal—the eating of the Paschal lamb with bitter herbs, bread, and the fruit mixture called *ᶜaroseth*—followed the table prayer and the word of interpretation over the broken bread. At the end of this central part, the father of the family took the "cup of blessing" and pronounced another prayer of thanksgiving over it. At this point Mark again begins to tell us of another unusual event: Jesus makes the giving and drinking of the cup of blessing a sign-action as well, for after saying the prayer of thanksgiving he interprets the cup as follows: "This is my blood, [the blood] of the covenant, that will be poured out for many."

The statement is replete with traditional motifs, almost too many for people today. But we should not fault the ancient text for it. Today's hearers would not know, either, that the background of the Aramaic words of interpretation Jesus cites is Deuteronomy 16:1-8. For Jewish ears at that time a few central words, often just one, were sufficient to evoke a broader biblical context. What is Mark's text saying?

First of all: Jesus again refers to his imminent death. He interprets the cup of red wine as his blood, soon to be shed. "Shedding blood" means "killing." Jesus will be killed. But here again the saying does not remain merely a prophecy of death. The text does not simply speak of Jesus' blood, but of his blood of the covenant, and "blood of the covenant" alludes to the event in Exodus 24:4-11. That is the story of the act of Israel's founding. Moses builds an altar at the foot of Sinai and sets up twelve pillars, dashes the blood of sacrifices against the altar, and reads the book of the covenant in the hearing of the twelve tribes. Finally, he also sprinkles the people with the blood and says, "See the blood of the covenant that the LORD has made with you in accordance with all these words" (Exod 24:8). After that, Moses and the elders of Israel are permitted to eat a meal with God himself on the mountain. At this point we do not need to ask about the original meaning of this sprinkling with blood; probably it was intended to show that Israel had become a nation of priests in the sense of Exodus 19:6: "You shall be for me a priestly kingdom and a holy nation."

Crucial to the later understanding of Exodus 24:8 is that it combines three motifs: the common meal, God's covenant with Israel, and the blood with which the covenant is sealed. In the Jewish interpretive tradition in Jesus' time this blood dashed onto the altar at the foot of Sinai was a means of atonement for the sins of Israel.[20]

Against this background Jesus' saying about the cup of blessing in Mark 14:24 can only mean that his life is being surrendered to death. But his blood, which flows out as a result, is not shed in vain and without meaning; it is "blood of the covenant," that is, it renews and perfects the covenant God once made with Israel at Sinai. This eschatological renewal of the covenant, which is simultaneously a new creation and a new founding of Israel, takes place through the blood of Jesus, which frees Israel from its sins and atones for it.

If we take seriously the connection to Exodus 24:8 the "many" of whom the cup saying in Mark speaks can initially refer only to Israel. Jesus interprets his violent death as dying for Israel, as an atoning surrender of his life for the life of the people of God. That reference to Israel was clear from the very fact that Jesus gave the cup of blessing to the Twelve, his chosen representatives of the people of the twelve tribes. But the reference to Israel is equally clear from the background of the Sinai covenant. That covenant was made with Israel, and if it is renewed, then it is renewed with Israel. The "many" are, then, in the first place, the people of the twelve tribes.

We cannot be content to say that, however, because the saying about the "many" comes from Isaiah 52:13–53:12, the so-called Fourth Servant Song. The Servant[21] suffers as representative of the many, and in this song, in which "many" is a *leitmotif*, they are clearly the Gentile nations.[22] So in redacting the Last Supper tradition available to him Mark must have had the nations in view in addition to Israel. That is not a problem, for Israel, in the theology of the Old Testament, is representative of the nations. It was not chosen for its own sake but for that of the world. The salvation that spreads throughout Israel is to become salvation for the whole world. Therefore the many can be Israel first of all, and then beyond Israel the nations as well. This universal statement becomes false only if it passes over the reference to Israel. And that is certainly not the case for Mark, nor is it for the other New Testament authors.

So we can also say that, according to Mark, in the course of the Paschal meal Jesus interprets the loaf of bread torn asunder and the red wine in terms of his approaching death, and by handing the bread and wine to the Twelve he gives them, and so Israel, a share in the power of his death. For this death is at the same time interpreted as atonement for Israel, which has fallen into sin, and as a renewal of the Sinai covenant. And by way of the eschatological Israel this new and ultimate salvation is to reach the many nations.

In Mark's gospel Jesus concludes this complex of interpretation with an eschatological outlook: "Truly I tell you: I will never again drink of the fruit of the vine until that day when I drink it new in the [reign] of God" (Mark 14:25). Here again Jesus utters a prophecy of his death: from now on he will drink no more wine, certainly not the wine of the Passover meal, because he will be killed. But the death prophecy is not the whole of the matter. Jesus points toward the great banquet of the end time as described, for example, in Isaiah 25:6-8. When that meal takes place, death will be destroyed forever. The shroud of sorrow that covers all the nations will be torn asunder. All disgrace will be removed from Israel (Isa 25:7-8). But above all, on that day God will finally and forever be shown to be king (Isa 24:23). The reign of God will dawn in its perfection, in all its fullness. With this eschatological outlook Mark concludes Jesus' last meal.

Since there is no serious reason to regard Mark's presentation of the Last Supper as a scribal construction by the early communities (who, after all, would have had the *chutzpah* to make up such a story about Jesus?), and since the tradition about the Last Supper that Paul cites in 1 Corinthians 11:23-25 agrees in essential points with Mark 14:22-24, we may say that this is how Jesus celebrated his last meal, and this is how he understood it.

Thus at the end of his life Jesus performs a last and crucial sign-action. He does so in face of his approaching death. It interprets that death, but at the same time it is the sum and climax of earlier sign-actions. It reaches back to the constitution of the Twelve, because Jesus celebrates the Passover meal with the group of the Twelve. But it also refers back to the preceding entry into the city and the action in the temple. Jesus had made himself known as the Messiah of Israel and as the one who was entitled to submit even the temple to the rule of God. He was thinking of the eschatological temple, which would be altogether holy and altogether fitting for God. Now, in his words of interpretation over the cup, he makes his own life and death the place of atonement for Israel (and thus also for the nations). In this way, of course, the concept of the temple is redefined and placed in a new frame of reference. Its innermost center is no longer the many sacrifices, but the one sacrifice of life, Jesus' surrender of his own life. He himself is the new and final "place" of atonement.

This is so bold, even outrageous, that a great many New Testament scholars simply deny that Jesus had any idea of atonement, not only in celebrating his last meal, but altogether. They still grant him an eschatological outlook in his last meal, but not the interpretation of his approaching death as an atoning action on behalf of Israel. The questions thus raised are so fundamental to an understanding of what Jesus wanted that we must devote an entire chapter to them.

Chapter 16

Dying for Israel

Skepticism and inability to understand the idea of atonement are widespread, not only in society, but also in many church circles.[1] At least in Germany the word "atonement" does not appear in newer prayers and hymn texts. We may say there is resistance to any formulation that alludes to atonement. This is connected, first of all, with the fact that the word "atonement" has become narrower and narrower in meaning. It was always a component of legal language, but in the medieval period Old High German *suona* and Middle High German *suone* acquired, besides the meaning "recompense," the additional nuances of "judgment," "contract," "settlement," "compensation," "conciliatory ending of a legal conflict," "making peace," and even "forgiveness."[2] Of this originally broad spectrum of meanings there remained, in the nineteenth and twentieth centuries, only the means by which a debt was paid. Atonement thus came to mean the punishment imposed by a judge so that the crime committed by the offender may be compensated for.

Modern people don't like such things. They don't want criminals to atone for their crimes, but instead that they be improved and resocialized or, if that is impossible, that the general public be protected from them. If they hear "atonement" in a theological context they connect it with the specter of a cruel God who is profoundly offended, mercilessly demands the payment due him, and can only be appeased by an infinite atonement. That, or something like it, is what many people imagine as "atonement" in a Christian context, and they turn away with a shudder.

A Jesus without Atonement

Something else must be added. In New Testament exegesis atonement often appears as a theological construct with whose aid the post-Easter community interpreted the otherwise unfathomable execution of Jesus on the cross. They thus gave meaning to Jesus' catastrophic death. Jesus himself understood his death much more simply—perhaps in the sense of the eschatological view in Mark 14:25 ("I will never again drink of the fruit of the vine until that day when I drink it new in the [reign] of God"). When we deny that Jesus thought of atonement we degrade the idea of atonement from the outset. We no longer need take the concept seriously since Jesus himself did not use it and the early church only did so in order to give a deeper meaning to Jesus' death.

That Jesus remained firm in his message of the coming reign of God and his love for human beings even to death is something we can appreciate, but not the thick theological web of blood, atonement, representation, and covenant embedded in the saying over the cup in Mark 14:24. After all, during the whole time of his previous activity Jesus never said anything of the kind.[3]

So it is that, for example, Herbert Braun's book on Jesus sees the Last Supper as nothing more than a banquet with friends, in continuity with Jesus' previous meals. After Jesus' death his followers took up this meal custom again and in doing so looked forward with great joy to Jesus' return. There were not yet any words of institution or "sacramental" food, nor was there any special "remembrance of Jesus' death," but simply a "breaking of bread." Only later did the Palestinian community interpret Jesus' death as atoning. The Hellenistic community then did something more: they saw these meals by analogy with the meals of the Greek mystery cults and "set back" the institution of "this sacrament, perceived in Hellenistic terms," to the last hours of Jesus' life.[4]

Nothing in this description can withstand a sober historical examination, from the schematic and undifferentiated distinction between Palestinian and Hellenistic communities[5] to the derivation of the early Christian eucharistic celebration from the meals of the Hellenistic mysteries.[6] It seems that for Braun the Old Testament had no part to play, nor did the fact that Jesus was a Jew who lived wholly on the basis of the Old Testament.

There is one position that radicalizes the objection to the idea of atonement in Jesus' Last Supper still further. It says that the idea of an atoning death was not only fully improbable for Jesus but is incompatible with his proclamation of the nature of God. Jesus, it is said, preached a Father who was ready to forgive without condition. That this loving Father then one day was no longer so generous and suddenly demanded atonement simply does not fit with Jesus' message and practice.[7]

A Gospel of Death?

Obviously this position says something correct with regard to Jesus' preaching. He by no means came preaching the message that "I have come into the world to suffer and so to atone for the sins of the world; follow me and suffer with me!" He certainly did not preach, "I have come into the world because God desires me to be a sacrifice for the redemption of the world. Death on the cross is the goal of my life." If Jesus' message had been anything like that it would have been masochism, glorification of suffering, a culture of death. That is *not* how Jesus spoke and acted. From the very beginning his proclamation was *evangelium*, Gospel, "good news." We have seen that Jesus saw himself as the messenger of joy in Isaiah 52:7. He summarized his activity with elements of Isaiah's text: "The blind receive their sight, the lame walk, the lepers are cleansed, the deaf hear, the dead are raised, and the poor have good news brought to them" (Matt 11:5). The blind, the lame, the lepers, the deaf, and the dead represent the suffering and misery of Israel and the world. Jesus acts against that suffering. He desires that God should be master of the world so that creation might become what it is really supposed to be. That is the impetus of his message and his actions.

This transformation of the world does not, however, come about by magic. It is brought about by Jesus' surrender to the will of God, his surrender to Israel, his living with his whole existence for the sake of the people of God. This "for" is realized in a great many ways, for example, in his healings of the sick or in the teachings of the Sermon on the Mount. These instructions, such as love of enemies, Jesus not only preached; he lived them. The disciples he gathered around him learned from him trust, forgiveness, reconciliation, compassion, service, turning away from the self, and turning toward the people of God. They are to make God's concern for the world their own.

So Jesus' message is thoroughly good news, but from the very beginning it contains within itself a radical "for others," "for Israel," "for the world." This "for" is inextricably bound up with the message itself. If one were to take it away, the message would be an empty husk.

What happens when such a message encounters indifference, resistance, even the will to destroy? Then it still remains good news, but at the same time the giving-oneself-for-others that is inherent in the message from the beginning emerges more clearly and sharply, even harshly.

The New Situation

We have to consider the whole matter still more radically. It is false, to begin with, to reduce Jesus' preaching of the reign of God to a timeless message about the timeless essence of God. That is as unbiblical as anything can be,[8] for the nearness of the reign of God is not something timeless, as far as Jesus is concerned. The reign of God is not something to be had always and everywhere. It has its hour. For him it is unique, self-contained, to be grasped now, not something that can be repeated at will, an eschatological offer from God. In that, it resembles John's baptism, which also had its unrepeatable hour. Jesus could build on the movement the Baptizer had begun. Without his call for repentance the good news would not have been possible. Like John's baptism, Jesus' preaching is a once-and-for-all address by God to Israel. The salvation offered by Jesus must therefore not be detached from its historical situation.

If Jesus encountered more indecision than faith in Galilee, and if now in Jerusalem Israel's representatives rejected him—indeed, made sure that he would be killed—then Israel was rejecting the reign of God. But if Israel refused to accept the reign of God it abandoned the whole meaning of its existence, squandered salvation for itself and the nations, and made God's action in choosing Israel absurd. That is the only way to explain the terrible seriousness of the judgment sayings Jesus spoke over Israel toward the end of his public activity. He must have reckoned with the definitive refusal of the people of God when, for example, he said:

> Jerusalem, Jerusalem, the city that kills the prophets and stones those who are sent to it! How often have I desired to gather your children together as a hen gathers her brood under her wings, and you were not willing! See, your house is left to you, desolate. (Matt 23:37-38)

"Your house" is the temple. The "your" only sharpens the point of the judgment saying. It is no longer the common sanctuary, the holy house for all Israelites, but "your house." It is *abandoned* to Israel; that is, it is *abandoned by God*.[9] At the hour when God's eschatological messenger was done away with there had to arise a situation in which nothing was any longer as it had been at the beginning of Jesus' appearance in Galilee—a situation in which Jesus' proclamation, "the reign of God has come near," could never again be simply repeated. Because in that case grace itself would have been rejected.[10] Indeed, we have to phrase it even more sharply: not only would grace have been rejected, but in the very moment in which God gives himself totally to his people Israel in Jesus, when, so to speak, he shows his innermost self and does his utmost—in that very moment the highest religious authorities of that very people he had cared for over the centuries and struggled for since Abraham reject him.

Therefore in this moment Jesus and Israel were faced with an entirely new situation, and that new situation demanded a new interpretation. To argue that Jesus never spoke before about his blood, about substitution and atonement, is not to the point. It assumes that the existence of individuals and of nations is carried on outside history. But the new interpretation Jesus gives in this very moment when the people of God is at the point of squandering its election for the sake of the world does not happen just anywhere and at any time. It happens at the Passover meal, at one of the holiest hours of the Jewish year. Jesus interprets his death as a final and definitive saving decree of God. Israel's guilt, concentrated in Jesus' death, is thus answered by God: he does not withdraw election from his people but instead truly allows that people to live, even though it has forfeited its life. That is precisely what the Bible means by "atonement."[11]

In this interpretation Jesus makes use of Scripture in masterful fashion. He is familiar, of course, with the texts about the Sinai covenant, sealed with atoning blood;[12] he knows the texts about the new (= renewed) covenant that sets aside Israel's sins after it has broken the Sinai covenant;[13] he knows above all the texts about the Suffering Servant who gives his life and takes the guilt of the many on himself.[14] The Servant, of course, is Israel,[15] but Jesus can see himself as the embodiment of the true Israel.

In interpreting his death in the light of the Torah and the prophets, did Jesus deny his previous message? Precisely the contrary is the case. Jesus had proclaimed the reign of God as a reign of God's mercy and kindness. When he now, in the crucial hour before his death, sets before the eyes of the participants in the meal in definitive signs that God is holding fast to the covenant with Israel, indeed, that God is renewing the covenant and assuring this people of new life in spite of everything, he reveals the true radicality of God's mercy. We must truly say that only in the interpretation Jesus gives to his approaching death does his message of the reign of God achieve its ultimate power and shape. And here, with utmost clarity, appears definitively the "being for others" that was implied in his message from the beginning.

If there are again and again exegetes who simply deny that Jesus could have understood his death as an existential representative substitution for the many and an atoning sacrifice for Israel, that is not really based on questions of historical criticism. Their decision has already been made beforehand, long before the historical discussion has begun. Rudolf Bultmann made that clear, with the honesty that was his, when in his famous essay on "New Testament and Mythology" he wrote:

> How can my guilt be atoned for by the death of someone guiltless (assuming one may even speak of such)? What primitive concepts of guilt and righteousness lie behind any such notion? And what primitive concepts of God? If what is said about Christ's atoning death is to be understood in terms of the idea of sacrifice, what kind of primitive mythology is it according to which a divine being who has become man atones with his blood for the sins of humanity?[16]

Precisely here the course is set for historical demonstrations that present themselves as logical and certain. People living in the wake of the European Enlightenment can no longer reconcile concepts such as representative substitution and atonement with the autonomy they have gained by so much struggle.[17] But are they really irreconcilable? What is meant by representative substitution and atonement only becomes an irritant when the experience of the people of God has been forgotten. For life in the people of God, representative substitution and atonement are simply elementary. They detract nothing from the dignity and independence of the human being.

Representative Substitution

Israel's existence always depended on individuals who believed with their whole existence. That the scarlet thread of salvation history was never broken depended on Abraham, Moses, Elijah, Amos, and Isaiah; on King Josiah, on John the Baptizer, and on many others. Others could enter into their faith and so come to believe in their own right. It is not a language game to say of Abraham that whoever blesses him will be blessed, and that through him all the families of the earth achieve blessing (Gen 12:3). Jesus' representative substitution for the many is no exotic exception but the culmination and ultimate distillation of a long history of representation in Israel. Only by way of representative substitution can faith be handed on at all.

Nevertheless, representative substitution never means dispensing others from their own faith and repentance; it is meant to make both those things possible. True representation does not infantilize; it desires nothing more strongly than that the other should be free to act. It is done so that one person takes the place of another, not to "replace" that one, but to enable the other person to take possession of her or his own place.[18]

In this sense we depend on others, our representatives, from the beginning of our lives to the end. As children we needed our parents, who fed and clothed us, wiped our noses, and enrolled us in school, until finally we could do all that for ourselves. Then we needed teachers, who with endless patience taught us to read and write and do arithmetic. And that others help us, introduce us to new knowledge, lead the way for us by their abilities, show us solutions—that will go on till the end of our lives. Even as adults we are constantly dependent on the competence and abilities of others.

We could add example to example here. Every person, every society lives through an infinite number of representatives. It is the same with the people of God, which is an even more dense network of representation. For it is still more true of the life of faith than it already is for everyone: a human being needs help; on our own we would inevitably shrivel and die. Every believer lives out of the faith of another who preceded her or him in faith—parents, friends, great models of faith, the faith of the saints. Even to believe in the first place we need the help of others. The statement abstracted from Kant's *Critique of Practical Reason*, "You can because you should,"[19] is highly questionable. Against the background of Jewish-Christian tradition it ought to be: "You can, if you are willing to be helped."[20] The supposedly "autonomous person" who thinks she or he needs no help and no representative, of course, does have them: for example, the media that all too often think for us, shape us according to their dominant images, and thus incapacitate us without our realizing it. People always have representatives. It is only a question of which ones.

Atonement

The aversion of people today to the idea of atonement is even greater than their discomfort with the idea of representative substitution. There is, as we have seen, a serious reason for this. For today's people atonement is only the "service" or "action" by which a debt is paid, or it is the "punishment" imposed by a judge as retribution for a crime committed. This puts a lot of baggage on the word "atonement" from the outset. Does God really want us to be punished for our sins? Or that someone else should be punished for our sins in our place?

The *biblical* idea of atonement means something different; in fact, it turns the notion of atonement common today on its head. Of course, that in turn raises the question whether we can still use a word when its content in the Bible is altogether different from what is understood by it today. Shouldn't we just replace it with a word we can understand better, such as "reconciliation"?

In what follows I will continue to talk of "atonement," because we are interested here not in the word itself but in the subject, what Jesus expressed in the sign-actions at his last meal and accomplished through his death. But I am fully aware of the language problem. Therefore in this section I will often put "atonement" in quotation marks, so that readers will know that this is not about the word as we understand it today. It is about what the Bible means when it uses the word.

What *does* the Bible mean by this word, so much misunderstood and so easily misinterpreted today? "Atonement" is nothing but representation carried to the ultimate, namely, representative substitution that often extends *even to death* for others. Of course, this description is inadequate; it is only an initial approach. We can only understand what "atonement" really means if we look at the difference between "atonement" in the Old Testament sense and in the world religions. In the latter the whole matter of sacrifice is often nothing more than a symbolic replacement to pay for sin, often even a self-punishment people impose on themselves to cause the deity to feel gracious toward them or to appease it. The religious person gives the gods something that belongs to her or him in order to receive something in return, something important to the person. Such people give something valuable, perhaps even what is dearest to them—even, it may be, one of their own children—in order to be certain of receiving what is desired.

With this sacrifice people seek to bring the powers that influence their lives to their own side. They perform an atoning sacrifice in order to be pure once more before the gods. Perhaps, they think, the punishments due them can be reduced by making a sacrifice. In any case, atonement falls within a diverse category of actions to be performed. The initiative comes from the human side, for the securing of one's own life. For that purpose people develop a whole variety of cultic mechanisms, and in doing so they always run the risk of making use of the deity and rendering it instrumental to their own purposes.

Israel was familiar with all the atonement mechanisms just described. After all, it had been in Egypt and it was familiar with the cultic sites in Canaan. It had been exiled to Babylon and was aware of the rituals of atonement practiced there. It had seen through it all and rethought it in light of its experience of God. Essentially, it had turned the concept of atonement in the religions on its head. For in Israel all "atonement" proceeds from God, as God's own initiative. "Atonement" is a new enabling of life given by God. "Atonement" is the gift of being able to live in the presence of the holy God, in the space where God is near, despite one's own unholiness and constant new incurring of guilt. Effecting "atonement" means *not* appeasing God or making God amenable to reconciliation, but allowing ourselves to be rescued by God's own self from the death we deserve.[21]

Israel knew that human beings cannot work off their own guilt and that both "atonement" and forgiveness must come from God. "Atonement," like covenant and the forgiveness of sins, is God's gracious order, into which the human being can only enter. In all this, biblical thought—at least as regards the power of distinction—is clearly different from the religions.

Certainly the real question has not yet been answered. We could state it somewhat as follows: If everything comes from God's initiative, why is there any need for "atonement" at all? If God himself has created "atonement," just as he created forgiveness, why not simply forgive? Why can God not simply decree: your guilt is absolved; everything is forgiven and forgotten? Why is it not enough for catechesis and preaching simply to speak of the immeasurable readiness of God to forgive, or of God's endless love, or even of God's "crucified love"?

The answer is: if I simply say "God forgives everything on condition that I acknowledge my guilt," the reality is too quickly covered up. The consequences of sin are not really taken seriously. Sin does not just vanish in the air, even when it is forgiven, because sin does not end with the sinner. It has consequences. It always has a social dimension. Every sin embeds itself in human community, corrupts a part of the world, and creates a damaged environment.[22]

Even if God has forgiven all sin, the consequences of sin are not eliminated. What Adolf Hitler set in motion was by no means eliminated from the world by his death in April 1945, even if he was contrite and even if he himself was forgiven. The fearful consequences of National Socialism poison society until today, and they are still nesting in the lives of the surviving victims, even in the lives of their children and grandchildren.

So the consequences of sin have to be worked off, and human beings cannot do so of themselves any more than they can absolve themselves. Genuine "working off" of guilt is only possible on a basis that God himself must create. And God has created such a base in his people, and in Jesus he has renewed and perfected it.

Dag Hammarskjöld, the second Secretary General of the United Nations, who died on 17 September 1961 in a plane crash near the border in Katanga while on a mission to try to resolve the civil war in the Congo, offers us a text that can help us better understand the connections we are discussing here. It is in his diary, published after his death under the title *Markings*:

> Easter, 1960. Forgiveness breaks the chain of causality because he who "forgives" you—out of love—takes upon himself the consequences of what *you* have done. Forgiveness, therefore, always entails a sacrifice.
>
> The price you must pay for your own liberation through another's sacrifice is that you in turn must be willing to liberate in the same way, irrespective of the consequences to yourself.[23]

This utterly penetrating observation, validated by Dag Hammarskjöld's own life and death, makes it clear what is at stake when we talk of representative *atonement*: love forgives, but it cannot forgive the consequences of sin because they are long since buried within history. The chain of causality set in place by sin continues of itself. If love is genuine it therefore not only forgives but takes responsibility for the consequences of what the other has done. And that costs something. It cannot happen without sacrifice, and it can only succeed if many work to heal the consequences of others' guilt. Dag Hammarskjöld indicates that when he says that one's own liberation obligates one to give oneself for the liberation of others. So arises a new chain of causality that works against the causal chain of guilt.

When the New Testament tradition speaks of Jesus' *atoning death*, it means that through his death—which was utterly and entirely death for others, self-emptying to the ultimate degree, *agapē* in the most radical sense—he broke through the causal chains of evil in the world and created a new basis on which it is possible to work off the consequences of sin.

"Atonement" and the People of God

So Jesus' death did not effect any magical redemption applied to the redeemed in some mysterious and opaque manner. That Jesus died for our sins does not mean that we ourselves need no longer die to sin. His death is not a substitute action but the cause and enabling of a process of liberation that goes on. But the social basis on which it continues is the eschatological people of God, which had already begun with the creation of the Twelve. But it was only Jesus' self-surrender for the sake of Israel, even to death, that made possible the new chain of causality and endowed the world definitively with redemption and liberation. The Fourth Evangelist says it in an impressive image:

> Standing near the cross of Jesus was his mother, and his mother's sister, Mary the wife of Clopas, and Mary Magdalene. When Jesus saw his mother and the disciple whom he loved standing beside her, he said to his mother, "Woman, here is your son." Then he said to the disciple, "Here is your mother." And from that hour the disciple took her into his own home. (John 19:25-27)

This scene may indeed signify the legitimation of the Beloved Disciple as witness to the tradition.[24] But there is something still more fundamental at work here: Jesus is founding a new family, the basis on which people who have nothing at all in common can join together in unreserved solidarity. It is the place where true reconciliation with God and one another is possible. But human beings cannot of themselves create that possibility. It must come from the cross and be founded in the death of Jesus.

I have tried to show that in Jesus' death his message of the reign of God reached its most profound depths. When, at the Last Supper, he interpreted his coming death as a representative "atoning death" he did not take back his previous proclamation of God's mercy but instead demonstrated the social reality of that mercy. God is not content merely to forgive. In the death of Jesus God bestows the social location where guilt and its consequences can be eliminated. A message about the loving Father God separated and isolated from that whole context not only fails to recognize the powers in society; it also ignores the web of evil in history. It takes no account of the world's reality. It is absolutely unworldly.

In view of Jesus' previous proclamation, however, his death shows something different: it reveals in all clarity the hidden and humble form of the reign of God as I spoke of it at the beginning of this book, in chapter 2.

The reign of God does not come without persecution and sacrifice. It comes precisely where Jesus himself can do no more, but surrenders and sacrifices himself for the sake of God's truth. How did Jesus' self-sacrifice look in its concrete form?

Chapter 17

His Last Day

It is impossible to write a life of Jesus with the fullness and linkage of events required by a biography. The gospels do not provide the material—with one exception, namely, Jesus' last day. That can be rather precisely reconstructed on the basis of the passion account in Mark's gospel. Behind Mark 14–15 there must stand ancient traditions, carefully handed down, and behind those traditions the memories of eyewitnesses, because these two chapters recount a connected set of events and offer an unusually large number of concrete details.

Merely a glance at the numerous personal names found in Mark's passion account is enlightening: Simon the Leper, Judas Iscariot, Peter, James, John, Pilate, Barabbas, Simon of Cyrene, Alexander, Rufus, Mary Magdalene, Mary the (daughter?/mother?) of James the Younger, Mary the mother of Joses, Salome, Joseph of Arimathea. On the other hand, Mark does not speak of the current high priest by name. Matthew and Luke saw this omission and corrected it. In contrast to Mark, they name the high priest: he was called Caiaphas (Matt 26:3; Luke 3:2; cf. John 11:49). This could be evidence that the passion narrative Mark is drawing on is very ancient. The New Testament scholar Rudolf Pesch argued that if someone telling a story today simply refers to *the* president, in general the reference is taken to be to the one currently in office and not an earlier one.[1] In the same way, the pre-Markan passion story spoke of *the* high priest. Does it then go back to the time when Caiaphas was still in office? He was high priest from 18 to 37 CE.

Gethsemane

The Passover meal ended, at that time, with the singing of the little *Hallel*, that is, Psalms 114(115)–118. Mark says that Jesus and his disciples went to the Mount of Olives after having sung the hymn (14:26). Even this rather minor observation, which seems almost an aside, shows that Jesus celebrated a Passover meal.

At the foot of the Mount of Olives, in a place called Gethsemane, Jesus was overcome with deep anxiety. "He began to be distressed and agitated" (Mark 14:33). Jesus sees death approaching, and he struggles with God in prayer: "Abba, Father, for you all things are possible; remove this cup from me; yet, not what I want, but what you want" (Mark 14:36). On the one hand this prayer depicts Jesus' profound trust in his Father: the Aramaic *abba* is not attested as an address in the prayers of Judaism at that time. It is the trusting and loving address of children, but also of adult sons and daughters, to their father.[2] So according to the text Jesus prays with childlike trust. On the other hand he struggles with God, because when he speaks of the "cup" he wants to have pass by him, that is biblical language. It is the cup of wrath and of desolation,[3] in this case the cup of death. This makes it clear that Jesus is pleading not to have to die. We dare not detract from that, and it must not be drained of its significance. Jesus—according to the narrative—fell into deep fear. On the other hand, he places his life completely in his Father's hand. It probably contributed to his fear and distress that the most trusted members of the group of the Twelve—Peter, James, and John—have left him alone in his time of crisis. They do not understand. They keep falling asleep.

Evidently the passion story has artistically united two things: on the one hand a precise recollection of what happened in Gethsemane, and on the other hand a theological interpretation of the event with the aid of biblical language. It will often be this way in the course of the passion story. A refined explication of how much language from the psalms and how much of the theology of the "suffering righteous one" has made its way into the passion narrative in no way proves that the early church freely invented these events on the basis of the Old Testament. The phenomenon should be interpreted otherwise: the passion story tells of real events, using *biblical* language, in order to make clear that what is happening here is history between God and God's people, just as it had always been, again and again, in the history of Israel.

Something else must also be maintained: the scene in Gethsemane is fundamentally different from later depictions of early Christian martyrdoms, which lack the motifs of temptation and struggle in prayer. We must also keep clearly in mind that Celsus, the philosopher and critic of Christianity, mocked Jesus' fear of death; the emperor Julian "the Apostate" found Jesus' behavior "pitiful."[4] In the eyes of antiquity, heroes must behave differently. For biblical authors of both the Old and New Testaments, on the contrary, the depiction of such existential crises is not only possible[5] but appropriate: that is how the righteous in Israel suffered, and that is how Jesus suffered.

Arrest

Immediately after Jesus' struggle in prayer, an armed troop appears and seizes him. There is not the least reason to disqualify the arrest scene, as Mark describes it, as unhistorical. The Judas kiss in particular is often regarded by critical scholars as a legendary narrative motif. Against this we must say that the arrest takes place at night. Having made a number of failed attempts, as John's gospel is aware (John 7:30, 32, 44; 10:39), Jesus' opponents want to be absolutely sure of getting their hands on Jesus this time. That Jesus is not arrested in the daytime but in the depths of night must also be the result of anxiety over the many Galilean festival pilgrims in Jerusalem. The Passover night was the most opportune time to seize Jesus without being seen. Mark writes: "Immediately, while he was still speaking, Judas, one of the twelve, arrived; and with him there was a crowd with swords and clubs, from the chief priests, the scribes, and the elders" (Mark 14:43). This sounds like an improvised posse, if not a group paid to act against Jesus. Biblical translators would do better to speak of "nightsticks" than of "clubs." That is what Mark means, and such a translation would make it clear that this is a police posse.

In addition to the regular temple guards, the Sanhedrin (the Council) apparently had at their disposal a larger police troop for keeping necessary order, making arrests, and guarding prisoners. This also makes it clear that this was an official arrest ordered by the Council and altogether part of the normal order of things. Because of the disciples, who we know were with Jesus at this time, a large number of armed men had been sent. It is possible that the posse was augmented by servants from the high-priestly families of Annas and Caiaphas (cf. Mark 14:47).

Apparently the disciples are surprised by Jesus' sudden arrest. They abandon him and flee. Peter makes an attempt to stay close to the events: he lingers for a while in the court of Annas's house,[6] where he denies Jesus and then vanishes from the scene—at any rate, from the scene Mark describes.

Before Annas

Jesus is led across the Kidron valley into the city. According to the report in Mark's gospel he was taken immediately to the house of the reigning high priest (that is, Caiaphas), where the Sanhedrin assembled for a night session to examine Jesus (Mark 14:53). The description in John's gospel differs. According to the Fourth Evangelist, Jesus was first presented to the former high priest, Annas, subjected to a kind of "hearing" before him, and only then taken to the reigning high priest, Caiaphas (John 18:12-24). The Fourth Gospel then has no further description of a session of the Council; it is, however, indirectly indicated by the fact that Jesus is sent to Caiaphas (John 18:24).

In fact, it is highly improbable that Jesus was brought before the Sanhedrin without first having been interviewed and at least an attempt having been made to obtain statements from him before the Council session. The experienced former high priest, Annas, would have played an important role in this. In all probability this pre-hearing also occupied the time that was necessary for the members of the Sanhedrin to be called together.[7] But apparently that was not a problem. It may be that they had already been informed ahead of time. In any case, the Council assembled during the night between Thursday and Friday.

Before the Sanhedrin

In itself a night session is unusual. Therefore it has often been argued that, in accordance with the Mishnah (cf. *m. Sanh.* IV.1), in cases involving the death penalty the Sanhedrin was not permitted to hold a night session. Against this we may say that the Mishnah was only edited around 200 CE under Rabbi Yehuda Hanasi and in many respects was more of an abstract theory of law. Its directions regarding penal law probably played scarcely any role in the trial of Jesus. He was brought to trial in accordance with Old Testament and Sadducean penal law, and we do not know that law, with the exception of Old Testament regulations for the penal process. But the Old Testament does not forbid night courts.[8]

Besides, the Sanhedrin was under severe time constraint because of the Passover feast. If we follow the Synoptics' chronology, Jesus died on 15 Nisan, that is, the Passover feast itself. A court session after daybreak of the feast day had to be avoided at all costs. The Sanhedrin had brought itself into this time constraint because of the late hour at which Jesus was arrested. There was probably no question, from the point of view of the Jewish officials, of waiting until after the feast day and the following Sabbath. Jesus' arrest could not remain secret for long, and it was to be feared that Jesus' sympathizers among the people would assemble. So the Council acted quickly and decisively, convening a night court. Mark 14:53 reads, "They took Jesus to the high priest; and all the chief priests, the elders, and the scribes were assembled."

Mark here names the three groups that made up the Council or Sanhedrin. The first group included the reigning high priest and the occupants of a number of important temple offices as well as former high priests no longer in office. The second group was made up of the elders, who came from the most influential lay families in the country. Both the first and the second group were primarily Sadducaic in their orientation. The third group within the Sanhedrin contained only scribes, and it was here, in this group, that the primary speakers for the Pharisees were to be found. What Mark calls the Sanhedrin, however, was not precisely the highest court for all Israel that the Mishnah would later describe, more in terms of legal theory than of practice; rather, it was a group the high priest gathered around himself for making important decisions. It was, so to speak, the Annas-clan's instrument for wielding power.

The only participant whose name we know with certainty was Caiaphas. He must have been a skillful diplomat and a highly pragmatic politician, because he managed to remain in power for nearly twenty years, from 18 to 37 CE. No other high priest in the first century achieved such a long term of office. Caiaphas would not have survived so long if he had not had a powerful clan behind him and had he not adopted a flexible position toward the Roman prefects. So Caiaphas presided at this night session of the Council.

Mark's report that witnesses appeared against Jesus during this trial corresponds exactly to Old Testament and Jewish trial law.[9] In contrast to Roman law, which focused on the examination of the accused, opposing and supporting witnesses were constitutive for Jewish judicial proceedings; the opposing witnesses played the role of district attorney. The statements of the witnesses had to agree in every detail; otherwise, they were irrelevant to the proceedings.

It is important to ask what accusation was brought against Jesus. Some things indicate that he was said to be "leading the people astray." Just such an accusation had been made against him in the past (cf. John 7:12), and it appears in Jewish sources long after his death. The Babylonian Talmud reads, "[Jesus] practiced magic and led Israel astray" (*b. Sotah*

47a). The charge of leading astray would have included such things as disregard for the Law and acting against the temple. Jesus' temple action in particular must have played a major role. People in Jerusalem were allergic to any kind of hostility to the temple. It secured the chief significance of the city as a pilgrimage center and the incomes of the population, especially of the local aristocracy, depended on pilgrims. In any case, according to Mark's account Jesus' saying about the temple played an important initial role in his trial. But apparently it was not easy for the Sanhedrin to condemn Jesus in a clean judicial action for what he had said about the temple. The accusing witnesses did not agree, and the trial came to a standstill.

Messiah and Son of Man

In this situation Caiaphas opened a new segment in the proceedings. Because the witnesses did not agree, the court was short of proof. This may have moved the high priest to take a step that would compel a decision. Caiaphas asked Jesus, "Are you the Messiah, the Son of the Blessed One?" (Mark 14:61). There is no reason not to believe that the high priest asked such a question. It is meaningful and plausible. It refers to opinions and rumors that had long been circulating about Jesus. His dramatic entry into the city in particular must have given a new currency to this evaluation of his person. In addition, Caiaphas's question follows on the temple action that had already been the subject of the proceedings, because that action had shown a sovereign and messianic character. So Caiaphas asks again about Jesus' authority.

Jesus had already been questioned about his authority soon after the temple action by a delegation from the Council. He had not answered, but instead had posed a counter-question: "I will ask you one question; answer me, and I will tell you by what authority I do these things. Did the baptism of John come from heaven, or was it of human origin? Answer me" (Mark 11:29-30). Jesus' counter-question is apparently based on the assumption that a public confession is not appropriate in every situation. The fact that the delegation from the Sanhedrin turned the question aside and refused to take a stand showed in retrospect that his reticence had been justified.

Now Jesus is asked again about his authority, but this time in a new and different situation. He now stands before the assembled Council, before the high priest, Israel's representative. The conclusive nature of this moment must have been perfectly clear to Jesus. Therefore he answers directly, and to the question whether he is the Messiah he confesses, "I am."

Naturally, the reader of the gospel wonders how Jesus can accept in the presence of the Sanhedrin a title of authority that is as enigmatic as it can possibly be, and as subject to political misunderstanding, one he has long avoided in public and even forbidden his disciples to use openly[10] and that he himself has hinted at only symbolically through his entry into the city and his action in the temple. The answer can only be that now, in the presence of the highest authority in Israel, the hour has come to speak openly. Now the possibility of misunderstanding and deliberate misinterpretation must be accepted. In any case, as Jesus had warded off all political interpretations of his entry into the city by riding on a donkey, so now before Caiaphas he guards against any false notion of his messianic character. Thus he is not content to say "I am." His immediate delimitation of the messianic title was compelling and urgently necessary: "and 'you will see the Son of Man seated at the right hand of the Power,' and 'coming with the clouds of heaven'" (Mark 14:62).

Whether Mark and his tradition repeat word for word what Jesus said at that time in this combination of Psalm 110:1 and Daniel 7:13 is a question that may remain open. In any case, it seems to me certain that Jesus made his authority clear in the presence of Caiaphas—the same authority that had always been concealed in his speaking and acting, an authority that extended far beyond anything superficially messianic. For this purpose the phrase "Son of Man" (or "Human One" or "Human Being") from Daniel 7 was ideally suited, for on the one hand this Son of Man is given "dominion and glory and kingship, that all peoples, nations, and languages should serve him. His dominion is an everlasting dominion that shall not pass away" (Dan 7:14). On the other hand this Human One, as we have already seen in chapter 3 above, represents an ultimate *human* society that signifies the end to all dominion by force and violence.

Jesus had repeatedly used the "Son of Man" title during his public life.[11] He employed it to express his lowliness—the Human One is the end of all societies built on force and violence—but he was also able, through it, to formulate his eschatological authority, to be given to him when the reign of God reaches its fulfillment. These two—lowliness and sovereignty—are not contradictory in Jesus' eyes. That the Human One in Daniel 7 is a collective personality was likewise no problem at that time. Jesus sees himself as the embodiment, the representative of that collective, namely, the eschatological Israel.

Thus when Jesus speaks of himself before the Council as the Human One to come he is correcting an idea of the Messiah that could be misunderstood: he emphasizes his nonviolence. But at the same time he reveals his sovereignty. In that sovereignty, given him by God, he will become the judge of the Sanhedrin and of all Israel. It is not *he* who is on trial; it is the Sanhedrin itself that now stands in the dock, and Jesus has forced it to face this moment of decision.

However Jesus shaped what he said, Caiaphas understood. Two avenues were now open to him: believe in Jesus' claims to sovereignty or be convinced that he has heard with his own ears a dreadful blasphemy against God. The high priest's decision is clear. For him, confessing that Jesus would soon appear at the right hand of God as judge was nothing but damnable and blasphemous presumption. Now at last had been proved before many witnesses what had long been suspected: Jesus is a false prophet, a blasphemer, someone who was leading Israel astray.

Therefore Caiaphas immediately does what the Law demands of someone forced to listen to blasphemy: he tears his clothes,[12] and he points the way to what the Torah prescribes for a false prophet, namely, that he be punished with death. Israel must remove the wickedness from its midst (Deut 13:2-6). The rest of the court joins in Caiaphas's decision: "All of them condemned him as deserving death" (Mark 14:64). At this point Mark inserts two scenes: first, very briefly and succinctly, the mocking and mistreatment of Jesus after his affirmation (Mark 14:65), and then, at much greater length, Peter's threefold denial (Mark 14:66-72). Then he takes up the thread of the Council's action again.[13] He now reports the end of the meeting—the Sanhedrin makes a formal decision to transfer Jesus to Pilate's jurisdiction: "As soon as it was morning, the chief priests held a consultation with the elders and scribes and the whole council. They bound Jesus, led him away, and handed him over to Pilate" (Mark 15:1). A new proceeding against Jesus then immediately begins before Pilate, this time according to Roman law and with a Roman official presiding.

Before Pilate

This seamless interlocking of the trial machinery was only possible because the Roman prefect, who otherwise resided at Caesarea Maritima on the Mediterranean, took up residence in Jerusalem for the Passover feast and because the Romans customarily began their court sessions at dawn. Of course, a whole series of questions arises at this point: Why were there two trials in the first place? Why was there need for a Roman trial after a Jewish one had just taken place? And the reverse: If the Jewish officials knew a Roman judicial process would be necessary, why did they carry out their own procedure during the night? Furthermore, what was the nature of the formal decision reached by the Sanhedrin? Was it an official sentence of death, or only a resolution to hand Jesus over, that is, a decision to accuse him before the Roman prefect?

We can best understand the whole situation if we assume, with many interpreters and on the basis of John 18:31, that at that time the Roman occupying power denied the Jews the power to impose capital punishment.[14] That is, they no longer had the right to carry out a death sentence; according to some exegetes they even lacked the right to pass a formal sentence of death. If the Jews had possessed the right at that time to execute Jesus according to their own legal system he would not have been crucified; he would have been stoned, for the method of execution by crucifixion, widespread in antiquity and especially characteristic of the Romans, was practiced by Jews only in a very few exceptional situations.

That the Jewish officials handed Jesus over to Pilate shows quite clearly that they considered him convicted of a capital crime, one that in their view could only be punished by death. In this case they had to let the matter pass from their own hands and allow the Roman prefect to investigate the guilt of the accused by his own judicial process and then pass sentence according to Roman law. The formal decision made by the Council toward the end of the night must have been one that formulated Jesus' guilt and ordered that he be handed over. It is obvious that Pilate could not avoid a process that was developed in this way; it most definitely put pressure on him to act.

But the Sanhedrin's decision probably had another meaning as well: by this means the members of the Council could justify to themselves the manner in which they presented their accusation of Jesus before the Roman prefect. After having carried out their own process of determining guilt they could say that Jesus was quite definitely a criminal deserving death, even if his condemnation by Pilate could only be achieved by highly questionable and by no means immaculate methods. We must now discuss these questionable methods used in presenting the accusation to Pilate.

The Council had condemned Jesus for blasphemy or, more precisely, had determined the fact of his having blasphemed. It is highly probable that the accusation of leading the people astray had also played a significant role in the trial. Within the Jewish legal system both were capital crimes. But if an accusation was to be brought against a Jew in a Roman court, both blasphemy and leading the people astray would count as crimes against Jewish religion, and no Roman judge could condemn a Jew to death merely for violating the internal laws of the Jewish religion. The Council saw this point very clearly; therefore, in a quite consistent strategy, it brought the "Jesus case" before the Romans under a different aspect. No more is said about "blasphemy," but fomenting unrest is still there. The Sanhedrin makes the religious seducer of the people into a political-messianic revolutionary. That is the only way to understand Pilate's ironic question to Jesus, namely, whether he was the "king of the Jews" (Mark 15:2), and that is the only way we can comprehend how Jesus was ultimately executed under a placard that read "the king of the Jews" (Mark 15:26).

The accusation that Jesus pretended to be the messianic king was so effective because during the Roman occupation every messianic movement almost inevitably fell under suspicion of being a national uprising against the Romans. "Messianic king" was pretty much the equivalent of "freedom fighter" and "rabble rouser"—and the Romans were inclined to react very quickly and effectively against anything bearing the scent of "sedition" (*seditio*). It is true that when Jesus was accused before Pilate of being a political messiah it was possible—in a superficial way—to appeal to his temple action and his confession of himself as Messiah, but in reality this was a distortion and perversion of Jesus' claim. After all, he had expressed himself clearly enough against any kind of revolt (cf. Mark 12:13-17), and he did not understand his temple action as a signal for a political uprising.

So with this accusation a second process, a political trial, began. The issue was now nothing less than "treason" (*perduellio*). How did Pilate react to the charge brought against Jesus? He apparently hesitated to accept it on its face. All four evangelists agree on that. Reasons for his hesitation can certainly be found.

First, as a Roman official Pilate could not be content to accept vague accusations. He was authorized to apply the death sentence only if Jesus could be proved to have committed a capital crime. He needed genuine proof that Jesus had called for political upheaval or participated actively in an uprising. Apparently such proof could not be produced, and Pilate probably saw that very quickly. It is likely that after a brief confrontation with Jesus he no longer took seriously the statement that the accused was a political revolutionary.

But there could be another reason why Pilate did not assent at once. He was, as we know from a variety of ancient witnesses, more hostile than friendly toward the Jews. The Jewish philosopher Philo wrote in his *Legatio ad Gaium* that "[he did not wish] to do anything which could be acceptable to his [Jewish] subjects" (XXXVIII, 303). We may suspect that as soon as Pilate determined that the Jewish authorities were trying to use him to get rid of their hated Galilean he immediately opposed their wishes.

Thus there are certainly reasons for Pilate's striking efforts to set Jesus free. But he could not permit himself simply to send the accusers home and release Jesus on the spot. The charge of political uprising was too serious for that. According to the evangelists Matthew, Mark, and John, the Roman prefect was accustomed to release a prisoner for the Jews at Passover (Matt 27:15; Mark 15:6; John 18:39). Perhaps the Jewish committee appointed to present the petition for pardon had already arrived at the praetorium early in the morning. It may be, however, that they only appeared at a later time (so Mark 15:8). In any case, the candidate had long since been chosen; he was a certain Barabbas, who was in prison with a number of other men who had started an "uprising" and in the process had committed murder. This uprising, which had probably occurred quite recently, could have been an assassination or an attack directed against the Romans. Mark's striking formulation (cf. 15:7) suggests that Barabbas was not the head of the group but an accomplice or—to speak cautiously—one of those accused of complicity. The delegation would have been made up primarily of relatives and friends of Barabbas.

Pilate must have known already that this year he would be asked to issue the usual Passover pardon to Barabbas, imprisoned for sedition. It would be naïve to suppose that on that Friday morning Pilate did not already know the concrete expectations of the delegation. Apparently, however, he wanted to avoid pardoning Barabbas. He probably saw a major risk in releasing a man who had been arrested while committing a terrorist act, a risk that ran absolutely contrary to his own interests and those of Rome. On the other hand, a prisoner had to be released at the Passover festival—the custom is much too firmly attested by the gospels to be in doubt. In this situation it must have impressed itself on Pilate as an utterly ideal solution to suggest that Jesus be released. At first glance such a solution would have seemed to him suited to his purposes in every respect: in this way Pilate would get rid of the altogether unpleasant "Jesus case" and at the same time avoid pardoning Barabbas.

The details of the prefect's calculated game can no longer be reconstructed, but we have good grounds for assuming that his efforts to release Jesus resulted, among other reasons, from the tactical calculation that he could thus avoid letting the rebellious Barabbas go, something that was much more dangerous to himself.

But then this very calculation proved to be a wrong estimate with serious consequences. Pilate apparently reckoned far too little with the fact that his opposite numbers in the deal could harden their support for Barabbas, and he had also probably underestimated by far the energy with which the Jewish officials were pursuing Jesus' execution. But above all, when he suggested that Jesus be pardoned rather than Barabbas, he had, in fact, confirmed Jesus' guilt to the public. His tactics had now really brought him into a situation in which pressure could be put on him.

Evidently this new situation was immediately perceived and seized upon by Jesus' opponents. The prefect was very quickly faced with a massed outcry that settled into chants against Jesus: "Crucify him! Crucify him!" (Mark 15:13-14). Suddenly the situation was different. Pilate, through his apparently clever strategy, had allowed the judicial decision to be taken out of his hands. He had not decided the guilt or innocence of the accused simply as an impartial judge. By trying to make the innocent man into a subject for pardon he had combined the judicial and political levels.

So it is no surprise that in the end, under the increasing pressure, he made his decision purely on the political level—and now against Jesus. He abandoned his original goal of securing Barabbas's execution by pardoning Jesus, and he condemned Jesus to death on a cross as a political rebel and traitor. Probably he uttered the usual formula: *Ibis in crucem* (You will go to the cross).

Execution

For Jesus, Pontius Pilate's failed stratagem meant death, and death by one of the most gruesome methods of execution ever devised by human beings to torture others. For Romans, death on the cross was regarded as so dreadful and dishonorable that it could be imposed only on slaves and non-Romans. Cicero wrote, "The executioner, and the veiling of the head, and the mere name of the gibbet, should be far removed, not only from the persons of Roman citizens—from their thoughts, and eyes, and ears" (*Pro Rabirio* 16). But even in the case of slaves and provincials crucifixion was generally reserved for serious crimes such as murder, temple robbery, treason, and rebellion.

It was the Roman custom to precede every crucifixion with an additional feature: scourging. Mark and Matthew report it in this sense (Mark 15:15; Matt 27:26). For them the scourging of Jesus clearly functions as an added punishment prior to crucifixion and part of the whole process.[15] Thus even before his actual execution Jesus received a punishment so horrible that it often resulted in death. Roman scourging was so dangerous because the number of strokes was not limited and the thongs of the whip often incorporated bits of bone or metal. That gives us a hint of what the brief statement "Pilate had Jesus scourged" means.

In addition, the Roman soldiers, after Jesus was handed over to them for execution, first played games with him. They dressed him as a king, imitated the solemn royal acclamation, and fell on their faces before him. They spat on him and cried, "Hail, king of the Jews!" while striking him brutally in the face (Mark 15:16-20). As a result of the scourging and the subsequent mistreatment, Jesus was no longer able to carry his own cross to the place of execution. Therefore the soldiers forced a certain Simon of Cyrene, who was just coming from the fields and accidentally crossed the path of the execution squad, to carry Jesus' cross for him (Mark 15:21).

We should not, however, imagine this carrying of the cross as Christian art has portrayed it. For regular executions the condemned did not carry the whole cross, but only the crossbeam. The upright beams were posts that were firmly rammed into the earth, usually as semi-permanent fixtures. When the delinquent arrived at the place of execution he was laid on the ground and his outstretched arms were nailed to the crossbeam; then the beam bearing the condemned man was hoisted onto the fixed upright pole. The crossbeam was fastened to the top; only then were the feet nailed fast. So Jesus and Simon of Cyrene did not carry the whole cross but only the crossbeam. That Jesus could not carry even this single beam shows that he was already at the limits of his physical strength after the scourging.

On the way to the place of execution someone carried a placard (*titulus*) in front of the condemned person giving the reason for the execution. For Jesus the *titulus* read, "Jesus of Nazareth, the King of the Jews" (John 19:19; cf. Mark 15:26). That Pilate had the *titulus* read "the King of the Jews" and not "he pretended to be the King of the Jews" can only be understood as a malicious mockery directed at the Jewish people. Apparently, after having drawn the short straw in his confrontation with the Sanhedrin, Pilate wanted to revenge himself at least in this way. But at the same time the wording of the *titulus* represented a spiteful irony against Jesus: the Roman soldiers had played their rough games with him, and now the mockery continues.

It should be noted that the information that Jesus was crucified between two rebels is part of the consistently maintained symbolism of mockery. A king cannot appear on solemn public occasions without his council. The "council" carefully placed to Jesus' "right" and "left" (Mark 15:27) is made up of two felons, with Jesus enthroned exactly in the middle. The two "thieves" were probably some of the terrorists or freedom fighters who had been imprisoned along with Barabbas. Although the gospels do not say so, we have to assume that Pilate had also condemned these two terrorists on that same Friday morning. Thus the prefect had not wasted much time on Jesus' condemnation; he made the trial a short one.

The hill on which Jesus was executed bore the name "Golgotha," simply translated "skull [hill]" (Mark 15:22), not because the skulls of people previously executed were lying around—something that would have been unthinkable in a place subject to Jewish laws of purity—but because the hill had the form of a skull. The Church of the Holy Sepulchre stands today on the place where Jesus died. As soundings in the area in 1961 have shown, there was in the time of Jesus an abandoned quarry from the royal period on the site, and to the west of this former quarry some private graves had been cut into the layers of stone. Eastward, in the direction of the city, a remaining part of the cliff arose; this was the "skull." Between the two were gardens (cf. John 19:41; 20:15). This makes it clear that we have to imagine the cliffs of Golgotha and their surroundings as lying outside the city walls as they were at that time. Excavations beneath the Church of the Redeemer have clarified the course of the walls. There was only a small valley between the western wall of Jerusalem and the height of Golgotha. Jesus' walk with the cross from the praetorium to the city wall, and from there to the place of execution, was not very long, assuming, of course, that the shortest way was chosen.

According to Mark the execution squad arrived at Golgotha in the forenoon; at about the third hour—that is, around nine o'clock—they nailed Jesus to the cross there. The gospels do not describe the crucifixion, with its misery and fearful suffering. The tact and stylistic feelings of the early church forbade it. Mark writes soberly and with extreme brevity: "and they crucified him" (15:24). Immediately before this Jesus was offered wine mixed with myrrh (Mark 15:23). This was an anesthetizing drink that, by Jewish custom, was given to condemned people before their execution.[16] The wine, with strong herbs mixed in, was supposed to make the pain of execution somewhat more bearable. But Jesus refused the wine.

This must be distinguished from a later event, when Jesus was already hanging on the cross and in his death struggle. At that point one of the bystanders tried to give Jesus something to drink by impaling a sponge on the end of a rod, soaking the sponge with sour wine, and holding it to Jesus' mouth (Mark 15:36). We can no longer be certain whether that person acted out of pity for Jesus or only wanted to refresh him in order to extend his death agony. But the incident clearly shows that Jesus was nailed to a high cross; the upright must have been tall and strong and was probably anchored firmly in the ground for long-term use.

After Jesus was nailed to the cross, the soldiers divided his clothing among themselves (Mark 15:24). One of the unwritten rules for execution squads was that they were permitted to take for themselves the property a condemned person wore to execution. In Jesus' case that would have been his outer and inner garments, his belt, sandals, and perhaps a headcloth.

While hanging on the cross Jesus was derided by passersby—the city wall was not far away—and by spectators who had gathered at the place of execution. As in the court of the praetorium, the scoffing was primarily about his messianic assertion, incorporated in the *titulus*, "the King of the Jews." Thus, for example, some said, "Let the Messiah, the King of Israel, come down from the cross now, so that we may see and believe!" (Mark 15:32). The background of this mockery was the idea that Jesus' crucifixion was the tangible refutation of his claim. The true messiah would never hang on a cross and suffer; he would destroy his opponents.

According to Mark, Jesus prayed the beginning of Psalm 22 at the ninth hour (that is, about three in the afternoon) in a loud voice: "My God, my God, why have you forsaken me?" Some of the bystanders misunderstood this prayer as a call for Elijah. It was probably already the case at that time that Elijah was seen as an aid at the hour of death. Because Jesus cried out the beginning of Psalm 22 in Aramaic ("Eloi, eloi") there must have been some kind of twisting of his cry; the mockery of Jesus continues.

In all probability Jesus did not merely pray the beginning of Psalm 22. He must have spoken parts of the whole psalm as his dying prayer, as far as his fading strength allowed, or stuttered it out in bits. At any rate, the opinion of some authors that the cry, "My God, my God, why have you forsaken me?" represents ultimate and final despair is contradictory to the practice of Old Testament prayer.[17] It is not only that Psalm 22 is shot through with cries of trust ("since my mother bore me you have been my God," v. 10), not merely that the end of the psalm speaks of the banquet of the nations in the reign of God (vv. 27-29); the beginning of the psalm is itself not a cry of despair, but a lament, and in the Psalms that is something completely different from despair. Psalm 22 contains both: that God is silent and yet replies, the horrible hiddenness of God and the showing of God's face (v. 24), the ultimate loneliness of the one praying and the new gift of community.

According to Mark, Jesus died at the ninth hour, that is, around three in the afternoon, with a loud cry (15:34, 37). It is in itself surprising that he died only six hours after being crucified, because usually the death struggle of a crucified person lasted much longer. The inhuman horror of execution on a cross consisted precisely in that crucifixion was meant to cause a very long, drawn-out death that was repeatedly delayed. If it was desired to make the crucified person die sooner, his legs would be broken; then the weight of the body hung completely from the arms and suffocation quickly resulted. The only remains of a crucified person from antiquity thus far discovered, in a surprising find in Jerusalem in 1968, included a single rusted nail that had been driven through both feet at once, but it also showed that both shins had been broken at the same height by heavy blows. This gave archaeological confirmation to the custom of *crucifragium*, the breaking of legs, attested by the evangelist John (John 19:32). According to John the death of the two terrorists crucified with Jesus was brought about by this breaking of their leg bones, but Jesus' legs were not broken because he was already dead. His quick death, after only a few hours, must have resulted from the severe flogging he had received and the loss of blood that resulted.

Burial

We have already seen that in antiquity burial was denied to those who had been crucified, and we also saw what Joseph of Arimathea's approaching Pilate meant in this context (chap. 6: "The Many Faces of Being Called"). Joseph, one of Jesus' sympathizers, also made sure that the shroud was purchased and Jesus' body taken down from the cross. Then Jesus was wrapped in the newly purchased shroud and placed in a tomb. Women who were part of Jesus' circle of disciples were present (Mark 15:42-47).

We can draw a vivid picture of Jesus' tomb on the basis of many archaeological parallels in and around present-day Jerusalem and from the reports in the four gospels. It was close to the Golgotha rise (John 19:41); it was hewn in one of the bands of rock that ran through the abandoned quarry west of Golgotha; it was in a garden; it was a tomb chamber with benches on the sides for bodies; it had a relatively low door opening through which one could only enter by bending over and that entry door was closed with a stone that could be rolled back and forth (Mark 15:46); it was a previously unused tomb in which no one had yet been laid (John 19:41). So we may be certain that Jesus' body did not remain on the cross, nor was it thrown into a common grave for criminals; it was placed in a family tomb whose location was known in Jerusalem. On the morning of the first weekday after the Sabbath, the women would go to this tomb.

Strategies

The events of the passion were crammed into a few hours: struggle in prayer, arrest, hearing before Annas, session of the Council, delivery to Pilate, condemnation by Pilate, scourging, mocking, execution, burial. All that took place in under twenty-four hours. Those who desired Jesus' death knew why it all had to proceed so swiftly, and they knew their business. That business included the strategies applied by Jesus' opponents. The Council internally considered Jesus deserving of death because he led the people astray and was a blasphemer. But before Pilate they made the religious seducer of the people into a political rebel, and Jesus' confession of his authority became an admission that he was a messiah with a political purpose. It was this strategy, which completely twisted Jesus' real claim, that brought him to the cross.

But Pilate followed his own strategies as well. He wanted to avoid pardoning Barabbas at the Passover festival, and Jesus became a means to his end. Pilate was so preoccupied with carrying out his strategy that he did not notice how, in suggesting that Jesus be pardoned in place of Barabbas, he was already declaring him guilty and so losing control of his own judicial powers. Pilate's political strategy also became deadly to Jesus in the end. But Pilate, despite his much greater power, is the weaker figure in this game of clashing moves. The Sanhedrin—quite unlike Pilate—never lost sight of its goal and pursued it unerringly. That goal was to bring Jesus to the cross.

But we can scarcely understand the unerring purpose of the Jerusalem temple aristocracy in seeking Jesus' crucifixion without considering the background in Deuteronomy 21:22-23, which is about the burial of those who are executed. It is presupposed that, after their execution, they will be hanged on a pole (as a warning?). The law in Deuteronomy 21:22-23 says that the bodies of those who are hanged in this way may not remain overnight but should be buried on the same day. In this context it is said that "anyone hanging on a tree is under God's curse." That sentence from Torah was already applied by pre-Christian Judaism to those who were crucified. As the "Temple Scroll" found at Qumran shows, the statement "anyone hanging on a tree is under God's curse" was applied to the crucifixion of Jews who betrayed their people to a foreign nation and brought evil upon them.[18] It must therefore have seemed appealing to the Council to have Jesus crucified with the help of the Roman occupying power as someone who was leading the people astray and corrupting them.

From this point of view the Passover festival with its masses of pilgrims represented an uncomfortable obstacle to having Jesus seized by the police, but on the positive side it offered the opportunity to expose Jesus publicly before assembled Israel as someone cursed by God. For once Jesus was hanging on the cross it would be obvious: God could by no means be behind a man like that.

All these strategies show that Jesus had fallen between the millstones of powers much stronger than he who (like Pilate) wanted nothing to do with any question of truth or who (like the Sanhedrin) saw it as their religious duty to expose Jesus and get rid of him. But were they really stronger than he? The Jerusalem temple aristocracy who condemned him have vanished from history. Jesus has not vanished. He started an unimaginable movement. He changed the world and goes on changing it. All those who have tried to get rid of him have been wrecked in the attempt. Their project continually turns into its opposite.

The Question of Guilt

Those who seek to reconstruct what happened on Jesus' last day cannot avoid the question of guilt. They cannot be content to note, coolly and clinically, what took place in Jerusalem on that day. They must think about the guilt of the Council and that of Pilate but also the guilt of all those who had encountered Jesus, since his appearance in Galilee, with unbelief, skepticism, or indifference. And they must reflect on the guilt of Jesus' disciples, who left him in the lurch and fled.

It will be clear to those who have read this book to this point that it is not intended to argue an anti-Jewish cause, certainly not to sow hatred against the Jews. Sadly, there has been such hatred in Christianity, a horrifying mass of it, throughout the centuries. But there can be no talk of any kind of collective guilt on the part of Israel, and even if there were such a thing the Christian response would have to have been completely different.

In reflecting on Jesus' death we must also refuse to simplify things the way the old passion plays did: here the Holy One, there the evil ones! Instead, we must assume that there were many among Jesus' opponents who desired nothing but to follow their consciences. The depth of the conflict with Jesus is not simply apparent from the fact that the general public here acted against the good—although, of course, one must always take the possibility into account. There is a kind of lust for evil, and it would be naïve to suppose that all people desire only the true and the good. At any rate, often they desire neither good nor evil but simply their own convenience. But to get back to the point: the real depth of the conflict emerges only if we see that here people who sought to defend the honor of God or God's Law set themselves against an individual who, in their opinion, was blaspheming God's honor and destroying the holy Law.

It appears that the Sanhedrin thought they had to defend the temple, the Torah, and the people against Jesus. But Jesus had not questioned the temple, the Torah, or the people of God. He did want to gather Israel together so that it might finally become what it was intended to be in the eyes of God. And he did not destroy the Torah but interpreted it radically in terms of God's will. He wanted the temple to finally become what the prophets had longed for: a place of true worship of God in whose forecourt even the Gentiles could worship. Certainly, behind all that lay the claim that the fulfillment of the Torah had arrived in his own person and that where he lived out the reign of God with his followers "something greater than the temple" (Matt 12:6) was present. Israel, and with it the Sanhedrin, were faced with this tremendous claim.

This makes it clear that the question of the guilt of Jesus' opponents is much more complex than it at first appears. For if all this is true, then it is a conflict we all face and in which we all must find ourselves guilty: we too constantly hear God's true claim, fully evident in Jesus, but we cover it up with our own ideas, habits, and convenience and so shove it out of the world. Therefore an examination of the passion of Jesus cannot be about diluting or downplaying the guilt of Jesus' opponents. On the contrary: it is about uncovering the depths of that guilt, because that is how we will uncover the guilt of us all.

Chapter 18

The Easter Events

This book is about Jesus' public life: What did he do? What did he want? Who was he? Is it even permissible to introduce the Easter events into this context? Shouldn't we stop with Jesus' death? Doesn't something completely different begin with his resurrection—something that can only be grasped in faith?

Such questions are urgent, and yet they only partly touch the reality of Jesus, since ultimately his activities in Galilee and later in Jerusalem can also be understood only by faith. Nevertheless, those matters have to be examined historically. In the same way, Jesus' resurrection belongs to the realm of faith, and yet theology, insofar as it works historically, may and must ask: what really happened among Jesus' followers after Good Friday? How can we understand the phenomenon that they first separated and then came back together again? How can we explain that, despite the catastrophe of Good Friday, they suddenly became a community? That was anything but a matter of course. It was evidently connected to the Easter faith. But how did that Easter faith come to be? And what did it look like in the concrete?

The events after Jesus' death are certainly part of his "life." Without those events he still could not be understood, even if we reconstructed only the external sequence. And within the imponderable history of Jesus' actions, which still goes on, these first days and weeks are a time of special focus. It is this particular period after Good Friday that the present chapter attempts to grasp.

The Flight of the Disciples

The evangelist Mark does not make the slightest attempt to conceal the dreadful loneliness in which Jesus' life ended. Judas Iscariot, one of the group of the Twelve, handed him over; he made Jesus' nighttime arrest possible. Then, when Jesus was taken into custody, all the disciples left him and fled (Mark 14:50). Only Peter followed at a distance, to the court of the high priest's house. Then he too left Jesus in the lurch—after having denied him. According to Mark, not one of the men from the group of disciples was present at the crucifixion, but some women from among Jesus' followers watched from a distance (Mark 15:40-41).

Jesus' burial was carried out, as we have seen, by Joseph of Arimathea, a Jesus sympathizer but not a member of the group of disciples (Mark 15:42-46). According to Mark, the Twelve took no part in the events at the empty tomb.[1] The oldest tradition associates those events exclusively with the women, especially Mary Magdalene (Mark 16:1-8).

So in Mark we can speak of an accelerating disappearance of the Twelve from the ending of the gospel. How should we interpret their vanishing? Did they simply hide in Jerusalem, so that we may still suppose they were in the city? Or did they leave Judea and flee to their homeland in Galilee? There are two texts that favor flight. The first is Mark 14:27, where Jesus, quoting Zechariah 13:7, says, "You will all become deserters; for it is written, 'I will strike the shepherd, and the sheep will be scattered.'" This text speaks about the scattering of the disciples in a kind of epic anticipation that, however, is historically retrospective. "Scattering"—that seems meant to say more than merely concealment in the capital city. A second text, John 16:32, says much the same. There Jesus prophesies, "The hour is coming, indeed it has come, when you will be scattered, each one to his [home], and you will leave me alone." This text too acquires its historical force only if we see it as retrospective. The translators of the NRSV have expanded the Greek expression "each to his own" to read "each one to his home," which captures the meaning; an alternate translation would be "each to his private interests." But that means that the disciples have fled, returned pell-mell to their homeland, and they have resumed their former occupations.[2]

But at this point we need also to take note of Mark 16:7 (cf. 14:28), where an angel orders the women, "Go, tell his disciples and Peter that he is going ahead of you to Galilee; there you will see him." Lived history lies behind these words as well. The disciples—or more precisely the

Galileans among them—have gone to Galilee. Why? Evidently because they have fled there. But the angel's words give their flight a positive meaning: the disciples flee and seem thereby to have abandoned Jesus, but in reality he is with them; he is even ahead of them. Precisely in the place where they appear to have lost him forever they will find him: in their home, in Galilee, when they have taken up their old occupations once more.

So Mark 16:7 in particular seems to presume the flight of the disciples to Galilee, and it is completely plausible. Jesus' execution would have had a shocking effect on his followers. As we have already seen, on the basis of Deuteronomy 21:23, "being hanged on a tree" would have seemed like God's judgment on Jesus. From that point of view the confusion of Jesus' associates and the pell-mell flight of the group of Twelve is easily understood. In addition, it was completely possible at the outset that the inner circle of disciples was threatened with a fate similar to that of Jesus himself. What was more likely than that the Galileans would return to Galilee? There they could feel safe; in Galilee they were far enough from the Sanhedrin's grasp.

The Beginning of the Appearances

One of the surest indicators of the flight of the Galilean disciples to their home country is, in fact, the phenomenon that the appearances to Peter and the Twelve did not take place in Jerusalem but in Galilee. It is true that the gospels give a contradictory picture in this regard: Mark 16:7 announces that the first appearance will be in Galilee, and Matthew 28:16-20 tells of the first appearance to the Eleven, which for him is a summary of all appearances, and locates it in Galilee. Luke, in contrast, places all the appearances in or near Jerusalem. But in doing so he betrays an obvious theological intention: for Luke, Jerusalem is a symbol of the continuity between the time of Jesus and the time of the church.[3] Therefore he omits the angel's order, according to which the disciples should go to Galilee, even though he read it in Mark, which he was using as a model.[4] According to Luke the disciples were to remain in the city (Luke 24:49). He thus says nothing about the Galilean appearances, which very certainly played as great a role in the tradition as did the accounts of appearances in Jerusalem.

John also locates the appearances in Jerusalem, but in this he appears to be directly or indirectly dependent on Luke. Finally, we are faced with the striking phenomenon that chapter 21, an addition to John's gospel, tells of an appearance to seven disciples in Galilee, on the Sea of Gennesareth. It is not introduced as a first appearance, but it might originally have been the story of such an initial encounter. The overall finding thus points clearly to Galilee as the place where appearances *to the inner group of disciples* began.

Here commenced a series of appearances in which the Risen One was seen. The first of these Galilean appearances apparently came to Simon Peter. Two texts favor this. First there is the very ancient confession of faith retained in 1 Corinthians 15:3-8. Paul himself had received it as a faith tradition and handed it on to the congregation in Corinth:

> I handed on to you as of first importance what I in turn had received: that Christ died for our sins in accordance with the scriptures, and that he was buried, and that he was raised on the third day in accordance with the scriptures, and that he appeared to Cephas, then to the twelve. (15:3-5)

Probably the ancient creed ended here, but Paul adds the following, on the basis of a good knowledge of the first period after Easter:

> Then he appeared to more than five hundred brothers and sisters at one time, most of whom are still alive, though some have died. Then he appeared to James, then to all the apostles. Last of all, as to one untimely born, he appeared also to me. (15:6-8)

The second text that speaks of an initial appearance to Peter is Luke 24:34. The context here is that the two disciples who had encountered the Risen One on the road from Jerusalem to Emmaus have returned immediately to the capital. There they have found the Eleven and a larger group of Jesus' followers gathered together, and the group says to them, "The Lord has risen indeed, and he has appeared to Simon." It is odd that Luke does not describe the appearance to Simon Peter but simply inserts a formulaic reference to it in a single sentence. What he is really telling about is the appearance to the disciples on the road to Emmaus, not the much more important appearance to Peter. How can we explain that? By no means can we say that he had no narrative of an appearance to Peter available to him. The matter is much more simply explained: the tradition that related the appearance to Peter was so clearly located in Galilee that Luke, who concentrates all appearances in Jerusalem or its neighborhood, simply could not include it at this point. A story that took place at the lake, with boats and a fisherman pursuing his task, was one that Luke with the best will in the world could not shift to the city of Jerusalem. It is true that John 21:1-14 does not tell of an appearance to Peter alone, but the text does clearly reflect the possible milieu of such a story.

So we can with good reason suppose that Peter, who had fled to Galilee with the rest of the inner group of disciples, experienced an appearance of the Risen One there. It banished all doubts and made Peter one of the first Easter witnesses. Apparently the high regard for Peter and his leading role in the early church rested, among other things, on that appearance, which was then followed by further appearance phenomena, including some in Jerusalem.

But before turning to the progress of events, I need first to offer some reflections on the structure of the Easter appearances.

The Structure of the Easter Experience

There is a current position that exercises a certain fascination because it makes things easier for people today. It could be described this way: After the death of Jesus there were no visions or appearances; Jesus' disciples came to their Easter faith through "experience" that, as regards its psychic structure, was wholly within the framework of religious experiences as they are commonly understood. There was nothing unusual or ecstatic about it. The disciples mourned, but in their sorrow the death of Jesus opened itself to them in a new way. They entered into a "disclosure situation."[5] Suddenly they knew that Jesus had not remained in death but was exalted to the right hand of God. God had justified him, contrary to the sentence of his judges in the Sanhedrin. They experienced the nearness of Jesus in their hearts and the grace of his forgiveness. They turned again to the Jesus they had abandoned. Then these "disclosure experiences," in which, of course, things drawn from Scripture played a role, were secondarily fitted into the existing narrative model of "appearances." Originally the Easter experiences had nothing visionary or ecstatic about them.

I consider the position thus described to be *theologically* possible. It would not destroy the Christian Easter faith. It by no means excludes God's action (or the action of the Risen One) in the world. But from a *historical* point of view this position is untenable. It is a way of currying favor with the Enlightenment mentality, which wants to explain away everything unusual. It is impossible to eliminate the basic structure of a vision from Paul's Damascus experience, for which we have personal testimony (1 Cor 9:1; 15:8). And the gospels also clearly show that we are dealing with typical phenomena of visions. That of Peter begins a long series of further visions that first affected the group of the Twelve and then a larger group of disciples who were later called apostles, and then no fewer than five hundred followers of Jesus at the same time. This could represent the original Jerusalem community. At some point the visionary phenomena even extended to Jesus' family: it is said of James, the "brother of the Lord" (Gal 1:19), that the Risen One appeared to him (1 Cor 15:7). Finally, Stephen's vision (Acts 7:55) is part of the long series of these early Christian visions.

Not far removed from the modern position of "disclosure experiences" as described above is a much older hypothesis according to which the Easter appearances were "subjective visions." That position can be described somewhat as follows: The disciples simply could not come to terms with the fact that their Lord and Master, Jesus, was no longer with them, and so there arose in their deep unconscious minds an image of a Jesus who returned to them to give them pardon and peace. Added to this was the profound hope for the imminent reign of God that Jesus had planted in them. Could all that be over? No! The desires and fears, the hopes and longings of the disciples were suddenly transformed into a certainty that Jesus had risen. This certainty paved the way for and erupted in visions within their souls in which the disciples saw what they longed for and dreamed of. This purely psychogenic process, extending into the innermost levels of the personality, began with Peter. He then drew his friends along with him by suggestion, and the result was a kind of enthusiastic chain reaction.

Christian faith has always taken its stance against this emptying of the Easter appearances that reduces them to *unusual* but purely *natural* phenomena. In its defense against the position described it has emphasized the supernatural character of the Easter appearances, stressed God's genuine action at Easter, and underlined the true revealedness of the Risen One in the sight of his disciples. So, since the Enlightenment, there have come to be two sharply opposed positions. On the one side it is asserted that the Easter visions were purely natural phenomena produced by the imagination or, more precisely, the unconscious of the disciples. Opposed to this, and in a constantly defensive position, stands the traditional view: no, the Easter appearances were purely supernatural events in which God, or the Risen One, intervened in history through revelation.

But it has become more and more clear that this alternative—either natural or supranatural—is most unfortunate and even falsely understood; a theological resolution to this false dilemma is long overdue. It is similar to what we saw in the case of Jesus' miracles: when God acts on people he does not make them passive objects of divine action but acts with and through them. That is, God does not eliminate the structures, laws, frameworks, and potentials of the world but acts with the aid of these and in common with them. Therefore a *real* vision is both entirely a human production and entirely a work of God.

A genuine vision is first of all totally a human production: it is a bringing into play of the person's history, past experiences, knowledge, hopes, imagination—and all this, obviously, in an unconscious process the person cannot control and in which the styles of the time and culturally conditioned forms of thinking play an important role.[6] The time is long since ripe for acknowledging visions as a genuine human possibility. Then one can likewise take them seriously as also a genuine divine possibility, a way of speaking to human beings within the structures of humanity. For just as every vision is wholly and entirely a human work it can at the same time be wholly and entirely a divine work, as God thereby uses the productive imaginative power of the human in order to reveal God's self in the midst of history.

The principle of the doctrine of grace, that God's action does not suppress human action but instead frees it, must be applied to the inner structure of the Easter appearances. This means that the disciples' Easter experiences can be regarded *theologically* as really and truly appearances of the Risen One in which God revealed his Son in power and in all his glory (Gal 1:16) but *psychologically* at the same time as visions in which the disciples' power of imagination constructed the appearance of the Risen One. By no means does the one exclude the other.

Only if we understand the Easter appearances as thus described do we take them seriously, both theologically *and* anthropologically. Then we need no longer shrink from the idea that visionary phenomena spread, after Good Friday, in a kind of chain reaction, and that they were altogether inculturated in the respective visual and linguistic abilities of the recipients. We can then understand, for example, how the disciples could "see" and "hear" the Risen One and even "touch" him.

The considerations presented in this section are important because they put interpreters in a position to look without historical prejudice at visionary, pneumatic, and ecstatic phenomena in the earliest community and not, out of pure fear of what is unusual, to turn immediately to magical words such as "legend" or "community construct." The Easter appearance phenomena really happened. That can be determined by purely historical means.

"Resurrection" as an Imaginative Model

In our inquiry into the structure of the Easter experience we have left one question open: namely, the problem of the imaginative model within which the Easter experience took place. That model must have been present already in the disciples' unconscious. It must have been available as an existing form, an imaginative and linguistic possibility. Otherwise there could have been no perception of Christ at all, and it would have remained unutterable. But what was available in the Judaism of the time with which one could grasp such a profound reality? There were three possibilities:

1. The idea of the "exaltation" by God of a person humiliated by suffering and death. This model is found, for example, in Isaiah 52:13-15: the "servant of God," crushed and pierced, is heard and exalted by God. But Psalm 110 was also an important background: this was about the true king of Israel, who is permitted to sit at God's right hand as God's throne companion and is thus exalted over all his foes.

2. Likewise available was a notion according to which an individual who stood out above others would be swept away from earth by God at the end of his or her life. The history of religions has adopted the concept of "rapture" or "translation" for this. The category of "rapture" also existed in the Old Testament: it is said of Enoch that God took him (Gen 5:24), and there is even a long narrative about Elijah's translation (2 Kgs 2:1-18).

3. Finally, there existed the idea of the general "resurrection of the dead" at the end of time. It is attested only marginally in the Old Testament, in Isaiah 26:19 and Daniel 12:2, but it began to play a larger role in the intertestamental literature. At the time of Jesus it had made its way into the thinking of large parts of the population. In contrast to the notions of exaltation and rapture, and also contrary to certain statements of hope in the psalms,[7] this is not about the fate of an individual but about the destiny of the many. And, also in contrast to the ideas of exaltation and rapture, the concept of the

resurrection of the dead applied to an eschatological event. That is, the place assigned to the resurrection of the dead was the end of history, or the end of the world.

In which of these three categories did the primitive church articulate its Easter faith? In fact, it employed all three categories. It said: God has exalted Jesus to his right hand;[8] it said: God has taken Jesus away into heaven;[9] but above all it said: God has raised Jesus from the dead.[10] It is highly revealing, however, that the idea of rapture is not present at the beginning of the history of tradition. It was introduced at a relatively late period, above all by Luke. It is only he who tells of a *visible* ascension into heaven, which is nothing but a kind of "rapture." His intention is thus to give a visible form to Jesus' exaltation and at the same time to set an end to the Easter appearances.

But the category in which the *immediate* Easter experience was received and put into words, the one that dominated the first visionary phenomena, was that of the general resurrection of the dead at the end of time. This is evident from the broad reception as well as the early dating of the texts in question. The oldest Easter creed was: God has raised Jesus from the dead. Certainly the idea of the exaltation of Jesus to the right hand of God and thus his affirmation as Messiah and Lord must have been intimately connected from the very beginning to the statement about his resurrection. But the original thought model in which the Easter experience was expressed—in which, indeed, it was "understood"—was that of the general resurrection of the dead.

This fact is of great significance for the description of the dimensions of the Easter events that are accessible to historians, because it makes clear that Peter, the Twelve, and the regathering community of disciples thought and acted within an extreme state of eschatological consciousness. They were deeply convinced that with the resurrection of Jesus the eschatological resurrection of the dead had already begun. But that meant that the end time, the period immediately before the end of the world, had broken upon them. The experience of the Risen One in the Easter visions in Galilee and Jerusalem must have been shocking, deeply moving, and all-shattering: now the dead will rise, the end of the world is near, the great eschatological turning has begun.

The following is important in this context: for Jewish thinking at the time the turn to a new era, to a new creation of the world by God, certainly did not have to take place on a single day. The end-time events could occur during a certain period. It is certainly not out of the question, and indeed it is quite likely, that Jesus' disciples, while seeing him as the first of those raised from the dead, at the same time expected that the universal resurrection of the dead and the end of the world would follow within days or weeks. This "extension" of the events is still evident in the ancient confessional statement: "Christ [is] the first fruits of those who have died" (1 Cor 15:20) or "the firstborn from the dead" (Col 1:18; Rev 1:5)—that is, the first, the beginning of the resurrection of the dead that is being introduced in him.

When we read through the Easter stories in the gospels, however, we find scarcely anything left of the eschatological tension and shock of the first Easter days. That could make everything I have said here seem like a construct far removed from reality. But we must consider that the four gospels were written decades after the Easter events. At the time they were composed people had long since begun to translate the expectations of the beginning into statements that projected the intent of the oldest eschatology into a new language horizon. So we cannot expect still to find in the Easter narratives of the gospels the eschatological tension of the earliest time. Nevertheless, there is a series of indicators showing that Jesus' resurrection was experienced as an end-time event and an immediate prelude to the general resurrection of the dead. I will trace these indicators in the next section.

The Resurrection of Old Testament Saints

In Matthew 27 we find an oddly unwieldy text with which today's readers for the most part cannot begin to cope. It follows immediately after Matthew's account of Jesus' death: "At that moment the curtain of the temple was torn in two, from top to bottom. The earth shook, and the rocks were split. The tombs also were opened, and many bodies of the saints who had fallen asleep were raised. After his resurrection they came out of the tombs and entered the holy city and appeared to many" (Matt 27:51-53). It is clear that this text, the second part of which works with a tradition unknown to Mark, is meant to indicate the salvation-historical significance of Jesus' death. It uses apocalyptic motifs: earthquake, splitting of rocks, graves opening. But that is by no means an adequate explanation of the text. It also reflects the atmosphere of the Easter days. The appearance of dead saints (namely, the righteous of the Old Testament), who can be seen as persons raised from the dead, must rest on visionary experiences in the earliest Jerusalem community. Apparently the Easter experiences were originally much more complex and experienced as far more apocalyptic than we would like to think today. Matthew 27:52-53 represents the highly tense eschatological atmosphere of the first days and weeks after the death of Jesus.

The Return of the Galileans

Another phenomenon points in the same direction and can substantiate what has been said thus far. We have seen that the appearances before the Twelve began in Galilee. On that basis we would have to assume that the original community assembled in Galilee and remained there. A number of scholars have, in fact, posited an original Galilean community in addition to the one in Jerusalem, but that has remained simply a postulate; thus far it has been impossible to offer historical proof of an initial community on the Sea of Galilee.

We are, however, faced with the fact that Peter, the Twelve (without Judas Iscariot, of course), and other disciples were in Jerusalem, at the latest on Pentecost. There, and not in Galilee, the first community gathered, and at first it was firmly tied to Jerusalem. Peter and the other disciples did not remain in Galilee. How can we explain their return to the capital city, which was still so dangerous for them?

A primary reason must have been the centering of the end-time events in the holy city, which was a matter of course in Jewish thought. It was from Zion that the conclusive gift of salvation would emanate, and from Jerusalem judgment and resurrection would take their beginning. It must therefore have been almost a necessity for the disciples in Galilee, when they saw the general resurrection of the dead beginning in their visions of the Risen One, to wait for those events in Jerusalem and nowhere else. So, at the latest in time for the feast of Pentecost, they returned with the other pilgrim caravans to the capital city, gathered together, and awaited the progress of the end-time events.

The Empty Tomb

Indeed, there may have been another reason for this return, in addition to the impulse given by the appearances of the Risen One: in all probability not all the disciples had fled to Galilee. Individuals among Jesus' followers and sympathizers had stayed in the capital city, especially those who were less threatened or whose families were resident in Jerusalem. We have firm evidence that a group of women remained in the city; these included Mary Magdalene (Mark 16:1; cf. Acts 1:14). On the morning of the first day of the week these women went to Jesus' tomb to anoint his body. They probably wanted to make up for what Joseph of Arimathea had been unable to do because of lack of time.[11] But they sought in vain for Jesus' corpse; they found the tomb empty.

That, at any rate, is what Mark says in 16:1-8. His account has repeatedly been called into question. Even in the first century the empty tomb was interpreted as a fantastic invention, a shameless fraud, or a simple mistake. Since the eighteenth century the empty tomb has had it even worse. Enlightened minds repeatedly declare it a legend or part of a great myth.

It is true that the tomb story contains fictive elements. The longer the story was told, the more they multiplied. The "stone rolled away" in Mark becomes in Matthew "an angel of the Lord, descending from heaven, [who] came and rolled back the stone and sat on it" (Matt 28:2). Mark's *one* angel becomes two in Luke (Luke 24:4). And the apocryphal Gospel of Peter describes how Jesus himself emerged from the tomb; his form reached not only to heaven, but beyond (*GosPet* 10:39-40).

But I do not see myself in a position to call the whole story that lies behind Mark 16:1-8 a fiction. There are elements in it that still bear the whiff of real events.

1. First of all, there is the burial by Joseph of Arimathea and thus certain knowledge of the location of the tomb. That knowledge cannot have vanished from the minds of the original Jerusalem community.

2. Then there is the date: the first day of the week. That day would from that time forth play an extraordinary role in the history of the church: the first day of the Jewish week became the Christian Sunday, the "day of the Lord." In the Jewish method of counting this was the "third day" after Jesus' death. The very oldest creedal formula we have speaks of Jesus' being raised "on the third day" (1 Cor 15:4). Where does that date come from? It is not "spun out" of the Old Testament, e.g., from Hosea 6:2,[12] nor does it date the first appearances of the Risen One. The dating on the "third day" can only come from events that took place at the tomb.

3. We should also note that anyone inventing a story from beginning to end would have been very unlikely to make women the witnesses to an empty tomb. In the Judaism of that time women were not

proper witnesses, as is abundantly clear from the resurrection traditions. According to Luke the apostles considered the women's report of the empty tomb "an idle tale"; they did not believe them (Luke 24:11). The following is also very revealing in this context: the attestation of the resurrection in 1 Corinthians 15:3-8 speaks only of men, naming Cephas, James, the Twelve, and more than five hundred "brothers." There were most certainly women among those five hundred, but they are not mentioned. Why? Because they were not regarded as qualified witnesses. Likewise unnamed in 1 Corinthians 15 is Mary Magdalene, although Matthew, John, and the "canonical ending" of Mark make it known that she had a vision of the Risen One at the tomb.[13] Luke says nothing about her vision; instead, in his account Peter runs to the tomb to seek proof of the women's testimony (Luke 24:12). All this shows how little value was placed on women's witness in the milieu of the time. From that point of view it is improbable that the early church would have invented a tomb story as a sign of Jesus' resurrection in which women appeared as the witnesses.

4. Finally, we should observe that there was polemic opposition to the story of the empty tomb. Significantly, that polemic never disputes the fact of the empty tomb as such; it is only reinterpreted: the disciples stole Jesus' body or a gardener had transferred it to another tomb.[14] All this presupposes an empty tomb. This supports the historical basis of the tomb story and speaks against the assertion sometimes heard that Jesus was tossed into a mass grave or that his tomb was unknown.

So, until there be proof to the contrary, we should posit an empty tomb that became a sign[15] and a signal for the disciples remaining in Jerusalem. Reports would then have been transmitted to and from Galilee. The coincidence of visionary experiences and the empty tomb led the disciples to a single interpretation of the Easter event, summarized in the statement "God has raised Jesus from the dead." The news of the empty tomb must at first have strengthened the apocalyptic expectations of the Galileans, because the spontaneous opening of graves was part of the general resurrection of the dead. At the same time, however, this news strengthened their resolve to return to the capital.

It has probably become clear long since that this chapter is attempting to make the elevated eschatological expectations of the disciples after

Easter the key to the sequence of Easter events. I do believe that without the end-time atmosphere I have described we can neither correctly order nor understand the sequence of events following immediately on the death of Jesus. Here is another example.

The Election of Matthias

In Acts 1:15-26 Luke writes that the first order of business within the community was the choice of Matthias to join the group of the Twelve, which was incomplete as a result of Judas's betrayal. We have no reason to question the very ancient tradition on which Luke relies for his account of this election. What is crucial to note is that there was never another such election afterward. It might have seemed like a good thing to augment the Twelve each time one of its members died and so continue the group as such. But that simply did not occur. Why? The information that the Twelve gradually came to play less and less of a role as a leadership group for the earliest community may not suffice as an explanation. Why did they so rapidly cease to play that role? Apparently because it was not their proper work. The original function of the Twelve within the earliest community was *eschatological* and can be read in Matthew 19:28: "Truly I tell you, at the renewal of all things, when the Son of Man is seated on the throne of his glory, you who have followed me will also sit on twelve thrones, judging the twelve tribes of Israel."

During Jesus' lifetime the Twelve were an institutionalized sign of Jesus' focus on the whole of Israel. He made them the official witnesses of his message and the personal symbol of the claims of the reign of God on the whole people of the twelve tribes. That was already a clearly eschatological function, one whose symbolic language was irrevocably linked to the number twelve. If the eschatological-symbolic function of the Twelve with respect to Israel continued after the death of Jesus—and the appearances of the Risen One must certainly have suggested that— then the group of the Twelve had to be augmented and made complete again *precisely because of the approaching end-time events*. Only in the number twelve was the sign visible, and only in the full power of the sign could the Twelve be witnesses for the Son of Man to Israel at the immediately approaching last judgment.

This offers the simplest explanation for why the group of the Twelve, though quickly restored to its full complement after Jesus' death, was not further augmented in later years: the first and only election took place in that particular historical phase of the earliest community when the disciples' expectations of the end had reached their highest degree of intensity. Again it proves to be a valid principle to regard the movements and activities within the earliest community entirely from the point of view of their highly expectant consciousness of the end time.

The Pentecost Event

This interpretive key applies also to the event that took place at the Jewish Feast of Weeks in Jerusalem. Luke tells of it immediately after he has recounted the choice of Matthias:

> When the day of Pentecost had come, they were all together in one place. And suddenly from heaven there came a sound like the rush of a violent wind, and it filled the entire house where they were sitting. Divided tongues, as of fire, appeared among them, and a tongue rested on each of them. All of them were filled with the Holy Spirit and began to speak in other languages, as the Spirit gave them ability. (Acts 2:1-4)

This narrative and its continuation make up a text that already had a long history of tradition behind it, in the course of which it had been changed and brought up to date; it was then reworked again and expanded by Luke himself. Let us for the moment set aside the motifs of wind and fire. They are part of an older, pre-Lukan layer of tradition that told of miraculous speech and whose model lay in Jewish interpretations of the Sinai story. God gave his Law on Sinai in fire and loud thunder, and despite all their different languages all the peoples of the world could understand what God spoke on Sinai.[16]

The earliest level of the narrative, however, was not about a miracle of speech but about the phenomenon of "speaking in tongues," or glossolalia. The final text says that they spoke "in other tongues," that is, in foreign languages, but behind that is an original *lalein glōssais*, a "speaking in tongues," namely, inarticulate, ecstatic speech.[17] We can take it as certain that the oldest narrative core of Acts 2:1-36 told of the outbreak of ecstatic praise of God in inarticulate speech within the original Jerusalem community.

In that case, however, we can imagine the whole context as follows: Peter, the Twelve, and other disciples returned to Jerusalem, at the latest for the Feast of Weeks. They were still in the thrall of their visions of the

Risen One and the impressions from what they had heard about the empty tomb. They arrived in a high-strung state of eschatological expectation, looking for the Parousia, the final, ultimate appearance of the Risen One, to take place publicly in the capital city itself.

They joined with the disciples, male and female, who had remained in the city. All of them gathered to exchange experiences and pray (cf. Acts 1:13-14), and then, on the Feast of Weeks (Pentecost), in the midst of such a gathering, there was an eruption of ecstatic speech that seized them all and shook them to the core. This prayer experience left them with a deep faith conviction. It formed the group of Jesus followers definitively into a community and—this is crucial—it was interpreted by the community as an experience of the Spirit. This was the beginning of such experiences of the Spirit in the church. There have again and again been glossolalic phenomena since then. In the course of the later mission they extended to other communities (cf. Acts 10:46; 19:6). Even twenty years later we find them in Corinth. It was probably at the same time, and in connection with the speaking in tongues, that the charism of prophecy appeared in the earliest community (cf. Acts 11:27), and it would accompany the development of communities for a long time.

What is decisive in our context is the following: In the Old Testament and in Judaism there was a clear-cut tradition that described the coming of the Spirit of God as a phenomenon of the end time, indeed, as a sign preceding the end of the world. We need only recall Joel 3:1-5, a text quoted by Peter in his Pentecost discourse. The quotation begins as follows: "then afterward [lit.: in the last days] I will pour out my spirit on all flesh; your sons and your daughters shall prophesy, your old men shall dream dreams, and your young men shall see visions" (Joel 2:28). This text clearly shows how, already in the Old Testament,[18] the coming of the Spirit can introduce the end time. It was against that background that the sudden and elemental experience of the Spirit was comprehensible to the earliest community in Jerusalem. The ecstatic phenomena of the day of Pentecost and their interpretation in terms of the Spirit of God would have been unthinkable without the firm conviction of the participants at that time that the end-time events had already begun. The ecstatic shock of the Pentecost assembly was immediately understood to be the eschatological outpouring of the Spirit of which the Old Testament prophets had spoken. This again supports our interpretive approach, which says that without the network of coordinates that made up the tense expectation of the Parousia the history of the earliest community cannot be understood at all.

Further Indications

What we have seen thus far could easily be expanded. We would then have to speak especially of baptism, which was practiced from the beginning of the earliest community and appeared as suddenly and abruptly as the experience of the Spirit. It can only be understood phenomenologically as an eschatological sacrament, a saving seal in view of the nearness of the end.[19]

We should also speak of the earliest community's self-perception, recorded in the terms it applied to itself. It would become clear that concepts such as "the saints" (Acts 9:13), "the elect" (Mark 13:19-27), or "the church of God" (Gal 1:13) reveal a fundamentally eschatological structure. They refer to the Israel of the end time, which God has created, chosen, and sanctified for God's self.

Finally, we would have to speak of the celebration of the Lord's Supper, which also points toward the *eschatōn*. The *maranatha*, "Our Lord, come!" (1 Cor 16:22), at worship sounded forth already in the earliest Jerusalem community. When we read in Acts 2:46, "they broke bread at home and ate their food with glad and generous hearts," we are reading of the end-time rejoicing of the community that erupted in their eucharistic celebrations; this is about the overflowing joy of people who rejoice and can be jubilant that in their meals they were permitted to anticipate the eternal banquet with God they expected to encounter in the very near future.

World-Altering Expectation

But none of that can be pursued here. Even this brief description has probably shown already what approach we need to take if we are to understand the course of the Easter events. Here I will propose only one more question: What happened in the long term to that understanding of Easter, that tense and eager expectation of the Parousia in the first weeks after Jesus' death? Did history invalidate it and lay it to rest? Was it an illusion? Was it all like a grass fire that blazes up suddenly and just as suddenly collapses?

It is helpful, in trying to answer this, if we recall a basic feature of all the appearance accounts. There is not a single Easter narrative in the New Testament that would point our attention to the "beyond," to heaven, to eternal happiness or the disciples' own resurrection. Nowhere in the Easter stories in the gospels do we find the basic idea of many of today's Easter sermons, meditations, hymns, and petitions: because Christ is risen we can be certain that we will also rise.

Instead, all the Easter texts culminate in the Risen One's sending of the disciples. "Go therefore and make disciples of all nations," says Matthew 28:19. "Go into all the world and proclaim the good news to the whole creation," says Mark 16:15. In the name of the Messiah "repentance and forgiveness of sins is to be proclaimed in his name to all nations, beginning from Jerusalem. You are witnesses of these things," reads Luke 24:47-48. Finally, "as the Father has sent me, so I send you," according to John 20:21. Even Paul said nothing in response to the question of why the Lord had appeared to him except that God "was pleased to reveal his Son to me, so that I might proclaim him among the Gentiles" (Gal 1:15-16). And to round off the whole, in Acts 1:11 the disciples who are staring after the vanishing Christ hear, "Men of Galilee, why do you stand looking up toward heaven?" That is, they should not fixate on heaven but be Jesus' witnesses "in Jerusalem, in all Judea and Samaria, and to the ends of the earth" (Acts 1:8).

Matching all these texts is the remarkable circumstance that it was precisely this original Jerusalem community—which, as we saw, expected the return of the Risen One and the end of the world in the immediate future—that stood up before Israel, preaching and missionizing (Acts 2:38-40). The expectation did not falter; rather, it compelled them to gather Israel and lead it to repentance in light of the approaching end. The same can easily be demonstrated in the case of Paul, who in spite of his imminent expectation of the end traveled the Mediterranean world to win as many people as possible for Christ (cf. Rom 15:17-21).[20]

Real, genuine *biblical* expectation of the approaching end does not grow lame, does not allow one to stand idly looking up to heaven, but instead draws our eyes directly to the world and its distress. So it was in the early communities; so it had already been for Jesus. We have seen that his proclamation of the reign of God (cf. chap. 2 above) was tied to the most intense expectation of the approaching end imaginable— namely, an expectation that was constantly being fulfilled "today." That kind of expectation knows that it must act because it is about "now," and because there is no time afterward. Every hour is then precious; the time must be used up entirely just because it has an end-time quality. Jesus' purpose was nothing else but to gather Israel in view of the already approaching reign of God and to lead it to repentance.

Jesus' disciples had experienced all that intimately; they had internalized it, and with the appearances of the Risen One it broke out in them anew. Their urgent expectation of the Parousia was therefore never pointed only to what was to come, but instead, just as in the mind of Jesus, always also to today. This is evident in their idea of the Holy Spirit and the sacraments. In earliest Christianity the Holy Spirit is certainly the beginning of the end time and the deposit on fulfillment, but at the same time that Spirit is the power of God for the new creation of the world. When the Spirit is received and given room in the church, the world will be created anew—toward its perfection.

The sacraments too are eschatological. That is evident in the Eucharist, which is characterized by the cry, "come, Lord Jesus!" and yet this very sacrament binds Christians together as brothers and sisters and so creates new community. Something similar is true of baptism. It is an eschatological sign; it seals one for the end, and yet precisely this sacrament obligates us to a new life in the world. Whoever has died with Christ in baptism is born into the new society of the church. The sacraments contain eschatological dynamite, and yet they are the place where the earliest church made real its present eschatology.

It is against this horizon of the coming of Christ, already being fulfilled and yet again and again delayed, that the anticipatory texts of the New Testament must be interpreted. Then the Easter expectation in Christian communities would mean anticipating that at every hour the Spirit of Christ will show the community new paths, expecting new doors to open at any moment, counting on it that at any hour the Spirit can transform evil into good, hoping at every hour that the impossible will become possible, and never saying "later!" but always "now!" Then the texts of expectation in the New Testament are not something embarrassing, something we need to be ashamed of, and also not something time-bound that we can leave behind us; instead, they are at the center of what it means to be Christian.

From this point of view I would never say that Jesus and the earliest church were misled or disappointed in their imminent expectation. Jesus was profoundly certain that God was acting now, and acting with finality and in unsurpassable fashion. He was certain that in that action God was expressing God's very self in the world, totally and without reservation. This "totality" and "finality" are, however, faced with the fact that human beings normally reject such a "totality" insofar as it applies to themselves and their own response. They do not want to commit themselves definitively but prefer to delay their own decisions and leave everything open for the time being. So there arises a deep discrepancy between God's "already" and the human "not yet." But because God has expressed God's self wholly and absolutely in Jesus there is no time left for "delaying the decision." Jesus' hearers and the apostles had to decide *now*, in this hour. And they had to decide not only for God's sake but also because of Israel's need and the immeasurable suffering of the world.

I wonder whether, within the eschatological thinking of his world, in which he himself was deeply rooted, Jesus could have formulated and expressed this urgent "now" for decision in any other language than that of imminent expectation.[21] We ourselves stand within an imaginative horizon of endlessly extended time in which there is no genuine *kairos*, but only events. Are we really closer to the truth of our existence and of human history than Jesus, with his eschatological emphasis? I doubt it very much indeed. Obviously we have to translate the eschatological language of Jesus and the early church. When we do, we see that it was not Jesus who was mistaken; it is we who constantly deceive ourselves, not only about the fragility and exposure of our lives, but also about the nearness of God.

Chapter 19

Jesus' Sovereign Claim

This chapter was originally to be titled "Jesus' Self-Awareness," but I erased that. "Self-awareness" is too close to "self-assurance" or "self-importance," and if we scarcely dare to say anything about the innermost thoughts of people around us we most certainly can say nothing about Jesus' self-awareness and "inner life." All that is open to a historical view is what emerges in Jesus' speech and action as his "claim."

Obviously we have spoken repeatedly about this claim in previous chapters; after all, it expresses itself in every one of Jesus' deeds and words. But now it needs to be addressed again as a single topic. Why only now? Why only after an attempt to reconstruct the sequence of the Easter events? Simply because for Jesus' disciples the appearances of the Risen One put everything in motion again. Only now did they begin to really understand. Only now could they see Jesus with complete clarity. That is by no means to say that in the time before his death he was a blank page that was only written on after and through Easter. No, everything was there before Easter. What Jesus wanted and what he was—all that was there to be heard and seen. But the disciples had not yet really grasped it.

The dialogues Jesus conducts with his disciples in John's gospel, as he approaches death, reflect this "already" and "not yet" with the finest theological precision. The Holy Spirit whom the Father will send will indeed "teach everything" to the disciples, but that teaching consists precisely[1] in "reminding" them of all Jesus had said (John 14:26). Thus after Easter nothing new is taught the disciples about the mystery of Jesus' person. They do not receive any new revelations, as the later Gnostic gospels would say they did. It was simply that the full profundity of who Jesus was became clear to them.

So this chapter (together with chaps. 20 and 21) belongs at the end of the book, in the time after Easter, we might say. But the method remains the same. My principal questions will be historical: what claims to sovereignty are evident in Jesus' words and actions?

Was Jesus a Prophet?

"Who do people say that I am?" Jesus, according to Mark 8:27, posed this question to his disciples one day: "Jesus went on with his disciples to the villages of Caesarea Philippi; and on the way he asked them, 'Who do people say that I am?' And they answered him, 'John the Baptist; and others, Elijah; and still others, one of the prophets' " (Mark 8:27-28). The disciples' answer is as unclear as are the identifications of Jesus circulating among the people: apparently many suppose Jesus is John the Baptizer. Do they merely think Jesus has appeared in the power and spirit of the Baptizer, or do they believe he has returned in Jesus as *Johannes redivivus* (cf. Mark 6:14)?

The disciples list a second popular opinion, that Jesus is the prophet Elijah. Here things are clearer. It is said of Elijah in 2 Kings 2:1-18 that he did not die but was raptured to heaven by God. This led to the opinion that in the end time Elijah would come again and appear once more in Israel (Mal 3:23; Sir 48:10). So part of the people of God regarded Jesus as the prophet Elijah, sent by God to introduce the end-time events.

The third position is again unclear. Many said that Jesus was one of the prophets. That, similarly to the second position, could mean that Jesus is another prophet, such as Jeremiah (cf. Matt 16:14), who had been taken up to heaven and has now returned. But probably it simply means that many people thought Jesus was a prophet like those who had appeared in Israel in times past (cf. Mark 6:15).

We may suppose that Mark 8:28 is a fairly accurate reflection of the speculations about Jesus that were circulating in Israel, with all their vagueness and attempts to grope toward the reality of Jesus' person. Many people must have thought and spoken in more or less these terms. There was also an opinion, appearing in the gospels and elsewhere,[2] that Jesus was a great prophet. For example, the inhabitants of Nain say, " 'A great prophet has risen among us!' and 'God has looked favorably on his people!'" (Luke 7:16), or John 7:40-41 reads, "Some in the crowd said, 'This is really the prophet.' Others said, 'This is the Messiah.' But some asked, 'Surely the Messiah does not come from Galilee, does he?'" We can see from these texts how divided opinions were. In the mind of the Fourth Evangelist, certainly, one may indeed say of Jesus that he is "the" prophet, because that phrase refers to the end-time prophet *per se*, the one who, on the basis of Deuteronomy 18:18, was awaited by some groups of Jews.[3]

Jesus does not seem to have shared the evaluation of his person as that of a prophet, or a raptured and returned prophet, or "the" end-time prophet. We can see this clearly from the fact that after the disciples have listed the people's opinions (Mark 8:28) he asks them, "But who do you say that I am?" (Mark 8:29). Jesus—at least in the narrative—expects a different answer, one not identical with what has been said before, and he receives that answer in Peter's confession of him as Messiah.

A still clearer answer to our question is the way Jesus estimates John the Baptizer, since for Jesus not even the Baptizer is simply a prophet. Jesus tells the crowd, regarding John:

> What did you go out into the wilderness [to the Baptizer] to look
> at? A reed shaken by the wind? What then did you go out to see?
> Someone dressed in soft robes? Look, those who wear soft robes are
> in royal palaces. What then did you go out to see? A prophet? Yes,
> I tell you, and [you have seen] more than a prophet. (Matt 11:7-9)

If even the Baptizer cannot be comprehended in the title "prophet" we may conclude that the same is certainly true of Jesus. And Jesus must have seen it the same way. The Baptizer spoke in his preaching of a Stronger One who would come after him: "I baptize you only with water, but the one who comes after me is stronger than I; I am not worthy to untie his sandals. He will baptize you with fire" (cf. Matt 3:11). That would have been more or less the original wording of the Baptizer's saying about the "Stronger One." Many interpreters ponder which of the exalted end-time figures in Judaism the Baptizer may have had in mind, but exegetically speaking that is impermissible. If the Baptizer does not use one of the existing titles of majesty (cf. also Luke 7:19) but only alludes to the one who is to come as the Stronger One—that is, he is unable to describe his mystery in a single concept—that must be respected and we should not attempt to correct it in hindsight.

We may suspect that since Jesus had probably spent a rather long time as a follower of the Baptizer he had at some point applied to himself the prediction of the Stronger One who was to come. And we may further suppose that he tended to avoid existing titles of majesty. As far as the mystery of his person was concerned, Jesus preferred to speak in veiled and indirect terms, just as the Baptizer had done in this regard.

At any rate, Jesus did not see himself as a prophet.[4] This is abundantly clear from the beatitude he spoke over his disciples: "Blessed are the eyes that see what you see! For I tell you that many prophets and kings desired to see what you see, but did not see it, and to hear what you hear, but did not hear it" (Luke 10:23-24). According to this saying, the turning of the age has already happened. Prophets and kings are contrasted to the disciples, the time of prophets and kings to the time of the reign of God. What previously was only longed for can now be seen. In light of these words it is out of the question that Jesus could have located himself within the time of the prophets or the phenotype of the prophet! This matches to the letter "something greater than Jonah is here . . . something greater than Solomon is here!" in Matthew 12:41-42.

In addition, the beatitude for the disciples just quoted makes it clear what reticence and veiled reference Jesus employed when speaking of the mystery of his own person. We will encounter this reticence again and again, also with regard to the question of whether Jesus saw himself as the Messiah. But first we need to mention another ground for concluding that Jesus could not have seen himself as a prophet. He had Scripture before his eyes. Like every pious Jew he recited a part of it every day. Every Sabbath he heard not only sections of the Torah but also readings from the prophets. Someone who constantly encounters Scripture in this way very quickly internalizes *how* the prophets speak. All the writing prophets in Israel point out persistently that "the word of the LORD" has come to them and is being communicated to Israel through them.[5] It is not their own words they are handing on but the word spoken to them.

Jesus makes no such statements. We do not find a single passage in which he says anything like "The LORD has spoken," or "the mouth of the LORD has spoken it," or "hear the word of the LORD," or "thus says the LORD." In place of these "messenger formulae," which repeatedly emphasize that the prophet is only a transmitter, Jesus created for himself his own opening formula, one so far not attested in the Judaism of the time: "Amen, I say to you."[6] In contrast to the "amen" that responds to someone else's speech and affirms it, this "amen" *begins* sayings of Jesus and introduces them as words spoken on his own authority. The result is a dialectic that is hard to describe: on the one hand, Jesus speaks in his own name like a sovereign and on his own authority. On the other hand, he speaks out of the most extreme intimacy with God.

Jesus the Messiah?

In preaching to the crowds, did Jesus make a kind of self-presentation of himself as the Messiah? The answer is clearly no. Jesus proclaimed the beginning of the reign of God but not himself as Messiah. There are not even very many reactions from the people showing that Jesus was regarded as the Messiah. In Mark's gospel, differently from that of Matthew,[7] there is but a single text in which someone from the crowd addresses Jesus as Messiah. This is the healing of the blind Bartimaeus outside Jericho. When Bartimaeus hears that Jesus is passing by, he cries out, "Jesus, Son of David, have mercy on me!" (Mark 10:47). That was a messianic confession, because the messiah could be called "Son of David."[8] The appeal shows that there were those in Israel, besides the ones who thought Jesus was a prophet or even a prophet *redivivus*, who conjectured that he was the expected messiah. According to the narrative, Jesus accepted the appellation and healed the blind man.

On the other hand, Jesus accepted Peter's confession of him as Messiah, which he himself had provoked, but he immediately emphasized to his disciples that they should not talk about the messiah (Mark 8:27-30). Of course, at that time he was alone with his disciples. If we take the two texts together—the cry of the blind Bartimaeus, his healing, and the previous command to silence in Mark 8:27-30—we may conclude that Jesus did not simply regard the notion that he was the messiah as false, but he did not want it to be applied thoughtlessly and prematurely.

Bartimaeus's cry then acts as a signal to readers of Mark's gospel that the situation has changed. At any rate, Jesus, as he approached Jerusalem soon afterward, gave his entry into the city a messianic character. I have already spoken about this at length (chap. 15). Jesus also accepted the messianic acclamation of those accompanying him, but he interpreted his messianic character in terms of Zechariah 9:9.

The crucial and decisive scene takes place before the Sanhedrin. Here Jesus is asked by the high priest himself, the highest religious authority in Israel, if he is the Messiah, and he answers, "I am" (Mark 14:61-62). He refines this confession, however, by saying that he will come in majesty as the Son of Man, the Human One.

In recent exegesis, especially since Rudolf Bultmann, both Peter's confession of Jesus as Messiah and Jesus' affirmation before the Sanhedrin have been presented as fictive scenes. All the gospel texts in which a messianic statement appears are said to be post-Easter constructions. But here a critique of the critique is in order. It is quite correct that Jesus did not proclaim himself as Messiah when he appeared in Galilee. That he always treated the messianic title with reticence and the highest degree of caution is also correct. But that in no way excludes what then occurred in the acute situation in Jerusalem, for we cannot avoid the fact that, after his sentencing by Pilate, Jesus was mocked by Roman soldiers as "king of the Jews" (Mark 15:16-20) and then executed under a placard reading "King of the Jews" (Mark 15:26). That *titulus* must very certainly have had a starting point in the events themselves, before the Sanhedrin as well as before the Roman prefect. When Jesus was formally charged by Caiaphas to say whether he was the Messiah, he could not say, "No, I am not." He could not do so even though he maintained a certain reserve toward the title. He could, however, give more precision to this title of majesty, and he did so.

What is the basis for Jesus' careful treatment of the title "messiah"? As we have indicated earlier, there were special political reasons for such caution. In the ears of many Jews, but most especially in the ears of the Roman occupying power, the word "messiah" sounded like uproar and rebellion against Rome. That was one-sided, of course: Jewish ideas of the messiah were much richer and more nuanced. The Old Testament itself sometimes paints its "messianic" figures[9] in quite different colors. But as disunified and multiple as the ideas of a messiah were, in Jesus' time the word had become a dangerous irritant. Jesus could not desire that his gathering of Israel could be even distantly interpreted in the direction of Zealot uprisings. That would have falsified his whole message. Probably in that case Jesus' effectiveness would have come to a quick and violent end, and it would already have happened in Galilee.

But the reasons for Jesus' reticence lay deeper: apparently the concept of a messiah was as inadequate as that of an eschatological prophet for explaining his mission, his claim, and his mystery—not only the mystery of his majesty but also that of his humility. So he preferred to speak indirectly of what was now happening before the eyes of all: "the blind receive their sight, the lame walk, the lepers are cleansed, the deaf hear, the dead are raised, and the poor have good news brought to them. And blessed is anyone who takes no offense at me" (Matt 11:5-6). That is thoroughly "messianic," and there can be no question that the designation "messianic," or as we may say, the Savior-figure of the Messiah, covers much of what Jesus was. Otherwise the early church would not have called him the "Christ" ("Anointed One") and so rapidly and earnestly that "Christ" became his proper name. We must even say that if Jesus had not made himself known as Messiah, at the latest before the Sanhedrin, the development of the early church's Christology would be beyond all understanding. And yet we cannot overlook the fact that here, as elsewhere, Jesus showed reserve and restraint, and that restraint is to be respected in raising historical questions and must not be swept aside.

Jesus, the "Son of Man"

It is quite different with regard to the concept of the "Son of Man" or "Human One." It is striking that in this case Jesus did use the title. The evidence is completely clear: the title "Son of Man" appears in the New Testament almost exclusively in the gospels,[10] and there only on the lips of Jesus.[11] But it is also important that it is found in every level of tradition: in the Sayings Source, in Mark, in Matthew, in Luke, in the Gospel of John, and even in the apocryphal *Gospel of Thomas* (logion 86).[12] If the church had first begun giving Jesus the exalted title "Son of Man" after Easter we would find a completely different picture within the New Testament. Apparently the earliest church was still aware that this was a usage particular to Jesus that had to be left with him and could not be freely thrown around, for example, in christological confessional statements.[13] Conclusion: Jesus used the title "Son of Man" as a self-designation in the presence of his disciples and then publicly as well.

This was, of course, also connected with the fact that "Son of Man" was enigmatic or coded speech. That was already the case in Daniel 7, where the great powers of history were presented as beasts, with a human being (= Son of Man or Human One) as their counter. As we have already seen (chap. 3), this "human being" is there a symbol of the ultimate human society God is creating in Israel and, through Israel, in the world.

In the apocalyptic secret literature of early Judaism, the Human One in Daniel 7 was regarded as a majestic figure who would hold judgment in God's name at the end of time and establish salvation and justice. This is attested by the imagery in Ethiopian Enoch (*1 En.* 37–71) and 4 Ezra.[14] But the latter was created only after the destruction of Jerusalem, and there is dispute about when the image discourses in *1 Enoch* were written. They come either from the first century before or the first century after Christ. It is also possible, however, that these image discourses have a history of redaction behind them, one that extended over a considerable period of time.

Even if these image discourses already existed in Jesus' time there remains the question whether Jesus knew them or not. It is much more plausible that he drew the symbol of the Human One/Son of Man not from some esoteric sources but from Sacred Scripture itself, for it is certain that Jesus had access to the picture of history in Daniel 7; its whole force was familiar to him. When he spoke of the *coming* of the reign of God, the interpretation of history in Daniel 7 was part of it. Nevertheless, Jesus modified it at the same time. What was different with Jesus?

First of all, there was the time scheme! In Daniel 7 the five empires or five societies succeed one another: first Babylon, then the Medes, then the Persians, then the Seleucids—and only when the rule of all the world empires has expired does the true kingship, the true *basileia*, the true society of God come to pass. Only then begins the rule of the Human One who is so deeply connected to the reign of God. For Jesus, in contrast, the reign of God is already beginning, in the midst of this history, in the midst of the still ongoing power of the world empires, represented at that time in the brutal and violent rule of the Roman Empire.

And there was still more in the scheme of Daniel 7 that changed for Jesus: the new society of the reign of God not only begins in the midst of the still existing epoch of the world empires; it is indissolubly linked to a single one. While the Human One in Daniel 7 was still a collective person, Jesus now speaks of himself as the Son of Man. "Son of Man/Human One" is thus no longer a mere symbol of the true eschatological Israel; at the same time it is a mysterious name for Jesus himself. He *is* the Son of Man; he embodies in himself the new society of the eschatological Israel.

Finally, there is a third modification, and an especially important one: it is ordained of the Human One in Daniel 7 that "all peoples, nations, and languages should serve him," as it says at the end of the vision. But Jesus says of himself, "The Son of Man came not to be served but to serve, and to give his life a ransom for many" (Mark 10:45). On this point Jesus has again surpassed the historical projection of Daniel 7. Jesus' rule is based on his service, his surrender even to death. So Jesus altered the statements made in Daniel 7, but those very changes—palpable especially in the motif of service—show that in speaking of the "Son of Man" he is referring directly to Daniel 7. For what one changes is already presupposed, and evidently the very symbol of the "Son of Man" was a welcome expression for what he had to say about himself. Why?

1. The concept of "Son of Man/Human One" could not be politically misinterpreted like that of "messiah." It was not meant to arouse passions.

2. Already in Daniel 7 this concept was associated with a majesty equal to that of the hoped-for messianic king if not even surpassing it: "His dominion is an everlasting dominion that shall not pass away" (Dan 7:14).

3. With this concept Jesus could simultaneously express his lowliness, his humility, for the Human One in Daniel 7 is also the end of all societies based on self-exaltation and violence. And a rule that abandons violence can only rely on God; it is helplessly delivered over to the powers and rulers of history. Thus the symbol of the "Son of Man/Human One" allows the linking of statements of majesty and those of lowliness.

4. In Daniel 7 the Human One is Israel's representative. He embodies the "people of the holy ones of the Most High" (Dan 7:27). This reference to Israel touches on something that is essential about Jesus. His purpose was to gather the eschatological Israel, something that had already begun with him and his group of disciples.

5. But what is crucial is that what Jesus says about himself thus remains coded. Talk of the Son of Man preserves his reticence. It remains enigmatic to a certain extent, and thus it provokes its hearers, who must ask themselves who this Son of Man really is. We have already noted Jesus' restraint in speaking of himself in a number of places.

In this connection we should look especially at the double saying in Luke 12:8-9 about confessing Jesus. Those who now, in the present, confess Jesus publicly will also be publicly acknowledged by Jesus at the final judgment. But here it seems that Jesus and the Son of Man are separate:

> "And I tell you, everyone who acknowledges me before others, the Son of Man also will acknowledge before the angels of God."

> "but whoever denies me before others will be denied before the angels of God." (Luke 12:8-9)

This double saying even today plays a central role in the endless and confusing debates over the "Son of Man." Rudolf Bultmann and others have concluded from Luke 12:8-9 that Jesus saw the Son of Man as a heavenly figure distinct from himself.[15] But that would be a deceptive conclusion. The shift from first to third person is by no means an indicator of a change in the figures but is part of the style of reticent, enigmatic speech. It was long the custom for an author, in beginning a book, not to say "I" but instead "the author." The direct use of "I" was considered impolite. In fact there are things that are better said in "he/she" style than in "I" style. We can see this exact usage in Paul when he writes in 2 Corinthians 12:1-5:

> It is necessary to boast; nothing is to be gained by it, but I will go on to visions and revelations of the Lord. I know a person in Christ who fourteen years ago was caught up to the third heaven—whether in the body or out of the body I do not know; God knows. And I know that such a person—whether in the body or out of the body I do not know; God knows—was caught up into Paradise and heard things that are not to be told, that no mortal is permitted to repeat. On behalf of such a one I will boast, but on my own behalf I will not boast, except of my weakness.

Paul here shifts twice between "I" and "he," and then speaks in "I" form again. In that form he speaks of his "weakness." In the "he" form he talks of things one prefers to keep back, things one cannot talk about in the same way as everyday, visible matters. He does not want to boast.

Thus there are situations in which tact and a sense of style demand that one speak in "he/she" style. Jesus betrays this very tact, discretion, and sense of style when he speaks of the Son of Man and thus of himself in the third person. It is superfluous to suppose he is speaking of two different figures.

With this note on Rudolf Bultmann I have taken a tiny step into the simply endless history of scholarly discussion about the "Son of Man/ Human One." But I do not want to continue the discussion in this form here. My position on the titles of majesty such as "prophet," "messiah," and "Son of Man/Human One" should have become clear by now, and nothing more is necessary for this book, because in the end the question of Jesus' claim to majesty need not be made dependent on whether Jesus used those titles or not. Much more important is the claim that emanates indirectly from Jesus' words and actions. I will now speak of this hidden and yet unmistakable and immense claim as a whole.

The Time Fulfilled

Eschatology speaks of the last things, of the hour toward which everything is moving, and thus also of the hour in which everything will be fulfilled and reveal its ultimate meaning. This utmost, ultimate hour includes judgment, because the confusions of history must be cleared up. All injustice must be uncovered, all evil revealed, and all guilt transformed. Jesus often spoke of judgment—not only the judgment to come, but also the judgment already in the making (see chap. 10). But more frequently and more fundamentally, he said that now all the time of Israel's waiting and longing was being fulfilled and as overflowing salvation (chap. 14). Jesus' appearance is shot through with the assurance that the promised time of salvation, of liberation, of fulfillment of the promises given by God is dawning. Let me quote once more the blessing of the eyewitnesses, which is so important: "Blessed are the eyes that see what you see! For I tell you that many prophets and kings desired to see what you see, but did not see it, and to hear what you hear, but did not hear it" (Luke 10:23-24 // Matt 13:16-17). In both Luke (10:23) and Matthew (13:10) this word is explicitly addressed to the disciples. Those called blessed are the *disciples* because they hear most directly what Jesus says and see what is happening in him.

How did the disciples understand the words spoken to them? They could only have understood them in the sense that now, with Jesus, the time of messianic salvation has come. The word "messiah" does not appear, of course, any more than does an equivalent of "messianic time." But both lie concealed behind this beatitude. The *Psalms of Solomon* describe the messianic time as follows:

> Happy are those who shall live in those days, to see the good things of Israel that God shall accomplish in the congregation of the tribes. (*PsSol* 17:44)

> Happy are those who shall live in those days, to see the good things of the LORD, which he will perform for the coming generation. Under the rod of discipline of the LORD's anointed in fear of his God, in wisdom of spirit and of righteousness and strength . . . (*PsSol* 18:6-7)

The *Psalms of Solomon* speak directly of the expected royal messiah, and they describe the messianic time, but the texts quoted show that this messianic time still lies in the future. It is only against the horizon of such future expectation that the whole explosive force of Luke 10:23-24 is evident. It is not *future* participants in the messianic time who are called blessed, but Jesus' disciples. That means the future is already here. The time is fulfilled. Jesus' saying about "new wine" also speaks of this fulfilled time: "No one puts new wine into old wineskins; otherwise, the wine will burst the skins, and the wine is lost, and so are the skins" (Mark 2:22). Normally wine was kept in amphorae, that is, in large, two-handled clay jars. Only for purposes of transport would one use "wineskins" made of tanned hides of goats or sheep. No rational person would transport young wine that was still fermenting in old wineskins. They were no longer elastic enough to sustain the shaking on a donkey or in a cart. In his images and similitudes Jesus loved to speak realistically; he even insisted on it. The same is true here.

The new wine points to the time of the reign of God that has now begun, its newness enrapturing, destroying everything that is worn out and broken. Compromises are impossible. The reign of God is full of power and bubbling like new wine. Jesus' answer to the question of fasting works within the same field of associations: "The wedding guests cannot fast while the bridegroom is with them, can they?" (Mark 2:19). As we saw already in chapter 14, Jesus regards the time that has dawned with his preaching of the reign of God as a wedding, God's wedding with God's people. The metaphor presumes that the wedding has already begun. The bridegroom has already brought the bride home. The wedding banquet is in full swing, and the days of the wedding will not end very quickly.

It would have been very natural for Jesus, when he was speaking within this metaphorical field, to have said: I myself am the bridegroom. This would have been a new and moving statement about the messiah. But Jesus holds back even here. He only says that the bridegroom is already here, and that itself is indirectly formulated. He certainly does not say, "It is I." With similar reticence he avoids saying that he himself is the messenger from Isaiah 52:7, and yet his talk about the good news that is now being preached makes it clear indirectly that he himself is that messenger of joy (cf. chap. 11 above). This way of speaking, which holds back and yet can be understood by those who trust, is characteristic of Jesus. He is the center of everything that is now happening; he pours the new wine (John 2:1-11), and he has the bride (John 3:29). Through him comes the fulfillment of everything Israel has desired to hear and see for many generations. He himself is the bringer of the time of salvation. What a claim to sovereignty that is!

A Time of Decision

But what is now coming with Jesus is not merely a time of salvation; it is also a time of decision—for the very reason that the reign of God, if not accepted, will become division, separation, and judgment. Therefore Jesus is concerned not only with rejoicing in the reign of God but also with radical conversion. The similitude of the barren fig tree is about the time of decision into which Israel has now entered:

> A man had a fig tree planted in his vineyard, and he came looking for fruit on it and found none. So he said to the gardener, "See here! For three years I have come looking for fruit on this fig tree, and still I find none. Cut it down! Why should it be wasting the soil?"
>
> He replied, "Sir, let it alone for one more year, until I dig around it and put manure on it. If it bears fruit next year, well and good; but if not, you can cut it down." (Luke 13:6-9)

In those days in Palestine shoots and vines were not trained on trellises as they are today. They simply proliferated on the ground or wound their way up the trunks of other trees. That is why trees, especially fig trees, were often planted in vineyards, making them doubly useful. Of course, that only made sense if the fig trees bore fruit and did not produce too much shade. In Luke 13:6-9 the barren fig tree gets a year's reprieve through the dialogue between the owner and the worker in the vineyard; after that it is threatened with the axe. A single year! It is clear that the point of the similitude lies here: Israel has only a short time left to repent; if it does not make use of the time it will have missed its own meaning and mission.

What is crucial in our context is that in this similitude of the barren fig tree the time is strictly limited. It becomes a provisional time, a time for ultimate decision, a deadline. We could also say that it is a grace-given deadline. Everything depends on whether the fig tree will produce fruit after all. The gospels contain a whole series of similar texts that call for radical conversion and so speak of the last chance to secure one's own existence.[16]

While the parable of the barren fig tree is only about the truth that the decision for conversion must happen immediately because God is allowing just a short period of time, the following little composition goes a step further:

> Do not think that I have come to bring peace to the earth;
> I have not come to bring peace, but a sword.

> For I have come to set a man against his father,
> and a daughter against her mother,
> and a daughter-in-law against her mother-in-law;
> and one's foes will be members of one's own household."
> (Matt 10:34-36; cf. Luke 12:51-53)

"I have not come to bring peace, but a sword." This saying of Jesus has led a whole series of twentieth-century writers astray, making them see Jesus as a social revolutionary—examples include the Social Democratic politician Karl Kautsky (1854–1938), the Austrian cultural historian Robert Eisler (1882–1949), or the English historian of religion Samuel G. F. Brandon (1907–1971). They, and others, saw Jesus as a kind of Marxist preacher of revolution who relied on violent exercise of force.[17] Why else would he have talked about a "sword"?

But this interpretation mistakes the metaphor in Jesus' words. "Sword" here stands for division, separation. That sense of "sword" needs explanation, of course. The discourse composition does this by means of a quotation from the prophet Micah, who depicts the judgment that will befall faithless Israel. That judgment includes the fact that no one can trust another any longer. The land is torn apart by fear and mistrust:

> Put no trust in a friend,
>> have no confidence in a loved one;
> guard the doors of your mouth
>> from her who lies in your embrace;
> for the son treats the father with contempt,
>> the daughter rises up against her mother,
> the daughter-in-law against her mother-in-law;
>> your enemies are members of your own household. (Mic 7:5-6)

This quotation from Micah within the composition of Matthew 10:34-36 says that this very condition has now arrived. Division and rejection are everywhere! But why? The reason is directly connected with Jesus himself. Jesus has come to unite the people of God under God's rule, and he has indeed brought many people together in this new condition. He has bridged chasms. He has assembled toll collectors and Zealots, sinners and saints, poor and rich at one table. His colorfully mixed band of disciples is a sign of this gathering movement.

But Jesus' work in Israel has another side: it has led to divisions. Jesus has come up against bitter opposition, and that opposition has cut across the land and even across families. His own family attempted to bring him back home by force and put him under house arrest. His relatives said, "He has gone out of his mind" (Mark 3:20-21). But unfortunately it is not only that his appearance has led to separation and division. The metaphor of the sword that Jesus flings into society[18] contains still more. Jesus has not only *factually* evoked division; he has desired it. Consider: "I have come to. . . ."

So Jesus *intended* the division; he desired the cleaving sword blade in the sense that he wanted decision, unambiguity, clarity before God. For him the reign of God is not some vague mist; it has clear contours. "No one can serve two masters," Jesus says (Matt 6:24). He demanded that his hearers make a clear decision for the reign of God, and that necessarily led to divisions, indeed, to such as reach deep into the milieu of the closest social relationships, the home, the community of the extended family. Behind the little composition in Matthew 10:34-36 is the experience that, in light of Jesus' appearance and his call to discipleship, the most intimate human connections have been broken. Jesus himself had to undergo that experience and it continued after Easter; it has not ceased even today.

The proclamation of the reign of God thus not only introduced a final time of decision; to say that would not be enough. Matthew 10:34-36 says also that Jesus himself is the reason why the time is coming to its end. He himself is the cause of the crisis. He himself tears apart the closest social ties. He himself compels decision. "I have come to set . . . against. . . ." Jesus would have had the opportunity to speak of this final decision in various other ways. He could have said, "You have to decide for or against repentance. You have to choose to believe in the good news, or not. You must decide for the reign of God and thus for God, or against God." And he did say all that. But Jesus dares to go beyond this and say: you have to choose *for me*—or *against me*. "Whoever is not with me is against me, and whoever does not gather with me scatters" (Matt 12:30 // Luke 11:23).

We have already had (in chap. 4) an overview of all that echoes in the concept of "gathering." Every one of Jesus' hearers who was even slightly familiar with Sacred Scripture necessarily associated this concept with the prophetic hopes for the "gathering of Israel," something that had become a central concept for salvation from the time of the exile. Gathering Israel from its Diaspora then was often paralleled with "uniting," "liberating," "saving," and "redeeming." Thus it was clear that it is God's own self who gathers Israel. That God is the one who gathers Israel even became a predicate, an attribute of God.

When Jesus now says that *he* is gathering Israel, he is claiming to do precisely what God himself will do at the end of time: gather, sanctify, and unite Israel. Then the word can only be interpreted to mean that Jesus speaks and acts as if he is standing in God's stead. In any event the saying "whoever is not with me is against me" betrays a claim that had to cause irritation, the claim to unconditional and direct authority. No prophet could ever have spoken that way. A prophet would have to say:

> Thus says the Lord GOD:
> I will gather you from the peoples,
> and assemble you out of the countries
> where you have been scattered. (Ezek 11:17; cf. 28:25; 34:13)

Jesus' Scandalous "I"

Jesus' "I" of his own authority has replaced the "I" speech of God that runs throughout the books of the writing prophets of the Old Testament. We really have to read through the first three gospels and note this phenomenon. Only then will we experience the "aha!" of recognizing what is actually happening:

"I came to bring fire to the earth, and how I wish it were already kindled!" (Luke 12:49). "I have come to call not the righteous but sinners" (Mark 2:17). "Do not think that I have come to abolish the law or the prophets; I have come not to abolish but to fulfill" (Matt 5:17). "You have heard that it was said to those of ancient times. . . . But I say to you . . ." (Matt 5:21-22). "Everyone then who hears these words of mine and acts on them will be like a wise man who built his house on rock" (Matt 7:24). "If any want to become my followers, let them deny themselves and take up their cross and [so] follow me" (Mark 8:34). "Whoever comes to me and does not hate father and mother, wife and children, brothers and sisters, yes, and even life itself, cannot be my disciple" (Luke 14:26). "I watched Satan fall from heaven like a flash of lightning" (Luke 10:18). "If it is by the finger of God that I cast out the demons, then the kingdom of God has [already] come to you" (Luke 11:20). "You spirit that keeps this boy from speaking and hearing, I command you, come out of him, and never enter him again!" (Mark 9:25). "See, I have given you authority to tread on snakes and scorpions, and over all the power of the enemy; and nothing will hurt you" (Luke 10:19). "See, I am sending you out like sheep into the midst of wolves" (Matt 10:16). "Whoever listens to you listens to me, and whoever rejects you rejects me" (Luke 10:16). "You are those who have stood by me in my trials; and I [hereby] confer on you, just as my Father has conferred on me, a kingdom" (Luke 22:28-29). "Truly [or: Amen] I tell you . . ." (Matt 11:11, and frequently elsewhere).

"And blessed is anyone who takes no offense at me" (Luke 7:23). "Whoever does the will of God is my brother and sister and mother" (Mark 3:35). "Let the little children come to me; do not stop them; for it is to such as these that the kingdom of God belongs" (Mark 10:14). "And I tell you, everyone who acknowledges me before others, the Son of Man also will acknowledge before the angels of God" (Luke 12:8).

To continue listing texts would be no problem. It is superfluous to ask whether each one of these sayings is authentic, because the relevant *logia* run throughout the gospels and belong to very different genres and situations. There are "I have come" sayings that are by no means retrospective summaries of the life of Jesus but have the sense of "it is my task to. . . ." There are the antitheses in the Sermon on the Mount, formulated with shocking authority,[19] in which Jesus places himself in the stead of the one who formerly gave the Torah at Sinai. There are the discipleship sayings in which Jesus does not urge his disciples to study Torah or grow in the love of God but to abandon everything, even father and mother, spouse and children, to follow him.

There are the sayings in which he sends out his disciples, the words of command to the demons, the amen-sayings that replace the way the prophets introduced their message and themselves as messengers, and above all the sayings in which he inextricably links the decision of the final judgment to the decision about his own person—still more, in which he presents himself, though reticently and in code, as the end-time judge.

For Christians who hear the Gospel every Sunday this "I" of Jesus is a matter of course. But in reality it is anything but. Why? Because the center of Jesus' message is not his own self. The heart, the center that dominates all of his preaching and his whole doing is the reign of God. And, as has already been made clear (chap. 11), the proclamation of the reign of God is nothing but the end-time realization of the primary commandment, namely, that Israel is to love its God as the only God, with its whole heart, soul, and strength. This one, this only God will now be master in Israel and, through Israel, in the whole world. So Jesus' message is not at all his own person. His entire, his sole concern is God the Father, the One, the Only. He corrected someone who addressed him as "Good Teacher" by saying, "Why do you call me good? No one is good but God alone" (Mark 10:18). Thus God, the one, the absolute Lord, is the center of Jesus' message, and for that very reason it is so appalling that Jesus unceasingly connects this One and his rule with his own person. This is the real stumbling block, then and now. It was because of that scandal that Jesus was brought to the cross. Many pious people, and especially the religious authorities in Israel, could not bear to hear that claim. Today also there are many who cannot stand to listen to this elementary link between God and a Jesus who spoke and acted as if he stood in God's stead and as if God were coming to his people in Jesus himself.

Consequently, Jesus has been made a simple rabbi, a Jewish Socrates, or an itinerant Galilean philosopher who spoke about God with infinitely wise words. Or people have overlooked his message about the reign of God and made of him only a preacher of himself. Neither does justice to the historical record. Jesus' radical proclamation of the reign of God contains an *implicit* Christology.

And it is not just his message; it is his actions as well. It is his coolness in authoritatively pronouncing the forgiveness of sins, when it is only God who can forgive sins.[20] It is the claim that underlies the fact that he appoints the Twelve as a sign of the gathering of Israel, though in the Old Testament and in many Jewish prayers that gathering is predicated of God: ". . . who gathers the dispersed of Israel." It is his deeds of power, the driving out of the demons of society and the many healing miracles along the way. He saw them as the works of God, and yet he accomplished them by his own power.

There was the messianic entrance into Jerusalem, the almost matter-of-fact taking possession of the temple, and the words of interpretation at the last meal, in which Jesus authoritatively declared his blood, now to be shed, to be "the blood of the covenant," that is, the blood of the renewal and completion of the covenant God had once made with Israel (cf. chap. 15). And then, above all, there is the acknowledgment before the Sanhedrin that he, Jesus himself, will come again and judge his accusers. At this point, at the very end, the Christology implicit throughout his activity is unveiled and becomes public.

But otherwise Jesus' claim retains its tactfulness. Jesus was clear and yet always discreet. He was clear and yet always reticent. It is from this very implicit, often hidden, often concealed, and yet all-penetrating Christology that a great power emerges. Fundamentally that power is much greater than if Jesus had spoken in the language of the Fourth Gospel, where everything is direct and immediate to the point of provocation. There Jesus says "whoever has seen me has seen the Father" (John 14:9), or still more clearly, "The Father and I are one" (John 10:30). In the course of the first century this explicit Christology became necessary, and it was altogether appropriate and accurate. But it was not the language of Jesus.

A Successful Break-In

The power of Jesus' language lies precisely in the fact that it only points the way. One last text can show us that. It is in Luke 12:39 and reads in some translations "if the owner of the house knew at what hour the thief was coming, he would prevent his house from being broken into." This image, or similitude, played an extraordinary role in the early church. It admonishes to watchfulness. It was intended to say: we know neither the day nor the hour in which Christ will appear in glory. He will come as suddenly and unexpectedly as a thief in the night. Therefore be ready at all times! Keep awake!

Naturally, Christ is not portrayed as a burglar here. The point of comparison is only the suddenness and unpredictability of his return. So it is not that Christ is a thief but rather that he will come as unexpectedly *as a thief* does. Just when no one is expecting him, he will appear. That is how Matthew and Luke, and Paul, and the early church understood it.[21] But there is good reason to think that Jesus himself understood the similitude differently.[22] That is to say, it can be translated (as does the NRSV) as "past contrary to fact": "if the owner of the house had known at what hour the thief was coming, he would not have let his house be broken into." If we remove the text from its present context (the return of Christ) and understand it in this latter sense, the similitude is not warning against a future break-in but is looking back at one that has already happened. Then it is talking about a burglary that succeeded. The successful break-in would then be the coming of the reign of God, and the text would say: the reign of God has already come. It is here. It has taken place.

In that case this similitude belongs within a series of texts that speak in similar fashion of the reign of God as having already come, for example: "If it is by the finger of God that I cast out the demons, then the kingdom of God has come to you" (Luke 11:20). The following metaphor also presumes the having-already-come of the reign of God. The background here is again Jesus' exorcisms of demons: "No one can enter a strong man's house and plunder his property without first tying up the strong man; then indeed the house can be plundered" (Mark 3:27). This image too does not speak of coming events; against the background of Luke 11:20 it means to say that everything is already happening. Jesus is already in the "house of the strong man," that is, he has pushed his way into the world ruled by demons.[23] The Satan is already bound, the power of the demons already broken.

Mark 3:27 in particular is especially close to the text we began with, Luke 12:39, because there too a "house" is invaded. Thus the interpretation of Luke 12:39 I have presented here fits thoroughly within Jesus' bold way of speaking, one that is not frightened of daring images. Similarly bold and "violent" is the so-called violence saying: "The prophets and the law [were in effect] until John. From then on the kingdom of heaven has broken its path with violence, and the violent take it by force" (cf. Matt 11:13, 12 // Luke 16:16). Against this whole background the similitude of the thief who breaks into a house during the night reveals an excellent sense. Jesus could, in the sense of the thing, have spoken as follows:

> To what shall I compare the reign of God? What image shall I use for it—for you doubters who think the reign of God is still far in the future? But it has already come. Its coming is like a break-in that could not be prevented. If the owner of the house had known at what hour the thief was coming he would, of course, have kept watch. But he did not know. And so the thief broke into his house.

In this similitude Jesus does not seem to be speaking about himself at all. As so often, he talks of the coming of the reign of God. And yet he speaks in the same similitude about his own activity.

If we read carefully and place the similitude in the context of his activity we have to say that yes, he broke into the spaces of the old society, the realm of the demons' power and that of the gods of the world, the taken-for-granted things from which people interested only in themselves build the houses of their lives. The old society would have defended itself; it would not have let him in; it would have secured itself, locked up everything, blocked all entrances. But he surprised it. He came like a thief in the night, secretly, in silence, unexpected, when no one was thinking about any of it. With him the reign of God was suddenly there, and the new had already begun—in the midst of the old world.

In this form it is an unbelievably bold similitude! And it is full of truth. The similitude of the burglar who comes in the silence of the night is a cry of victory. Jesus has broken into the model images, the self-deceptions and compulsions of a society far from God. He has succeeded, and he goes on succeeding. No one is safe from him.

What a self-awareness speaks in this text from Jesus! And yet he keeps his restraint, and that very restraint is what fascinates me about Jesus. It makes his language tactful and yet lends it an enormous power. Above all, this incognito allows for the necessary space in which one can decide for him, or not.

Chapter 20

The Church's Response

The church confesses and teaches: Jesus Christ is true human and true God—the latter, of course, in full unity with the Father and the Holy Spirit. It has said that not just since the Council of Chalcedon in the year 451.[1] The New Testament says the same.

It is not hard to believe that Jesus is truly human, at least not in the West. In the sphere of the Orthodox churches, however, things are different. There the image of Jesus is projected more powerfully in terms of his divinity; it can draw Jesus' humanity into itself and almost conceal it altogether. Orthodox believers sometimes admit that they have difficulties with Jesus' radical humanity. Apparently a long history of theology and belief has left its traces here.

In the West, theology and the history of devotion have acquired different accents. We only have to think of the late medieval images of the crucifixion that depict its horrors with ultimate realism. Scriptural interpretation is differently weighted in the West as well. It holds to the saying that Jesus "increased in wisdom and in years, and in divine and human favor" (Luke 2:52). That means Jesus learned. He struggled to gain insight, he prayed, he wept, he sorrowed, he was tempted by the Evil One, he suffered unspeakably. It really should not be difficult to believe that he was a true human being.

Jesus Deified?

But true God? Isn't it the case that here a Jew who was certainly deeply believing and charismatic has been retrospectively made into a super-human, divine figure? We read and hear that statement over and over, not only from our non-Christian contemporaries but even from quite a few Christian theologians. In the year 2000 Gerd Theissen published a book titled *Die Religion der ersten Christen. Eine Theorie des Urchristentums.*[2] Part 1, section 3 in the book is titled "How Did Jesus Come to Be Deified?" Theissen's intention in this book is not to write a "theology of the New Testament," that is, to consider early Christianity from within, but to analyze it in strictly religious-historical terms from a deliberately chosen external perspective. Obviously that is a legitimate effort. It even makes good sense. But it seems to me that he does not respect the boundaries of such a perspective. A historian of religions can say that the early church, using Jewish concepts and forms of thought, confessed Jesus as Messiah, as Son of God, even as true God, and was convinced that in doing so it was adopting Jesus' own claim and developing its implications.

All that can be said from an external perspective. But when Theissen writes that the early church deified Jesus he is adopting a concept from the Hellenistic ruler cult, namely, "apotheosis." In the Roman imperial cult this deification of great heroes and rulers, exemplified by the celebration of Alexander the Great, developed a specific shape: a series of Roman emperors were elevated to the status of state deities by *consecratio.* Their divinization took place as follows: The emperor's body was brought in a magnificent wagon to an artistically constructed pyre several stories high. On the uppermost platform stood a *quadriga*, a chariot that would conduct the emperor to Olympus. Alongside it were two cages, each containing an eagle. As the pyre began to burn, the two eagles were released. Their upward flight was regarded as a symbol of the deification of the dead person. The ascension of the emperor in question was then affirmed in a solemn public act by means of eyewitnesses, and reviewed by the Roman Senate. Finally, the emperor was declared a god.[3] That is the religious-historical background of the idea of "deification." It in no way applies to the development and nature of the early church's Christology. The concept is altogether inappropriate for it, even purely from the point of view of religious phenomenology.

On the other hand, it is understandable that Theissen speaks of deification. Probably every serious Christian has thought in this direction at least once. It seems so natural that one day the question would arise in our minds: could it be that talk about "Jesus' divinity" was simply a culturally conditioned language pattern whose only function was to attempt to describe Jesus' outstanding importance? Was the statement "Jesus is true God" perhaps meant to say nothing more than that he is the most important person for every Christian, the one who shows us the way, the one who is the guideline and measure of our lives?

We must not suppress such doubts; we must engage with them. This chapter is meant to serve that purpose: not as if it could prove Jesus' divinity in the way proofs are developed by the natural sciences. *Faith* must always remain, faith that is open and trusting, because—and this is often forgotten—we can only encounter the truly great things in life through trust. Love can never be proved. We can only entrust ourselves to it. It is only when we trust ourselves to another that we truly know him or her. Knowing another person presupposes openness, looking within, listening within, moving toward the other: sympathy, in fact.

Nevertheless, faith must not be blind, just as love for another human being must not be blind and indifferent. In this particular case that means that theology can remove difficulties that stand in the way of belief in Jesus Christ's divine sonship. It can protect the christological statements against misunderstandings. It can point to areas of agreement. It can clarify concepts and statements. It can investigate historical processes. It can, for example, ask *how*, historically speaking, it came about that Jesus was affirmed as true God. In that way alone it can show the false-hood of a whole series of repeated assertions. Before we undertake that, to a very modest extent, in what follows, and since the proper theme of this book is not early church Christology, let me offer three preliminary remarks:

1. If Jesus was only a human being and nothing else, from the perspec-tive of religious phenomenology he would have been a kind of "prophet." And then it would be impossible to understand why God would not one day send other prophets who might be still more important than Jesus was, more eloquent, with better answers to the questions of our time—prophets who would one day surpass Jesus.

If Jesus had been merely a prophet, then, theologically speaking, he would not have been God's final word. God would indeed have spoken through him but only in preliminary fashion. God would not yet have said everything through Jesus; crucial things would have been held back. God would by no means have spoken God's complete mind through

Jesus. Christian faith confesses that Jesus Christ is the "Word" in whom God has expressed himself entirely and with finality. But in this case that is precisely what would not have happened. We would be living in an ultimate insecurity, because even the best prophet can be surpassed and corrected by a newer prophet.

Certainly it is beyond the scope of this religious-historical phenomenology to speak of a "last prophet" who represents the summit of all prophecy. That is the case, for example, in Islam. Muhammad called himself "the seal of the prophets" (*Sura* 33.40)—that is, the last of all Jewish, Christian, and Arab prophets.[4] With him, it is said, all prophecy is completed, for he received the Qu'ran, the perfect and final revelation. But in the view of Islam, Muhammad in no way *embodied* this perfect truth. It was only conveyed to him. Still, he is the "last" prophet and no other can come after him.

Moreover, Jews would not accede to either position, the Christian or the Muslim. They would say: God had expressed himself definitively long before Jesus. The Torah tells human beings everything they must know and live in order to achieve salvation. They might quote Micah 6:8: "He has told you, O mortal, what is good; and what does the Lord require of you but to do justice, and to love kindness, and to walk humbly with your God?" That is, in fact, one of the great texts of the Old Testament. Jesus would have agreed heartily. But probably he would have added: if Israel is really following its path with God—alertly, willingly, and attentively—its path will lead it exactly to the place where now, in this hour, the signs of the reign of God are appearing: to the place toward which the history of the people of God was always on the way and where Torah and prophets are fulfilled because their whole meaning is now illuminated for all to see.

2. If Jesus were only a human being and nothing else, then the church, which regards itself, after all, as "made holy by Jesus Christ" (cf. Eph 5:26-27), can only be a human endeavor and nothing else. Then God does not dwell in the midst of it, even though the whole Old Testament had said that ultimately God will dwell wholly and entirely in the midst of God's people.[5] Then there are no sacraments in which God acts; then the assemblies of Christian congregations are merely human assemblies, no different from millions of other gatherings. Then the church is ultimately a religious society, a community of opinion, an organization for mutual assistance, an agent of meaning, or still worse, an umbrella organization in pursuit of Christian interests.

3. If Jesus was only a human being and nothing else, then there is no redemption in the Christian sense. Then God has not become "one of us"; then the distance between God and the world remains an unbridgeable chasm. Then the miracle that God can already be seen in the face of the man Jesus Christ (John 14:7-9) does not exist.

Stating these consequences is simply meant to make the weight of the question clear. Jesus is true human and true God: infinitely much depends on that statement, far more than one suspects at first glance. For Christians this is not a purely theoretical question. On it depends, for them, whether there really is liberation and rescue. On it depends whether the church is a purely human coalition or the "body of Christ" (Eph 1:22-23). On it depends whether the world contains only the chaos of opinions constantly chasing their tails and eternally contradicting each other, or whether there is a revealed and ultimate truth to be found because God has completely opened God's self to the world.

Hellenistic Thought?

But enough preconsiderations! Much more important is the following: that Christians, only a few decades after the death of Jesus, said that he was truly God and yet at the same time truly human is one of the most remarkable and exciting phenomena in the history of religions. Why? Because faith in the divinity of Jesus Christ arose within Israel, that is, within the sphere of the strictest monotheism, of the strictest belief in one God. Israel confesses the uniqueness of God. Over centuries it had wrestled its way to the knowledge that there is only the one unique God who made heaven and earth and leads his people through history. Israel very rightly said that the many gods do not exist, and the church holds inexorably to this confession along with Israel. There are not many deities, many divine entities like those that fill the world of other religions; there is only the one God who is Lord of the world but is not identical with the world.

And now, on the soil of this very Israel, in the midst of Judaism, Jesus is confessed and called upon as true God—and by Jews. From the religious-historical perspective that is an unbelievable phenomenon. Precisely because it runs counter to every expectation of the Judaism of the time and also to everything that could have been anticipated, a broad current of liberal theology has tried to explain it away with the phrase "Hellenization of Christianity." This trend asserted for a long time that in the oldest church, that is, in the Jewish-Christian communities, the confessional tradition that ultimately came consistently to assert that Jesus was true God did not exist at all. That, it is said, is Greek thought and only forced its way gradually into the church by way of the Gentile Christian communities. Such thought was utterly foreign to the Jewish-Christian church. In pure Jewish Christianity, it is asserted, Jesus was regarded simply as a great wisdom teacher or an eschatological prophet or the longed-for messiah. It was Hellenistic thought that deified Jesus. For the Greek world—in contrast to Judaism—that was supposedly no problem because the Greeks saw something divine in everything out of the ordinary and unusual, in everything great and beautiful. There were many "divine men," *theioi andres*, and the title "Son of God" was said to have been common. Was Alexander the Great not revered as "son of Zeus," Julius Caesar in Ephesus as "the god made manifest, offspring of Ares and Aphrodite, and common saviour of human life," and Augustus—at least in the East—as "god of god"?[6]

In fact, there was no dearth in antiquity of self-proclaimed sons of God or rulers who were deified after their deaths or even before. But this knowledge does not take us a single step farther, for "Jesus, true human and true God" is not a Greek idea. That confession arose in the midst of Israel, in a spiritual milieu that loathed divinized humans. We only need to compare John 5:18; 10:33 and Acts 12:21-23; 14:8-18. Certainly this confession "grew," but in such a way that the knowledge of the mystery of Jesus that was present from the beginning developed more and more clarity.

Why does the assertion that Jesus was not deified in Jewish-Palestinian but instead in Gentile-Christian "Hellenistic" communities miss the point entirely? Simply because this opens a cleft between Jewish-Christian and Gentile-Christian communities that never existed in such a form. Israel's conflicts with Hellenism had begun much earlier, not at the time when Gentile-Christian communities were created. Since Alexander the Great (356–323 BCE) Israel had been confronted with Hellenistic ideas and had adapted many of them to its own uses. That is unquestionably true. But the question is: *what* was adapted? Most surely it was not anything that touched the center of Israel's faith. It is true that, especially in its mission literature, Israel had taken over Hellenistic stylistic figures, literary genres, Greek concepts and patterns of thought—but it never employed Hellenism to water down its faith in the one unique God, creator of heaven and earth.

The clear separation of communities—"Jewish-Christian here, Gentile-Christian Hellenistic there"—is also, for another reason, a construct that does not stand up to comparison with historical reality: the great successes of the mission in the Mediterranean region did not happen, at least in the first decades, by means of Paul and other apostles and missionaries having converted a large number of Gentiles. The people they gained for the Gospel were overwhelmingly drawn from the so-called God-fearers, that is, Gentiles who had long sympathized with Judaism, who attended the synagogue on the Sabbath, heard the readings from the Torah and the prophets, tried to live according to the Ten Commandments, and felt themselves drawn to the monotheism of Judaism. From a purely religious-historical perspective they did, of course, remain Gentiles; the men had not yet accepted circumcision. Nevertheless, they were already immersed in the Jewish faith tradition.[7] At least as far as the time of Paul is concerned, the notion that there was such a thing as a "pure" Gentile Christianity is a phantasm. And yet it was precisely in that period that the basic substance of the christological confession developed. Thus what the early Christian communities said about Jesus must be understood entirely in terms of *internal Jewish* forms of thought.

How could the apostles and Jewish-Christian teachers express the fact that God himself had spoken and acted *totally and in unsurpassable fashion* in Jesus? That God had uttered himself completely in him, so that Jesus was the never-to-be-surpassed self-definition of God, the final image and definitive place of God in the world? Because that is exactly what Jesus' disciples had experienced, and that same experience had to be "appropriately" expressed after Easter. There were two basic possibilities for this in Israel, eschatological and protological:

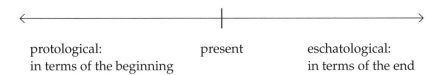

protological: present   eschatological:
in terms of the beginning   in terms of the end

In Terms of the End

In this case "eschatological" means: the end of time is here. Therefore, God is now acting *conclusively*, because these are the "last times," that is, the hour for God's concluding word and final action has come. The definitive, conclusive, unrepeatable, in which everything, without exception, is said and done, is expressed precisely in the fact that it takes place at the end, that it is the last in time, that nothing more can be added afterward. Jewish apocalyptic literature in particular sees the end of the world and what happens at the end as the definitive revelation of God. To take one example, in chapters 24–27 of the book of Isaiah, often called the "Isaian apocalypse," the glory of God shines forth at the end of time over all peoples. This glory is, however, also a dreadful judgment on the nations. And yet what took place on Sinai for the elders of Israel and thus for all Israel (Exod 24:9-11) is now repeated in worldwide dimension: God will spread a banquet on Zion for all peoples, and there all tears will be dried, the shroud of sadness that covers all the nations will be taken away, and death will be destroyed. God's royal glory will be revealed to the whole world (Isa 25:6-8; 24:23). What is promised in Isaiah 24–27 is definitive and unrepeatable. Therefore it reveals the true nature of God. The whole and conclusive truth about God is evident in that it is located "at the end."

The oldest post-Easter Christology that is still entirely Jewish-Christian formulated the mystery of Jesus within this same thought pattern: namely, within an *eschatological* horizon. It says not only that God raised Jesus from the dead, that is, that the general resurrection of the dead at the end of time has already begun in him, but beyond that, "God has made both Lord [*kyrios*] and Messiah this Jesus whom you crucified" (Acts 2:36). As the context shows, this means that God has made the crucified Jesus Lord and Messiah *in that* God raised him from the dead and exalted him to God's right hand. In this way God has shown that this very Crucified One, who appeared to have failed and been discredited in every respect, has been approved in God's eyes, and not only approved but made Lord of all. The exaltation Christology of Matthew 28:18 belongs here also: "All authority in heaven and on earth has been given to me." And we should mention here the confessional formula Paul received, which he quotes in Romans 1:3-4: "the gospel concerning his Son, who was descended from David according to the flesh and was declared to be Son of God with power according to the spirit of holiness by resurrection from the dead."

This very early Christology would be totally misunderstood if we were to leap to the conclusion that Jesus only became, through his exaltation, something he was not beforehand. For such confessional formulae do speak of an event, but not one that can be compared to the promotion of a human being to a higher position. Jesus' exaltation, his heavenly installation as "Son of God"—in Acts 2:36 even *kyrios*—is in no way to be compared with the awarding of a PhD or the inauguration of a president. Instead, Jesus' exaltation is an eschatological event, that is, here God is acting *conclusively* in Jesus inasmuch as God shows who Jesus truly is and thus demonstrates eschatologically, i.e., definitively, that he is who he always has been. In this way the one exalted through resurrection is proved and shown to be the final, conclusive, and unrepeatable truth of God, God's final Word and God's last act. That is precisely what these oldest Christian confessions are trying to say.

They definitely did not intend to say that Jesus was not the Messiah previously, that he was not the Son of God and *kyrios* but became all that only through his resurrection and exaltation. Enthronement here signifies confirmation, justification, proof, recognition. Jesus is, so to speak, publicly elevated to the status his opponents had denied that he possessed. We must on no account introduce into these very ancient confessional formulae the much later adoptionist Christology of the second century. That existed within a different context and did not simply reflect the earliest time of Christian beginnings.[8]

Thus, inasmuch as the oldest christological statements are formulated in terms of the end, eschatologically, they said who Jesus truly is. But their thinking was entirely and utterly Jewish. The Greeks did not think eschatologically at all, but rather in the system of an eternal cycle: at the beginning the golden age, then the silver, bronze, and iron—and then everything starts over from the beginning.

In Terms of the Beginning

It is important to note that in Judaism the true nature of a thing or a person could be expressed not only *eschatologically* but *protologically*. The latter means thinking not from the end but from the beginning. For Christology that means it could be formulated not only in terms of the end of time but also in terms of a "time before time." In that case it does not say that at the end, thus conclusively, God shows who Jesus is, but that from the very beginning, before all creation, Jesus was the whole truth of God and the absolute measure of the world.

Protological thinking developed in Israel in the so-called Wisdom literature and was personified in the figure of "Wisdom." In the book of Proverbs, Wisdom speaks of herself and tells of her cooperation in creation:

> The LORD created me at the beginning of his work,
> > the first of his acts of long ago.
> Ages ago I was set up,
> > at the first, before the beginning of the earth.

When there were no depths I was brought forth,
  when there were no springs abounding with water.
Before the mountains had been shaped,
  before the hills, I was brought forth—
  when he had not yet made earth and fields,
    or the world's first bits of soil.
When he established the heavens, I was there,
  when he drew a circle on the face of the deep,
  when he made firm the skies above,
    when he established the fountains of the deep,
  when he assigned to the sea its limit,
    so that the waters might not transgress his command,
  when he marked out the foundations of the earth,
    then I was beside him, like a master worker;[9]
  and I was daily his delight,
    rejoicing before him always,
  rejoicing in his inhabited world
    and delighting in the human race. (Prov 8:22-31)

Thus Wisdom is God's creature, but she precedes the creation of the world. Thus she can be present at all the work of creation; she plays about God and creation. In this very way it is made clear that all creation was formed in wisdom. Because the figure of Wisdom was always prior to creation, it is filled with meaning, with order, with beauty—and reflects the wisdom of God.

While the book of Proverbs only echoes at its end the truth that it is Wisdom's whole joy to be with the human race, the motif is broadly developed in Sirach 24:1-22:

"I came forth from the mouth of the Most High,
  and covered the earth like a mist.
I dwelt in the highest heavens,
  and my throne was in a pillar of cloud.
Alone I compassed the vault of heaven
  and traversed the depths of the abyss.
Over waves of the sea, over all the earth,
  and over every people and nation I have held sway.
Among all these I sought a resting place;
  in whose territory should I abide?

"Then the Creator of all things gave me a command,
  and my Creator chose the place for my tent.
He said, 'Make your dwelling in Jacob,
  and in Israel receive your inheritance.'" (Sir 24:3-8)

Thus in the book of Sirach itself, but even more in the continuing process of Jewish thinking, this Wisdom whom God had created before all creation was equated with the Torah. Thus, for example, in the great Jewish commentary on Genesis, *Bereshit Rabbah*, we read of Genesis 1:1:

> [T]he Torah speaks, "I was the work-plan of the Holy One, blessed be he." In the accepted practice of the world, when a mortal king builds a palace, he does not build it out of his own head, but he follows a work-plan. And [the one who supplies] the work-plan does not build out of his own head, but he has designs and diagrams, so as to know how to situate the rooms and the doorways. Thus the Holy One, blessed be he, [first] consulted the Torah [and then] created the world.

This commentary alludes to the text quoted above from Proverbs (8:30: "then I was beside him, like a master worker"). Creative Wisdom playing before God is thus identified with the Torah. Torah existed even before the creation of the world. It is thought of as preexistent, prior to the cosmos. God creates the universe according to the building plan of the Torah.

What did Israel express in this discourse on Wisdom, i.e., Torah? It is intended to say that inasmuch as Torah was present before anything was created it is the absolute measure of all created reality, its internal order, its meaning. Thus the thought scheme of protology clearly presents the priority of Torah over all creation. From this starting point it was possible and even unavoidable to speak of Jesus, too, protologically, that is, "in terms of the beginning."

A Song of the Logos

The gospel text that does this most urgently is the beginning of the Fourth Gospel, its so-called Prologue. That text speaks simply of the *logos*, the Word in which God has fully expressed the divine self—and the Johannine Prologue is referring to Jesus Christ. Nearly everything is said of this *logos* that was said also of preexistent Wisdom in Judaism:

The *logos* was present with God at the beginning, as a mediator of creation when the world was made. The *logos* came to Israel as to its own property, its inheritance. It took up its dwelling there—literally, "pitched its tent." It is absolutely clear that all this is presented according to the same model in which creation's Wisdom speaks of itself in Proverbs 8 and Sirach 24.

But there are three differences: Wisdom, in Proverbs 8 and Sirach 24, speaks in the first person, while John 1 tells its story in a hymnic third person until, beginning in verse 14, the hymn shifts to the confessional "we" of the community. The second difference is that in contrast to creation's Wisdom, the *logos* is not made welcome by all Israel. "He came to what was his own, and his own people did not accept him" (John 1:11). The third and decisive difference is that, in contrast to creation's Wisdom, it is not said of the *logos* that it was created. The *logos* was with God "in the beginning." Everything was created through the *logos*, but the *logos* was not created.

Passages about John the Baptizer have been inserted into the *logos* hymn in the Fourth Gospel. If we omit them, the text reads:

> In the beginning was the *logos*,
> and the *logos* was with God,
> and the *logos* was God.
> It was in the beginning with God.
>
> Everything came into being through him,
> and without him not one thing came to be
> that has come to be.
>
> He was the life in it [i.e., what has come to be],
> and the life was the light of humanity.
> And the light shone in the darkness,
> but the darkness did not comprehend it. [. . .]
>
> It was the true light
> that enlightens every human being—
> [the light] that comes into the world.
>
> He was in the world,
> and the world came into being through him,
> but the world did not recognize him.
>
> He came to what was his own,
> but his own did not accept him.
>
> But to those who did accept him
> he gave power to become children of God,
> those who believe in his Name,
> who have been begotten not of blood [of parents]
> and not of the will of the flesh
> and not of the will of a man,
> but of God.

And the *logos* became flesh
and took up its dwelling among us,
and we have seen his glory,
the glory of the only-begotten of the Father,
full of grace and truth. [. . .]

For of his fullness we have all received,
grace following upon grace.

For the Law
was given through Moses,
grace and truth
have come through Jesus Christ.

No one has ever seen God.
The only-begotten, who is God
and rests in the bosom of the Father,
he has borne witness. (John 1:1-18)[10]

This speaks explicitly of Jesus' divinity: "The *logos* was God" (1:1; cf. 1:18), but this divine predicate is embedded in an idea that at the time was deeply rooted in Judaism, that of Wisdom's preexistence. Those who say that all this would have been impossible in Jewish-Christian communities have to contend with these texts, and they cannot argue that such statements must be placed very late.

A Song of the Kyrios

Clearly against such a position is the so-called hymn in Philippians 2:6-11, in which the Jewish pattern of exaltation, that is, the eschatological view, *and* preexistence-Christology, the protological view, are combined. Thus the world of ideas behind the Philippians hymn is also entirely Jewish and feeds on the Old Testament.

The letter to the Philippians was probably written around the year 55 CE, but the hymn it quotes is still older. Between the Philippians hymn and the death of Jesus lay perhaps twenty years. In this hymn Christ is not called God, but he is called *kyrios*. The whole hymn points toward that confession:

Therefore God also highly exalted him
and gave him the name
that is above every name,
so that at the name of Jesus

> every knee should bend,
> in heaven and on earth and under the earth,
> and every tongue should confess
> that Jesus Christ is Lord,
> to the glory of God the Father. (Phil 2:9-11)

Here Jesus is clearly on the same level with God. How so? The last part of the hymn clearly alludes to a text from Isaiah 45:23: "To me every knee shall bow, every tongue shall swear." In Isaiah it is God who speaks; it is before God that one day every knee shall bend. When the hymn alludes to this statement from Isaiah, Jesus is set in place of God, but in the sense that when every knee bends before *Jesus*, then *God the Father* is thereby glorified.

It should also be noted that in the Septuagint, that is, the Greek translation of the Bible, *kyrios*, LORD, is used to replace YHWH, in accordance with the precept that the tetragrammaton, YHWH, is not to be spoken aloud; it is replaced by Hebrew *adonaj* (= LORD). When Jesus here, against the background of the Septuagint, is publicly acknowledged and called upon as Lord, this says that in this Jesus, God himself has become tangible, visible, audible. He is the eternal and conclusive presence of God in whom and through whom all creatures adore God.

A Jewish Way of Thinking and Nothing Else

Result: in the texts so briefly discussed here (Acts 2:36; Matt 28:18; Rom 1:3-4; John 1:1-18; Phil 2:6-11), despite the christological novelty, everything is formulated in Old Testament–Jewish forms of thought. And all these texts except John 1:1-18 are very old. They all say, on either the eschatological or the protological level, that Jesus is the final word and conclusive action of God, definitive of creation, definitive of all history. He is the Lord. In him God has fully uttered God's own self. This conviction lays the groundwork for the confession "Jesus: true human and true God."

The assertion that the first Jewish-Christian communities honored Jesus only as a simple rabbi, a teacher of wisdom, or a prophet, and that it was only Greek thought, rooted in Gentile-Christian communities, that divinized Jesus' person, is therefore inaccurate fore and aft. The same truth is illustrated by the titles given to Jesus: Messiah, Son of Man, Son of God, and Lord. All of them are Jewish; they come from the Old Testament or at least have their basis there. Also important in this regard would be a close examination of the early Christian interpretation of Psalm 110:1 ("The LORD says to my lord, 'Sit at my right hand'") and Psalm 2:7 ("You are my son; today I have begotten you"). It would show how accurately the formulations of early Christology could be developed out of Old Testament–Jewish texts.

Incidentally, the statement in Psalm 2:7, "You are my son; today I have begotten you," very probably assumes an ancient component of Israelite family law: when a son was born in Israel the father took him on his knee and spoke this very formula (Gen 30:3; 50:23; Ps 22:11). Only thus was the child acknowledged as a legitimate son. Adoption of a child from outside the family or even of an adult was only a special case of this common practice. Normally it was one's own child, but even so it had to be legally acknowledged, affirmed, and legitimated. In this precise sense in the earliest Christian exaltation Christology Jesus, who was already Son of God, was publicly legitimated as God's Son and installed in his rightful position.

This should make it clear that New Testament Christology is Jewish. From the very beginning the apostles and disciples and, after them, Jewish-Christian prophets and teachers sought to grasp who Jesus was. They attempted to express the overwhelming experience they had of Jesus, during his lifetime and then in the Easter appearances, in the existing Jewish categories available to them. Unless we are completely deceived, it seems that the insight that the formation of early Christology was an internal process within Judaism and not a Hellenization of Christianity is gaining more and more ground. Thus, for example, Gerd Theissen writes in his book *The Religion of the Earliest Churches*:

> The deification of Jesus did not contradict the Jewish sign world, but consistently "built up" and "fulfilled" it. Those who enthroned Jesus at the right hand of God were not Gentiles but Jews; and they did this in the awareness not of forsaking their Jewish monotheism but rather of consummating it.[11]

This insight represents a crucial scholarly advance over the liberal positions of the nineteenth and twentieth centuries. The question, however, remains, and Theissen's words about the "deification of Jesus" and his "enthronement" by Christians make it all the more urgent: was the Christology of the first communities and the early church based on Jesus' own claim and awareness of his sovereignty? Or is that Christology pure ideology, that is, was it simply imposed on the real Jesus after Easter?

The latter appears to be Theissen's opinion. He speaks of "experiences of dissonance," by which he means that Jesus' disciples and the first communities could only overcome the horrible contradiction between the hopes Jesus had awakened, "between the expectations of a charismatic surrounded with a messianic aura" and his shameful and painful failure on the cross by assigning him an infinitely higher status than that they had originally attributed to him. They had to "enthrone" him at the right hand of God; they had to "deify" him; they had to give him a central place: the rank of the universal redeemer.[12]

It certainly makes good sense to illuminate the psychological and sociological structure of processes in the history of theology. But Theissen's overall description can only lead ordinary readers to a serious misunderstanding. Or is he really convinced that Jesus was simply a charismatic, a prophet, a healer, a poet, a teacher, a founder of a cult, and a martyr,[13] and that early Christology was a "deification" *theologically* as well?

This should make it clear, once again, why this chapter had to treat Jesus' sovereign claim so extensively. Everything depends, after all, on the question of the claim *Jesus himself* advanced and what the eyewitnesses at the time observed him to be. At a later time, 1 John 1:1 reflects what a profound and fundamental experience this represented: "We declare to you what was from the beginning, what we have heard, what we have seen with our eyes, what we have looked at and touched with our hands, concerning the *logos* of life."

The Fundamental Experience of the First Witnesses

But in what did that experience consist? What was it that the first witnesses saw and heard? It makes sense at this point to summarize briefly what we already said in chapter 19.

1. Jesus *spoke* as one who stood in the place of God. Jesus did not speak like a prophet who hands on a word received from God. Nor did he speak like a precursor who points to one greater who is coming after him but instead as one who speaks with sovereign authority. We may remember especially the very frequent authoritative "I" in Jesus' words, and also his cries of woe over the cities that rejected him. Judgment will be measured by a decision for or against him.

2. Jesus *acted* like one who stands in God's stead. According to the theology of Ezekiel, God himself will gather his people (Ezek 36:24).

Jesus began the gathering of Israel by authoritatively, in a symbolic act, installing and sending forth twelve men as representatives of eschatological Israel. According to the theology of the book of Isaiah, in the now-dawning time of salvation God will heal his people (Isa 57:18-19), bind up their wounds (30:26); then no one in Israel will again say, "I am sick" (33:24). The whole people will see what the hand of God is accomplishing in their midst (29:23). Jesus' appearance was accompanied from the very beginning by healing miracles. He cured the blind, the lame, the lepers, and the possessed among the people of God. In Mark 2:7 the scribes quite correctly ask, "Who can forgive sins but God alone?" But evidently Jesus assured people that their sins were forgiven (cf. Mark 2:5; Luke 7:47), and in consequence he entered into community with sinners (Mark 2:13-17; Luke 19:1-10). Here again he acts as if he stood in the place of God.

3. But for all this we should finally consider that Jesus spoke and acted not only as someone who stood in God's stead. He acted *eschatologically*, that is, conclusively. This end-time-conclusive or eschatological character is evident especially in the claim that the decision about his own person would become salvation or judgment for those who decide. We may refer once more to Luke 12:8-9: "And I tell you, everyone who acknowledges me before others, the Son of Man also will acknowledge before the angels of God; but whoever denies me before others will be denied before the angels of God." Jesus' disciples and the first witnesses heard this claim; they saw, and they internalized it. It was their fundamental experience of Jesus. The church has preserved that fundamental experience, protected it against misinterpretation, and in the process has plumbed and reflected on it more and more deeply. It is true that in subsequent centuries this was done also with the aid of Greek concepts, but the church used those concepts precisely in order to hold fast to the confession of the first witnesses.[14]

The Dilemma

In closing, let me once again clarify the point at issue. The question was: was the Christology of the first communities and the early church based on a sovereign claim by Jesus himself? Or is this Christology pure ideology, that is, was it placed like a golden cloak over the real Jesus after Easter?

Historical criticism here stands before a parting of the ways that may lead in very different directions. If it posits that the biblical God exists, acts in the world, and does so through human beings, it also posits that there could be a pure "present," a presence in the world—perhaps even to an extent that is unimaginable and absolutely unheard of—and then it can at least accept Jesus' claim *as a claim* and not attempt to use historical criticism to weaken it or eliminate it entirely.

But if historical criticism does not accept that God can act radically as present in the world it will regard the irritating claim of Jesus as historically improbable and explain the corresponding texts from the early church as later "community constructions" or as myths arising in the minds of early Christian teachers. Or it will describe Jesus as the true image of the human and humanity that God wanted to put before our eyes. And so on. There are countless possibilities for accommodating the image of Jesus painted by the gospels to one's own desires and imaginings.

The hermeneutics of the Enlightenment, which became dominant in eighteenth-century Europe, is still deeply rooted in many people's heads, including those of Christians. The Enlightenment posited that what does not correspond to reality as it is *always* and *everywhere* to be found cannot be historical. There are sages, there are prophets, there are great teachers, and therefore Jesus can have been all those things. But he cannot have been what the Christian creed says about him, because that is not found anywhere else in history. Thus the texts of the gospels that furnish material for an examination of the question of the real Jesus must be subjected to a process of reduction.

Those who work with this Enlightenment premise are faced with a dilemma: what is historical determines our primary category of decision, which tells us from the beginning what *can* be historical. Only what has existed always and everywhere in the world *can* be historical. Everything that does not match this self-created preliminary conception is not historical.

An adequate theology does not bow to such prior conceptions because it posits that God acts in the world, indeed, that God can be present in the world in a way that is irritatingly *unique* and therefore can surpass all previous experience. Jesus was confronted even in his own lifetime with the prior conceptions of many of his contemporaries who knew for certain how God would act and how God had to act if God did act. Because they knew all that for certain, they rejected Jesus. But Jesus found others who saw what was happening through him and who he was. He could say to them:

Blessed are the eyes that see what you see! For I tell you that many prophets and kings desired to see what you see, but did not see it, and to hear what you hear, but did not hear it. (Luke 10:23-24 // Matt 13:16-17)

Chapter 21

The Reign of God: Utopia?

I spoke of Jesus' proclamation of the reign of God at the beginning of this book (chap. 2). But that subject then continued like a scarlet thread through every chapter. It was for the reign of God that Jesus lived. For its sake he gave his all. He spoke of nothing else. It was for that end that he began to gather Israel. Nevertheless, his own person was inextricably linked to the reign of God. He spoke as one who stands in the place of God. The mystery of his person is precisely the interweaving of "God alone" and "but I say to you." Anyone who dissolves that tension abandons the opportunity even to approach an understanding of Jesus.

But if we try to maintain the tension, at some point the question inevitably arises: what became of Jesus' preaching of the reign of God? It is true that an imponderable multitude of Christians throughout the world believe him to be the eternal Word of God, the Son of God, true God. But the reign of God he announced: did it come? Has the world changed for the better? Has the beatitude pronounced over the poor been fulfilled? Have the hungry been filled? Have the demons been banished from society? Can the lame walk and the blind see? Have his disciples received their hundred brothers and hundred sisters already in this world? Or was what Jesus announced nothing but a utopia? What he wanted was undoubtedly revolutionary. It was also shockingly beautiful and profoundly moving—but was it not just a utopia? And doesn't that mean that his sovereign claim is also dead?

The Notion of Utopia

But what *is* a utopia? The word, as we have seen, was coined by Thomas More, who also gave the genre of "utopias" their classic form. With his work *Utopia* in 1516 he began the unending series of utopias written since then. The word "utopia" represents the Greek *ou topos* = "non-place," or simply "nowhere." That is, what is dreamed of as a utopia does not exist anywhere in the real world. Therefore Thomas More's country of Utopia is far, far away, on an unknown island scarcely accessible to traffic. Distant islands are favorites for utopian literature, and since the nineteenth century these have been replaced by planets and since the twentieth by virtual worlds.

All utopias have one thing in common: the utopian society does not exist within the world we know, or else it *does not yet* exist, in which case it is located in the future. Consequently, students of utopias distinguish between those that are *spatially* distant and those distant *in time*, in short, between space- and time-utopias. Ultimately, the intent is the same: what the utopia depicts is far, far away.

In terms of this basic structure of all utopias we must say that the reign of God, as Jesus sees it, is no utopia, because utopia means "nowhere." The reign of God of which Jesus speaks, however, has a location: its place is Israel, the people of God (see chap. 3). Obviously Israel is not an end in itself. The Old Testament already sees the people of God as the entry-way for the whole world. The "pilgrimage of the nations to Zion" shows that Israel is God's way to reach all peoples (see chap. 4). So also the concept of the reign of God ultimately always applies to the whole world. But the transformation of the world that is at stake in the proclamation of the reign of God begins in Israel because what is to happen in the whole world must begin in a concrete and strictly defined place.

That is why Jesus does not go to the Gentiles but concentrates on the people of God. And he sends the Twelve not to the Gentiles but to the twelve tribes of the house of Israel. That is his program. That is precisely why he chose the Twelve.

So for Jesus the reign of God has a fixed place that is not somewhere in the distance but precisely where he proclaims the reign of God, where he heals the sick, where he drives out the demons of society (chap. 9). In reality the place of the reign of God is even more concretely defined: Jesus begins, from the very first day of his public activity, to gather disciples around him (chap. 5). He wants the signs of the reign of God to be immediately present to every eye; he wants those signs to be tangible, visible, the objects of experience. Hence the group of disciples to whom Jesus says, "Do not be afraid, little flock, for it is your Father's good pleasure to give you the kingdom" (Luke 12:32). All that speaks against the idea of calling the reign of God a utopia. But I have already indicated that, in the long series of utopias produced in the West, the utopian society is sometimes set spatially at a distance and sometimes in the future—thus either in a spatial not-here or in a temporal not-yet. How did Jesus view the *temporal* aspect of the reign of God? When is it coming?

We have seen that there are many texts from Jesus showing that the reign of God is not yet announced, it is still coming, people in Israel must first open themselves to it, so that from a certain point of view it is not yet here. But that was only one side of the coin, because much more prominent were all the texts in which Jesus speaks of the *presence* of the reign of God. For Jesus the reign is not "coming" in the sense that it lies somewhere in the unattainable future; that future is already dawning, is already visible in Jesus and his deeds. Everyone can already share in the reign of God now (chap. 2).

So in terms of the temporal dimension also the reign of God is not a utopia, but a future already in realization. Future hopes, promises, prophetic proclamations had existed in Israel for a long time. What is new with Jesus is precisely that he says: *today* it is all beginning, *today* it is fulfilled in your midst. That is, the longed-for future is here. The people of God need only believe and repent. Utopia means "not here" or "not yet." But Jesus says instead: "today already" and "really here!"

The Function of Utopias

Thus far I have based my remarks primarily on the Greek roots of the word "utopia," but such purely linguistic considerations are inadequate since the real impetus for the conception of utopias was not the pleasure of fantasizing but the desire to change the present. Thomas More himself, when he wrote his *Utopia*, had in mind the English society of his time. This is evident in the first book of *Utopia*, in which he gives no account at all of his distant island but instead criticizes the bad social conditions in England. We should not be overly influenced by the fact that he called his work "Nowhere." He was altogether concerned with the society in which he lived.

Such is the case, fundamentally, with all those who write utopias. They are depicting something that does not exist in order to change society as they find it. All utopias are counter-projects that are critical of the authors' own societies. Hence I must pose my question anew.

Was Jesus not simply one of the many who try to renew their own societies with the aid of a utopia? In that case, his talk about the reign of God would have accomplished only what all inventors of utopias do: propose to the eyes of his contemporaries new ideas for changing society in the form of images, guidelines, and visions. If Jesus thought that way, would it be so bad to call the reign of God a utopia? In that case, could we not say that yes, the reign of God is a utopia and Jesus is one in the long sequence of those who projected utopias in order to change the present injustice, misery, and critical deficiency of society? Then the question would be, at most, whether this was the best and most beneficial of all utopias. If we want to get past this we cannot avoid the task of comparing Jesus' proclamation of the reign of God more closely with the textual genre of utopias.

Abundance of Detail in Utopias

I will therefore make another foray into the enormous fund of utopian material[1] and look more closely at Thomas More's *Utopia*. To understand his intention one must imagine the conditions in London at the time: the misery of the poor and the arrogance of the rich, the numerous fires, poisoned wells, unbearable hygienic conditions, the power of those who could afford lawyers. It was against these conditions in his own time that More projected the new society of "Utopia." There, everything is different. The cities are not a chaos of narrow, twisting alleys but are laid out on a broad geometric plan. They accommodate themselves to nature and are surrounded by farm fields. The water conduits are lined with brick. The roofs of houses are flat and made of a sort of cement that renders them both weatherproof and fireproof. The doors of the houses have no locks; anyone can enter at any time, since private property has been eliminated.

Every city is divided into four equal quarters. At the center of each quarter is a market for every kind of wares; there the head of each family obtains what is needed for the family and receives everything asked for without payment. No one needs to carry luggage on a journey because the people of Utopia are at home everywhere. The whole island is a single family.

The story continues with the same degree of concrete detail. Money does not play much of a role. Everyone works, but only very limited hours, and everyone rests for two hours after the midday meal. The Utopians sleep eight hours per night; they take their meals together in large dining halls. The nobility have no more privileges. The laws are very simple and clear, so that no lawyers are needed. The governing law of the island nation is also detailed: its foreign policy, how wars are conducted (they happen only in self-defense), how a family is started (only after the couple have received careful advice and counseling), how divorce is punished (with forced labor), how people dress (simply, but in high-quality and valuable materials).

We could go on for a long time in this way, but probably it is already clear that More's *Utopia* is concrete. It overflows with detail; nothing is omitted. There is even consideration for how people approaching marriage get to know each other. *Utopia* is, in fact, made up of countless details. This was probably the reason for its breakthrough success, though that can also be attributed to its satirical features and More's sense of humor. He wanted to make his readers laugh too. So his *Utopia* is bursting with details. It is concrete. And it is precisely this concrete and detailed description that characterizes the whole textual genre of utopias. To offer another example:

In 1975 the Californian Ernest Callenbach published his *Ecotopia*, in which he projects a detailed image of a society on the Pacific coast of the former states of California, Oregon, and Washington dedicated entirely to ecology.

> The society of excess and waste has been eliminated. People live modestly, dress simply though imaginatively in a material developed from cotton. There are no more synthetic fibers. Microwave ovens are illegal. There is no use of metals (other than iron) or of synthetic colors. Food is sugar-free. . . . San Francisco has become a city-state. Smaller streams have been opened up, skyscrapers that were once corporate offices have been transformed into apartment buildings and linked by footbridges. . . . Public transportation is free. Bicycles are available everywhere at no cost. Major transport is conducted with container ships and through a subterranean system of conveyor belts.[2]

I need not look further into the world of today's utopias. The principle is clear: an effective utopia is detailed. That in itself secures it attention, fascination, or horror. The details themselves delight the readers and lead them to ask whether they themselves could live this way.

And it is precisely this crucial feature of the genre that is missing from Jesus' proclamation. We find nothing of the sort with him. One must read the utopias of the modern age to understand clearly how little Jesus describes the reign of God. He does not picture how Israel will look under God's rule: how people will live together, how families will look, how society itself will look, how things will be when God alone is sovereign. There is almost only a single image he uses for the reign of God: the common table, the shared meal (Matt 8:11; Luke 14:15-24). And even that does not remain merely an image, because Jesus already makes it a reality among his disciples and with toll collectors and sinners (Mark 2:15).

Jesus does not project any imaginative scenes of the future society. He acts. He gathers disciples around him, brings them together around a table, and practices with them the table customs of the reign of God: that one should not choose the best place but instead wait to see what place one is given (Luke 14:7-11); that the one who wants to be first must be the servant of all (Luke 22:24-27); that disciples should wash each other's feet, just as he has done—that is, do the dirty work for others (John 13:14-15); that disciples must forgive each other seventy-seven times, that is, always and without ceasing (Matt 18:21-22); and that they should look out not for the splinter in a sister's or brother's eye but for the beam in their own (Matt 7:3-5).

Jesus does not portray a utopian "realm of freedom," but he leads those who follow him into freedom. He does not describe the condition in which all alienation will be miraculously overcome, but he says, "Those who want to save their life will lose it, and those who lose their life for my sake will save it" (Luke 9:24). This is how Jesus projects society under the rule of God. He sets no preconditions: the reign of God is already beginning; its powers are already at work; it gives a new way of being together, even a new society, but not one that needs to be dreamed up. It takes place in the daily companionship of the one table, in common discipleship, in daily reconciliation. It happens out of joy in what God is doing. And it is by no means the case that this coming of the reign of God happens purely within. No, sick people are being healed, demonic forces are being overcome, the hungry are being filled, and enemies are being reconciled.

Jesus did not participate in preparations for a revolt against the Roman occupation (chap. 11). He and his disciples went about the country barefoot and unarmed and without any equipment so as to distance themselves from the Zealots' preparations for war (Matt 10:10). This again makes it clear that life in the reign of God has political consequences and social dimensions; it inserts itself into real life. It is already concrete, and for that very reason it has no need of the concreteness of a utopia.

Utopian Faith in Progress

When Thomas More's *Utopia* was printed in 1516, Christopher Columbus had already discovered America. Nicolaus Copernicus had probably written his *Commentariolus* in 1509; in it he proved that the planets revolve around the sun. The Age of Discovery had begun, and it opened up completely new perspectives. The English statesman and philosopher Francis Bacon published his own utopia, *Nova Atlantis*, in 1626. It too took place far away, on a lonely island, Bensalem.

In *Nova Atlantis* a society had been established that placed the highest value on scientific research. The island of Bensalem is practically a single institution for research. It includes "collections, laboratories, botanical gardens, places for the cultivation and manipulation of seeds, parks for animals and birds, high towers for meteorological and astronomical observations."[3] Science is to rely only on observation and planned research.

Thomas More had already anticipated technical advances, but it was Francis Bacon who first put science, technology, and the systematic investigation of nature at the center of his utopian society. He projected it as "a perfect scientific society." The goal of the research and technical innovations was for him "a better life for all."[4]

Since Bacon, no utopia can lack faith in reason and progress. It is true that beginning in the twentieth century there are also negative projections, "dystopias" that warn against the baser aspects of progress: consider only Aldous Huxley's *Brave New World* (1932) and George Orwell's *1984* (1949). The number of these dystopias is growing. But the majority of utopias, now as ever, assign great and even decisive significance for the advancement of humanity to science and technology. On the whole, the utopias project an image of a progressive society in which, through human reason, learning lessons from history, and the application of science and technology, a better and easier life for all will be made possible.

What is the relationship of Jesus' proclamation of the reign of God to all that? If he had only thought of something that comes after death, the question would, of course, make no sense. But for Jesus the reign of God first of all means this life, this world, this history within which the rule of God is to expand. But that necessarily raises the question whether his idea of the reign of God includes anything like progress and development. Let us look once more, briefly, at the parable of the mustard seed (cf. chap. 7 above).

To interpret this parable in Mark 4:30-32, it is crucial to compare the reign of God not simply with the mustard seed but with the whole process by which the tiny seed becomes a mighty shrub. The reign of God is neither like the mustard seed alone nor like the full-grown bush but resembles the whole process from seed to shrub. Thus the parable does not speak about the reign of God in static terms; it is about the way in which it comes, the "silent revolution" of the reign of God. It speaks of how God realizes his plan, his rule, his salvation in the world. God starts small, but at the end the tiny beginning will become something unexpectedly great, in whose sheltering shadow the birds of the air build their nests.

Does that represent faith in progress? Not at all! Jesus does not say that culture or morality grows, world peace or the well-being of human beings increase. Nor does he say that people will become steadily healthier and have to work less and less. He says: the reign of God is growing.[5] And the reign of God means that in the end God alone is Lord, that all honor is given to God and God alone is served. But at this point Jesus would say: When all that happens, then human life will be at its best. When God alone is Lord, the mastery of human beings over one another in the bad sense will cease. And he would add: "Seek first the kingdom of God, and all other things will be given to you as well" (cf. Matt 6:33 // Luke 12:31).

Faith in progress, together with a mania for whatever is technically feasible and the corresponding fantasies of universal power, is not to be found in Jesus. But he does possess the knowledge that God's salvation will succeed because it is more fascinating than anything else in the world. To that extent, certainly, the proclamation of the reign of God releases a dynamic in the world that, beyond the utopian, introduces unstoppable salvation and creates a new thing.

The Perfection of the Human

Closely associated with the faith in progress of Western utopias is belief in the perfection of the human being. That means not only the improvement of their physical constitution, which, of course, takes up quite a bit of space in the bio-technical utopias. It refers also to the human psyche with its confusions and destructive desires. Here too the modern utopia, increasingly combined with science fiction, offers a rich fund of material.

Despite all our recent experience of totalitarian societies, the optimal new human plays an astonishingly important role in current utopias. Humanity becomes more and more perfect. Many utopias even dream that the boundaries between the "real" and the "virtual" world will increasingly vanish. The individual is gradually dissolved into a constantly networked, super-individual reality until there remains only a single world-intelligence.

I cannot find anything like belief in human perfection with Jesus. Here especially his incorruptible realism is evident. He knows that human beings are evil (Luke 11:13); he speaks of this "evil and adulterous generation," with adultery of course serving as an image for turning away from God (Matt 12:39). He speaks of the persecution and even the violent death of those who follow him and do the will of God. In the end he himself was killed. His death is the final interpretive element added to his proclamation of the reign of God (chap. 2). Without what Jesus had said about slander, persecution, and suffering, his idea of the reign of God might insinuate an almost magical success story; it could lead one astray to believe in the possibility of perfecting humanity.

Jesus did not believe in the perfecting of the human, but only that it is possible to become perfect (Matt 5:48), though "perfect" does not mean simply moral perfection; it means an undivided surrender to the will of God (chap. 13). Jesus believed not in the constant "improvement" of human beings but that in the people of God all could help one another, repeatedly forgive one another, and show one another the way. Precisely because Jesus counted not on the optimization of the human but on joy over the reign of God and constant conversion and reconciliation we do not find in him anything like the contempt for reality that characterizes so many utopias—the same contempt for reality that began with Plato in the utopian sections of his *Politics*. Precisely because Jesus always had the weakness and fragility of human existence before his eyes the society he began with his group of disciples was not totalitarian, as are so many utopian societies from More to Lenin. With the Zealots, with whom Jesus was much more powerfully confronted than is usually assumed (chap. 5), one can speak of a "terror of ideas" and also of genuine terrorism. There is nothing like that with Jesus. He even warns people against following him.

Utopia almost always demands a total or at least a closed system. Therefore the old world must first be demolished. But with Jesus the tensions within reality are maintained: the fruitful tension between the state, which Jesus did not fundamentally question (Mark 12:17), and the people of God; the tension between the individual and the community; between the *already* of the reign of God and its *not yet*; and finally the tension between grace and freedom, that is, between the reign of God as pure gift and the fact that human beings can work in freedom and yet with ultimate passion for the reign of God. He did not destroy any of these tensive arcs; he maintained them. Jesus was very well aware of the "impossibility" of God's cause in the world, but he knew that God's possibilities are infinitely greater than all human possibilities (Mark 10:27).

Was the reign of God that Jesus proclaimed a utopia? Most certainly it was not. We can see this also from the fact that his proclamation, sealed with his death and resurrection, immediately after his execution brought forth communities on Israel's soil everywhere around the Mediterranean, communities that lived his message. What began in those communities is still alive and world-altering in the church even today, despite all the weakness and deficits of the church, despite its constant failure. That must be connected with the fact that the Risen One is present in the church—always, to the end of the age of the world (Matt 28:20). And it must be connected with the truth that Jesus' proclamation and practice of the reign of God is more radical than any utopia. It is more realistic, it is more critical, it knows more about human beings. It is the only hope for the wounds and sicknesses of our planet.

Notes

Chapter 1

1. The text that follows uses material from Gerhard Lohfink, *Der letzte Tag Jesu. Was bei der Passion wirklich geschah* (Freiburg: Herder, 1981), 71–98. The material was reworked and updated for this book. For an English translation of that book see Gerhard Lohfink, *The Last Day of Jesus: An Enriching Portrayal of the Passion* (Notre Dame, IN: Ave Maria Press, 1984).

2. Story in the *Frankfurter Allgemeine Zeitung* 289 (11 December 2010): 33.

3. Translator's note: Scripture quotations are based on the NRSV but adapted to match the author's German translation. Cf. v. 24 above, where NRSV reads: "What have you to do with us, Jesus of Nazareth? Have you come to destroy us?"

4. This is the fifth Sunday in the cycle for Year B. Unfortunately, the liturgists broke up Mark's composition and spread it over the fourth and fifth Sundays.

5. *Stauffenberg* won the prize for best German television film of 2004. Its international English title is *Operation Valkyrie*.

6. Frank Schirrmacher, "Was fehlt. Die entdramatisierte Geschichte. Jo Baiers 'Stauffenberg'-Film und wie es gewesen ist," *Frankfurter Allgemeine Zeitung* 47 (25 February 2004): 33.

7. Cf. Jan Assmann, *Das kulturelle Gedächtnis. Schrift, Erinnerung und politische Identität in frühen Hochkulturen* (Munich: Beck, 1997; 6th ed., 2007). Cf. idem, *Religion and Cultural Memory: Ten Studies*, trans. Rodney Livingstone (Stanford, CA: Stanford University Press, 2006).

8. Thomas Meurer, "Wer zu spät kommt . . ." *Christ in der Gegenwart* 54 (2002): 369–70.

9. Romano Guardini, "Das Gleichnis vom Säemann," [3–13], 159–69, in idem, *Wahrheit und Ordnung. Universitätspredigten* 7 (Würzburg: Werkbund Verlag, 1956).

10. "The Infancy Gospel of Thomas," quotations and comments from Oscar Cullmann, "Infancy Gospels," in Wilhelm Schneemelcher, *New Testament Apocrypha*, trans. R. McLean Wilson (Louisville: Westminster John Knox, 1963–65), 1:439–52, at 444.

11. This has been demonstrated especially well by David Trobisch. See his *The First Edition of the New Testament* (Oxford and New York: Oxford University Press, 2000).

12. Joseph Ratzinger, "Israel, die Kirche und die Welt," 152–67, in *Heute. Pro ecclesia viva. Das Heft der Integrierten Gemeinde 1: Vom Wieder-Einwurzeln im Jüdischen als einer Bedingung für das Einholen des Katholischen* (Bad Tölz: Urfeld Verlag, 1994), at 156.

Cf. also Joseph Ratzinger/Pope Benedict XVI, *Jesus of Nazareth: From the Baptism in the Jordan to the Transfiguration*, trans. Adrian J. Walker (New York: Doubleday, 2007), xxii.

Chapter 2

1. For an extensive presentation see Norbert Lohfink, "Der Begriff des Gottesreichs vom Alten Testament her gesehen," 152–205, in idem, *Studien zur biblischen Theologie*, SBAB 16 (Stuttgart: Katholisches Bibelwerk, 1993).

2. On this cf. especially Helmut Merklein, *Jesu Botschaft von der Gottesherrschaft. Eine Skizze*, 2nd ed., SBS 111 (Stuttgart: Katholisches Bibelwerk, 1984), 28–33.

3. Cf. Exod 15:17; 2 Sam 7:10; Isa 60:21; 61:3; Jer 32:41; 42:10; Matt 15:13; *Jub.* 36:6; *PsSol* 14:3-5.

4. According to the Sayings Source used by Matthew and Luke the coming judge baptizes "with the Holy Spirit and fire" (Matt 3:11 // Luke 3:16). This is probably an updating to conform to Christian experience of the Spirit. The Greek *pneuma* can mean not only "spirit" but also "wind" and even "storm." The Baptizer must have spoken of a baptism of judgment "by storm and fire."

5. The next seven sections in this chapter refer to Gerhard Lohfink, *Does God Need the Church? Toward a Theology of the People of God*, trans. Linda M. Maloney (Collegeville, MN: Liturgical Press, 1999), 134–39; and Gerhard Lohfink, "Die Not der Exegese mit der Reich-Gottes-Verkündigung Jesu," 383–402, in idem, *Studien zum Neuen Testament*, SBAB 5 (Stuttgart: Katholisches Bibelwerk, 1989).

6. On this see Joachim Jeremias, *New Testament Theology*, vol. 1: *The Proclamation of Jesus*, trans. John Bowden (London: SCM, 1974), 43–46.

7. For this paraphrase of "a new teaching—with authority!" cf. Marius Reiser, "Die Charakteristik Jesu im Markusevangelium," *TTZ* 119 (2010): 43–57, at 44.

8. I draw the concept of a "humbled shape" from the article by Heinz Schürmann, "Jesu ureigenes Basileia-Verständnis," 191–237, in Hans Waldenfels, ed., *Theologie— Grund und Grenzen. FS Heimo Dolch* (Paderborn: Schöningh, 1982), at 219.

Chapter 3

1. Andreas Lindemann, "IV. Neues Testament und spätantikes Judentum," in "Herrschaft Gottes/Reich Gottes," *TRE* 15:172–244, at 196–218.

2. Erich Zenger, "II. Altes Testament," in "Herrschaft Gottes/Reich Gottes," *TRE* 15:172–244, at 176–89.

3. For the interpretation of Daniel 7 I am making use of previously published material. Cf. Gerhard Lohfink and Ludwig Weimer, *Maria—nicht ohne Israel. Eine neue Sicht der Lehre von der Unbefleckten Empfängnis* (Freiburg: Herder, 2008), 218–23. Here I was guided by Norbert Lohfink, "Der Begriff des Gottesreichs vom Alten Testament her gesehen," 152–205, in idem, *Studien zur biblischen Theologie*, SBAB 16 (Stuttgart: Katholisches Bibelwerk, 1993), at 196–99.

4. For what follows, see further development in Gerhard Lohfink, *Does God Need the Church? Toward a Theology of the People of God* (Collegeville, MN: Liturgical Press, 1999), 26–39.

5. Quotations are from Adolf von Harnack, *Das Wesen des Christentums*, GTB 227 (Gütersloh: Gütersloher Verlagshaus Mohn, 1977). The lecture texts were translated into English and published as *What Is Christianity*, trans. Thomas Bailey Saunders (London: Williams and Norgate; New York: Putnam, 1901). English quotations are from that publication.

6. *What Is Christianity*, 37.

7. Ibid., 60.

8. Ibid., 15.

9. Ibid., 60–61. With these statements Harnack placed himself within a broad current of the mentality of his time. Cf., for example, Wilhelm Bousset, *Jesus*, trans. Janet Penrose Trevelyan (New York: G. P. Putnam's Sons, 1911), 149–50: "His [Jesus'] ethics are the ethics of lofty individualism. Beside these two entities of God and the individual everything else sinks into the background. No account is taken of the history of man as a whole or of the connected labour of the human race in the wider or narrower forms of its social life—marriage, the family, society, the state, the nation. Jesus makes his moral demands as if the individual stood free and naked before God, absolved from all these relationships and customary standards—except as regards the direct relationship of man to man,—as in fact Jesus and his disciples in their wandering life lived free from all such forms and relationships."

10. Ibid., 74.

11. Ibid., 154.

12. Ibid., 66.

13. Ibid., 125–26.

14. Ibid., 120.

15. Ibid., 17.

16. Ibid., 190.

17. Ibid., 192.

18. Cf. Colin H. Roberts, "The Kingdom of Heaven (Lk xvii.21)," *HTR* 41 (1948): 1–8; Hans Klein, *Das Lukasevangelium*, KEK 1.3 (Göttingen: Vandenhoeck & Ruprecht, 2006), 570–71; and especially Alexander Rüstow, "Zur Deutung von Lukas 17, 20-21," *ZNW* 51 (1960): 197–224.

19. Origen, *De oratione* 25.1. The translation is adapted from that by William Curtis in the Christian Classics Library, available online at www.ccel.org/ccel/origen/prayer.xvi.html. In his homilies on Luke's gospel also, Origen finds the soul or the heart to be the place for the reign of God. Cf. Origen, *Homilies on Luke; Fragments on Luke*, trans. Joseph T. Lienhard, SJ (Washington, DC: Catholic University of America Press, 1996), 151–52.

20. Cf., for example, Rudolf Schnackenburg, *Gottes Herrschaft und Reich. Eine biblisch-theologische Studie* (Freiburg: Herder, 1959), 62–65.

21. Rudolf Bultmann, *Jesus and the Word*, trans. Louise Pettibone Smith and Erminie Huntress Lantero (New York: Scribner, 1958), chap. 2: "The Teaching of Jesus: The Coming of the Kingdom of God," 35–36.

22. Ibid., 37.

23. Ibid.

24. Gershom Scholem, *Über einige Grundbegriffe des Judentums*, Edition Suhrkamp 414 (Frankfurt: Suhrkamp, 1970), 121.

25. Cf. Augustine, *City of God*, 20, 9.

26. Johannes Weiss, *Jesus' Proclamation of the Kingdom of God* (Philadelphia: Fortress Press, 1971).

27. Cf. *Lumen Gentium* 1, 3, 5.

Chapter 4

1. For what follows, see more detail in Gerhard Lohfink, *Does God Need the Church? Toward a Theology of the People of God* (Collegeville, MN: Liturgical Press, 1999), 51–66.

2. See chap. 2 above.

3. Thus Albert Schweizer, *The Quest of the Historical Jesus*, trans. John Bowden (Minneapolis: Fortress Press, 2001), 340.

4. Ulrich Luz, *Matthew 8–20*, trans. James E. Crouch, Hermeneia (Minneapolis: Fortress Press, 2001), 205.

5. Thus, correctly, Michael Wolter, *Das Lukasevangelium*, HNT 5 (Tübingen: Mohr Siebeck, 2008), 420.

6. The Fourth Gospel makes it impossible fully to exclude this possibility. The so-called calendar of feasts in John envisions at least three Passovers during the time of Jesus' public activity: the so-called pre-Synoptic Passover (2:13), the Passover of the multiplication of the loaves (6:4), and finally the death Passover (11:55; 12:1; cf. also 5:1; 7:10).

7. Cf. Isaiah 13–23; Jeremiah 46–51; Ezekiel 25–32; Amos 1:3–2:3.

8. The translation follows W. A. M. Beuken, *Jesaja 1–12*, HTKAT (Freiburg: Herder, 2003), 212, 226–28.

Chapter 5

1. This chapter owes much to Martin Hengel's book, *The Charismatic Leader and His Followers*, trans. James C. G. Greig (New York: Crossroad, 1981; repr. Eugene, OR: Wipf & Stock, 2005).

2. Translator's note: English "disciple" comes from Latin *discipulus*, which also means "pupil" or "apprentice" or "learner."

3. *b. Berakhot* 34b. Further citations in Hengel, *Charismatic Leader*, 51–53 and n. 54.

4. *m. Abot.* 1.6b.

5. For more detail see chaps. 11 and 12 below.

6. The time at which the concept of a "Zealot" became current (as early as Judas Galilaeus, who appeared in the year 6 CE, or only with the resistance movement in Jerusalem in the years 66–70) is disputed among scholars. Josephus, to whom we owe nearly all our information on this subject, restricts the term to a particular resistance group in the years 66–70. In what follows I am using the concept without entering into this special terminological question, joining some scholars in employing it in a general sense as an umbrella term for the theologically and socially motivated resistance movement against Roman rule that began with Judas Galilaeus.

7. Josephus, *Bell.* 2, 8.1 (§118).

8. Here I am indebted to Martin Hengel, *The Zealots: Investigations into the Jewish Freedom Movement in the Period from Herod I until 70 A.D.* (Edinburgh: T & T Clark,

1989), 88. Cf. idem, *The Charismatic Leader and His Followers* (New York: Crossroad, 1981), 59–60.

9. See chap. 11 below, "Jesus and the Old Testament."

10. Cf. Hengel, *Charismatic Leader*, 17.

11. Proclamation of the reign of God: Matt 10:7; Luke 9:2; 10:9; healing: Matt 10:8; Luke 10:9; expelling demons: Matt 10:8; Mark 6:7; Luke 9:1.

12. Cf., e.g., Joel 4:13; Matt 13:30, 39; Rev 14:15.

13. As in Prov 6:26; Jer 16:16; Ezek 13:18; Amos 4:2; Hab 1:14-15.

Chapter 6

1. Disciple = Christian: Acts 6:7; 9:1, 10, 26b; 16:1; 21:16b. Disciple = community member: Acts 6:1; 11:29; 19:30; 20:30; 21:16a. The disciples = community: Acts 6:2; 9:19, 26a, 38; 13:52; 14:22, 28; 18:23, 27; 20:1; 21:4.

2. In previous publications I have generally identified church and disciples. Cf., e.g., Gerhard Lohfink, *Wem gilt die Bergpredigt? Beiträge zu einer christlichen Ethik* (Freiburg: Herder, 1988), 32–35, 73. The present chapter corrects my previous approach.

3. Cf. Mark 1:17; 2:14; 10:21; Luke 9:59; John 1:43.

4. In this passage we could also associate the verb *akolouthein* with: "and the scribes of the Pharisees followed him." But that is less likely. Mark reserves *akolouthein* for discipleship of Jesus, with a single exception in 14:13, and even there those "following behind" are the disciples and not opponents.

5. The manuscript tradition varies between seventy-two and seventy. The number seventy-two is more difficult and therefore the more probable reading. In the ancient world the number in a defined group was often given as seventy, hence the correction in many manuscripts. Possibly in choosing the number seventy-two Luke was simply thinking of a multiple of twelve (6 x 12). Cf. the number 120 (10 x 12) in Acts 1:15.

6. Luke read in Mark of the mission of the "Twelve" (Mark 6:7), while the Sayings Source speaks of the sending out of "disciples" (cf. Matt 9:37). Both refer to the same event, but Luke has created two missions out of them.

7. In Luke 19:8 Zacchaeus is not describing his good behavior in the past but making a promise for the future.

8. Josephus, *Bell.* 2, 12.3-7 (§§ 232–46); *Ant.* 20, 6.1-3 (§§ 118–36). The *Antiquities*, in contrast to the presentation in the *Bellum Judaicum*, speaks of *many* being murdered. The event took place in the fall of the year 51 CE.

9. The mission discourse occurs in the New Testament in a variety of forms and stages of tradition. Cf. Matt 10:5-42; Mark 6:8-11; Luke 9:3-5; 10:2-16.

10. Cf. Josef Blinzler, *The Trial of Jesus: The Jewish and Roman Proceedings against Jesus Christ Described and Assessed from the Oldest Accounts* (Westminster, MD: Newman Press, 1959), 256–57 and n. 39. See also Rudolf Pesch, *Das Markusevangelium II*, HTKNT II/2 (Freiburg: Herder, 1977), 513: "The characterization of Joseph, which seems slightly distant (as if the community that handed on the tradition knew this high-ranking man only from afar; cf. also Acts 13:29) makes it improbable that after Easter he was a member of the community of Jesus Messiah in Jerusalem."

11. Cf. Matt 10:2; Mark 6:30; Luke 6:13; 9:10; 17:5; 22:14; 24:10. Of course, the oldest concept of "apostle" is a great deal broader.

12. Cf. Gottfried Wenzelmann, *Nachfolge und Gemeinschaft. Eine theologische Grundlegung des kommunitären Lebens*, CTM.PT 21 (Stuttgart: Calwer, 1994), 45.

13. The following section rests in part on Gerhard Lohfink, *Does God Need the Church?* (Collegeville, MN: Liturgical Press, 1999), 170–73.

14. For a fuller discussion of the biblical concept of "perfection," see Lohfink, *Wem gilt die Bergpredigt?*, 69–75.

Chapter 7

1. See examples in Michael Wolter, *Das Lukasevangelium*, HNT 5 (Tübingen: Mohr Siebeck, 2008), 422.

2. Cf. Ulrich Luz, *Matthew 8–20: A Commentary*, trans. James E. Crouch, *Hermeneia* (Minneapolis: Fortress Press, 2001), 516 n. 59.

3. For more detail on the following exegesis, especially the phenomenon of "stocking," see Gerhard Lohfink, "Das Gleichnis vom Sämann (Mk 4, 3-9)," *BZ* 30 (1986): 36–69.

4. Cf., e.g., 2 Esdr 4:26-27: "for the age is hurrying swiftly to its end. It will not be able to bring the things that have been promised to the righteous in their appointed times, because this age is full of sadness and infirmities."

5. For the following section. see more detail in Gerhard Lohfink, "Die Metaphorik der Aussaat im Gleichnis vom Sämann (Mk 4, 3-9), 131–47, in idem, *Studien zum Neuen Testament*, SBAB 5 (Stuttgart: Katholisches Bibelwerk, 1989).

Chapter 8

1. "[He] loved him" in this passage does not correspond correctly to the Greek *ēgapēsen*, which here refers to a concrete action: he embraced, he caressed the rich man. Cf. BDAG, 5.

2. Not "[he] put saliva on his eyes," as the NRSV nicely has it.

3. Quoted from Peter Brown, *The World of Late Antiquity: From Marcus Aurelius to Muhammad* (London: Thames and Hudson, 1971), 96.

4. Athanasius, *Vita Antonii* 45: "When he was about to eat and sleep and provide for the needs of the body, shame overcame him as he thought of the spiritual nature of the soul. Often when about to partake of food with many other monks, the thought of spiritual food came upon him and he would beg to be excused and went a long way from them, thinking that he should be ashamed to be seen eating by others. He did eat, of course, by himself because his body needed it; and frequently, too, with the brethren—embarrassed because of them, yet speaking freely because of the help his words gave them." Translation from *St. Athanasius: The Life of St. Antony*, trans. Walter J. Burghardt and Robert T. Meyer, ACW (Westminster, MD: Newman Press, 1950), 58.

5. Josef Ratzinger, "Pastoralblatt" (Cologne, March 1988), quoted in Rudolf Pesch, *Über das Wunder der Brotvermehrung, oder: Gibt es eine Lösung für den Hunger in der Welt* (Frankfurt: Knecht, 1995), 40.

6. The next section is treated more fully in Gerhard Lohfink and Rudolf Pesch, "Volk Gottes als 'Neue Familie,'" 227–42, in Josef Ernst and Stephan Leimgruber,

eds., *Surrexit Dominus vere. Die Gegenwart des Auferstandenen in seiner Kirche. FS Erzbischof Johannes Joachim Degenhardt* (Paderborn: Bonifatius, 1995).

7. Cf. Norbert Lohfink, *Church Dreams: Talking against the Trend,* trans. Linda M. Maloney (North Richland Hills, TX: BIBAL Press, 2000), chap. 2, "The Will of God," 15–46.

8. Cf. Bernhard Lang, "Ehe," *NBL* 1: 475–78, at 476.

9. Cf., e.g., Exod 18:25; 1 Sam 12:6; 1 Kgs 12:31; 13:33; 2 Chr 2:17.

10. In regard to this problem, which I have only hinted at here, everything depends on what one means by "church." If by it we mean a new entity, a "new people" that has taken the place of Israel (substitution or supercessionist theory), then Jesus did not found a church. But if, in line with the New Testament writings, one understands the church as the eschatological Israel, then Jesus laid the foundations of the church by gathering Israel and constituting the Twelve. Of course, we could only speak of "church" in the modern sense at the moment when it became evident, after Easter, that the greater part of Israel had not come to believe. As a result, the church remained only a *part* of Israel. It rightly understood itself as the true eschatological Israel, but historically it only became what it was because the majority in Israel had not believed. This must necessarily be maintained in regard to the concept of the church. It is true that the church must be defined entirely in terms of Israel, but not only as the eschatological Israel that believed in Jesus; at the same time it must be seen as a fragment born out of the crisis of history and remaining, in its innermost being, entirely oriented to the whole Israel. Perhaps one may say that it is already the whole, but it is still the "whole in fragments." For more on this, see Gerhard Lohfink, "Jesus und die Kirche," in Walter Kern, Hermann Josef Pottmeyer, and Max Seckler, eds., *Handbuch der Fundamentaltheologie,* UTB 8172, 2nd ed. (Tübingen and Basel: Francke, 2000), 3:27–64.

Chapter 9

1. "Deeds of power" (*dynameis*): Matt 7:22; 11:20, 21, 23; 13:54, 58; Mark 6:2, 5; 9:39; Luke 10:13; 19:37. "Signs" (*sēmeia*): John 2:11, 23; 3:2; 4:48, 54; 6:2, 14, 26, 30; 7:31; 9:16; 10:41; 11:47; 12:18, 37; 20:30.

2. There is a detailed and substantive discussion of the problems in the *Testimonium Flavianum* in Gerd Theissen and Annette Merz, *The Historical Jesus: A Comprehensive Guide,* trans. John Bowden (Minneapolis: Fortress Press, 1998), 65–74.

3. Cf. Michael Wolter, *Das Lukasevangelium,* HNT 5 (Tübingen: Mohr Siebeck, 2008), 495–96.

4. In the Hebrew text, however, it is ridiculed by being misspelled as "Beelzebub," that is, "lord of the flies."

5. For the whole cf. Martin Ebner, *Jesus von Nazaret. Was wir von ihm wissen können* (Stuttgart: Katholisches Bibelwerk, 2007), 107–12.

6. For what follows cf. Marius Reiser, "Die Wunder Jesu—eine Peinlichkeit?" *EuA* 73 (1997): 425–37.

7. I am adopting this list, with small alterations, from Martin Hengel and Anna Maria Schwemer, *Jesus und das Judentum* (Tübingen: Mohr Siebeck, 2007), 462–63.

8. Cf. Otto Böcher, "Dämonen I," *TRE* 8: 271.

9. This is described in detail by Albert Schweitzer, *The Quest of the Historical Jesus,* trans. John Bowden (Minneapolis: Fortress Press, 2001), 37–55.

10. Tacitus, *Histories* IV, 81; Suetonius, *Vespasian*, 7.

11. Josephus, *Ant.* 8, 2.5 (§§46-49).

12. The only text in which Jesus prays in connection with a miracle is the raising of Lazarus (cf. John 11:41-42). But this text is composed altogether on the level of Johannine reflection.

13. Rudolf Bultmann, *The History of the Synoptic Tradition*, trans. John Marsh (New York: Harper & Row, 1963), 221–26.

14. Cf. Theissen and Merz, *The Historical Jesus*, 283–84.

15. Marius Reiser has pointed this out to me.

16. For what follows see, more fully, Gerhard Lohfink and Ludwig Weimer, *Maria— nicht ohne Israel. Eine neue Sicht der Lehre von der Unbefleckten Empfängnis* (Freiburg: Herder, 2008), 358–63.

17. For the history of this formula and the ideal-typical forms in which it appears in the history of theology cf. Ludwig Weimer, *Die Lust an Gott und seiner Sache. Oder: Lassen sich Gnade und Freiheit, Glaube und Vernunft, Erlösung und Befreiung vereinbaren?* (Freiburg: Herder, 1981), 146–74, 223–303.

18. Romano Guardini had already thought and written along these lines in his book, *Wunder und Zeichen* (Würzburg: Werkbund-Verlag, 1959). Cf. Bernhard Bron, *Das Wunder. Das theologische Wunderverständnis im Horizont des neuzeitlichen Natur- und Geschichtsbegriffs* (Göttingen: Vandenhoeck & Ruprecht, 1975), 188–89. Bron summarizes Guardini as follows: "Therefore the miracle does not destroy the unity of the world or set aside the natural order; instead it brings them to fulfillment and allows the eschatological aspect to be made manifest as the true meaning of the miraculous event" (p. 189).

19. Certainly nature contains "not only linear cause-and-effect relationships, but also networked or functional retroactive causality, which is why complementary explanations (including 'top-down' ones) are necessary," Siegfried Wiedenhofer, "Wunder III," *LThK* (Freiburg: Herder, 3d ed. 2006), 10: 1318.

20. Cf. Matt 8:10, 13; 9:2, 22, 28, 29; 15:28; 17:20; 21:21; Mark 2:5; 5:34, 36; 9:23, 24; 10:52; 11:22, 23; Luke 5:20; 7:9, 50; 8:48, 50; 17:6, 19; 18:42; John 4:50.

21. C. S. Lewis describes what I mean by "malleability" here in *Miracles. A Preliminary Study* (New York: Macmillan, 1947; repr. in *The Complete C. S. Lewis Signature Classics* [San Francisco: HarperCollins, 2002], 242): "If I knock out my pipe I alter the position of a great many atoms: in the long run, and to an infinitesimal degree, of all the atoms there are. Nature digests or assimilates this event with perfect ease and harmonises it in a twinkling with all other events. . . . I have simply thrown one event into the general cataract of events and it finds itself at home there and conforms to all other events." Natural scientists will describe what Lewis is getting at in more professional terms, but unless they are monists and determinists they will say the same thing.

22. Theissen and Merz, *Historical Jesus*, 312.

23. Cécile Ernst, *Teufelsaustreibungen: die Praxis der katholischen Kirche im 16. und 17. Jahrhundert* (Bern: Huber, 1972).

24. Cf., e.g., Joachim Gnilka, *Das Evangelium nach Markus*, vol. 1, EKK II/1 (Zürich: Benziger; Neukirchen-Vluyn: Neukirchener Verlag, 1978), 226: "The demonic worldview is unacceptable to us."

25. I cannot at this point enter into the question of the reality of evil as a *personal* power, since it is something that cannot be summarized in a few sentences. Let me

instead refer to the work of Jürgen Bründl, *Masken des Bösen. Eine Theologie des Teufels*, BDS 34 (Würzburg: Echter, 2002).

26. See Hengel and Schwemer, *Jesus und das Judentum*, 479. [Translator's note: "Mirakel" in German is dismissive, unlike English "miracle," which is equivalent to German "Wunder."]

27. Mark 11:12-14, 20-21 is, of course, not a miracle on his own behalf. The difficult narrative depicts a punishment miracle. Perhaps it rests on a saying of Jesus about an Israel that bore no fruit: cf. Mic 7:1-2.

28. See, e.g., the Infancy Gospel of Thomas 3, 4, 8; Acts of Andrew: Gregory of Tours, *Liber de miraculis* 4, 12; Acts of Paul: Heidelberg Coptic Papyrus, 32; Acts of Thomas 8–9.

29. *Ant.* 20, 8.6 (§§ 167–170). Translations of Josephus in this book are by William Whiston in *The Works of Josephus, Complete and Unabridged*, new updated ed. (Peabody, MA: Hendrickson, 1987). Cf. also *Bell.* 2, 13.4-6 (§§ 258–264).

30. Cf. Hengel and Schwemer, *Jesus und das Judentum*, 194, 257–58.

31. Philostratus, *Vita Apollonii* IV, 45. Translation by F. C. Conybeare.

32. Ibid., IV, 10.

33. For what follows cf. Christoph Kleine, "Wunder I," *TRE* 36: 380–81.

34. Reference is made here to Ernst Bloch, *The Principle of Hope*, vol. 3 (Cambridge, MA: MIT Press, 1986), 1265.

35. For the referential context of Jesus' mighty deeds cf. also Peter Stuhlmacher, *Biblische Theologie des Neuen Testaments*, vol. 1 (Göttingen: Vandenhoeck & Ruprecht, 1992), 81–83. See also Marius Reiser, "Die Wunder Jesu," 434–37, on Jesus' miracles as sign actions.

Chapter 10

1. The Jesus Seminar has engaged intensively with the question of the authenticity of the traditional sayings of Jesus and published the results in a book. All the words of Jesus declared to be genuine are printed in red, all those considered ungenuine are in black. One result is that all Jesus' sayings about judgment are printed in black. The accompanying commentary grounds this by saying, "The vindictive tone of these sayings is uncharacteristic of Jesus." No other reason is given. See Robert W. Funk, Roy W. Hoover, and the Jesus Seminar, *The Five Gospels: What Did Jesus Really Say? The Search for the Authentic Words of Jesus* (New York: HarperCollins, 1996), 188.

2. "Up in the Gallery," in Franz Kafka, *The Metamorphosis, In the Penal Colony, and Other Stories: With Two New Stories*, trans. Joachim Neugroschel (New York: Scribner Paperback Fiction, 2000), 244–45.

3. Marius Reiser, *Jesus and Judgment: The Eschatological Proclamation in Its Jewish Context*, trans. Linda M. Maloney (Minneapolis: Fortress Press, 1997). For the statistics, see pp. 303–4.

4. "Glutton and drunkard," Luke 7:34; "friend of sinners," Luke 7:34; "possessed," Mark 3:22; possessed "Samaritan," John 8:48; "impostor," Matthew 27:63; "deceiver of the people," John 7:12; "apostate to the faith," cf. Mark 3:22. We can conclude from Matthew 19:12 that people accused Jesus of being a eunuch; in that passage Jesus reacts to the accusation in his own way.

5. Reiser, *Jesus and Judgment*, 289–90.

6. For discussion of the details, see Anton Vögtle, *Gott und seine Gäste. Das Schicksal des Gleichnisses Jesu vom grossen Gastmahl. (Lukas 14, 16b-24; Matthäus 22,2-14)*, BThS 29 (Neukirchen-Vluyn: Neukirchener Verlag, 1996). There is a general consensus that in his version Matthew reshaped the parable secondarily and made of it an allegory of salvation history.

7. The last sentence of the parable says literally, "For I tell you: none of those men who were invited will taste of my meal" (v. 24). In narrative terms, the "you" here is problematic because it is still the servants who are being addressed. Did Luke have in mind a shift in the audience, so that in this sentence Jesus himself is speaking to those listening to him? In that event Luke failed to mark the shift. But for us the problem is more or less irrelevant, because v. 24 touches precisely the essential meaning of the parable.

8. Cf. Reiser, *Jesus and Judgment*, 258–62.

9. Norbert Lohfink, "'Ich komme nicht in Zornesglut' (Hos 11,9). Skizze einer synchronen Leseanweisung für das Hoseabuch," 163–90, in *Ce Dieu qui vient. Mélanges offerts à Bernhard Renaud*, LD 159 (Paris: Cerf, 1995), at 188. I am following this essay in interpreting the text of Hosea.

Chapter 11

1. Cf. Gunther Wanke, "Bibel I. Die Entstehung des Alten Testaments als Kanon," *TRE* 6: 1–8.

2. For the reasons for this translation and the intent of the text, cf. Norbert Lohfink, "Der Glaube und die nächste Generation. Das Gottesvolk der Bibel als Lerngemeinschaft," 144–66, in idem, *Das Jüdische am Christentum. Die verlorene Dimension* (Freiburg: Herder, 1974).

3. Here I am following Henry M. Shires, *Finding the Old Testament in the New* (Philadelphia: Westminster, 1974), 66, 70–71.

4. Raymund Schwager wrote a moving book some years ago in which he attempted to tell Jesus' inner history in the form of a free meditation. What is crucial in this depiction is how Jesus learns to understand himself and his task through Scripture. Raymund Schwager, *Jesus of Nazareth: How He Understood His Life* (New York: Crossroad, 1998).

5. For the oral Torah and the means of its transmission, cf. Hermann L. Strack and Günter Stemberger, *Introduction to the Talmud and Midrash*, trans. and ed. Markus Bockmühl (Edinburgh: T & T Clark, 1991).

6. For more detail, see Peter Stuhlmacher, *Biblische Theologie des Neuen Testaments* I (Göttingen: Vandenhoeck & Ruprecht, 1992), 68–70.

7. Cf. Erich Zenger, "Herrschaft Gottes / Reich Gottes II. Altes Testament," *TRE* 15: 172–244, at 187.

8. Cf. Ismar Elbogen, *Jewish Liturgy: A Comprehensive History* (Philadelphia: Jewish Publication Society, 1993), §9a.

9. Matt 11:5; cf. Isa 35:5-6; 61:1-2.

10. E.g., in the writings and fragments found at Qumran; cf. Martin Hengel and Anna Maria Schwemer, *Jesus und das Judentum* (Tübingen: Mohr Siebeck, 2007), 410,

467. Now fundamental to this topic is Johannes Zimmermann, *Messianische Texte aus Qumran. Königliche, priesterliche und prophetische Messiasvorstellungen in den Schriftfunden von Qumran*, WUNT 2d ser. 104 (Tübingen: Mohr Siebeck, 1998), esp. 389–412, 467–69.

11. For more detail on this subject, see Gerhard Lohfink, *Das Vaterunser neu ausgelegt*, Urfelder Reihe 7 (Bad Tölz: Verlag Urfeld, 2007).

12. For extensive discussion of the ʿ*Amida* (= *Tefilla*) see Elbogen, *Jewish Liturgy*, §§8, 9.

13. Introduction and text: Svend Holm-Nielsen, *Die Psalmen Salomos*, JSHRZ IV/2 (Gütersloh: Mohn, 1977); for a critical English edition, see Robert B. Wright, *The Psalms of Solomon: A Critical Edition of the Greek Text*, Jewish and Christian Texts in Contexts and Related Studies 1 (London, et al.: T & T Clark, 2007).

14. Cf. János Bolyki, *Jesu Tischgemeinschaften*, WUNT 96 (Tübingen: Mohr Siebeck, 1998), 181.

15. Cf. Erich Zenger, et al., *Einleitung in das Alte Testament*, 2nd ed. (Stuttgart: Kohlhammer, 1996), 22–24.

16. For what follows, see Norbert Lohfink, "Death at the River Frontier: Moses' Incomplete Mission and the Contours of the Bible," 1–14, in idem, *In the Shadow of Your Wings: New Readings of Great Texts from the Bible*, trans. Linda M. Maloney (Collegeville, MN: Liturgical Press, 2003).

17. Cf. Rainer Albertz, *A History of Israelite Religion in the Old Testament Period*, 2 vols., trans. John Bowden (Louisville: Westminster John Knox, 1994), 2:472.

18. For what follows, see Norbert Lohfink, "Distribution of the Functions of Power," 55–75, in idem, *Great Themes from the Old Testament*, trans. Ronald Walls (Chicago: Franciscan Herald Press, 1982); idem, *In the Shadow of Your Wings*, 1–14.

19. This is demonstrated in terms of Psalms 137 and 138 in Gerhard Lohfink, *Beten schenkt Heimat. Theologie und Praxis des christlichen Gebets* (Freiburg: Herder, 2010), 162–64.

20. This is the formulation in "Gerechter Friede [Just Peace]," a pastoral letter of the German Catholic Conference of Bishops of 27 September 2000 (Bonn: Sekretariat der Deutschen Bischofskonferenz), 24.

21. The confession of the kings and nations is announced by God himself in Isa 52:15. It comprises Isa 53:1-11a. Then God speaks again. The beginning of the confession remains unclear in our Bible translations because it is simply translated "what we have heard," but in Hebrew the phrase can mean either "what we have said" or "what we have heard." In light of the context the second translation is more probable.

22. "Gerechter Friede," 25.

23. Cf. the brief summary of the discussion in Zenger, et al., *Einleitung in das Alte Testament*, 14–16.

Chapter 12

1. We are in the fortunate position of possessing records of the trial of Justin and his companions before the city prefect Junius Rusticus and of their martyrdom. For an English translation, see E. C. E. Owen, *Some Authentic Acts of the Early Martyrs* (Oxford: Clarendon Press, 1927), 47–52.

2. Cf. Stefan Heid, "Justinos, Märtyrer," *LThK*[3] 5: 1112–13.

3. Justin, *Dialogue with Trypho*, 11, 2. Translation from *Early Christian Writings*, http://www.earlychristianwritings.com/text/justinmartyr-dialoguetrypho.html.

4. "New lawgiver": *Dial*. 14, 3; 18, 3; cf. 12, 2; "new law": *Dial*. 11, 4; 12, 3; "eternal law": *Dial*. 122, 5. For Tertullian (see *De praescriptione haereticorum* 13, 4) the "preaching of the new law" by Jesus is even considered the rule of faith.

5. The New Testament does not yet speak of a "new people of God," but the expression appears already in the Letter of Barnabas and then in many of the Fathers. Cf., e.g., *Barn*. 7.5; Justin, *Dial*. 119, 3; Clement of Alexandria, *Paidagogos* I, 14.5; 58.1; Eusebius, *Eccl. Hist*. I, 4.2; Augustine, *John*, 65.1; Zeno of Verona, *Tractates* II, 14.4. The expression "new people of God" achieved renewed popularity in twentieth-century theology. The documents of Vatican II use it unquestioningly. Cf. *Lumen gentium* 10.13.26; *Nostra aetate* 4.

6. We find the pericope with the question about the highest commandment in Mark 12:28-34; Matt 22:34-40; and (in a different context) Luke 10:25-28. In this particular case (because of a number of minor agreements between Matthew and Luke), there is dispute about whether Mark or Matthew contains the oldest tradition. For the sake of simplicity, I will base my analysis on Matthew's version.

7. Already in the Pentateuch the commandment to worship Yнwн alone is the crystallizing core and the focus of meaning for all the law collections. Cf. Gerhard Lohfink, *Does God Need the Church? Toward a Theology of the People of God*, trans. Linda M. Maloney (Collegeville, MN: Liturgical Press, 1999), 78–79.

8. For what follows, cf. Norbert Lohfink, "Love: The Ethos of the New Testament: More Sublime Than That of the Old?," 239–54, in idem, *Great Themes from the Old Testament*, trans. Ronald Walls (Edinburgh: T & T Clark, 1982).

9. Cf. the collection of Jewish texts on this subject in Gerd Theissen and Annette Merz, *The Historical Jesus: A Comprehensive Guide*, trans. John Bowden (Minneapolis: Fortress Press, 1998), 381–87.

10. The parallel in Matthew is 5:38-48, though its antithetical form there is probably secondary.

11. The entire problem is treated in detail in Gerhard Lohfink, *Wem gilt die Bergpredigt? Beiträge zu einer christlichen Ethik* (Freiburg: Herder, 1988).

12. For the following sections on love and hatred in the Greek and Roman world I am much indebted to Marius Reiser's essay, "Love of Enemies in the Context of Antiquity," *NTS* 47 (2001): 411–27.

13. Mary Whitlock Blundell, *Helping Friends and Harming Enemies: A Study in Sophocles and Greek Ethics* (Cambridge: Cambridge University Press, 1989), 26.

14. Hesiod, *Works and Days*, ll. 353-54.

15. The extent to which the "Golden Rule" (Luke 6:31) also fits quite naturally in the Lukan context has been demonstrated by Michael Wolter: cf. Wolter, *Das Lukasevangelium*, HNT 5 (Tübingen: Mohr Siebeck, 2008), 258.

16. Plato, *Great Dialogues of Plato*, trans. W. H. D. Rouse (New York: Signet Classic, 1999), *Meno* 71E.

17. Archilochos, Fragment 23, 14 (West) = POxy 2310. Translation in Guy Davenport, *Archilochos, Sappho, Alkman: Three Lyric Poets of the Seventh Century B.C.* (Berkeley: University of California Press, 1980), 30.

18. Plato, *The Republic* I, 332A–336A.

19. Plato, *Crito* 48E–49E.

20. Seneca, *On Benefits*, trans. Aubrey Stewart (London: George Bell and Sons, 1905), IV, 26.1; VII, 31.1.

21. Cf. Georg Fischer and Dominik Markl, *Das Buch Exodus*, NSKAT 2 (Stuttgart: Katholisches Bibelwerk, 2009), 261–62, and especially Gianni Barbiero, *L'asino del nemico. Rinuncia alla vendetta e amore del nemico nella legislazione dell' Antico Testamento (Es 23,4-5; Dt 22,1-4; Lv 19,17-18)*, AnBib 128 (Rome: Pontifical Biblical Institute, 1991).

22. Thus correctly Erich Zenger, *A God of Vengeance? Understanding the Psalms of Divine Wrath*, trans. Linda M. Maloney (Louisville: Westminster John Knox, 1996), 31–32.

23. Following Theissen and Merz, *The Historical Jesus*, 393.

24. Among the six antitheses in Matthew's Sermon on the Mount, the antithetical form is secondary to the third (divorce), fifth (revenge), and sixth (love of enemies). Was Matthew also the one who introduced the antithetical form in the first (murder), second (adultery), and fourth (swearing)? It cannot be excluded. Even if he did so, everything favors the idea that he precisely reflected Jesus' language act and intention. There are many indicators of this: for example, Jesus' prohibition of divorce already in the Sayings Source, in the form of a legal decree, cf. Matt 5:32 // Luke 16:18. This already showed an affinity to the antithesis form.

25. That anger here does not refer to insults or blows to someone's honor that could be pursued through the justice system is signaled by the continuation of the discourse in v. 22bc. Apparently it is about insults in common use, such as "you dummy." I have deliberately omitted the continuation of the discourse in v. 22bc because it is very much disputed among exegetes. They have discussed whether v. 22bc was part of the original antithesis at all and also whether this is an intensification or not. If it is an intensification, then certainly the anger in v. 22a must be a purely internal act. For the problem of v. 22bc, see Ulrich Luz, *Matthew 1–7: A Commentary*, trans. Wilhelm C. Linss (Minneapolis: Augsburg Press, 1989), 282–86.

26. Author's translation.

27. Cf. n. 24 above.

28. Luke 16:18 reads: "Anyone who divorces his wife and marries another commits adultery, and whoever marries a woman divorced from her husband commits adultery." The phrase "and marries another" probably comes from Mark 10:11. If we eliminate that phrase and the adultery clause from Matt 5:32 the difference between Matt 5:32 and Luke 16:18 is limited. I have chosen the Matthean version as closer to the original. For what follows, cf. Gerhard Lohfink, "Jesus und die Ehescheidung. Zur Gattung und Sprachintention von Mt 5,32," 207–17, in *Biblische Randbemerkungen. Schülerfestschrift für Rudolf Schnackenburg zum 60. Geburtstag* (Würzburg: Echter Verlag, 1974).

29. Cf. Hos 2:4 and *ThWAT* 7, 834.

30. For this whole complex, cf. Frank Crüsemann, *The Torah: Theology and Social History of Old Testament Law*, trans. Allan W. Mahnke (Minneapolis: Fortress Press, 1996), 292–94. On the content of the fourth commandment, cf. Rainer Albertz, "Hintergrund und Bedeutung des Elterngebots im Dekalog," *ZAW* 90 (1978): 348–74.

31. Martin Hengel, *The Charismatic Leader and His Followers*, trans. John Riches (Edinburgh: T & T Clark; New York: Continuum, 1981), 14.

32. This is about people who use the *corban* formula against their parents: "'Whatever support you might have had from me is Corban' (that is, an offering to God)."

They thus take from their parents part of the support due to them by declaring it to be a temple offering.

33. Cf. the interpretation by Michael Wolter, *Das Lukasevangelium*, 483–84.

34. Ernst Käsemann, "The Problem of the Historical Jesus," first published as "Das Problem des historischen Jesus," *ZTK* 51 (1954): 125–53; reprinted in idem, *Essays on New Testament Themes*, trans. W. J. Montague, SBT 41 (London: SCM Press, 1964), 15–47, at 39.

35. Ibid., 37.

36. Cf. the study by Ulrich Kellermann, *Messias und Gesetz. Grundlinien einer alttestamentlichen Heilserwartung. Eine traditionsgeschichtliche Einführung*, BibS(N) 61 (Neukirchen-Vluyn: Neukirchener Verlag, 1971). The clearest tie between Messiah and Torah is established in *PsSol* 17, and there the Messiah calls for the strictest observance of the Torah; cf. esp. *PsSol* 17:27, 32. The two passages in Midrash cited in Hermann L. Strack and Paul Billerbeck, *Kommentar zum Neuen Testament aus Talmud und Midrasch* (Munich: Beck, 1922–61), 4/1, 2 for a "new Torah" and a "Torah of the Messiah" are late and are completely downplayed by Billerbeck himself.

37. Cf. the reference to this possibility in Martin Hengel, "Jesus und die Tora," *TBei* 9 (1978): 152–72, at 164, as well as in Theissen and Merz, *Historical Jesus*, 365–67.

38. See the prohibitions of mixing things in Lev 19:19 and Deut 22:5, 9-11.

39. Frank Crüsemann, *The Torah*, 366.

Chapter 13

1. I do so because here I want to set aside the question of how Jesus and the evangelists evaluate the position of John the Baptizer in salvation history. For a reconstruction of the logion in the Sayings Source, see especially Helmut Merklein, *Die Gottesherrschaft als Handlungsprinzip. Untersuchung zur Ethik Jesu*, FB 34, 3rd ed. (Würzburg: Echter Verlag, 1984), 80–96. For a more recent probing of the vocabulary, cf. Gerd Häfner, "Gewalt gegen die Basileia? Zum Problem der Auslegung des 'Stürmerspruches' Mt 11,12," *ZNW* 83 (1992): 21–51.

2. Translator's note: This is, in fact, the wording given in Editorial Board of the International Q Project, *The Sayings Gospel Q in English Translation* (Minneapolis: Fortress Press, 2001), online at http://homes.chass.utoronto.ca/~kloppen/iqpqet.htm.

3. Cf. Mark 8:35; Matt 16:25; Luke 9:24, and for the Sayings Source's version Matt 10:39 // Luke 17:33. See also John 12:25.

4. Cf. Homer, *Iliad* V, 529-32, and other examples in Michael Wolter, *Das Lukasevangelium*, HNT 5 (Tübingen: Mohr Siebeck, 2008), 348.

5. For details see Hermann L. Strack and Paul Billerbeck, *Kommentar zum Neuen Testament aus Talmud und Midrasch* (Munich: Beck, 1922–61), 2:37–46.

6. Literally, "Go (away) behind me!" Many interpreters seek (because of Mark 1:17, 20 and the immediately following "become my followers," lit., "go behind me," in Mark 8:34) to read these words to mean that Jesus calls Peter back to discipleship: "Go behind me [again]!" But the immediate appellation of Peter as "Satan" speaks against this. Such a word in no way fits with the motif of discipleship. The Greek preposition *opisō* has a very broad spectrum of meanings, as we can see from the

reading *hypage opisō mou* in Matt 4:10. That is a variant, it is true, but that Satan can be so addressed in a considerable number of textual witnesses reveals the breadth of meanings this preposition can have.

7. So, for example, *The Living Bible,* but also the NAB.—Tr.

8. Cf. Lev 22:24, which forbids the castration of sacrificial animals, and Deut 23:2-3 on the exclusion of *castrati* from Israel's worship.

9. *b. Yebam.* 63b, a saying of Rabbi Eliezer.

10. *b. Yebam.* 63a. Cf. Gen 5:2.

11. For what follows, cf. esp. Josef Blinzler, "*Eisin eunouchoi*: zur Auslegung von Matt 19:12," *ZNW* 48 (1957): 254–70.

Chapter 14

1. For the frequent occurrence of two-part sayings in the words of Jesus cf. Martin Hengel and Anna Maria Schwemer, *Jesus und das Judentum* (Tübingen: Mohr Siebeck, 2007), 380–96.

2. When Luke writes "earth" here he means the world. Jesus might originally have meant the "land (of Israel)."

3. Cf. Matt 6:19-20; 24:43; Luke 12:39.

4. Cf. Hermann L. Strack and Paul Billerbeck, *Kommentar zum Neuen Testament aus Talmud und Midrasch* (Munich: Beck, 1922–61), 1:971–72.

5. This could be quite accurate on the level of the intention of Matthew's gospel. Cf. Ulrich Luz, *Matthew 8–20,* trans. James E. Crouch, Hermeneia (Minneapolis: Fortress Press, 2001), 278–79.

6. This is the position defended by Tim Schramm and Kathrin Löwenstein, *Unmoralische Helden. Anstössige Gleichnisse Jesu* (Göttingen: Vandenhoeck & Ruprecht, 1986), 42–49.

7. Thus Joachim Jeremias, *The Parables of Jesus,* trans. Samuel H. Hooke, 6th ed. (New York: Charles Scribner's Sons, 1962), 201.

8. This is the point of Ludwig Weimer's book, *Die Lust an Gott und seiner Sache. Oder: Lassen sich Gnade und Freiheit, Glaube und Vernunft, Erlösung und Befreiung vereinbaren?* (Freiburg: Herder, 1981).

9. For what follows, cf. Norbert Lohfink, *Das Jüdische am Christentum. Die verlorene Dimension* (Freiburg: Herder, 1987), esp. 12.

10. In the next three sections I am making use of my book, *Does God Need the Church? On the Theology of the People of God,* trans. Linda M. Maloney (Collegeville, MN: Liturgical Press, 1999), 139–50.

11. Feeding of the five thousand: Mark 6:30-44; Matt 13:13-21; Luke 9:10-17; John 6:1-15; the feeding of the four thousand is a variant narrative: Mark 8:1-10; Matt 15:32-39.

12. Joseph Ratzinger, *Introduction to Christianity* [1968] (San Francisco: Ignatius Press, 2004), 257.

13. Ibid., 260.

14. This alludes to ibid., 261–62.

15. Cf. esp. John 12:23-24; 13:31-32; 17:1.

Chapter 15

1. Another and a whole newer version is offered by John 12:12-19. Matthew and Luke are both dependent on the Markan version.

2. In John 12:12-19 the Zechariah text is explicitly cited; Mark only alludes to it.

3. There are many ancient parallels for this. Cf. esp. Erik Peterson, "Die Einholung des Kyrios," *ZST* 7 (1930): 682–702. For spreading out garments as a sign of respect cf. 2 Kgs 9:13 and *Acta Pilati* I.2.

4. So Jürgen Roloff, *Jesus*, 4th ed. (Munich: Beck, 2007), 107.

5. In Matthew's gospel the action in the temple follows *immediately* on the entry into the city (Matt 21:10-12), as it does in Luke's (Luke 19:37-46). Mark (or the model he was following) inserts a day between the two (Mark 11:11-15).

6. Martin Hengel and Anna Maria Schwemer, *Jesus und das Judentum* (Tübingen: Mohr Siebeck, 2007), write correctly (p. 554): "Why, in view of the temple and the holy city that lay before him in all their beauty, should Jesus himself not have carried out a—messianic—parable-action, as he had done previously in establishing the Twelve, as he would a little later in cleansing the temple, and then at the Last Supper?"

7. Marius Reiser pointed out to me that under Roman rule Herod, the tetrarch Archelaeus, the Syrian legate Quirinius, the Roman governors, Kings Agrippa I and II, and Herod of Chalcis all installed and removed the high priests at will. The full list with all the evidence, arranged according to the person who made the appointment, can be found in Emil Schürer, *The History of the Jewish People in the Age of Jesus Christ (175 B.C.–A.D. 135)*, new English version rev. and ed. Geza Vermes, Fergus Millar, and Matthew Black (Edinburgh: T & T Clark, 1979), 2:229–32. Cf. Josephus, *Ant.* 20.224-51.

8. See the details in Christiana Metzdorf, *Die Tempelaktion Jesu. Patristische und historisch-kritische Exegese im Vergleich*, WUNT 2d ser. 168 (Tübingen: Mohr Siebeck, 2003), but esp. also Jostein Ädna, *Jerusalmer Tempel und Tempelmarkt im 1. Jahrhundert n. Chr.*, ADPV 23 (Wiesbaden: Harrassowitz, 1999), and idem, *Jesu Stellung zum Tempel. Die Tempelaktion und das Tempelwort als Ausdruck seiner messianischen Sendung*, WUNT 2d ser. 119 (Tübingen: Mohr Siebeck, 2000).

9. Cf. esp. Zech 6:9-15; 14:20-21. Chapters 40–48 of the book of Ezekiel set out in detail the plan of an eschatological temple. In the book of Tobit the eschatological Jerusalem is painted in glowing colors in 13:17. A little later it says: "But God will again have mercy on them, and God will bring them back into the land of Israel; and they will rebuild the temple of God, but not like the first one until the period when the times of fulfillment shall come. . . . [the house of God will be rebuilt in Jerusalem, a glorious edifice for all the generations forever], just as the prophets of Israel have said concerning it" (Tob 14:5, Codex Vaticanus).

10. Thus also Joachim Gnilka, *Das Evangelium nach Markus* 2, EKK II/2 (Zürich: Benziger; Neukirchen-Vluyn: Neukirchener Verlag, 1979), 131.

11. Cf. esp. 1 Cor 3:9, 16-17. The Essenes also saw their community as the eschatological temple; cf. 1QS 8.4-10; CD 3.19, and elsewhere.

12. For the remainder of this chapter I am using material from my book, *Does God Need the Church? On the Theology of the People of God*, trans. Linda M. Maloney (Collegeville, MN: Liturgical Press, 1999), 190–201.

13. The quotation is adapted from Gustaf Dalman, *Jesus-Jeshua, Studies in the Gospels*, trans. Paul P. Levertoff (New York: Ktav, 1971), 168. The age of the saying is disputed.

Günther Stemberger, "Pesachhaggada und Abendmahlsberichte des Neuen Testaments," 357–74, in idem, *Studien zum rabbinischen Judentum*, SBAB 10 (Stuttgart: Katholisches Bibelwerk, 1990), at 360–61, proposes a later dating. Nevertheless, Exod 13:8 (cf. Exod 12:26-27) suggests that very early there was a Passover ritual with extensive interpretation.

14. Thus Hengel and Schwemer, *Jesus und das Judentum*, 582. John 18:28 is crucial.

15. Cf. the brief summary of the major arguments for a Paschal meal in ibid., 582–86. Joachim Jeremias, *The Eucharistic Words of Jesus*, trans. Norman Perrin (Philadelphia: Trinity Press International, 1990), 15–88, remains fundamental.

16. Thus Gerd Theissen and Annette Merz, *The Historical Jesus*, trans. John Bowden (Minneapolis: Fortress Press, 1998), 426.

17. Mark probably offers the oldest account. The differences between Mark and 1 Cor 11:23-26 are more easily explained as further development of the Markan version than the reverse. Cf. Rudolf Pesch, *Das Markusevangelium* 2, HTKNT II/2 (Freiburg: Herder, 1977), 369–77.

18. For the sequence of the Passover meal, see Jeremias, *Eucharistic Words*, 84–88. Rudolf Pesch has shown that Mark 14:22-25 is an integral part of a more extensive text that saw Jesus' last meal as a Passover meal, most recently in "Das Evangelium in Jerusalem: Mk 14:12-26 als ältestes Überlieferungsgut der Urgemeinde," 113–55, in Peter Stuhlmacher, ed., *Das Evangelium und die Evangelien. Vorträge vom Tübinger Symposium 1982*, WUNT 28 (Tübingen: Mohr Siebeck, 1983), esp. 146–55.

19. Luke 22:19-20; 1 Cor 11:23-26.

20. Targum Onkelos (and similarly Targum Yerushalmi I) says of Exod 24:8: "And Mosheh took half of the blood which was in the basins, and sprinkled it upon the altar, to expiate the people, and said, Behold, this is the blood of the Covenant which the Lord hath made with you upon all these words." Cf. Peter Stuhlmacher, *Biblische Theologie des Neuen Testaments* 1 (Göttingen: Vandenhoeck & Ruprecht, 1992), 137.

21. In Isaiah the Servant is always Israel, including in the so-called Servant Songs. For more detail, see Gerhard Lohfink and Ludwig Weimer, *Maria—nicht ohne Israel. Eine neue Sicht der Lehre von der Unbefleckten Empfängnis* (Freiburg: Herder, 2008), 223–30.

22. Within Isa 52:13–53:12 we encounter the "many" in 52:14, 15; 53:11, 12. Isaiah 52:15 shows that this is about the "nations." We should also consider that even within the Old Testament itself the noun "many" can stand both for eschatological Israel (Dan 9:27; 11:33; 12:3) and for the "many" from among the Gentile nations (Isa 52–53). The expression is similarly open in the New Testament: in the Last Supper tradition the first referent can only be Israel, but in Matt 8:11 the word clearly refers to the Gentiles. Cf. also Mark 10:45 with 1 Tim 2:6. For a correct interpretation of Isa 52:13–53:12, see also above, chap. 11 n. 21.

Chapter 16

1. An exception to this are the church communities that are Evangelical in nature. These generally hold to biblical language.

2. Cf. Jakob and Wilhelm Grimm, *Deutsches Wörterbuch* (Leipzig: S. Hirzel, 1854–1962), 10:1012–22.

3. This position is most fully developed and emphasized at present by, for example, Werner Zager, "Die theologische Problematik des Sühnetods Jesu. Exegetische und dogmatische Perspektiven," 35–61, in idem, *Jesus und die frühchristliche Verkündigung. Historische Rückfragen nach den Anfängen* (Neukirchen-Vluyn: Neukirchener Verlag, 1999). Zager tries to show that the second part of Mark 10:45, "to give his life as ransom for many," is a post-Easter construction, as is the cup saying in Mark 14:24. According to him (pp. 36–45), the sole original cup saying is the eschatological prospect in Mark 14:25.

4. Herbert Braun, *Jesus of Nazareth: The Man and His Time* (Philadelphia: Fortress Press, 1979), 56–57.

5. This schematic distinction, which played a major role for Rudolf Bultmann, is outdated. Cf. esp. Martin Hengel, *Judaism and Hellenism: Studies in Their Encounter in Palestine during the Early Hellenistic Period* (Philadelphia: Fortress Press, 1974).

6. There were certainly influences from Hellenistic cultic meals, but there were also profound differences. The sole basis for the early Christian eucharistic celebration is Jesus' last meal. Cf. Hans-Josef Klauck, *Herrenmahl und hellenistischer Kult. Eine religionsgeschichtliche Untersuchung zum 1. Korintherbrief*, NTA n.s. 15, 2nd ed. (Münster: Aschendorff, 1986).

7. Thus Peter Fiedler, "Sünde und Vergebung im Christentum," *Concilium* 10 (1974): 568–71; idem, *Jesus und die Sünder*, BET 3 (Frankfurt: Peter Lang, 1976), 277–81.

8. For what follows, see also Rudolf Pesch, *Das Abendmahl und Jesu Todesverständnis*, QD 80 (Freiburg: Herder, 1978), 103–11.

9. Cf. Michael Wolter, *Das Lukasevangelium*, HNT 5 (Tübingen: Mohr Siebeck, 2008), 498.

10. Pesch, *Abendmahl*, 106.

11. Cf. Hartmut Gese, "The Atonement," 93–116, in idem, *Essays on Biblical Theology*, trans. Keith Crim (Minneapolis: Augsburg, 1981); Bernd Janowski, *Sühne als Heilsgeschehen. Studien zur Sühnetheologie der Priesterschrift und zur Wurzel KPR im Alten Orient und im Alten Testament*, WMANT 55 (Neukirchen-Vluyn: Neukirchener Verlag, 1982); idem, *Stellvertretung. Alttestamentliche Studien zu einem theologischen Grundbegriff*, SBS 165 (Stuttgart: Katholisches Bibelwerk, 1997); Peter Stuhlmacher, *Biblische Theologie des Neuen Testaments* 1 (Göttingen: Vandenhoeck & Ruprecht, 1992), 136–43.

12. Exod 24:4-11.

13. Jer 31:31-34; cf. Jer 34:40; Ezek 16:59-63; 37:21-28.

14. Isa 52:13–53:12.

15. See in more detail Gerhard Lohfink and Ludwig Weimer, *Maria—nicht ohne Israel. Eine neue Sicht der Lehre von der Unbefleckten Empfängnis* (Freiburg: Herder, 2008), 223–30.

16. Rudolf Bultmann, "New Testament and Mythology: The Problem of Demythologizing the New Testament Proclamation," 1–44, in idem, *New Testament and Mythology and Other Basic Writings*, ed. and trans. Schubert M. Ogden (Philadelphia: Fortress Press, 1984).

17. Immanuel Kant is frequently cited in this connection by many authors: "Religion within the Boundaries of Mere Reason," II.1.c., in idem, *Kant: Religion within the Boundaries of Mere Reason: And Other Writings*, trans. Allen Wood, et al., Cambridge Texts in the History of Philosophy (Cambridge: Cambridge University Press, 1998).

18. Cf. the comprehensively informative work of Karl-Heinz Menke, *Stellvertretung. Schlüsselbegriff christlichen Lebens und theologische Grundkategorie* (Einsiedeln: Johannes,

1991), 17. At this point he refers to Dorothee Sölle, *Stellvertretung. Ein Kapitel Theologie nach dem "Tode Gottes,"* 2nd ed. (Stuttgart: Kreuz-Verlag, 1982), English: *Christ the Representative: An Essay in Theology after the "Death of God"* (London: SCM, 1967).

19. Or "you can because you must." Cf. Immanuel Kant, *Critique of Practical Reason and Other Works on the Theory of Ethics*, trans. Thomas Kingsmill Abbott (London: Longmans, Green, 1898; repr. Charleston, SC: Forgotten Books, 2008), 25: "He [= one who in a difficult situation and must decide according to conscience—Author] judges, therefore, that he can do a certain thing because he is conscious that he ought, and he recognizes that he is free—a fact which but for the moral law he would never have known." Apparently "you can because you should/must" was later abstracted from this text. At any rate, in 1942 Walter Schmidkunz edited a collection of Kant citations in the *Münchner Lesebogen* 11, titled "I. Kant, Du kannst, denn du sollst. Vom Ethos der Pflicht." The phrase in the title did not, however, appear within the collection. I am grateful to Fr. Giovanni Sala, SJ, for this information.

20. I thank Ludwig Weimer for this formulation.

21. Cf. Gese, "The Atonement," 95–96, 106.

22. For an extended discussion of this point see Lohfink and Weimer, *Maria*, 37–64.

23. Dag Hammarskjöld, *Markings*, trans. Leif Sjöberg and W. H. Auden (New York: Ballantine Books, 1983), 173.

24. Thus, e.g., Jürgen Becker, *Das Evangelium nach Johannes. Kapitel 11–21*, ÖTK 4/2 (Gütersloh: Mohn, 1981), 592.

Chapter 17

1. Cf. Rudolf Pesch, *Das Markusevangelium*, Part 2, HTKNT II/2 (Freiburg: Herder, 1977), 21.

2. Cf. Gerhard Lohfink, *Das Vaterunser neu ausgelegt*, Urfelder Reihe 7 (Bad Tölz: Verlag Urfeld, 2007), 29–34. Still fundamental is Joachim Jeremias, *Abba. Studien zur neutestamentlichen Theologie und Zeitgeschichte* (Göttingen: Vandenhoeck & Ruprecht, 1966), 15–67. Available in English in idem, *Jesus and the Message of the New Testament*, ed. K. C. Hanson (Minneapolis: Fortress Press, 2002), esp. 39–74.

3. Ps 11:6; Isa 51:17, 22; Ezek 23:32-33.

4. Cf. Martin Hengel and Anna Maria Schwemer, *Jesus und das Judentum* (Tübingen: Mohr Siebeck, 2007), 588. The references for Celsus and Julian can also be found there.

5. Cf. in the Old Testament the distress of the prophet Jeremiah (e.g., Jer 20:7-18) and in the New Testament Paul's statements about himself (e.g., 2 Cor 4:7-18).

6. Thus, probably correctly, John 18:12-15.

7. Thus Hengel and Schwemer, *Jesus und das Judentum*, 593.

8. Cf. esp. Josef Blinzler, *The Trial of Jesus: The Jewish and Roman Proceedings against Jesus Christ Described and Assessed from the Oldest Accounts* (Westminster, MD: Newman Press, 1959), 117–21; also 86–89. In my description of Jesus' last day I am grateful to be able to follow this foundational work in many details.

9. Cf. in the Old Testament: Num 35:30; Deut 17:6; 19:15.

10. Thus Mark 8:29-30; 9:7-9.

11. The suggestion that Jesus did not use the Son of Man title is utterly unfounded. It appears in the New Testament almost nowhere but on the lips of Jesus. And later Christology had no idea what to do with the title. Cf. the persuasive and well-

considered presentation in Hengel and Schwemer, *Jesus und das Judentum*, 526–41; see also chap. 19 below.

12. Cf. *m. Sanh.* VII, 5. The command, however, is older than the law in the Mishnah: cf. 2 Kgs 18:37–19:1.

13. There is no basis in the Markan text for two different meetings of the Council; it is also improbable that the Sanhedrin only assembled in the early morning, as supposed by Willibald Bösen, *Der letzte Tag des Jesus von Nazaret. Was wirklich geschah* (Freiburg: Herder, 1994), 174–77.

14. An overview of the shifting discussion on this point can be found in Pesch, *Markusevangelium*, Part 2, 418–19.

15. In the Fourth Gospel account Jesus' scourging precedes the death sentence (John 19:1; cf. Luke 23:16). In that case it would have been a final attempt on the part of Pilate to avoid sentencing Jesus to death.

16. See *b. Sanh.* 43a: "When one is led out to execution, he is given a goblet of wine containing a grain of frankincense, in order to benumb his senses, for it is written, Give strong drink unto him that is ready to perish, and wine unto the bitter in soul" (*Sanhedrin*, trans. Jacob Schachter and Harry Freedman, ed. Isidore Epstein [London: Soncino, 1987]).

17. Thus Hengel and Schwemer, *Jesus und das Judentum*, 617; Schalom ben Chorin, *Brother Jesus: The Nazarene through Jewish Eyes* (Atlanta: University of Georgia Press, 2001), 184.

18. 11Q Temple 64, 6-10. Cf. Peter Stuhlmacher, *Biblische Theologie des Neuen Testaments* 1 (Göttingen: Vandenhoeck & Ruprecht, 1992), 155–56.

Chapter 18

1. Only in the so-called canonical ending of Mark (Mark 16:9-20), which, however, stems from the second century, is anything said (at v. 14) about the eleven (disciples).

2. Since there is probably an existing tradition behind John 16:32 the redactional tension with John 20, in which the disciples remain in Jerusalem after all, need not exclude this interpretation.

3. See in detail Gerhard Lohfink, *Die Himmelfahrt Jesu. Untersuchungen zu den Himmelfahrts- und Erhöhungstexten bei Lukas*, SANT 26 (Munich: Kösel, 1971), 262–65.

4. Cf. Luke 24:6 (which retains a reminiscence of Galilee) with Mark 16:7.

5. "Disclosure situation" is the phrase used by Ian T. Ramsey, Wilhelmus A. de Pater, and others. It refers to a moment in which, through a concrete event, a new view of things suddenly appears. For extensive discussion, see Tullio Aurelio, *Disclosures in den Gleichnissen Jesu. Eine Anwendung der disclosure-Theorie von I. T. Ramsey, der modernen Metaphorik und der Theorie der Sprechakte auf die Gleichnisse Jesu*, RST 8 (Frankfurt: Peter Lang, 1977), 28–41.

6. The natural aspect of genuine visions is treated extensively in Karl Rahner, *Visions and Prophecies*, trans. Charles H. Henkey and Richard Strachan (London: Burns & Oates, 1964).

7. Cf., e.g., Pss 16:10-11; 17:15; 27:13; 41:13; 49:16; 73:24; 143:7. All these passages oscillate between hope for newly given life in this time and hope for life beyond the bounds of death. The speaking subject is always an individual.

8. John 12:32; Acts 2:33; 5:31; Rom 1:4; Eph 1:20-22; Phil 2:9; Heb 1:3; 2:9; 5:5-6; 8:1; 10:12-13.

9. Luke 24:51; Acts 1:9; 3:21; 1 Tim 3:16.

10. Luke 24:34; Acts 10:40; Rom 4:24, 25; 8:11; 10:9; 1 Cor 6:14; 15:4; Gal 1:1; 1 Thess 1:10; 1 Pet 1:21, and frequently elsewhere.

11. Thus Rudolf Pesch, *Das Markusevangelium*, Part 2, HTKNT II/2 (Freiburg: Herder, 1977), 529.

12. The Hosea passage is cited nowhere in the New Testament, and even possible allusions are uncertain.

13. Cf. Matt 28:9-10; Mark 16:9; John 20:11-18.

14. For the opponents' assertion of theft of the body, see Matt 28:11-15; for transfer by a gardener, see John 20:15. The sudden and unexplained appearance of the "gardener" in the text is an allusion to the polemic of the Jewish opposition.

15. "A sign" because the fact of the empty tomb is not the resurrection itself. The earliest Christian tradition held that opinion also. In all four gospels the meaning and significance of the empty tomb must first be explained by angels.

16. The Jewish texts, especially those of Philo, are handily summarized in Rudolf Pesch, *Die Apostelgeschichte*, Vol. 1, EKK V/1 (Einsiedeln: Benziger; Neukirchen-Vluyn: Neukirchener Verlag, 1986), 101–2.

17. Paul speaks of this in 1 Corinthians 14 in the same terminology: *lalein glōssais*, "speaking in tongues." The pre-Lukan narrative layer made this into a *lalein heterais glōssais* (Acts 2:4), "speaking in other tongues," that is, foreign languages.

18. It is true that Luke, or the tradition that preceded him, has inserted "in the last days," but the context in Joel speaks unmistakably of the end time.

19. Cf. Gerhard Lohfink, "Der Ursprung der christlichen Taufe," *TQ* 156 (1976): 35–54.

20. Behind this is, of course, the complex of ideas surrounding the pilgrimage of the nations: at the end of time the nations will come as pilgrims to Zion to hear the word of God. Cf. esp. Isa 2:1-5; 60:1-6, and frequently elsewhere. The success of the Gentile mission (= the self-fulfillment of the promise of the pilgrimage of the nations) was also part of the end-time horizon of the early church.

21. I am here adopting a reflection by Karl Rahner. Cf. his "Warum gerade ER? Anfrage an den Christusglauben," *TG* 22 (1979): 65–74, at 66–67. English: "Why Him?," 85–104, in Karl Rahner and Karl-Heinz Weger, *Our Christian Faith: Answers for the Future* (London: Burns & Oates, 1980).

Chapter 19

1. The Greek *kai* is a *kai explicativum*, i.e., an explanatory "and."

2. Cf. also Matt 21:11, 46; Luke 24:19; John 4:19; 6:14; 9:17.

3. Deuteronomy 18:18 only means to say that Israel will always have a prophet, but later, in light of Deut 34:10, the text was read to indicate the coming of a single end-time prophetic figure.

4. Mark 6:4 and Luke 13:33 seem to contradict this statement, but both these passages are about "rule sayings" (Odil Hannes Steck) that do not permit us to draw

any conclusions about Jesus' sovereign claim. Mark 6:4 in particular is similar to other proverbial expressions in Hellenistic culture.

5. Cf. Horst Dietrich Preuss, *Old Testament Theology*, vol. 2, trans. Leo G. Perdue (Louisville: Westminster John Knox, 1996), 73.

6. Or "truly I tell you." See the details in Joachim Jeremias, *Abba. Studien zur neutestamentlichen Theologie und Zeitgeschichte* (Göttingen: Vandenhoeck & Ruprecht, 1966), 148–51. For an English translation, see idem, *Jesus and the Message of the New Testament*, ed. K. C. Hanson (Minneapolis: Fortress Press, 2002), 10.

7. Cf. Matt 9:27; 12:23; 15:22; 21:9, 15.

8. The oldest and clearest evidence is *PsSol* 17:21.

9. For "messianic" texts in the Old Testament, see esp. Ps 72; Isa 9:1-6; 11:1-10; Jer 30:8-9; 33:14-16; Ezek 34:23-24; 37:24-25; Mic 5:1-4; Zech 9:9-10. Others, such as Gen 49:10-12; Num 24:17-19; or Amos 9:11-12 were interpreted as messianic, at least later. "Messianic" here does not mean that the title "messiah" was used. That title for a future figure who will bring salvation appears for the first time in the first century BCE in the *Psalms of Solomon*.

10. "Son of Man" appears in the NT in only four passages outside the gospels; of these, Heb 2:6 and Rev 1:13; 14:14 are quotations from the Old Testament, leaving only Acts 7:56.

11. The exception is John 12:34.

12. Joachim Jeremias collected the precise findings; cf. his *New Testament Theology, Part 1: The Proclamation of Jesus*, trans. John Bowden (London: SCM, 1974), 257–76, at 260. In his search, however, Jeremias looked for instances that are certainly authentic and his method was much too mechanical. He separated out a number of *logia* in which the parallel tradition has "I" instead of "Son of Man." These should instead be discussed case by case. Cf. the lists in Martin Hengel and Anna Maria Schwemer, *Jesus und das Judentum* (Tübingen: Mohr, 2007), 534–41.

13. This does not exclude the possibility that *within* the transmission of the Jesus tradition the Son of Man title could be replaced by an "I" or the reverse, that "Son of Man" could be introduced in place of an "I." Cf., e.g., Matt 16:13, differently Mark 8:27.

14. Cf. *1 En.* 45:3-6; 46:1-6; 48:2-7; 49:2-4; 61:5–62:16; 71:13-17; 4 Ezra 13.

15. Cf. Rudolf Bultmann, *Theology of the New Testament* (Waco, TX: Baylor University Press, 2007), 9; also, e.g., Günther Bornkamm, *Jesus of Nazareth* (Minneapolis: Fortress Press, 1995), 176; Ferdinand Hahn, *The Titles of Jesus in Christology: Their History in Earliest Christianity* (Cambridge: James Clarke, 2002), 23.

16. Cf. Matt 5:25-26; Mark 9:43-48; Luke 12:54-57; 13:1-5, 25-27; 16:1-8; 17:26-30.

17. For this whole literary genre, see Martin Hengel, *Was Jesus a Revolutionist?* (Philadelphia: Fortress Press, 1971), 4–9.

18. A literal translation of Matt 10:34 would be: "I have not come to *cast* peace, but the sword."

19. At least the first and second antitheses (Matt 5:21-22, 27-28) are regarded by many scholars as authentic. There is no genuine parallel among the rabbis for Jesus' "but I say to you."

20. Mark 2:1-12; Luke 7:36-50. This corresponds to Jesus' table fellowship with toll collectors and sinners. In Mark 2:5, the most important text, Jesus does say to the lame man "your sins are forgiven," that is, "they are forgiven you *by God*," but it is Jesus himself who asserts it and thus acts authoritatively.

21. Cf. Matt 24:43-44; Luke 12:40; 1 Thess 5:2, 4; 2 Pet 3:10; Rev 3:3; 16:15.

22. For the following interpretation, see Tim Schramm and Kathrin Löwenstein, *Unmoralische Helden. Anstössige Gleichnisse Jesu* (Göttingen: Vandenhoeck & Ruprecht, 1986), 50–53. Previously C. H. Dodd, *The Parables of the Kingdom* (New York: Scribner, 1961), 126, had exegeted the text in the same sense.

23. Interpreters disagree about who it is that is entering the strong man's house. Is it God, or Jesus? Cf. Michael Theobald, "'Ich sah den Satan aus dem Himmel stürzen . . .'" *BZ* 49 (2005): 174–90, at 189–90. But the two are really inseparable. Obviously Jesus himself conquers and binds Satan, but he does it "in the power of God" (cf. Luke 11:20).

Chapter 20

1. The problem at Chalcedon was the relationship of the two "natures" in Christ, that is, the relationship of divinity and humanity. That Jesus Christ is true human and true God is already stated in the New Testament, especially in the Christology of the Gospel of John.

2. English: *The Religion of the Earliest Churches: Creating a Symbolic World*, trans. John Bowden (Minneapolis: Fortress Press, 2000), 41–60.

3. For the signs required to confirm the ascension, cf. Gerhard Lohfink, *Die Himmelfahrt Jesu. Untersuchungen zu den Himmelfahrts- und Erhöhungstexten bei Lukas*, SANT 26 (Munich: Kösel, 1971), 45–50.

4. Cf. Carsten Colpe, "Jesus und die Besiegelung der Prophetie," *BTZ* 4 (1987): 2–18; idem, *Das Siegel der Propheten: historische Beziehungen zwischen Judentum, Judenchristentum, Heidentum und frühen Islam*, ANTZ 3, 2nd ed. (Berlin: Institut Kirche und Judentum, 2007), 12–16; 200–203.

5. Cf., e.g., Isa 25:6-8 or Ezek 43:1-7. Exod 29:45 could also be mentioned here, if the text is read *eschatologically* on the canonical level.

6. For these instances, see Adolf Deissmann, *Light from the Ancient East: The New Testament Illustrated by Recently Discovered Texts of the Graeco-Roman World* (Grand Rapids, MI: Baker Book House, 1965 [orig. pub. 1909]), 343–45.

7. See Marius Reiser, "Hat Paulus Heiden bekehrt?," *BZ* 39 (1995): 76–91.

8. For the question of these so-called adoptionist formulae, cf. Peter Stuhlmacher, *Biblische Theologie des Neuen Testaments* 1 (Göttingen: Vandenhoeck & Ruprecht, 1992), 185–88; Martin Hengel and Anna Maria Schwemer, *Der messianische Anspruch Jesu und die Anfänge der Christologie. Vier Studien*, WUNT 138 (Tübingen: Mohr Siebeck, 2001), 13; Walter Kasper, *Jesus the Christ* (New York: Paulist Press, 1976), 233–34; Karl-Heinz Menke, *Jesus ist Gott der Sohn. Denkformen und Brennpunkte der Christologie* (Regensburg: Pustet, 2008), 166–68.

9. The translation of this passage is uncertain. The Septuagint has rendered the Hebrew *ʾamôn* with *harmozousa*, "the one who orders all things." Aquila's later Greek translation substituted *tithēnoumenē*, "nursling, darling child." Both refer *amon* to Wisdom, as have all interpreters up to modern times. But the word can also apply to God, in which case the text speaks of God as the artist, the master builder of the world.

10. For the basis of this translation, cf. Gerhard Lohfink and Ludwig Weimer, *Maria—nicht ohne Israel. Eine neue Sicht der Lehre von der Unbefleckten Empfängnis* (Freiburg: Herder, 2008), 350–51, 433. [Translator's note: The gender inflection in Greek and German of "*logos*/word" (masculine) creates difficulties for English translation, since in English most inanimate things and abstractions are "it."]

11. Theissen, *Religion of the Earliest Churches*, 42.

12. Ibid., 41–47.

13. These are the titles of chapters 8–14 in part 3 of Gerd Theissen and Annette Merz, *The Historical Jesus: A Comprehensive Guide* (Minneapolis: Fortress Press, 1998).

14. For the whole question of the "Hellenization of Christianity," see the essay by Alois Grillmeier, "'Christus licet uobis inuitis deus.' Ein Beitrag zur Diskussion über die Hellenisierung der christlichen Botschaft," 81–111, in idem, *Fragmente zur Christologie. Studien zum altkirchlichen Christusbild*, ed. Theresia Hainthaler (Freiburg: Herder, 1997); also Karl-Heinz Menke, *Jesus ist Gott der Sohn*, 8, 89–90, 168–72, and elsewhere.

Chapter 21

1. For what follows, see esp. Alfred Zänker, *Der lange Weg nach Utopia. Vom Vormarsch des politisch Vernünftigen* (Asendorf: Mut-Verlag, 2003).

2. Ibid., 143–44, summarizing material from Ernest Callenbach, *Ecotopia: The Notebooks and Reports of William Weston* (Berkeley, CA: Banyan Tree Books, 1975).

3. Ibid., 51. Cf. Francis Bacon, *The New Atlantis: Or, Voyage to the Land of the Rosicrucians* (1627).

4. Ibid., 53.

5. For a long time exegesis tried to keep the process of growth totally separate from the parable and therefore spoke of a "contrast parable." It was all about the tiny beginning and the astonishing size at the end. But the fear of discovering anything like growth in the "growth parables" rests on the fact that before World War I the reign of God was repeatedly equated with civilizing, intellectual, and moral entities.

Index of Biblical Citations